Standard Catalogue of British Coins

COINS OF
ENGLAND

AND

THE UNITED KINGDOM

25th Edition

Edited by

Stephen Mitchell and Brian Reeds

adapted, with additional material, from catalogues originally

compiled by H. A. and P. J. Seaby

Seab

D0831018

London

A Catalogue of the Coins of Great Britain
and Ireland
first published 1929

Standard Catalogue of British Coins
Coins of England and the United Kingdom

25th edition, 1989

© B.A. Seaby Ltd.
8 Cavendish Square
London W1M 0AJ

Distributed by
B. T. Batsford Ltd.
P.O. Box 4, Braintree, Essex CM7 7QY, England

Typeset by Latimer Trend & Co Limited, Plymouth.
Printed and bound in Great Britain
by Mackays of Chatham, Kent.

ISBN 1 85264 0413

CONTENTS

PREFACE

Over twenty years ago we prepared the text for the first issue of *Coins of England and the United Kingdom* as the first volume of Seaby's 'Standard Catalogue of British Coins', which itself had been an adaptation and improvement upon our *Standard Catalogue of the Coins of Great Britain and Ireland*, first published in 1945. Over the years the text has been subject to considerable change, the most important being in 1978 when the first of the current series of revised editions was published in a format consistent with our other catalogues on Greek, Roman and Byzantine coins.

For the collector the principal improvements may be seen in the steady increase of detailed information; in values being stated in more than one grade of preservation; in the constant improvement and revision of the text to take into account new coins found each year, and to keep abreast of current numismatic research.

We do not try to lead the market or consciously to anticipate demand for any particular series of coins; we try to reflect the market, taking note of fixed and auction prices during the year. As only a very few of the coins herein actually turn up in any one year, our aim, as far as possible, is to present to the collector our opinion of what he may reasonably expect to pay for a particular coin.

The catalogue, then, is primarily intended for the collector, but it will also be found to be a compact general handbook for the archaeologist, museum curator and amateur coin finder and, for that matter, any person who has a coin to identify and who wishes to know its approximate value.

We would like to acknowledge the help we have received from a number of collectors and specialists in certain series – Peter Wallwork, David Fletcher and Barry Windsor – and we have particularly valued the comments and suggestions of those who have used previous editions of the catalogue.

THIS CATALOGUE

Arrangement

The arrangement of this catalogue is not completely uniform, but generally it is divided into metals (gold, silver, copper, etc) under each reign, then into coinages, denominations and varieties. In the Celtic section the uninscribed coins are listed before the dynastic coins; under Charles II all the hammered coins precede the milled coinage; the reign of George III is divided into coins issued up to 1816 and the new coinage from 1816 to the end of the reign; and under Elizabeth II the decimal issues are separated from the £.s.d. coinages.

Every major coin type is listed though not every variety. We have endeavoured to give rather more coverage to the varieties of relatively common coins, such as the pence of Edward I, II and III, than to the very much rarer coins of, for instance, King Offa of Mercia.

Values

The values given represent the scale of **retail prices** at which Seaby's are offering coins **for sale** at the time of going to press, and *not* the price that Seaby's pay. These prices are based on our knowledge of the numismatic market, the current demand for particular coins, recent auction sale prices and, in those cases where certain coins have not appeared for sale for some years, our estimation of what they would be likely to sell at today, bearing in mind their rarity and appeal in relation to somewhat similar coins where a current value *is* known. Values are given for two grades of preservation from the end of the 10th century and for three grades of preservation for most coins of the 19th and early 20th centuries (except for Ancient British where the price is for the condition in which the coin usually appears).

Seaby's endeavour to be reasonably conservative in grading the state of preservation of coins, as our clients well know. Collectors normally require coins in the best condition they can afford and, except in the case of a really rare coin, a piece that is considerably worn is not wanted and has little value. The values given in the catalogue are for the exact state of preservation stated at the head of each column; and bearing in mind that a score of identical coins in varying states of wear could be lined up in descending order from mint condition (FDC, *fleur de coin*), through *very fine* (VF) to *poor* state, it will be realized that only in certain instances will the values given apply to particular coins. A 'fine' (F) coin may be worth anything between one quarter and a half of the price quoted for a 'very fine' (VF), on the other hand a piece in really mint condition will be valued substantially higher than the price quoted for 'extremely fine' (EF).

We emphasize again that the purpose of this catalogue is to give a general value for a particular class of coin in a specified state of preservation, and also to give the collector an idea of the range and value of coins in the English series. The value of any particular piece depends on three things:

Its exact design, legend, mintmark or date.
Its exact state of preservation; this is of prime importance.
The demand for it in the market at any given time.

Some minor varieties are much scarcer than others, and, as the number of coins issued varies considerably from year to year, coins of certain dates and mintmarks are rarer and of more value than other pieces of similar type. The prices given for any type are for the commonest variety, mintmark or date of that type.

Ordering coins from this catalogue

We obviously do not have every coin in stock that is listed in this catalogue. A large selection is, however, always available for viewing by personal callers and coins may be ordered by post on seven days' approval from time of delivery by known clients who have a credit account with us.

When making enquiries please ensure that the number of the coin is quoted correctly and that the reference is to the 25th edition.

A BEGINNER'S GUIDE TO COIN COLLECTING

The Scope

Coin collecting is a fascinating recreation. It requires little physical exertion and only as much mental effort as one wishes to give at any time. Numismatics has vast scope and boundless ramifications and byways. It encompasses not only things historical and geographical, but also touches on economics, metallurgy, heraldry, literature, the fine arts, politics, military history and many other disciplines. This catalogue is solely concerned with British coinage, but from the start the beginner should appreciate that the coinage of our own nation may be seen as a small but important part of the whole gamut of world currency.

The first coins, made of electrum, a natural alloy of gold and silver, were issued in western Asia Minor about the middle of the seventh century B.C. Over the next century or so coinage of gold and silver spread across the Aegean to mainland Greece, southwards to the eastern Mediterranean lands and eventually westward to the Adriatic cities and the Greek colonies in southern Italy, Sicily and beyond. The coins of the Greeks are noted for their beautiful, sometimes exquisite craftsmanship, with many of the coin types depicting the patron deities of their cities. Coins of Philip II of Macedon (359–336 B.C.), father of Alexander the Great, circulated amongst the Celtic peoples of the Danubian basin and were widely copied through central Europe and by the Gauls in France. Gold Gaulish staters were reaching Britain around the beginning of the first century B.C. and the earliest gold to be struck in the island must have been produced shortly afterwards.

The coins of the Romans cover some seven centuries and comprise an enormous number of different types current throughout a major part of the civilized world from Spain to further Syria and from the Rhine in the north to the Sudan in the south. The Roman province of Britain was part of this vast empire for four hundred years and innumerable Roman coins have been recovered from sites in this country, most being made of brass or bronze and many being quite inexpensive.

Following the revival of commerce after the Dark Ages, coinage in Western Europe was virtually restricted to silver until the thirteenth century, though gold was still being minted at Byzantium and in the Islamic world. In the Middle Ages many European cities had their own distinctive coinage, and money was issued not only by the kings but also by many lesser nobles, bishops and abbots. From the time of the later Crusades gold returned to the west; and the artistic developments of the Renaissance brought improved portraiture and new minting techniques.

Large silver crown-size thalers were first minted at Joachimsthal in Bohemia early in the sixteenth century. With substantial shipments of silver coming to Europe from the mines of Spanish America over the next couple of centuries a fine series of larger coins was issued by the European states and cities.

Both Germany and Italy became unified nation states during the nineteenth century but balancing the reduction in European minting authorities were the new coins of the indpendent states of South and Central America. Over the past quarter century many new nations have established their independence and their coinage provides a large field for the collector of modern coins.

It can be seen that the scope for the collector is truly vast, but besides the general run of official coinage there is also the large series of token coins—small change unofficially produced to supplement the inadequate supply of authorized currency. These tokens were issued by merchants, innkeepers and manufacturers in many towns and villages in the 17th, 18th and 19th centuries and many collectors specialize in their local issues.

Some coins have designs of a commemorative nature; an example being the recent Royal Wedding crown, but there are also large numbers of commemorative medals which, though never intended for use as coinage, are sometimes confused with coins, being metal objects of a similar shape and sometimes a similar size to coins. This is another interesting field for collectors as these medals may have excellent portraits of famous men or women, or they may commemorate important events or scientific discoveries. Other metallic objects of coin-like appearance may be reckoning counters, advertising tickets, various other tickets and passes, and items such as brass coin weights.

Minting processes

From the time of the earliest Greek coins to about the middle of the 16th century coins were made by hand.

The method of manufacture was simple. The obverse and reverse designs were engraved or punched into the prepared ends of two bars of iron, shaped or tapered to the diameter of the required coin. The obverse die, known as the *pile*, was usually spiked to facilitate its being anchored firmly into a block of wood or metal. The reverse die, the *trussel*, was held by hand or grasped by tongs.

The coin was struck by placing a metal blank between the two dies and striking the trussel with a hammer. Thus, all coinage struck by this method is known as 'hammered' money. Some dies are known to have been hinged to ensure exact register between the upper and lower die. Usually a 'pair of dies' consisted of one obverse die (normally the more difficult to make) and two reverse dies. This was because the shaft of iron bearing the reverse design eventually split under the constant hammering; two reverse dies usually being needed to last out the life of the obverse die.

Some time toward the middle of the 16th century, experiments, first in Germany and later in France, resulted in the manufacture of coins by machinery.

The term 'milled' which is applied to all machine-made coins comes from the type of machinery used, the mill and screw press. With this machinery the obverse die was fixed and the reverse die brought into contact with the blank by heavy vertical pressure applied by a screw or worm-drive connected to a cross bar with heavy weights at each end. These weights usually had long leather thongs attached which allowed a more powerful force to be applied by the operators who revolved the arms of the press. New blanks were placed on the lower die and struck coins were removed by hand. The screw press brought more pressure to bear on the blanks and this pressure was evenly applied.

Various attempts were made during the reigns of Elizabeth I and Charles I to introduce this type of machinery with its vastly superior products. Unfortunately problems associated with the manufacture of blanks to a uniform weight greatly reduced the rate of striking and the hand manufacture of coins continued until the Restoration, when Charles II brought to London from Holland the Roettiers brothers and their improved screw press.

The first English coins made for circulation by this new method were the silver crowns of 1662, which bore an inscription on the edge, DECVS ET TVTAMEN, 'an ornament and a safeguard', a reference to the fact that the new coins could not be clipped, a crime made easier by the thin and often badly struck hammered coins.

The mill and screw press was used until new steam powered machinery made by Boulton and Watt was installed in the new mint on Tower Hill. This machinery had been used most successfully by Boulton to strike the 'cartwheel' two- and one-penny pieces of 1797 and many other coins, including 'overstriking' Spanish eight real pieces into Bank of England 'dollars', the old Mint presses not being able to exert sufficient power to do this. This new machinery was first used at the Mint to strike the 'new coinage' halfcrowns of 1816, and it operated at a far greater speed than the old type of mill and screw presses and achieved a greater sharpness of design.

The modern coining presses by Horden, Mason and Edwards, now operating at the new mint at Llantrisant, are capable of striking at a rate of up to 300 coins a minute.

Condition

One of the more difficult problems for the beginner is accurately to assess the condition of a coin. A common fault among collectors is to overgrade and, consequently, overvalue their coins.

Most dealers will gladly spare a few minutes to help new collectors. Dealers, such as ourselves, who issue price lists with illustrations, enable collectors to see exactly what the coins look like and how they have been graded.

Coins cannot always be graded according to precise rules. Hammered coins often look weak or worn on the high parts of the portrait and the tops of the letters; this can be due to weak striking or worn dies and is not always attributable to wear through long use in circulation. Milled coins usually leave the mint sharply struck so that genuine wear is easier to detect. However a × 8 or × 16 magnifying glass is essential, especially when grading coins of Edward VII and George V where the relief is very low on the portraits and some skill is required to distinguish between an uncirculated coin and one in EF condition.

The condition or grade of preservation of a coin is usually of greater importance than its rarity. By this we mean that a common coin in superb condition is often more desirable and more highly priced than a rarity in poor condition. Few coins that have been pierced or mounted as a piece of jewellery have an interest to collectors.

One must also be on the lookout for coins that have been 'plugged', i.e. that have been pierced at some time and have had the hole filled in, sometimes with the missing design or letters re-engraved.

Badly cleaned coins will often display a complexity of fine interlaced lines and such coins have a greatly reduced value. It is also known for coins to be tooled or re-engraved on the high parts of the hair, in order to 'increase' the grade of coin and its value. In general it is better to have a slightly more worn coin than a better example with the aforementioned damage.

Cleaning coins

Speaking generally, *don't* clean coins. More coins are ruined by injudicious cleaning than through any other cause, and a badly cleaned coin loses much of its value. A nicely toned piece is usually considered desirable. Really dirty gold and silver can, however, be carefully washed in soap and water. Copper coins should never be cleaned or washed, they may be lightly brushed with a brush that is not too harsh.

Buying and selling coins

Swopping coins at school or with other collectors, searching around the antique shops, telling your relatives and friends that you are interested in coins, or even trying to find your own with a metal detector, are all ways of adding to your collection. However, the time will come for the serious collector when he wants to acquire specific coins or requires advice on the authenticity or value of a coin.

At this point an expert is needed, and generally the services of a reputable coin dealer will be sought. There are now a large number of coin dealers in the U.K., many of whom belong to the B.N.T.A. or the I.A.P.N. (the national and international trade associations) and a glance through the 'yellow pages' under 'coin dealer' or 'numismatist' will often provide local information.

We at Seaby's have been buying and selling coins for over sixty years, and have been publishing a priced catalogue since 1929. In addition to our books on English, Greek, Roman and Byzantine coins and on British tokens, we also publish 'Seaby's Coin and Medal Bulletin', a magazine containing articles, and lists of coins for sale.

Our stock of coins for sale represents every period from Greek and Roman times to the present day, and individual prices of coins range from a pound or so to several thousands. Callers at our premises are always made very welcome.

When buying coins Seaby's reckon to pay a fair proportion of the retail value; generally speaking we will pay a higher proportion of the selling price for better quality pieces.

Useful suggestions

Security and insurance. The careful collector should not keep valuable coins at home unless they are insured and have adequate protection. Local police and insurance companies will give advice on what precautions may be necessary.

Most insurance companies will accept a valuation based on the Standard Catalogue. It is usually possible to have the amount added to a householder's contents policy. A 'Fire, Burglary and Theft' policy will cover loss only from the assured's address, but an 'All Risks' policy will usually cover accidental damage and loss anywhere within the U.K. We can recommend a Lloyd's broker, if requested.

Coins deposited with a bank or placed in a safe-deposit box will usually attract a lower insurance premium.

Keeping a record. All collectors are advised to have an up-to-date record of their collection, and, if possible, photographs of the more important and more easily identifiable coins. This should be kept in a separate place from the collection, so that a list and photographs can be given to the police should loss occur. Note the price paid, from whom purchased, the date of acquisition and the condition.

Storage and handling. New collectors should get into the habit of handling coins by the edge. This is especially important as far as highly polished proof coins are concerned.

Collectors may initially keep their coins in paper or plastic envelopes housed in boxes, albums or special containers. Many collectors will eventually wish to own a hardwood coin cabinet in which the collection can be properly arranged and displayed. If a home-made cabinet is being constructed avoid oak and cedar wood; mahogany, walnut and rosewood are ideal. It is important that coins are not kept in a humid atmosphere; especial care must be taken with copper and bronze coins which are very susceptible to damp or condensation which may result in a green verdigris forming on the coins.

From beginner to numismatist

The new collector will feel that he has much to learn. He can best advance from tyro to experienced numismatist by examining as many coins as possible, noting their distinctive features and by learning to use the many books of reference that are available. It will be an advantage to join a local numismatic society, as this will provide an opportunity for meeting other enthusiasts and obtaining advice from more knowledgeable collectors. Most societies have a varied programme of lectures, exhibitions and occasional auctions of members' duplicates.

Those who become members of one or both of the national societies, the Royal Numismatic Society and the British Numismatic Society, can be sure of receiving an annual journal containing authoritative papers.

Many museums have coin collections available for study and a number of museum curators are qualified numismatists.

SOME COIN DENOMINATIONS

Gold

Angel	Eighty pence (6s. 8d.) from 1464; later 7s. 6d., 10s. and 11s.
Aureus	Roman currency unit (originally $\frac{1}{60}$th lb), discontinued A.D. 324.
Britain Crown	Five shillings, 1604–12; 5s. 6d. (66d.) 1612–19.
Broad	Twenty shillings, Cromwell, 1656.
Crown	Five shillings, from 1544 (and see below and Britain crown above).
Crown of the Rose	Four shillings and 6 pence, 1526.
Crown of the Double Rose	Five shillings, 1526–44.
Florin (Double Leopard)	Six shillings, Edward III.
George Noble	Eighty pence (6s. 8d.) 1526.
Gold 'Penny'	Twenty to twenty-four pence, Henry III.
Guinea	Pound (20s.) in 1663, then rising to 30s. in 1694 before falling to 21s. 6d., 1698–1717; 21s., 1717–1813.
Halfcrown	Thirty pence, 1526 intermittently to 1612; 2s. 9d. (33d.), 1612–19.
Helm (Quarter Florin)	Eighteen pence, Edward III.
Laurel	Twenty shillings, 1619–25.
Leopard (Half florin)	Three shillings, Edward III.
Noble	Eighty pence (6s. 8d., or half mark), 1344–1464.
Pound	Twenty shillings, 1592–1600 (see also Unite, Laurel, Broad, Guinea and Sovereign).
Quarter Angel	1s. 10½d., 1544–7 and (or Ryal)
Ten shillings, 1464–70.	
Rose-Ryal	Thirty shillings, 1604–24.
Ryal	Ten shillings, Edward IV and Henry VII; fifteen shillings under Mary and Elizabeth I (see also Spur Ryal).
Solidus	Roman currency unit ($\frac{1}{72}$nd lb) from A.D. 312; the 's' of the £.s.d.
Sovereign	Twenty shillings or pound, 1489–1526 (22s. 6d., 1526–44), 1544–53, 1603–04 and from 1817 (see also Pound, Unite, Laurel, Broad and Guinea, and Fine Sovereign below).
'Fine' Sovereign	Thirty shillings, 1550–96 (see also Rose-Ryal).
Spur-Ryal	Fifteen shillings, 1605–12; 16s. 6d., 1612–25.
Stater	Name commonly given to the standard Celtic gold coin.
Third guinea	Seven shillings, 1797–1813.
Thistle Crown	Four shillings, 1604–12; 4s. 5d., 1612–19.
Thrymsa	Early Anglo-Saxon version of the late Roman tremissis (one-third solidus).
Triple Unite	Three pounds, Charles I (Shrewsbury and Oxford only, 1642–4)
Unite	Twenty shillings, 1604–12 and 1625–62; 22s., 1612–19.

Silver (and Cupro-Nickel)

Antoninianus	Roman, originally 1½ denarii in A.D. 214 (later debased to bronze).
Argenteus	Roman, a revived denarius.
Crown	Five shillings, 1551–1965.
Denarius	Roman, originally 10 then 16 asses (25 to the aureus), later debased: the 'd' of the £.s.d.

Farthing	Quarter penny, 1279–1553.
Florin	Two shillings, from 1849–1967.
Groat	Four pence, 1279–*c.* 1305 and 1351–1662 (Halfgroat from 1351). 'Britannia' groat, 1836–55 (and 1888 for Colonial use only). See also Maundy.
Halfcrown	Thirty pence (2s. 6d.), 1551–1967.
Halfpenny	Intermittently, *c.* 890–*c.* 970, *c.* 1108, short cross and, more generally, 1279–1660.
Maundy money	Four, three, two and one penny, from 1660.
New pence	Decimal coinage: 50p from 1969, 25p. (crown) 1972 and 1977, 80, 81, 10p. and 5p. from 1968. 'New' removed in 1982.
Quinarius	Roman, half denarius or 8 asses; later debased.
Penny (*pl.* pence)	Standard unit of currency from *c.* 775/780 A.D.
Sceat	Early Anglo-Saxon, small, thick penny.
Shilling	Twelve pence, 1548–1966.
Siliqua	Roman, $\frac{1}{24}$th solidus.
Sixpence	From 1551–1967.
Testern (Portcullis money)	One, two, four and eight testerns for use in the Indies (and equal to the Spanish 1, 2, 4 and 8 reales); 1600 only.
Testoon	Shilling, Henry VII and VIII.
Threefarthings	Elizabeth I, 1561–82.
Threehalfpence	Elizabeth I, 1561–82, and for Colonial use, 1834–62.
Threepence	From 1551–1944 (then see Maundy).
Twenty pence	Decimal coinage from 1982.

Copper, Bronze, Tin, Nickel-Brass, etc.

As	Roman, an early unit of currency; reduced in size and equal to $\frac{1}{16}$th denarius in Imperial times.
Centenionalis	Roman, replaced the depleted follis in A.D. 346.
Dupondius	Roman, brass two asses or one-eighth of a denarius.
Farthing	Quarter penny: Harrington, Lennox, Richmond, Maltravers and 'rose' farthings, 1613–49; regal issues, 1672–1956 (tin, 1684–92).
Follis	Roman, silver-washed bronze coin, $\frac{1}{5}$th argenteus, introduced *c.* A.D. 290, later debased.
Half Farthing	Victoria, 1839–56 (and for Colonial use 1828–37).
Halfpenny	From 1672 to 1967 (tin, 1685–92).
New Pence	Decimal coinage; 2p., 1p. and $\frac{1}{2}$p. from 1971. 'New' removed from 1982.
Penny	From 1797 to 1967 (previously a silver coin).
Pound	Decimal coin from 1983.
Quadrans	Roman, quarter as or $\frac{1}{64}$th denarius.
Quarter Farthing	For Colonial use only, 1839–53.
Semis	Roman, half as or $\frac{1}{32}$nd denarius.
Sestertius	Roman, brass four asses or quarter denarius.
Third Farthing	For Colonial use only, 1827–1913.
Threepence	Nickelbrass, 1937–67.
Twopence	George III, 'Cartwheel' issue, 1797 only.

SOME NUMISMATIC TERMS EXPLAINED

Obverse	That side of the coin which normally shows the monarch's head or name.
Reverse	The side opposite to the obverse.
Blank	The coin as a blank piece of metal, i.e. before it is struck.
Flan	The whole piece of metal after striking.
Type	The main, central design.
Legend	The inscription.
Field	That flat part of the coin between the main design and the inscription or edge.
Exergue	That part of the coin below the main design, usually separated by a horizontal line, and normally occupied by the date.

Die	The block of metal, with design cut into it, which actually impresses the coin blank with the design.
Die variety	Coin showing slight variation of design.
Mule	A coin with the current type on one side and the previous (and usually obsolete) type on the other side, or a piece struck from two dies that are not normally used together.
Graining	The crenellations around the edge of the coin, commonly known as 'milling'.
Proof	Carefully struck coin from special dies with a mirror-like or matt surface. (In this country 'Proof' is *not* a term used to describe the state of preservation, but the method of striking.)
Hammered	Refers to the old craft method of striking a coin between dies hammered by hand.
Milled	Coins struck by dies worked in a coining press.

ABBREVIATIONS

Archb.	Archbishop	*mm.*	mintmark
Bp.	Bishop	mon.	monogram
cuir.	cuirassed	*O., obv.*	obverse
d.	penny, pence	p.	new penny, pence
diad.	diademed	pl.	plume
dr.	draped	quat.	quatrefoil
ex.	exergue	qtr.	quarter
grs.	grains	rad.	radiate
hd.	head	Ŗ., *rev.*	reverse
i.c.	inner circle	s.	shillings
illus.	illustration	var.	variety
l.	left	wt.	weight
laur.	laureate		

CONDITIONS OF A COIN

(i.e. grade of preservation) in order of merit as generally used in England.

Proof. See above.

FDC = *Fleur-de-coin.* Flawless, unused, without any wear, scratches or marks. Usually only applied to proofs.

Unc. = *Uncirculated.* A coin in new condition as issued by the Mint but, owing to modern mass-production methods of manufacture and storage, not necessarily perfect.

EF = *Extremely Fine.* A coin that shows little sign of having been in circulation, but which may exhibit slight surface marks or faint wear on very close inspection.

VF = *Very Fine.* Some wear on the raised surfaces; a coin that has had only limited circulation.

F = *Fine.* Considerable signs of wear on the raised surfaces, or design weak through faulty striking.

Fair. A coin that is worn, but which has the inscriptions and main features of the design still distinguishable, or a piece that is very weakly struck.

Poor. A very worn coin, of no value as a collector's piece unless extremely rare.

EXAMPLES OF CONDITION GRADING

EXTREMELY FINE

VERY FINE

FINE

FAIR

Edward III groat   *George II halfcrown*   *Victoria halfcrown*

BRITISH MINTS

LEGEND

Anglo Saxon and Norman, including Angevin mints (to 1279)   •

Edwardian and later mints (after 1279)   ○

Mints operating in both periods   ◉

Charles I and Civil War mints.   ✻

Map drawn by Alan Mil

CELTIC COINAGE

PERIOD OF BELGIC MIGRATION

The earliest uninscribed coins found in Britain were made in Gaul and brought to this country by trade and by the migration of Belgic peoples from the continent (Gallo-Belgic issues A to F). The earliest may date from some time late in the second century B.C., coinciding with Germanic tribes pushing westward across the Rhine and ending with refugees fleeing from the Roman legions of Julius Caesar. Certain of these coins became the prototypes for the first gold staters struck in Britain, their designs being ultimately derived from the gold staters (M) of Philip II, King of Macedonia (359–336 B.C.).

The following list is based on the 1975 edition of R. P. Mack, *The Coinage of Ancient Britain*, which now incorporates the classification for the uninscribed coins published by D. F. Allen, *The Origins of Coinage in Britain: A Reappraisal*, and from information kindly supplied by H. R. Mossop, Esq.

The new 'V' reference in this series relates to a forthcoming work by R. Van Arsdell, to be published by Spink in the near future. We hope to give more information next year.

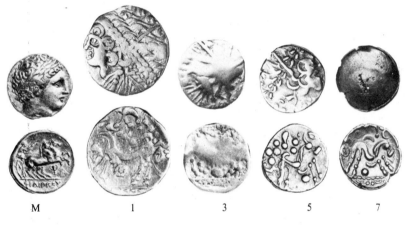

| | M | 1 | 3 | 5 | 7 |

Gold Gallo-Belgic Issues
£*

1   Gallo-Belgic A. (Ambiani), *c.* 125–100 B.C. *Stater*. Good copy of Macedonian stater, large flan. Laureate hd. of Apollo to l. or r. R̶. Horse to l. or r. *M. 1, 3; V. 10, 12* 750

2   — *Quarter stater.* As last. *M. 2, 4; V. 15, 20* 300

3   — B. (Ambiani), *c.* 115 B.C. *Stater*. Somewhat similar to 1, but small flan and "defaced" *obv.* die, some with lyre shape between horse's legs on *rev.* *M. 5, 7; V. 30, 33* 400

4   — — *Quarter stater.* As last. *M. 6, 8; V. 35, 37.* 250

5   — C. (Ambiani), *c.* 100–70 B.C. *Stater*. Disintegrated face and horse. *M. 26; V. 44* 325

6   — D. *c.* 80 B.C. *Quarter stater*. Portions of Apollo head. R̶. Unintelligible mixture of stars, crescents, pellets, zig-zag lines; often referred to as "Geometric" types. (See also British 'O', *S. 49.*) *M. 37, 39, 41, 41a, 42; V. 65/7/9/146.* 100

7   — E. (Ambiani), *c.* 57–45 B.C. *Stater*. Blank *obv.* R̶. Disjointed curved horse, pellet below. *M. 27; V. 52, 54.* 200

8   — F. (Suessiones), *c.* 50 B.C. *Stater*. Disintegrated head and horse to r. *M. 34a; V. 85* 250

*The price in this section is for the condition in which the coin usually appears

£*

9   — Xc. *c.* 80 B.C. *Stater.* Blank except for VE monogram at edge of coin, ℞.
     S below horse to r. *M. 82a*   400
10   — — *Quarter stater.* Similar, but horse to l. *M. 83; V. 355*   250
11   — Xd. *c.* 50 B.C. *Quarter stater.* Head l. of good style, horned serpent
     behind ear. ℞. Horse l. *M. 79; V. 78.*   500

13   18

Armorican (Channel Isles and N.W. Gaul), *c.* 75–50 B.C.   £*

12   *Stater.* Class I. Head r. ℞. Horse, boar below, remains of driver with
     Victory above, lash ends in one or two loops, or "gate"   45
13   Class II. Head r. ℞. Horse, boar below, remains of Victory only, lash ends
     in small cross of four pellets   40
14   Class III. Head r., anchor-shaped nose. ℞. Somewhat similar to Class I .   45
15   Class IV. Head r. ℞. Horse with reins, lyre shape below, driver holds
     vertical pole, lash ends in three prongs   50
16   Class V. Head r. ℞. Similar to last, lash ends in long cross with four pellets   50
17   Class VI. Head r. ℞. Horse, boar below, lash ends in "ladder"   60
18   *Quarter stater.* Similar types to above . . . . *from*   85

Celtic Coins Struck In Britain
Uninscribed gold staters

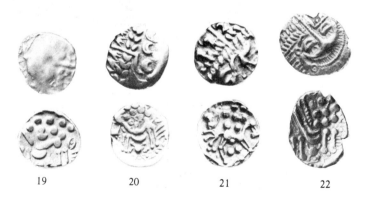

19   20   21   22

*The price in this section is for the condition in which the coin usually appears

£*

19 A. Westerham type, *c.* 95–65 B.C. As 5, but horse more disjointed. *M. 28, 29; V. 200, 202.* 325

20 B. Chute type, *c.* 85–55 B.C. Similar but crab-like figure below horse. *M. 32; V. 1205.* 140

21 C. Yarmouth (I.O.W.) type, *c.* 80–70 B.C. Crude variety of 5. *M. 31; V. 1220* 600

22 D. Cheriton type, *c.* 80–70 B.C. Variety of 20 with large crescent face. *M. 33; V. 1215.* 600

23 E. Waldingfield type, *c.* 90–70 B.C. Annulet and pellet below horse. *M. 48, V. 1462.* . . . . *Extremely rare*

24 F. Clacton type 1, *c.* 90–70 B.C. Similar to Westerham type but rosette below horse to l. *M. 47; V. 1458* 400

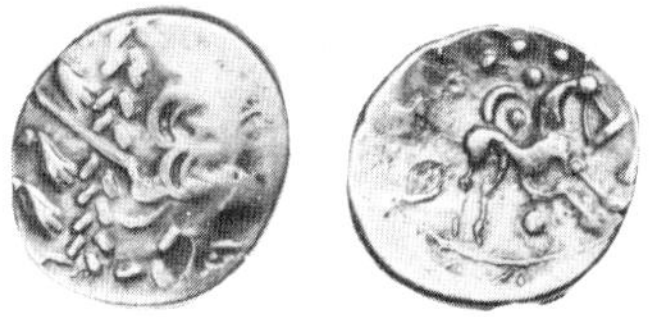

25 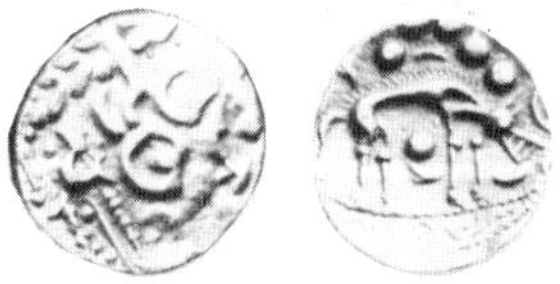   28

25 G. Clacton type 2. Similar, but horse r., with pellet, or pellet with two curved lines below. *M. 46, 46a; V. 30, 1455.* 350

26 H. North East Coast type, *c.* 75–30 B.C. Variety of 5, pellet or rosette below horse to r. *M. 50, 50a, 51, 51a; V. 800* 350

27 I. — — Similar, horse l., pellet, rosette or star with curved rays below. *M. 52–57; V. 804, 805, 807* 400

28 J. Norfolk wolf type, *c.* 65–45 B.C. ℞. Crude wolf to r. or l. *M. 49, 49a, 49b; V. 610.* 650

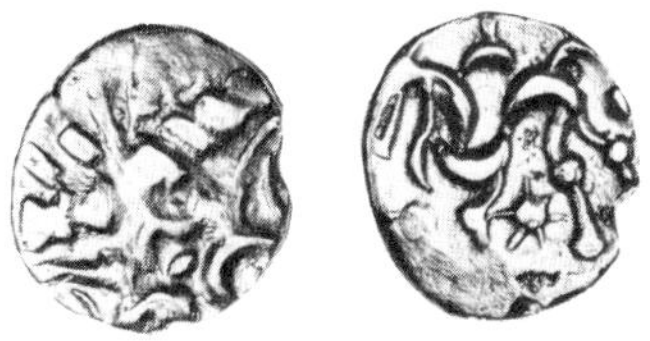

30    31

29 Ka. Coritani, South Ferriby type, *c.* 30 B.C.–A.D. 10. Crude wreath. ℞. Disjointed horse l., rectangular compartment enclosing four pellets above. *M. 447–448; V. 825, 829* 450

30 Kb. — — Similar, but star or rosette below horse. *M. 449–450a; V. 809, 811, 815, 817.* 500

30A — — — Trefoil with central rosette of seven pellets. ℞. Similar to last. *M. 450a; V. 821.* In auction 1985 £5500. (this coin) . . . . *Unique*

*The price in this section is for the condition in which the coin usually appears

4 CELTIC COINAGE

Uninscribed gold staters *continued* £*

31   L. Whaddon Chase type, *c*. 45–20 B.C. R̵. Spirited horse r. of new style,
various symbols below. *M. 133–138a, 139a; V. 1470–6, 1485/7/91/93* . . .   350

32   — — *O*. Plain. R̵. Horse r., with ring ornament below or behind. *M. 140–
143; V. 1498–1505*   325

33   Lx. North Thames group, *c*. 40–20 B.C. *O*. Blank apart from reversed SS.
R̵. Similar to last. *M. 146; V. 1509* . . . .   *Extremely rare*

34   Ly. North Kent group, *c*. 45–20 B.C. *O*. Blank. R̵. Horse l. or r., numerous
ring ornaments in field. *M. 293, 294; V. 142, 157*   350

35   Lz. Weald group, *c*. 35–20 B.C. *O*. Blank. R̵. Horse l., panel below. *M. 84,
292; V. 150, 144*   600

36   Lz. *O*. Blank with some traces of Apollo head. R̵. Horse r., large wheel
ornament below. *M. 144–145; V. 1507*   400

37

37   M. Wonersh type. *c*. 35–20 B.C. Crossed wreath design with crescents back
to back in centre. R̵. Spiral above horse, wheel below. *M. 148; V. 1520* .   375

38   39

38   39

38   Na. Iceni, *c*. 30 B.C.–A.D. 10. Double crescent design. R̵. Horse r. *M. 397,
399; V. 620*   600

39   Nb. — Trefoil on cross design. R̵. Similar to last. *M. 401–403a; V. 626* .   550

40   Nc. — Cross of pellets. R̵. Similar to last. *M. 400; V. 624*   625

41   43

*The price in this section is for the condition in which the coin usually appears

£*

41 QA. British "Remic" type, *c.* 45–25 B.C. Crude laureate head. ℞. Triple-
tailed horse, wheel below. *M. 58, 60, 61; V. 210–14* 400
42 QB. — Similar, but *obv.* blank. *M. 59, 62; V. 216, 1526* 250
43 R. Dobunni, *c.* 30 B.C.–A.D. 10. Similar, but branch emblem or ear of
corn on *obv. M. 374; V. 1005* 600

Uninscribed Quarter Staters

44

45

46

43A F. Clacton type. *O.* Plain, traces of pattern. ℞. Ornamental cross with
pellets. *M. 35; V. 1460* 375
44 LX. N. Thames group, *c.* 40–20 B.C. Floral pattern on wreath. ℞. horse l.
or r. *M. 76, 151, 270–271; V. 234, 1608, 1623, 1688* 250
45 LY. N. Kent group, *c.* 45–20 B.C. *O.* Blank. ℞. Horse r. *M. 78, 284–285;
V. 158/163/170* 250
46 LZ. Weald group, *c.* 35–20 B.C. Spiral design on wreath. ℞. Horse l. or r.
M. 77, 80–81; V. 250, 254, 366 250
47 — — *O.* Blank. ℞. Horse l., panel below. *M. 85; V. 151* 300
48 N. Iceni, *c.* 30 B.C.–A.D. 10. Floral pattern. ℞. Horse r. *M. 404; V. 628.* 300

49

50

51

49 O. Geometric type, Sussex group, *c.* 80–60 B.C. Unintelligible patterns
(some blank on *obv.*). *M. 40, 43–45; V. 143, 1425/27/29* 85
50 P. Kentish group, *c.* 65–45 B.C. *O.* Blank. ℞. Trophy design. *M. 36, 38;
V. 145/7* 175
51 Qc. British "Remic" type, *c.* 40–20 B.C. Head or wreath pattern, ℞.
Triple-tailed horse, l. or r. *M. 63–67, 69–75; V. 220–32, 36, 42–6, 56, 1015* 200
52 R. Dobunni, *c.* 30 B.C.–A.D. 10. *O.* Blank. ℞. Somewhat as last. *M. 68;
V. 1010* 325

Uninscribed Silver

53

55

56

58

*The price in this section is for the condition in which the coin usually appears

CELTIC COINAGE

Uninscrib⌐d silver *continued*

£*

52A (L) North Thames group. Head r. with headband (or diadem) and flowing
hair. Ŗ. New style horse of Whaddon Chase type (See *S. 31a*). *M.* — . . *Unique*

52B — — Similar. Ŗ. Pegasos. *M.* —. 200

53 Lx. Head l. or r. Ŗ. Horse l. or r. *M. 280, 435, 436, 438, 441; V. 80, 1546,*
1549, 1555 125

54 — — Head l. Ŗ. Goat r., with long horns. *M. 437; V. 1552* 175

55 — — Two horses or two beasts. *M. 442, 443, 445; V. 474, 1626, 1948* . . 150

56 — — Star of four rays or wreath pattern. Ŗ. Horse or uncertain animal r.
M. 272a, 414, 439, 440; V. 164, 679, 1543, 1611. 125

56A — — Hd. r. with corded hair and headband. Ŗ. Horse l., leaf (?) below,
ornaments in field. (Somewhat similar to *S. 77*).) *M.* — . . . . *Extremely rare*

56E — — *Half unit.* Cruciform pattern with ornaments in angles. Ŗ. Horse l.,
ear of corn between legs, crescent and pellets above. *M.* — . . . . *Extremely rare*

57 Lz. South Thames group. Wreath or head of serpent. Ŗ. Horse *M.* —
(*Allen L 28-10*). 150

58 — — Helmeted head r. Ŗ. Horse. *M. 89; V. 264* 200

58A — — Facing hd. of Celtic god with horns, wheel between. Ŗ. Triple-tailed
horse. l., ornaments in field. *M.* — . . . . *Extremely rare*

58B — — Two swans (or cranes), boar and eel (?) below. Ŗ. Reindeer l., boar
on hindquarters. *M.* — . . . . *Unique*

59 — — *Quarter unit* (3½–4 grains). Similar to 58. *M. 90–91; V. 268–70* . . . 150

60 Durotriges, *c.* 60 B.C.–A.D. 20. Size and type of Westerham staters (nos.
19 and 81 above). *M. 317; V. 1235* Quality of Æ varies, price for good Æ. 60

61 — Size and type of Sussex Geometric type (no. 49 above). *M. 319; V. 1242/*
49. 50

61A — 'Starfish' design. Ŗ. 'Geometric' pattern. *M. 320; V. 1270* 100

62 — Very thin flans, *c.* 55 B.C. Crude hd. of lines and pellets. Ŗ. Horse
similar. *M. 321; V. 1280.* 200

63 Dobunni, *c.* 30 B.C.–A.D. 10. Head r., with recognisable face. Ŗ. Triple-
tailed horse l. or r. *M. 374a, b, 375, 376, 378; V. 1558, 1020, 1042* 125

64 — Very crude head. Ŗ. Similar to last. *M. 378a–384d; V. 1035, 37, 45, 49,*
74, 75, 78, 85, 95. 75

65 — *Quarter unit.* As last. *M. 384c; V. 1080.* . . . . *Extremely rare*

66 Coritani, *c.* 50 B.C.–A.D. 10. I. Prototype issue of good style and
execution. Boar r., with rosette and ring ornaments. Ŗ. Horse. *M. 405,*
405a, b, 406, 451; V. 855, 57, 60, 64 200

*The price in this section is for the condition in which the coin usually appears

£*

67 — — *Half unit.* Similar. *M. 406a, 451a; V. 862/6*   135
68 — II. South Ferriby type. Vestiges of boar on *obv.* R. Horse. *M. 410, 452,*
    453; V. 875/7   175
69 — — *O.* Plain. R. Horse. *M. 453a, 454; V. 884/7*   140
70 — — *Half unit.* Similar. *M. 455–456; V. 879/89*   110
71 — — *Quarter unit.* Similar. *M. 456a; V. 881*   110

72   Iceni, *c.* 10 B.C.–A.D. 60. Boar r. R. Horse r. *M. 407–409; V. 655/7/9* . .   75
73   — *Half unit.* Similar. *M. 411; V. 661.*   75
73A — — Antlered deer. R. Horse r. *M.* — . . . .   *Unique*
73B — Quarter unit. Similar to 73. *M.* — . . . .   *Unique*
74   — Head r. R. Horse. *M. 412–413e; V. 665, 790, 792, 794*   100
74A — Large bust of good style. R. Horse r.   125
74B — Similar, but inverted ear of corn between legs of horse on *rev. M.* —
     (413 variety). . . . .   *Extremely rare*
75   — Double crescent and wreath pattern. R. Horse. *M. 414–415, 440;*
     V. 675/79/1611.   40
76   — *Half unit.* Similar. *M. 417a; V. 683*   135
76A — — Three crescents back to back. R. Horse r. *M. 417; V. 681.*   175

Uninscribed Bronze

77 Lx. North Thames group. Head l. with braided hair. R. Horse l. *M. 273,*
    274, see also *M. 281; V. 1615, 1646*   90
78 — — Horned pegasus l. R. Pegasus l. *M. 446; V. 1629.* . . . .   *Extremely rare*
79 — — Other types . . . . *from*   225
80 Ly. North Kent group. Boar. R. Horse. *M. 295–296; V. 154*   150
81 Durotriges, *c.* A.D. 20–50. Debased form of Æ stater (no. 60). *M. 318;*
    V. 1290.   35
82 — Cast coins, *c.* A.D. 50–70. As illustration. *M. 322–370; V. 1322–70* . .   60

Potin (bronze with high tin content)

83 Thames and South, *c.* 1st century B.C. Cast. Class I. Crude head. R. Lines
    representing bull. (*Allen,* types A–L.) *M. 9–22a; V. 104, 106, 108, 112, 114,*
    115, 117, 119, 120, 122, 123, 125, 127, 129, 131, 133   35
84 Kent and N. Thames, *c.* mid. 1st century A.D. Cast. Class II. Smaller flan,
    large central pellet. (*Allen,* types M–P.) *M. 23–25*   80

*The price in this section is for the condition in which the coin usually appears

CELTIC DYNASTIC ISSUES

The Celtic dynastic issues are among the most interesting and varied of all British coins. A great deal is known about some of the issuers from Julius Caesar's *Commentaries* and other sources—chiefly the kings of the Atrebates, Regni and Catuvellauni—while many are issues of kings quite unknown to history bearing legends which defy interpretation.

Roman influence in coinage design is particularly noticeable in the reign of Cunobelin (c. A.D. 10–40), but the Icenian revolt of A.D. 61 in which Colchester and London were sacked with the massacre of over 70,000 Romans resulted in the termination of British Celtic coinage which previously had been allowed to circulate along with Roman coins.

The dates given for the various rulers are, in most cases, very approximate. Staters and quarter staters are gold coins of varying quality.

N.B. Bronze coins in poor condition are worth very much less than the values given. All coins, even good specimens, are worth less if they lack clear legends, are struck off-centre or have striking cracks.

SOUTHERN BRITAIN

Atrebates and Regni. *Berks., Hants., Surrey and Sussex*

£*

85 **Commius,** *c.* 35–20 B.C. *Stater.* Portions of laureate hd. r. ℞. COMMIOS
around triple tailed horse r. *M. 92; V. 350*   2500
Copied from the "Remic" type Qᴀ *(no. 41), this is the first inscribed British coin.*

85   86   88

86 **Tincommius,** *c.* 20 B.C.–A.D. 5. Celtic style. *Stater.* Similar, but TINC
COMMI F, or TIN DV around horse. *M. 93, 94; V. 362, 363.*   850
87 — *Quarter stater.* TINCOM, zig-zag ornament below. ℞. Horse l. *M. 95;*
V. 365.   500
88 Classical style. *Stater.* TINC or COM · F on tablet. ℞. Horseman with
javelin. *M. 96, 98, 100; V. 375, 376, 385.*   900
89 — *Quarter stater.* TINC on a tablet, C above, A or B below. ℞. Medusa
hd. facing. *M. 97; V. 378*   550
90 — — *O.* As 88. ℞. Horse l. or r. *M. 99, 101–104; V. 379, 387–90*   325
91 — *Silver.* Head r., TINCOM. ℞. Eagle facing. *M. 105; V. 397*   500
91A — — Head l. ℞. Bull charging l., TINC. *M. 106; V. 396.*   400
92 — — Facing hd. with ornate hair. ℞. As last. *M. —.*   200
92A — — Laureate head l. ℞. Boar standing r., pentagram, TINCO in ex. . . .   *Extremely rare*
92B — — Similar, but head r., C (?) behind. ℞. Bull charging r. *M. —*   500
92C — — — TINCOMMIVS. ℞. Horse l. *M. 131b; V. 473.* (Listed in Mack
under Verica.) . . . .   *Extremely rare*
93 — — TINC. ℞. Animal prancing l. *M. 106a; V. 382.*   200
93A — Victory r., TIN. ℞. CO.F. within wreath. *M. —.*   225
93B — — TINC in angles of four rays, pellets in centre. ℞. Lion on hippocamp
l. *M. —.*   250
93C — — Five pointed star, pellet in centre. ℞. Boy on a dolphin r., TIN below.
M. —.   100
94 — *Silver quarter unit.* C F within two interlinked squares. ℞. Dog to r.,
TINC. *M. 118; V. 383.* . . . .   *Extremely rare*
94A — — Eagle r., TINC. ℞. Two handled krater, REX above. *M. —*   250

*The price in this section is for the condition in which the coin usually appears

£*

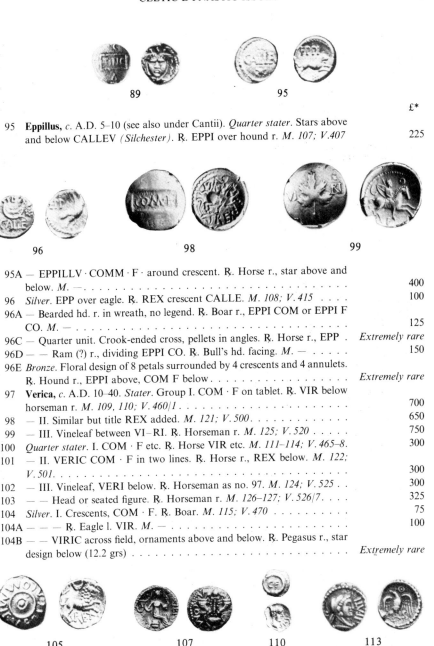

89   95

96   98   99

95   **Eppillus,** *c.* A.D. 5–10 (see also under Cantii). *Quarter stater.* Stars above
     and below CALLEV *(Silchester).* ℞. EPPI over hound r. *M. 107; V.407*   225

95A — EPPILLV · COMM · F · around crescent. ℞. Horse r., star above and
     below. *M. —*   400
96   *Silver.* EPP over eagle. ℞. REX crescent CALLE. *M. 108; V.415*   100
96A — Bearded hd. r. in wreath, no legend. ℞. Boar r., EPPI COM or EPPI F
     CO. *M. —*   125
96C — Quarter unit. Crook-ended cross, pellets in angles. ℞. Horse r., EPP .   *Extremely rare*
96D — — Ram (?) r., dividing EPPI CO. ℞. Bull's hd. facing. *M. —*   150
96E *Bronze.* Floral design of 8 petals surrounded by 4 crescents and 4 annulets.
     ℞. Hound r., EPPI above, COM F below. . . . .   *Extremely rare*
97   **Verica,** *c.* A.D. 10–40. *Stater.* Group I. COM · F on tablet. ℞. VIR below
     horseman r. *M. 109, 110; V.460/1*   700
98   — II. Similar but title REX added. *M. 121; V.500.*   650
99   — III. Vineleaf between VI–RI. ℞. Horseman r. *M. 125; V.520*   750
100 *Quarter stater.* I. COM · F etc. ℞. Horse VIR etc. *M. 111–114; V.465–8.*   300
101 — II. VERIC COM · F in two lines. ℞. Horse r., REX below. *M. 122;*
     V.501.   300
102 — III. Vineleaf, VERI below. ℞. Horseman as no. 97. *M. 124; V.525* . .   300
103 — — Head or seated figure. ℞. Horseman r. *M. 126–127; V.526/7.*   325
104 *Silver.* I. Crescents, COM · F. ℞. Boar. *M. 115; V.470*   75
104A — — — ℞. Eagle l. VIR. *M. —*   100
104B — — VIRIC across field, ornaments above and below. ℞. Pegasus r., star
     design below (12.2 grs) . . . .   *Extremely rare*

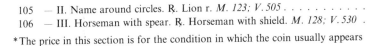

125   107   110   113

105 — II. Name around circles. ℞. Lion r. *M. 123; V.505*   120
106 — III. Horseman with spear. ℞. Horseman with shield. *M. 128; V.530* .   150

*The price in this section is for the condition in which the coin usually appears

Atrebates and Regni *continued* £*

107 — — Seated figure. ℞. Two cornucopiae. *M. 129; V. 531* 90
107A — — Bird l. ℞. As last. *M.* — . . . . *Extremely rare*
108 — — Head r. ℞. Seated or standing figure. *M. 130–131; V. 532/3* 150
108A — — Head r. ℞. Eagle. *M. 131a; V. 534* . . . . *Extremely rare*
108B — — Bull butting r. ℞. Figure standing l. *M.* — . . . . *Extremely rare*
108C — — Bull dividing VERICA REX. ℞. Stg. fig. with head on a standard,
    COMMI F. *M.* — 150
109 *Silver quarter unit.* I. *O.* Various. ℞. Animal. *M. 116–117; 119–120e;*
    V. 480/2/4, 510/11, 552 100
109A — — Eagle l., VE. ℞. Boar's hd. r., CF. *M.* — . . . . *Extremely rare*
109B — Sphinx C.F. ℞. Dog or wolf curled head to tail. VERI. . . . . *Extremely rare*
109C Eagle r. VERCA COMMI F. ℞. Wine krater. *M.* — . . . . *Extremely rare*
110 — III. C · F in wreath. ℞. Head r., VERI. *M. 132; V. 551.* 100
111A — IV. VIR/VAR on tablet. ℞. Pegasus r., CO below. *M.* — . . . . *Extremely rare*
111B — — VERICA around bucranium. ℞. Tomb, or altar, C.F. *M.* — . . . . *Extremely rare*
111C — — 'Maltese cross' design, pellets in angles. ℞. Hand grasping trident,
    VER REX. 300
111D — Two corpucupiae. ℞. Eagle. *M.* . . . . *Extremely rare*
111E Acorn pattern r. ℞. RVER CA, seahorse?. . . . . *Extremely rare*
111F Interlinked C's or crescents, standard between dividing CR at top. ℞.
    Hippocamp, VERICA. *M.* — 175
111G Human headed Sphinx, VERIC. ℞. Hd. r., SCF(?). *M.* — 175
111H Helmeted bust r. in Roman style. ℞. Horse r., CF between legs. *M.* — . 175
112 **Epaticcus,** *c.* A.D. 25–35. *Stater.* TASCI · F, ear of wheat. ℞. EPATICCV,
    horseman r. *M. 262; V. 575.* 1250
113 *Silver.* Head of Hercules r., EPATI. ℞. Eagle stg. on snake. *M. 263; V. 580* 50
114 — Victory seated r. ℞. Boar. *M. 263a; V. 581* 100
114A — EPATI in panel. ℞. Lion r. *M.* — . . . . *Extremely rare*
115 *Silver quarter unit. O.* EPATI. ℞. Lion's head (?), TA below. *M. 264;*
    V. 585. 250
115A — Lion (?) r., EPA. ℞. TA in centre of double lozenge. *M.* — . . . . . . *Rare*
116 *Bronze.* Head r. ℞. Horseman charging r., EPA. *M.* — . . . . *Unique*
    Known only from P. W. P. Carlyon-Britton, sale, 1913, lot 65.
117 **Caratacus,** *c.* A.D. 35–40. *Silver.* As 113, CARA. *M. 265; V. 593.* 600
    The above two rulers were brother and son of Cunoblin (see Catuvellauni), but their
    coins appear in the same area as Verica's.
117A *Silver quarter unit.* CARA around pellet in circle. ℞. Pegasus r., no legend.
    M. —; *V. 595* 450
Cantii *Kent*
118 **Dubnovellaunus,** *c.* 15–1 B.C. *(See also under Trinovantes.) Stater. O.* Blank.
    ℞. Horse r., DVBNOVELLAVNOS or DVBNOVI. *M. 282–283; V. 169/76.* 450
119 *Silver.* Griffin r. or horned animal. ℞. Horse l. or seated figure. *M. 286–*
    287; V. 171/8. 250
120 — Head l. ℞. Pegasus. *M. 288; V. 165.* 250
121 *Bronze.* Boar. ℞. Eagle, horseman or horse. *M. 289, 291, 291a, V. 173,*
    180/1 175
122 — Animal. ℞. Horse or lion l., DVBN on tablet below. *M. 290; V. 166* . 175

117   117A   118   124

*The price in this section is for the condition in which the coin usually appears

£*

123 **Vosenios**, *c.* A.D. 5. *Stater. O.* Blank. ℞. Serpent below horse. *M. 297;*
    V. 184. . . . . *Extremely rare*
124 *Quarter stater.* Similar. VOSII below horse. *M. 298; V. 185*   450
125 *Silver.* Griffin and horse. ℞. Horse, retrograde legend. *M. 299a; V. 186* .   350
126 *Bronze.* Boar l. ℞. Horse l., SA below. *M. 299; V. 187*   250

128   130   131

127 **Eppillus**, *c.* A.D. 10–25. *(See also under Atrebates.) Stater.* COM · F in
    wreath. ℞. Horseman l., EPPILLVS. *M. 300; V. 430.*   900
128 — Victory in wreath. ℞. Horseman r. Illustrated above. *M. 301; V. 431* .   1100
129 *Quarter stater.* EPPIL/COM · F. ℞. Pegasus. *M. 302; V. 435*   225
130 — EPPI around wreath, or COM · F. ℞. Horse. *M. 303–304; V. 436/7.* .   250
131 *Silver.* Head r. or l. ℞. Lion or horseman. *M. 305–306; V. 417/41*   275
132 — Diademed head l. or r., IOVIR. ℞. Victory or capricorn. *M. 307–308a;*
    V. 442/3   275
133 *Bronze.* Head l. ℞. Victory holding wreath. *M. 311; V. 452*   200
134 — Cruciform ornament or bull. ℞. Eagle. *M. 309–310; V. 450/1*   200
135 — Bearded head l. ℞. Horse r. *M. 312; V. 453*   200

136

136 **Amminus**, *c.* A.D. 15? *Silver.* Plant. ℞. Pegasus r. *M. 313; V. 192*   650
137 — A within wreath. ℞. Capricorn r. *M. 314; V. 194*   500
138 *Silver quarter unit.* A within curved lines. ℞. Bird. *M. 316; V. 561*   250
139 *Bronze.* Head r. ℞. Capricorn r. *M. 315; V. 195*   250
139A 'B' within octagonal pattern. ℞. Bird. *M.—*. . . . . *Extremely rare*

Unattributed coins of the Cantii

140 *Silver quarter unti.* Horseman. ℞. Seated figure wearing belt and holding
    spear or staff. *M. 316e; V. 153* . . . . *Extremely rare*
141 *Bronze.* Boar or head. ℞. Lion to r. or l. *M. 316a, c; V. 154.*   150
142 — Animal r. ℞. Horse l. *M. 316b*   150
143 — *O.* Uncertain. ℞. Ring ornaments. *M. 316d; V. 154* . . . . *Extremely rare*
144 *Bronze quarter unit.* Quatrefoil pattern. ℞. Horse r. *M. 316f; V. 154* . . .   150

145   148

*The price in this section is for the condition in which the coin usually appears

£*

Durotriges   *W. Hants., Dorset, Somerset and S. Wilts*

145	**Crab.** Silver. CRAB in angles of cross. ℞. Eagle. *M. 371; V. 1285*	600
146	*Silver quarter unit.* CRAB on tablet. ℞. Star shape. *M. 372; V. 1286* ...	500
147	**Uncertain.** *Silver.* Two boars back to back. ℞. Ring ornaments etc. in field. *M. 373*	Unique

NORTH THAMES

Trinovantes   *Essex and counties to the West*

150   152   154

148	**Addedomaros,** *c. 15–1 B.C. Stater.* Crossed wreath or spiral. ℞. Horse, wheel or cornucopiae below. *M. 266–267; V. 1605/20*	700
149	— Double crescent ornament. ℞. Horse, branch below. *M. 268; V. 1635.*	700
150	*Quarter stater.* Similar, but rectangle or wheel below horse. *M. 269; V. 1638*	700
	[Note. For uninscribed bronze, sometimes attributed to Addedomaros, see S. 77 (M. 273/274; V. 1646).]	
151	**Diras?,** *c. A.D. 1? Stater. O.* Blank. ℞. DIRAS and snake (?) over horse, wheel below. *M. 279; V. 162*	Extremely rare
152	**Dubnovellaunus,** *c. A.D. 1–10. (See also under Cantii.) Stater.* Wreath design. ℞. Horse l., branch below. *M. 275; V. 1650.*	500
153	*Quarter stater.* Similar. *M. 276; V. 1660*	275
154	*Bronze.* Head r. or l. ℞. Horse l. or r. *M. 277–278,* see also *M. 281; V. 1665, 1667, 1669*	75
155	— Without legend but associated with the Trinovantes. Head or boar. ℞. Horse or horseman. *M. 280a, b, d*	120

Catuvellauni   *N. Thames, Herts., Beds., spreading East and South*

157

Tasciovanus, *c. 20 B.C.–A.D. 10, and associated coins*

157	*Stater.* Crescents in wreath. ℞. TASCIAV and bucranium over horse. *M. 149–150; V. 1680/2*	750
158	— Similar, sometimes with VER *(Verulamium).* ℞. Horseman r., TASC. *M. 154–156; V. 1730/2/4*	700
159	— Similar, but T, or V and T. ℞. Similar to last. *M. 157; V. 1790*	Extremely rare
160	— As 157. ℞. Horse, CAMV monogram *(Camulodunum). M. 186; V. 1684* .	800
161	— TASCIOV / RICON in panel. ℞. Horseman l. *M. 184; V. 1780*	900
162	— TASCIO in panel. ℞. Horseman r., SEGO. *M. 194; V. 1845*	900

*The price in this section is for the condition in which the coin usually appears

163	*Quarter stater.* Wreath, TASCI or VERO. R̶. Horse, TAS or TASC. *M. 152–153; V. 1690/2*	300
164	—*O*. As 160. R̶. CAMVL mon. over horse. *M. 187; V. 1694*	300
165	— *O*. As 161, omitting RICON. R̶. Pegasus l. *M. 185; V. 1786*	300
166	— *O*. As 162. R̶. Horse l. omitting SEGO. *M. 195; V. 1848*	300
167	*Silver.* Bearded head l. R̶. Horseman r., TASCIO. *M. 158; V. 1745*. . . .	175
168	— Pegasus l., TAS. R̶. Griffin r., within circle of pellets. *M. 159; V. 1790*	175
169	— Eagle stg. l., TASCIA. R̶. Griffin r., *M. 160; V. 1792*	175
170	—VER in beaded circle. R̶. Horse r., TASCIA. *M. 161; V. 1699*	135
171	— — R̶. Naked horseman, no legend. *M. 162; V. 1747*	135

172   175   178

172	— Laureate hd. r., TASCIA. R̶. Bull butting l. *M. 163; V. 1794*	135
173	— Cruciform ornament, VERL. R̶. Boar, r. TAS. *M. 164; V. 1796*. . . .	135
173A	— Saltire over cross within square, serpentine design around. R̶. Similar to last. *M.* —	500
174	— TASC in panel. R̶. Pegasus l. *M. 165; V. 1798*.	125
175	— — R̶. Horseman l. carrying a long shield. *M. 166; V. 1800*.	125
176	— SEGO on panel. R̶. Horseman. *M. 196; V. 1851*	250
177	— DIAS / C / O. R̶. Horse, VIR (?) below. *M. 188; V. 1877*	250
178	*Bronze.* Two heads in profile, one bearded. R̶. Ram l., TASC. *M. 167; V. 1705*.	75
179	— Bearded head r. R̶. Horse l., VIIR, VER or TAS. *M. 168–169*.	75
180	— Head r., TASC. R̶. Pegasus l., VER. *M. 170*.	75
181	— — TAS ANDO. R̶. Horse r. *M. 170a*	Unique
182	— Head r., TAS. R̶. Horseman r., VER. *M. 171*	75
183	— VERLAMIO between rays of star-shaped ornament. R̶. Bull l. *M. 172*	75

185   190   191

184	*Bronze.* Similar, without legend. R̶. Sphinx l., legend SEGO? *M. 173; V. 1855*.	75
185	— Similar. R̶. Bull r. *M. 174; V. 1810*.	75
186	— Similar. R̶. Horse l., TASCI. *M. 175; V. 1812*.	75
187	— Head r., TASC... R̶. Horse r. in double circle. *M. 175a; V. 1873* . . .	Extremely rare
188	— Laureate hd. r., TASCIO. R̶. Lion r., TASCIO. *M. 176; V. 1814* . . .	75
189	— Head r. R̶. Figure std. l., VER below. *M. 177; V. 1816*	85
190	— — TASCIAVA. R̶. Pegasus l., TAS. *M. 178; V. 1818 (double bronze denomination)*	Extremely rare

*The price in this section is for the condition in which the coin usually appears

Tasciovanus *continued*   £*

191	— Cruciform ornament of crescents and scrolls. ℞. Boar r., VER. *M. 179; V. 1713*	100
192	— Laureate head r. ℞. Horse l., VIR. *M. 180; V. 1820.*	80
193	— Raised band across centre, VER or VERL below, uncertain objects above. ℞. Horse grazing r. *M. 183a; V. 1717*	100
194	— RVII above lion r. within wide beaded circle. ℞. Eagle looking l., sometimes reading RVE. *M. 189; V. 1890.*	100
195	— Bearded head r., RVIIS. ℞. Horseman r., VIR. *M. 190; V. 1892.* . . .	90
196	— RVIIS on panel. ℞. Animal l. *M. 191; V. 1895*	100
197	— Head r., TASC DIAS. ℞. Centaur r. playing double pipe, or sometimes horses. *M. 192; V. 1882.*	100
198	*Bronze half denomination.* Lion? r. ℞. Sphinx l. *M. 181; V. 1824*	*Extremely rare*
199	— Bearded head l. or r., VER. ℞. Goat or boar r. *M. 182–183; V. 1715, 1826*	100
200	— Head l. ℞. Animal l. with curved tail. *M. 183b, c; V. 1822*	100
201	— Annulet within square with curved sides. ℞. Eagle l., RVII. *M. 193; V. 1903*	100

202   203   205

202	**Andoco,** *c.* A.D. 5–15. *Stater.* Crossed wreath design. ℞. Horse r., AND. *M. 197; V. 1860*	1000
203	*Quarter stater.* Crossed wreaths, ANDO. ℞. Horse l. *M. 198; V. 1863* . .	325
204	*Silver.* Bearded head l. in looped circle. ℞. Pegasus l., ANDOC. *M. 199; V. 1868*	400
205	*Bronze.* Head r., ANDOCO. ℞. Horse r., AND. *M. 200; V. 1871.*	130
206	*Bronze half denomination.* Head l. ℞. Horse r., A between legs, branch in exergue. *M.* —	175

207   208

207	**Cunobelin** *(Shakespeare's Cymbeline).* c. A.D. 10–40. *Stater.* CAMVL on panel. ℞. Leaf above two horses galloping l., CVNOBELIN on curved panel below. *M. 201; V. 1910.*	800
208	— Ear of corn dividing CA MV. ℞. Horse prancing r., CVNO below. *M. 203, 206, 210–213. V. 2010/25/1925/31/33/2020* Varying in style, from— .	600
209	— Similar, but horse l. *M. 208; V. 2029*	1000
210	*Quarter stater.* Similar to 207. *M. 202; V. 1913*	250
211	— Similar to 208. *M. 204, 209; V. 1927, 2015.*	275
212	— Similar to 208 but CAM CVN on *obv. M. 205; V. 2017*	400
213	*Silver.* Two bull headed snakes intertwined. ℞. Horse l., CVNO. *M. 214; V. 1947.*	200

*The price in this section is for the condition in which the coin usually appears

£*

214 — Head l., CAMVL before. ℞. CVNO beneath Victory std. r. *M. 215; V. 2045*.   125

215 — CVNO BELI in two panels. ℞. CVN below horseman galloping r. (legends sometimes retrograde). *M. 216, 217; V. 1951/3*   175

216 — Two leaves dividing CVN. ℞. CAM below horseman galloping r. *M. 218; V. 2047*   200

217 — Flower dividing CA MV. ℞. CVNO below horse r. *M. 219; V. 2049* .   200

218 — CVNO on panel. ℞. CAMV on panel below griffin. *M. 234; V. 2051* .   175

219 — CAMVL on panel. ℞. CVNO below centaur l. carrying palm. *M. 234a; V. 1918*   175

219A CAMVL on panel. ℞. Figure seated l. holding wine amphora, CVNOBE. *M. —*   200

219B 🌿 Plant, CVNOBELINVS (see no. 136 Amminus). ℞. Hercules stg. r. holding club and thunderbolt, dividing CA MV. *M. —* . . . . *Extremely rare*

219C — Laur. hd. r., CVNOBELINVS. ℞. Pegasus springing l., CAMV below. *M. —* . . . . *Extremely rare*

220 — CVNO on panel. ℞. TASC F below Pegasus r. *M. 235; V. 2053*   200

221   225

221 — Head r., CVNOBELINI. ℞. TASCIO below horse r. *M. 236; V. 2055*   300

222 — Winged bust r., CVNO. ℞. Sphinx std. l., TASCIO. *M. 237; V. 2057* .   90

223 — Draped female figure r., TASCIIOVAN. ℞. Figure std. r. playing lyre, tree behind. *M. 238; V. 2059*   200

224 — Male figure stg. dividing CV NO. ℞. Female std. side saddle on animal, TASCIIOVA. *M. 239; V. 2061*   200

224A — Laur. hd. r., CVNOBELINVS. ℞. Victory r., TASCIO[VAN . . .] . . .   200

225 — Figure r. carrying dead animal, CVNOBELINVS. ℞. Figure stg. holding bow, dog at side, TASCIIOVANI. *M. 240; V. 2063*   225

226 — CVNO on panel, horn above, two dolphins below. ℞. Figure stg. r., altar behind. *M. 241a; V. 2065*   250

227 *Silver.* CVNO on panel. ℞. Fig. walking r., CV N. *M. 254; V. 2067* . . .   225

228 — — ℞. Animal springing l. *M. 255; V. 1949*.   285

229 — CVN in centre of wreath. ℞. CAM below dog or she-wolf stg. r. *M. 256; V. 2069*   285

230 — CVNO, animal l. ℞. CA below figure std. r. holding caduceus. *M. 258; V. 2071*   425

231 — SOLIDV in centre of looped circle. ℞. Standing figure l., CVNO. *M. 259; V. 2073*   450

232 *Bronze.* Head l., CVNO. ℞. Boar l., branch above. *M. 220; V. 1969* . . .   65

233 — CVNOB ELINI in two panels. ℞. Victory std. l., TASC · F. *M. 221; V. 1971*   65

234 — Winged animal l., CAM below. ℞. CVN before Victory stg. l. *M. 222a; V. 1973*   65

235 — Bearded head facing. ℞. Similar to no. 232. *M. 223; V. 1963*.   100

236 — Ram-headed animal coiled up within double ornamental circle. ℞. CAM below animal l. *M. 224; V. 1965*   125

237 — Winged animal r., CAMV. ℞. CVN below horse galloping r. *M. 225; V. 2081*   80

*The price in this section is for the condition in which the coin usually appears

£*

238 — Bearded head l., CAMV. R̩. CVN or CVNO below horse l. *M. 226, 229, V. 2085/2131*   75
239 — Laureate head r., CVNO. R̩. CVN below bull butting l. *M. 227; V. 2083.*   100
240 — Crude head r., CVN. R̩. Figure stg. l., CVN. *M. 228; V. 2135*   75
241 — CAMVL / ODVNO in two panels. R̩. CVNO beneath sphinx crouching l. *M. 230; V. 1977*   80

242   247   251

242 — Winged beast springing l., CAMV. R̩. Victory stg. r. divides CV NO. *M. 231; V. 1979.*   80
243 — Victory walking r. R̩. CVN below, horseman r. *M. 232; V. 1981.*   80
244 — Beardless head l., CAM. R̩. CVNO below eagle. *M. 233; V. 2087* . . .   80
245 — Laureate head l., CVNOBELINI. R̩. Centaur r., TASCIOVANI · F. *M. 242; V. 2089*   75
246 — Helmeted bust r. R̩. TASCIIOVANII above, sow stg. r., F below. *M. 243; V. 2091*   75
247 — Horseman galloping r. holding dart and shield, CVNOB. R̩. Warrior stg. l., TASCIIOVANTIS. *M. 244; V. 2093*   60
248 — Helmeted bust l., CVNOBII. R̩. TASC . FIL below boar l. std. on haunches. *M. 245; V. 1983*   125
249 — Bare head r., CVNOBELINVS REX. R̩. TASC below bull butting r. *M. 246; V. 2095*   75
250 — Bare head l., CVNO. R̩. TASC below bull stg. r. *M. 247; V. 1985.* . . .   100
251 — Winged head l., CVNOBELIN. R̩. Metal worker std. r. holding hammer, working on a vase, TASCIO behind. *M. 248; V. 2097*   75
252 — Pegasus springing r., CVNO. R̩. Victory r., sacrificing bull, TASCI. *M. 249; V. 2099*   75
253 — CVNO on panel within wreath. R̩. CAMV below horse, full faced, prancing r. *M. 250; V. 2101.*   95

254

254 *Bronze.* Bearded head of Jupiter Ammon l., CVNOBELIN. R̩. CAM below horseman galloping r. *M. 251; V. 2103.*   90
255 — Janus head, CVNO below. R̩. CAMV on panel below, sow std. r. beneath a tree. *M. 252; V. 2105*   150
256 — Bearded head of Jupiter Ammon r., CVNOB. R̩. CAM on panel below lion crouched r. *M. 253; V. 2107.*   90
257 — Sphinx r., CVNO. R̩. Fig. stg. l. divides CA M. *M. 260; V. 2109* . . .   175
258 — Animal stg. r. R̩. CVN below horseman r. *M. 261; V. 1987*   175

*The price in this section is for the condition in which the coin usually appears

£*

259 *Bronze half denomination.* Animal l. looking back. ℞. CVN below horse l.
    M. 233a; V. 1967. 200

S.W. MIDLANDS

Dobunni   *Glos., Here., Mon., Oxon., Som., Wilts. and Worcs.*

260

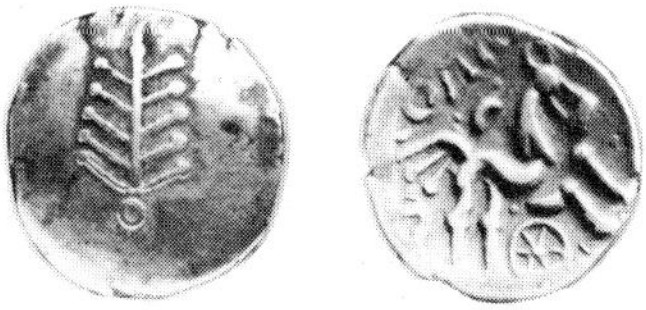

267

		£*
260	**Anted.** *Stater.* Ear of corn. ℞. ANTED or ANTEDRIG over triple-tailed horse r. *M. 385–386; V. 1062/6.*	700
261	*Silver.* Crude head r., as 64. ℞. AN TED over horse l. *M. 387; V. 1082* .	250
262	**Eisu.** *Stater.* Similar to 260 but EISV or EISVRIG. *M. 388; V. 1105* . . .	1300
263	*Silver.* Similar to 261 but EISV. *M. 389; V. 1110.*	225
264	**Inam.** (or Inara). *Stater.* Similar to 260 but INAM (or INARA). *M. 390; V. 1140*	*Extremely rare*
265	**Catti.** *Stater.* Similar to 260 but CATTI. *M. 391; V. 1130*	800
266	**Comux.** *Stater.* Similar to 260 but COMVX outwardly. *M. 392; V. 1092.*	950
267	**Corio.** *Stater.* Similar to 260 but COŘIO. *M. 393; V. 1035*	875
268	*Quarter stater.* COR in centre. ℞. Horse r. without legend. *M. 394; V. 1039*	1250

269

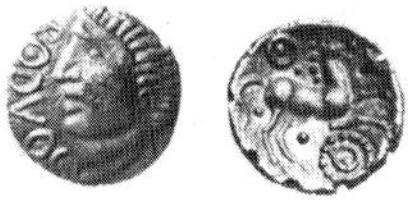

270

		£*
269	**Bodvoc.** *Stater.* BODVOC across field. ℞. As last. *M. 395; V. 1052.*	1200
270	*Silver.* Head l., BODVOC. ℞. As last. *M. 396; V. 1057*	200

EASTERN ENGLAND

Iceni   *Cambs., Norfolk and Suffolk*   *c.* A.D. 10–61

272

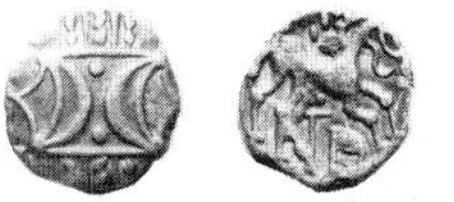

273

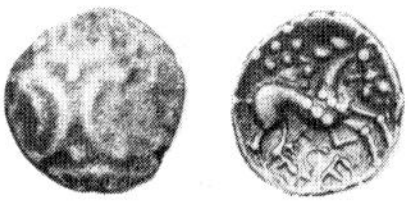

279

*The price in this section is for the condition in which the coin usually appears

£*

271 **Duro.** *Silver.* Boar. Ɍ. Horse r., CAN(s) above, DVRO below. *M. 434; V. 663.* 500

272 **Anted.** *Stater.* Triple crescent design. Ɍ. ANTED in two monograms below horse. *M. 418; V. 705* . . . . *Extremely rare*

273 *Silver.* Two crescents back to back. Ɍ. ANTED as last. *M. 419–421; V. 710/11/15* 40

274 *Silver half unit.* Similar to last. *M. 422; V. 720* 60

275 **Ecen.** *Silver.* As 273. Ɍ. Open headed horse r., ECEN below. *M. 424; V. 730.* 40

276 *Silver half unit.* Similar, but legends read ECE, EC, or ECN. *M. 431; V. 736* . 65

277 **Ed.** *Silver.* Similar to 275 but ED (also, E, EI and EDN) below horse. *M. 423, 425b; V. 734/40.* 150

278 **Ece.** *Silver.* As 273. Ɍ. Stepping horse r., ECE below. *M. 425a; V. 761.* . 60

279 — Similar, but "Y" headed horse r., ECE below. *M. 426–427; V. 762/4* . 50

280 — Similar, but horse l. *M. 428; V. 766* 50

281 **Saemu.** *Silver.* As 273. Ɍ. "Y" headed horse r., SAEMV below. *M. 433; V. 770.* 200

282 **Aesu.** *Silver.* As 273. Ɍ. As last, AESV. *M. 432; V. 775* 300

283

283 **Prasutagus,** Client King of the Iceni under Claudius; husband of Boudicca. *Silver.* Head of good style l. SUB RII PRASTO. Ɍ. Rearing horse r., ESICO FECIT. *M. 434a; V. 780* 1100

The attribution by H. Mossop of these rare coins to King Prasutagus has been made after a study of the legends on the ten known specimens and is published in "Britannia", X. 1979.

284 **Iat Iso.** *Silver.* IAT ISO (retrograde) on tablet, rosettes above and below. Ɍ. Horse r., E above. *M. 416; V. 998* 600

285 **Ale Sca.** *Silver.* Boar r., ALE below. Ɍ. Horse, SCA below. *M. 469; V. 996.* 300

Coritani *Lincs., Yorks. and E. Midlands c. A.D. 10–61*

291   292   298

286 **Aun Cost.** *Stater.* Crude wreath type. Ɍ. Disjointed horse l., AVN COST. *M. 457; V. 910.* 750

287 *Silver. O.* Blank or crude wreath design. Ɍ. AVN above horse l. *M. 458; V. 914.* 300

288 *Silver half unit.* Similar. *Vide M. p. 166 .* . . . . *Extremely rare*

289 **Esup Asu.** *Stater.* As 286 but IISVP ASV. *M. 456b; V. 920* 1100

290 *Silver.* Similar. *M. 456c; V. 924.* . . . . *Extremely rare*

*The price in this section is for the condition in which the coin usually appears

£*

291 **Vep Corf.** *Stater.* As 286. R. Disjointed horse, VEP CORF. *M. 459, 460;*
   V. 930.   550
292 *Silver.* Similar. *M. 460b, 464; V. 934, 50.*   250
293 *Silver half unit.* Similar. *M. 464a; V. 938* . . . .   *Extremely rare*
294 **Vepos Comes**(?). *Silver.* Similar but VEPOC (M)ES, pellets below horse.
   M. —   250
295 *Silver half unit.* Similar. *M. —* . . . .   *Extremely rare*
296 **Vep.** *Stater. O.* Blank. R. VEP. (Only plated coins are known.) *M. 460a;*
   V. 905.   375
297 *Silver.* As 286 or blank. R. VEP only. *M. —*   200
298 *Silver half unit.* Similar. *M. 464b; V. 967*   250
299 **Dumno Tigir Seno.** *Stater.* DVMN (OC)? across wreath. R. Horse l.,
   TIGIR SENO. *M. 461; V. 972.*   1000
300 *Silver. O.* DVMNO(C)? R. Horse r., legend as last. *M. 462; V. 974.*   350

299   301   305

301 **Volisios Dumnocoveros.** *Stater.* VOLI / SIOS in two lines. R. Horse,
   DVMNOCOVEROS across crude wreath. *M. 463; V. 978.*   750
302 *Silver.* As last. *M. 463a; V. 978 or 80*   350
303 *Silver half unit.* As last but DVMNOCO. *M. 465; V. 984*   350
304 **Volisios Dumnovellaunos.** *Stater.* As 301. R. Horse, DVMNOVELAV-
   NOS. *M. 466; V. 988*   700
305 Silver half unit. As last but DVMNOVE. *M. 467; V. 992*   250
306 **Volisios Cartivel.** *Silver half unit.* As 301. R. Horse, CARTIVEL. *M. 468;*
   V. 994. . . . .   *Extremely rare*

*The price in this section is for the condition in which the coin usually appears

ROMAN BRITAIN

From the middle of the first century A.D. until the early part of the fifth century, Britannia was a province of the vast Roman Empire—a single state encompassing the whole of the Mediterranean basin. In common with other western provinces, no local coinage was officially produced in Britain during this period (unlike the Eastern part of the Empire where hundreds of towns were permitted to issue muncipal currency) until the latter part of the third century. It was, therefore, the regular Imperial coinage produced mainly at Rome until the mid-third century, that supplied the currency requirements of the province, and no representative collection of British coins is complete without some examples of these important issues.

Although Britain was on the fringe of the Roman World, and never entirely subdued by the legions, a surprisingly large number of coin types allude to events in the province—usually frontier wars in the north. In the closing years of the third century, the usurper Carausius established two mints in Britain; one in London, the other not yet certainly identified (either Camulodunum: Colchester or Clausentum: Bitterne, Southampton). After the defeat of the rebellion London became an official Roman mint, with a substantial output of bronze coinage until its closure, by Constantine the Great, in A.D. 325. Other coins were produced unofficially in Britain at various times: soon after the conquest (copies of bronze coins of Claudius, etc.), in the troubled times of the early 270s (copies of Claudius II and the Tetrici, i.e., "Barbarous radiates") and the final years of the occupation (mostly imitated from the bronze coinage of Constantius II—"soldier spearing fallen horseman" type).

The Roman legions were withdrawn to the continent by Honorius in A.D. 411, but a Romano-British civil administration continued to operate for some time afterward until disrupted by the Teutonic invasions.

For general information on Roman coinage see *Roman Coins and their Values* by D. R. Sear and *Roman Coins* by J. P. C. Kent; for more detailed works consult *Roman Imperial Coinage*, the British Museum Catalogues of Roman coins, *Roman Silver Coins* (5 vols.), the first four by H. A. Seaby and Vol. V by Dr C. E. King, and *The Coinage of Roman Britain* by G. Askew (2nd Edition).

An invaluable companion volume for anyone studying Roman coinage is S. W. Stevenson's *A Dictionary of Roman Coins*.

THE REPUBLIC

Only a few representative examples are listed. Many Republican coins circulated well into the Imperial period and found their way to Britain.

	F	VF
	£	£
451 C. Naevius Balbus, moneyer, 79 B.C. Æ *denarius*. Diad. hd. of Venus r. ℞. Victory in triga r.	10	25

452   454

452 C. Calpurnius Piso, moneyer, 67 B.C. Æ *denarius*. Head of Apollo r. ℞. Horseman galloping r.	10	30
453 **Julius Caesar,** dictator, †44 B.C. Made two expeditions to Britain in 55 and 54 B.C. Æ *denarius*. Laur. head r. ℞. Venus stg. l.	120	300
454 Æ *denarius*. Elephant stg. r. ℞. Sacrifical implements	30	80
455 **Mark Antony,** triumvir, †30 B.C. Æ *denarius*. Galley r. ℞. Legionary eagle between two standards	22	65

Known for all Legions from I (PRImus) to XXIII, though only the following are known to have served in Britain during the Roman occupation—II Augusta, VI Victrix, IX Hispania, XIV Gemina Martia Victrix and XX Valeria Victrix.

THE EMPIRE

456   461

		F £	VF £
456	**Augustus,** 27 B.C.–A.D. 14. Æ *denarius.* ℞. Caius and Lucius Caesars . .	22	65
457	Æ *as.* ℞. The altar of Lugdunum	20	60
458	**Divus Augustus Pater,** commemorative issue. Æ *as.* ℞. PROVIDENT S . C. Altar	20	60
459	**Livia,** wife of Augustus. Æ *dupondius.* ℞. Legend around S . C	40	150
460	**Agrippa,** general and statesman, †12 B.C. Æ *as.* ℞. Neptune stg. l.	25	75
461	**Tiberius,** A.D. 14–37. Æ *denarius.* ℞. Livia seated r.	35	85
	This coin is often referred to as the "Tribute Penny" of the Bible.		
462	**Drusus,** son of Tiberius, †A.D. 23. Æ *as.* ℞. Legend around S . C.	30	90
463	**Nero Claudius Drusus,** father of Claudius, †9 B.C. Æ *sestertius.* ℞. Claudius seated amidst arms	80	300
464	**Antonia,** mother of Claudius, †A.D. 37. Æ *dupondius.* ℞. Claudius stg. l.	45	125
465	**Germanicus,** father of Caligula, †A.D. 19. Æ *as.* ℞. Legend around S . C..	25	80
466	**Agrippina Senior,** wife of Germanicus, †A.D. 33. Æ *sestertius.* ℞. Two mules drawing covered carriage	150	500
467	**Caligula,** 37–41. Æ *as.* ℞. VESTA. Vesta seated l.	35	100

468   474

468	**Claudius,** 41–54. Invaded Britain A.D. 43. Æ *aureus.* ℞. DE BRITANN on triumphal arch.	500	1500
469	Æ *denarius.* Similar	120	350
470	Æ *didrachm* of Caesarea. ℞. DE BRITANNIS below Emperor in quadriga r.	95	300
471	Æ *sestertius.* ℞. SPES AVGVSTA S . C. Spes walking l., of barbarous style, struck in Britain.	50	180
472	Æ *dupondius.* ℞. CERES AVGVSTA S . C. Ceres seated l., of barbarous style, struck in Britain.	30	85
473	Æ *as.* ℞. S . C. Minerva brandishing javelin	25	75
474	**Nero,** 54–68. Æ *denarius.* ℞. SALVS. Salus seated l..	45	125
475	Æ *as.* ℞. S . C. Victory flying l.	20	70
476	**Galba,** 68–69. Æ *denarius.* ℞. DIVA AVGVSTA. Livia stg. l.	50	150

		F £	VF £
477	**Otho,** 69. Æ *denarius*. ℞. SECVRITAS P . R. Securitas stg. l.	80	250
478	**Vitellius,** 69. Æ *denarius*. ℞. XV . VIR SACR . FAC. Tripod with dolphin	40	110

479   483

479	**Vespasian,** 69–79. Commanded one of the legions in the Claudian invasion of Britain. Æ *denarius*. ℞. ANNONA AVG. Annona seated l.	12	35
480	Æ *as*. ℞. PROVIDENT. S . C. Large altar	20	60
481	**Titus,** 79–81. Æ *denarius*. ℞. FORTVNA AVGVST. Fortuna stg. l. . . .	20	60
482	**Domitian,** 81–96. Æ *denarius*. ℞. IMP . XI. COS . XI . CENS . P . P . P. Minerva fighting.	10	30
483	Æ *dupondius*. ℞. VIRTVTI AVGVSTI. S . C. Virtus stg. r.	16	45
484	**Nerva,** 96–98. Æ *denarius*. ℞. CONCORDIA EXERCITVVM. Clasped hands.	20	60

485   489

485	**Trajan,** 98–117. Æ *denarius*. ℞. P . M . TR . P . COS . III . P . P. Victory standing r. on prow	10	30
486	Æ *sestertius*. ℞. S . P . Q . R . OPTIMO PRINCIPI. S . C. Fortuna stg. l. .	25	90
487	**Hadrian,** 117–138. Visited Britain *c*. A.D. 122 and constructed his famous wall from the Tyne to the Solway. Æ *denarius*. ℞. FIDES PVBLICA. Fides stg. r.	10	35
488	Æ *sestertius*. ℞. ADVENTVI AVG . BRITANNIAE. S . C. Emperor and Britannia sacrificing over altar	*Extremely rare*	
489	— ℞. BRITANNIA. S . C. Britannia seated l.	*Extremely rare*	
490	— ℞. EXERC . BRITANNI. S . C. Emperor on horseback addressing soldiers.	*Extremely rare*	
491	Æ *as*. ℞. PONT . MAX . TR . POT . COS . III . BRITANNIA. S . C. Britannia seated l.	100	300

	F £	VF £

492 **Sabina,** wife of Hadrian, Æ *denarius.* R. CONCORDIA AVG. Concordia seated l.   20   55

493 **Aelius Caesar,** 136–138. Æ *as.* R. TR . POT . COS . II . S . C. Fortuna stg. l.   25   80

494 **Antoninus Pius,** 138–161. His generals in Britain pushed the Roman frontier forward to the Forth–Clyde line (the Antonine Wall). Æ *aureus.* R. IMPERATOR II . BRITAN. Victory stg. on globe.   450   1200

495 Æ *denarius.* R. AEQVITAS AVG. Aequitas stg. l..   8   25

496   499

496 Æ *sestertius.* R. BRITANNIA. S . C. Britannia seated l. on rocks   350   1000

497 — R. IMPERATOR II . BRITAN. S . C. Victory stg. on globe   150   450

498 Æ *as.* R. Victory l. holding shield inscribed BRI · TAN   75   225

499 — R. BRITANNIA COS . III . S . C. Britannia seated l. in attitude of sadness.   45   135

  This coin was very possibly struck at a temporary travelling mint in Britain.

500 **Faustina Senior,** wife of Antoninus Pius, Æ *denarius.* R. AVGVSTA. Ceres stg. r.   8   25

501 Æ *sestertius.* R. IVNO S . C. Juno stg. l.   18   55

502 **Marcus Aurelius,** 161–180. Æ *denarius.* R. COS III. Jupiter seated l. . . .   10   30

503 Æ *sestertius.* R. IMP . VI . COS . III. S . C. Roma seated l.   25   80

504   510   515

		F	VF
		£	£
504	**Faustina Junior,** wife of Marcus Aurelius. Æ *denarius*. ℞. IVNONI REGINAE. Juno and peacock	8	25
505	Æ *as*. ℞. DIANA LVCIF . S . C. Diana stg. l.	10	30
506	**Lucius Verus,** 161–169. Æ *denarius*. ℞. CONCORD . AVG . COS . II. Concordia seated l.	15	45
507	**Lucilla,** wife of Lucius Verus. Æ *dupondius*. ℞. SALVS S . C. Salus stg. l..	12	35
508	**Commodus,** 177–192. There was considerable military activity in northern Britain in the early part of his reign. Æ *denarius*. ℞. MARTI VLTORI AVG. Mars stg. l.	15	45
509	Æ *sestertius*. ℞. BRITT . etc. Britannia stg., holding sword and wreath .	*Extremely rare*	
510	— ℞. VICT . BRIT . etc. Victory seated r., inscribing shield	75	225
511	**Crispina,** wife of Commodus, Æ *as*. ℞. IVNO LVCINA S . C. Juno stg. l	18	55
512	**Pertinax,** 193. One time governor of Britain, under Commodus. Æ *denarius*. ℞. LAETITIA TEMPOR COS . II. Laetitia stg. l	175	500
513	**Didius Julianus,** 193. Æ *sestertius*. ℞. CONCORD MILIT S . C. Concordia stg. l.	200	600
514	**Clodius Albinus,** 195–197. Proclaimed emperor while governor of Britain. Æ *denarius*. ℞. MINER . PACIF . COS . II. Minerva stg. l.	45	120
515	**Septimius Severus,** 193–211. Campaigned in Britain with his sons Caracalla and Geta; died at York. Æ *aureus*. ℞. VICTORIAE BRIT. Victory l., holding wreath and palm	850	2500
516	Æ *denarius*. ℞. Similar .	20	60
517	— ℞. Similar, but Victory seated l.	20	65
518	— ℞. Similar, but Victory stg. beside palm tree.	24	70
519	— ℞. VIRT . AVG. Roma stg. l.	9	25

520   528

520	Æ *sestertius*. ℞. VICTORIAE BRITANNICAE S.C. Two Victories affixing shield to palm tree, two captives below	140	375
521	Æ *dupondius*. ℞. Similar, but Victory inscribing shield on palm tree . . .	85	250
522	Æ *as*. ℞. Similar, Victory stg. r. holding vexillum	85	250
524	**Julia Domna,** wife of Septimius Severus. Æ *denarius*. ℞. PIETAS PVBLICA. Pietas stg. l..	7	20
525	**Caracalla,** 198–217. Personally led the campaign of A.D. 210. Æ *aureus*. ℞. VICTORIAE BRIT. Victory seated l., holding shield	850	2500

	F £	VF £
526 *N quinarius*. ℞. VICTORIAE BRIT. Victory advancing l., holding wreath and palm	1100	3000
527 *Æ denarius*. ℞. MARTI PACATORI. Mars stg. l.	9	25
528 — ℞. VICTORIAE BRIT. Victory advancing l., holding wreath and palm	22	65
529 — ℞. VICTORIAE BRIT. Victory advancing r., holding trophy	22	65
530 *Æ sestertius*. ℞. VICT . BRIT . P . M . TR . P . XIII . COS . III . P . P . S . C. Victory stg. r., erecting trophy	140	375
531 — ℞. VICT . BRIT . etc. Victory inscribing shield on tree.	130	350
532 — ℞. VICTORIAE BRITANNICAE. S . C. Two Victories erecting shield on tree	150	450
533 *Æ dupondius*. ℞. VICTORIAE BRITANNICAE. S . C. Victory seated l., on shields	28	80
534 **Plautilla**, wife of Caracalla. *Æ denarius*. ℞. PIETAS AVGG. Pietas stg. r..	16	45
535 **Geta**, 209–212. *Æ denarius*. ℞. PONTIF . COS . II. Genius stg. l.	18	50
536 — ℞. VICTORIAE BRIT. Victory advancing r., holding wreath and palm	28	75
537 *Æ sestertius*. ℞. VICTORIAE BRITANNICAE. S . C. Victory seated r., inscribing shield	150	450

537   541

538 — ℞. VICTORIAE BRITANNICAE. S . C. Victory standing r., erecting trophy; Britannia stg. facing with hands tied	150	450
538A **Geta**, 209–212. Billon *tetradrachm* of Alexandria, Egypt. ℞. NEIKH . KATA . BPET. Victory flying l.	200	600
539 **Macrinus**, 217–218. *Æ denarius*. ℞. SALVS PVBLICA. Salus seated l., feeding snake	20	60
540 **Diadumenian**, *as Caesar*, 217–218. *Æ denarius*. ℞. PRINC IVVENTVTIS. Diadumenian holding sceptre.	50	150
541 **Elagabalus**, 218–222. *Æ denarius*. ℞. FIDES MILITVM. Fides stg. l., head r., holding standards	10	30
542 **Julia Paula**, wife of Elagabalus. *Æ denarius*. ℞. CONCORDIA. Concordia seated l.	30	85
543 **Aquilia Severa**, wife of Elagabalus. *Æ denarius*. ℞. CONCORDIA. Concordia stg. l.	55	135
544 **Julia Soaemias**, mother of Elagabalus. *Æ denarius*. ℞. VENVS CAELESTIS. Venus stg. l.	25	65
545 **Julia Maesa**, grandmother of Elagabalus. *Æ denarius*. ℞. IVNO. Juno stg. l.	15	40

546   550

558   563

		F £	VF £
565	**Hostilian Caesar**, 251. Æ *antoninianus*. R̨. PIETAS AVGVSTORVM. Sacrificial implements	20	55
566	**Trebonianus Gallus**, 251–253. Æ *antoninianus*. R̨. LIBERTAS AVGG. Libertas stg. l.	7	20
567	**Volusian**, 251–253. Æ *antoninianus*. R̨. CONCORDIA AVGG. Concordia seated l.	7	20
568	**Aemilian**, 252–253. Æ *antoninianus*. R̨. PACI AVG. Pax stg. l.	45	95
569	**Valerian I**, 253–260. Billon *antoninianus*. R̨. VICTORIA AVGG. Victory stg. l.	4	10

570   576

570	**Gallienus**, 253–268. Æ *antoninianus*. R̨. DIANAE CONS . AVG. Antelope	3	8
571	**Salonina**, wife of Gallienus. Æ *antoninianus*. R̨. PIETAS AVG. Pietas stg. l.	3	8
572	**Valerian II Caesar**, 253–255. Billon *antoninianus*. R̨. PIETAS AVGG. Sacrificial implements	7	20
573	**Saloninus Caesar**, 259. Billon *antoninianus*. R̨. SPES PVBLICA. Spes advancing l.	7	20
574	**Macrianus**, usurper in the East, 260–261. Billon *antoninianus*. R̨. SOL. INVICTO. Sol stg. l.	26	75
575	**Quietus**, usurper in the East, 260–261. Billon *antoninianus*. R̨. ROMAE AETERNAE. Roma seated l.	26	75
576	**Postumus**, usurper in the West, 259–268. Æ *antoninianus*. R̨. MONETA AVG. Moneta stg. l.	5	15
577	**Laelianus**, usurper in the West, 268. Æ *antoninianus*. R̨. VICTORIA AVG. Victory advancing r.	60	185
578	**Marius**, usurper in the West, 268. Æ *antoninianus*. R̨. VICTORIA AVG. Victory advancing r.	20	60
579	**Victorinus**, usurper in the West, 268–270. A/ *aureus*. R̨. LEG . XX . VAL . VICTRIX. Boar l	3,500	10,000
580	Æ *antoninianus*. R̨. SALVS AVG. Salus stg. l.	4	10
581	**Claudius II Gothicus**, 268–270. Æ *antoninianus*. R̨. MARTI PACIF. Mars advancing l.	3	8
582	**Tetricus I**, usurper in the West, 270–273. Æ *antoninianus*. LAETITIA AVG. Laetitia stg. l.	3	8
583	**Tetricus II Caesar**, usurper in the West, 270–273. Æ *antoninianus*. R̨. SPES AVGG. Spes advancing l.	4	10

584A   584B   584C

		F £	VF £
584	**Barbarous radiates.** British and Continental copies of Æ *antoniniani*, mostly of Claudius II (A), Tetricus I (B) and Tetricus II (C)	2	4
585	**Quintillus,** 270. Æ *antoninianus*. ℞. FIDES MILIT. Fides stg. l..	10	25
586	**Aurelian,** 270–275. Æ *antoninianus*. ℞. SECVRIT . AVG. Securitas stg. l..	4	10

587   596

587	**Severina,** wife of Aurelian. Æ *antoninianus*. ℞. PROVIDEN . DEOR. Fides and Sol stg.	10	25
588	**Tacitus,** 275–276. Æ *antoninianus*. ℞. CLEMENTIA TEMP. Clementia stg. l.	7	20
589	**Florianus,** 276. Æ *antoninianus*. ℞. SALVS AVG. Salus stg. l..	18	55
590	**Probus,** 276–282. Æ *antoninianus*. ℞. ABVNDANTIA AVG. Abundantia stg. r..	4	10
591	**Carus,** 282–283. Æ *antoninianus*. ℞. PAX EXERCITI. Pax stg. l.	8	25
592	**Numerian,** 283–284. Æ *antoninianus*. ℞. ORIENS AVG. Sol advancing l..	7	22
593	**Carinus,** 283–285. Æ *antoninianus*. ℞. AETERNIT . AVG. Aeternitas stg. l.	6	18
594	**Diocletian,** 284–305, London mint reopened *c.* 297. Æ *argenteus*. ℞. VIRTVS MILITVM. Tetrarchs sacrificing before camp gate	75	200
595	Æ *antoninianus*. ℞. CLEMENTIA TEMP. Diocletian and Jupiter stg. . .	4	12
596	Æ *follis*. ℞. GENIO POPVLI ROMANI. Genius stg. l., LON (London) *mm*.	8	28

597   600

Diocletian *continued*

		F	VF
		£	£
597	Æ *follis.* ℞. Similar, no *mm.* (London)	8	25
598	— ℞. Similar, other *mms..*	6	20
599	**Maximianus, 286–310.** Æ *argenteus.* ℞. VIRTVS MILITVM. Tetrarchs sacrificing before camp gate	50	150
600	Æ *antoninianus.* ℞. SALVS AVGG. Salus stg. l.	4	12
601	Æ *follis.* ℞. GENIO POPVLI ROMANI. Genius stg. l., LON. *mm.*	10	30
602	— ℞. Similar, no *mm..*	7	24
603	**Carausius,** commander of the Roman Channel fleet, who took power in Britain and Northern Gaul, 287–293. *London mint* Æ *aureus.* ℞. PAX AVG. Pax stg. l., no *mm..*	7500	17500

604   623

604	Æ *denarius.* ℞. CONSER AVG. Neptune seated l.	550	1500
605	Æ *antoninianus.* ℞. ADVENTVS AVG. Emperor riding l.	55	160
606	— ℞. COHR . PRAEF. Four standards	70	200
607	— ℞. COMES AVG. Victory stg. l.	25	70
608	— ℞. CONCORD . EXERCI. Four standards	40	120
609	— ℞. CONCORDIA MILITVM. Clasped hands.	40	120
610	— ℞. CONSERVAT . AVG. Sol stg. l.	55	160
611	— ℞. FELICIT . TEMP. Felicitas stg. l.	25	70
612	— ℞. FIDES MILITVM. Fides stg. l..	55	160
613	— ℞. FORTVNA AVG. Fortuna stg. l..	20	55
614	— ℞. GENIVS AVG. Genius stg. l.	55	160
615	— ℞. GERMANICVS MAX . V. Trophy between captives	130	360
616	— ℞. LAETITIA AVG. Laetitia stg. l.	20	55
617	— ℞. LEG . II . AVG. Capricorn l.	55	160
618	— ℞. LEG XX . V . V. Boar r.	65	175
619	— ℞. MARS VLTOR. Mars walking r..	55	160
620	— ℞. MONETA AVG. Moneta stg. l..	20	55
621	— ℞. ORIENS AVG. Sol walking r.	25	70
622	Æ *antoninianus.* ℞. PACATOR ORBIS. Bust of Sol r..	95	280
623	— ℞. PAX AVG. Pax stg. l.	16	50
624	— ℞. PIAETAS AVG. Pietas sacrificing at altar	25	70
625	— ℞. SALVS AVG. Salus feeding serpent	20	55
626	— ℞. SECVRIT . PERP. Securitas stg. l.	25	70
627	— ℞. VICTORIA AVG. Victory walking r.	25	70

628   643

		F £	VF £
628	Æ *antoninianus*. Struck in the name of Diocletian. ℞. PAX AVGGG. Pax stg. l.	20	60
629	Æ *antoninianus*. Struck in the name of Maximianus. ℞. PROVIDENTIA AVG. Providentia stg. l.	20	60
630	*Colchester or Clausentum mint*. Æ *denarius*. ℞. CONCORDIA MILITVM. Clasped hands	350	1000
631	Æ *antoninianus*. ℞. ABVNDANTIA AVG. Abundantia stg. l.	25	70
632	— ℞. APOLINI CON . AV. Griffin walking r.	90	240
633	— ℞. CONCORDIA AVGGG. Two emperors stg.	110	320
634	— ℞. CONSTANT . AVG. Nude male stg. r.	55	160
635	— ℞. EXPECTATE VENI. Britannia stg. r.	90	240
636	— ℞. FELICITAS AVG. Galley.	40	120
637	— ℞. GENIO BRITANNI. Genius stg. l.	120	340
638	— ℞. HILARITAS AVG. Hilaritas stg. l.	20	55
639	— ℞. IOVI CONSERV. Jupiter stg. l.	25	70
640	— ℞. LEG. I. MIN. Ram stg. r.	55	160
641	— ℞. LIBERALITAS AVG. Carausius seated with subordinates	70	200
642	— ℞. PAX AVG. Pax stg. l.	20	55
643	— ℞. PROVID . AVG. Providentia stg. l.	20	60
644	— ℞. RENOVAT . ROMA. She-wolf suckling Romulus and Remus.	65	175
645	— ℞. RESTIT . SAECVL. Carausius and Victory stg.	65	175
646	— ℞. ROMAE AETER. Roma seated l.	28	72
647	— ℞. SAECVLARES AVG. Lion walking r.	55	160
648	— ℞. SOLI INVICTE. Sol in quadriga	55	168
649	— ℞. SPES PVBLICA. Spes walking r.	20	60
650	— ℞. TEMP . FELICIT. Felicitas stg. l.	20	60
651	— ℞. VIRTVS AVG. Mars stg. r.	20	55
651A	Æ *antoninianus*. Struck in the name of Diocletian. ℞. PAX AVGGG. Pax stg. l.	20	60
652	Æ *antoninianus*. Struck in the name of Maximianus. ℞. PAX AVGGG. Pax stg. l.	20	60

653   662

		F £	VF £
653	**Carausius, Diocletian and Maximianus.** Æ *antoninianus*. Struck by Carausius. CARAVSIVS ET FRATRES SVI. Jugate busts of three emperors l. R. PAX AVGGG. Pax stg. l.	600	1750
654	**Allectus,** chief minister and murderer of Carausius, 293–296. *London mint.* N *aureus*. R. PAX AVG. Pax stg. l.	7500	20,000
655	Æ *antoninianus*. R. AEQVITAS AVG. Aequitas stg. l.	20	55
656	— R. COMES AVG. Minerva stg. l.	20	55
657	— R. FORTVNA AVG. Fortuna seated l.	52	145
658	— R. HILARITAS AVG. Hilaritas stg. l.	18	50
659	— R. LAETITIA AVG. Laetitia stg. l.	25	65
660	— R. LEG . II. Lion walking l.	130	360
661	— R. ORIENS AVG. Sol stg. l.	55	160
662	— R. PAX AVG. Pax stg. l.	25	65
663	— R. PIETAS AVG. Pietas stg. l.	20	55
664	— R. PROVIDENTIA AVG. Providentia stg. l.	35	72
665	— R. SAECVLI FELICITAS. Emperor stg. r.	45	36
666	— R. SALVS AVG. Salus feeding serpent	20	55
667	— R. SPES PVPLICA. Spes holding flower	18	52
668	— R. TEMPORVM FELICI. Felicitas stg. l.	18	52
669	— R. VICTORIA AVG. Victory stg. r.	18	52
670	— R. VIRTVS AVG. Mars stg. r.	20	55
671	Æ *quinarius*. R. VIRTVS AVG. Galley	16	50
672	*Colchester or Clausentum mint.* Æ *antoninianus*. R. ABVND . AVG. Abundantia stg. l.	25	65
673	— R. ADVENTVS AVG. Emperor riding l.	70	190
674	— R. DIANAE REDVCI. Diana leading stag	55	160
675	— R. FELICITAS SAECVLI. Felicitas stg. l.	55	160
676	— R. FIDES EXERCITVS. Four standards	45	130
677	— R. IOVI CONSERVATORI. Jupiter stg. l.	55	160

678   681

678	— R. MONETA AVG. Moneta stg. l.	28	80
679	— R. PAX AVG. Pax stg. l.	25	65
680	— R. ROMAE AETERN. Roma in temple.	65	185
681	Æ *quinarius*. R. LAETITIA AVG. Galley.	25	65
682	— R. VIRTVS AVG. Galley.	18	70

683   698

		F £	VF £

683 **Constantius I,** Caesar 293–305. Augustus 305–306, campaigned in Britain and died at York. Æ *follis.* ℞. GENIO POPVLI ROMANI. Genius stg. l., no *mm.* 9 28

684 Æ *follis.* ℞. MEMORIA FELIX. Eagles beside altar. PLN. *mm.* 8 25

685 Æ *radiate.* ℞. CONCORDIA MILITVM. Constantius and Jupiter stg. . 7 20

686 **Galerius,** Caesar 293–305, Augustus 305–311. Æ *follis.* ℞. GENIO IMPERATORIS. Genius stg. l. 5 12

687 — ℞. GENIO POPVLI ROMANI. Genius stg. l., no *mm.* 6 16

688 **Galeria Valeria,** wife of Galerius. Æ *follis.* ℞. VENERI VICTRICI. Venus stg. l. 26 70

689 **Severus II,** 306–307. Æ *follis.* ℞. FIDES MILITVM. Fides seated l. . . . 25 70

690 Æ *follis.* ℞. GENIO POPVLI ROMANI. Genius stg. l., no *mm.* 28 75

691 Æ *radiate.* ℞. CONCORDIA MILITVM. Severus and Jupiter stg. 15 45

692 **Maximinus II,** 309–313. Æ *follis.* ℞. GENIO AVGVSTI. Genius stg. l.. . 4 12

693 — ℞. GENIO POP . ROM. Genius stg. l., PLN. *mm.* 7 20

694 **Maxentius,** 306–312, Æ *follis.* ℞. CONSERV . VRB SVAE. Roma in temple 7 20

695 **Licinius I,** 308–324. Æ *follis.* ℞. GENIO POP . ROM. Genius stg. l., PLN. *mm.*. 5 15

696 Æ 3. ℞. SOLI INVICTO COMITI. Sol stg. l. 3 8

697 **Licinius II Caesar,** 317–324. Æ 3. ℞. PROVIDENTIAE CAESS. Camp gate. 4 12

698 **Constantine I, the Great,** 307–337. Came to power in Britain following his father's death at York. London mint closed 325. Æ *follis.* ℞. SOLI INVICTO COMITI. Sol stg. l., PLN *mm.*. 8 25

699 Æ 3. ℞. BEATA TRANQVILLITAS. Altar. PLON *mm.* 4 12

700 Æ 3. ℞. VOT . XX. in wreath 2 5

701

701 **Commemorative issues,** Æ 3/4, commencing A.D. 330. Bust of Roma. ℞. She-wolf suckling Romulus and Remus 3 6

702 Æ 3/4. Bust of Constantinopolis. ℞. Victory stg. l. 3 6

703 **Fausta,** wife of Constantine. Æ 3. ℞. SPES REIPVBLICAE. Fausta stg.. . 8 25

704 — ℞. Similar. PLON *mm.* 18 50

F	VF
£	£

705 **Helena,** mother of Constantine. Æ 3. ℞. SECVRITAS REIPVBLICE.
     Helena stg. l.   7   22
706 — ℞. Similar. PLON *mm.*   18   50

707   714

707 **Theodora,** second wife of Constantius I, struck after her death. Æ 4. ℞.
     PIETAS ROMANA. Pietas holding child   4   12
708 **Crispus Caesar,** 317–326. Æ 3. ℞. CAESARVM NOSTRORVM VOT . V.
     Wreath   3   10
709 — ℞. PROVIDENTIAE CAESS. Camp gate. PLON *mm.*   5   12
710 **Delmatius Caesar,** 335–337. Æ 3. ℞. GLORIA EXERCITVS. Two soldiers
     stg.   8   25
711 **Hanniballianus Rex,** 335–337. Æ 4. ℞. SECVRITAS PVBLICA. Euphrates
     reclining   60   180
712 **Constantine II Caesar,** 317–337. Æ 3. ℞. BEAT . TRANQLITAS. Altar.
     PLON *mm.*.   5   12
713 Æ 3/4. ℞. GLORIA EXERCITVS. Two soldiers stg.   7   20
714 **Constans,** 337–350. Visited Britain in 343. Æ *centenionalis.* ℞. FEL .
     TEMP . REPARATIO. Constans stg. on galley   5   12

715   723   733   741

715 **Constantius II,** 337–361. Æ *centenionalis.* ℞. FEL . TEMP . REPARATIO.
     Soldier spearing fallen horseman   4   10
716 Æ 3. ℞. PROVIDENTIAE CAESS. Camp gate. PLON *mm.*   10   30
717 **Magnentius,** usurper in the West, 350–353. Æ *centenionalis.* ℞. VICTOR-
     IAE DD . NN. AVG . ET CAE. Two Victories.   7   18

		F £	VF £
718	**Decentius Caesar**, usurper in the West, 351–353. Æ *centenionalis*. ℞. VICTORIAE DD . NN . AVG . ET . CAE. Two Victories	10	30
719	**Constantius Gallus Caesar**, 351–354. Æ *centenionalis*. ℞. FEL . TEMP REPARATIO. Soldier spearing fallen horseman	8	22
720	**Julian II**, 360–363. Æ *siliqua*. ℞. VOT . X . MVLT . XX with wreath . .	18	50
721	Æ 3. ℞ Similar.	7	18
722	**Jovian**, 363–364. Æ 3. ℞. VOT . V . within wreath	18	50
723	**Valentinian I**, 364–375. Æ 3. ℞. SECVRITAS REIPVBLICAE. Victory advancing l.	4	10
724	**Valens**, 364–378. Æ *siliqua*. ℞. VRBS ROMA. Roma seated l.	14	40
725	Æ 3. ℞. GLORIA ROMANORVM. Valens dragging captive.	4	10
726	**Gratian**, 367–383. Æ *siliqua*. ℞. VRBS ROMA. Roma seated l.	18	50
727	Æ 3. ℞. CONCORDIA AVGGG. Constantinopolis seated l.	7	18
728	**Valentinian II**, 375–392. Æ *siliqua*. ℞. VICTORIA AVGGG. Victory advancing l.	22	60
729	Æ 2. ℞. GLORIA ROMANORVM. Valentinian stg. on galley	9	22
730	Æ 4. ℞. SALVS REIPVBLICAE. Victory advancing l.	3	8
731	**Theodosius I**, 379–395. Æ 2. ℞. GLORIA ROMANORVM. Theodosius stg. on galley.	9	22
732	Æ 4. ℞. SALVS REIPVBLICAE. Victory advancing l.	2	6
733	**Magnus Maximus**, usurper in the West, 383–388, proclaimed emperor by the Roman army in Britain, Ν solidus. ℞. VICTORIA AVGG. Two emperors seated. Victory between them; AVGOB *mm*. (London)	2750	8000
734	Æ *siliqua*. ℞. VICTORIA AVGG. Victory advancing l. AVGPS *mm*. (London).	225	600
735	— ℞. VIRTVS ROMANORVM. Roma seated l..	25	65
736	**Flavius Victor**, usurper in the West, 387–388. Æ 4. ℞. SPES ROMA- NORVM. Camp gate	18	50
737	**Eugenius**, usurper in the West, 392–394. Æ *siliqua*. ℞. VIRTVS ROMA- NORVM. Roma seated l..	90	250
738	**Arcadius**, 383–408. Æ 2. ℞. GLORIA ROMANORVM. Arcadius stg. r..	9	22
739	**Honorius**, 393–423, during whose reign the so-called "Roman withdrawal" from Britain took place. Æ *siliqua*. ℞. VIRTVS ROMANORVM. Roma seated l.	25	65
740	Æ 3. ℞. VIRTVS EXERCITI. Honorius stg. r..	7	20
741	**Constantine III**, usurper in the West, proclaimed emperor in Britain, 407– 411. Æ *siliqua*. ℞. VICTORIA AVGGGG. Roma seated l.	100	300
742	**Valentinian III**, 425–455, during whose reign the last vestiges of Roman rule in Britain disappeared. Æ 4. ℞. VOT . PVB. Camp gate	18	50

EARLY ANGLO-SAXON PERIOD, c. 600–c. 775

The withdrawal of Roman forces from Britain early in the 5th century A.D. and the gradual decline of central administration resulted in a rapid deterioration of the money supply. The arrival of Teutonic raiders and settlers hastened the decay of urban commercial life and it was probably not until late in the 6th century that renewed political, cultural and commercial links with the kingdom of the Merovingian Franks led to the appearance of small quantities of Merovingian gold *tremisses* (one-third solidus) in England. A purse containing such pieces was found in the Sutton Hoo ship-burial. Native Anglo-Saxon gold *thrymsas* were minted from about the 630s, initially in the style of their continental prototpyes or copied from obsolete Roman coinage and later being made in pure Anglo-Saxon style. By the middle of the 7th century the gold coinage was being increasingly debased with silver, and gold had been superseded entirely by about 675.

These silver coins, contemporary with the *deniers* or *denarii* of the Merovingian Franks, are the first English pennies, though they are commonly known today as *sceattas* (a term more correctly translated as "treasure" or "wealth"). They provide important material for the student of Anglo-Saxon art.

Though the earliest sceattas are a transition from the gold thrymsa coinage, coins of new style were soon developed which were also copied by the Frisians of the Low Countries. Early coins appear to have a standard weight of 20 grains (1.29 gms) and are of good silver content, though the quality deteriorates early in the 8th century. These coins exist in a large number of varied types, and as well as the official issues there are mules and other varieties which are probably contemporary imitations. Many of the sceattas were issued during the reign of Aethelbald of Mercia, but as few bear inscriptions it is only in recent years that research has permitted their correct dating and the attribution of certain types to specific areas. Some silver sceats of groups II and III and most types of groups IV to X were issued during the period (A.D. 716–757) when Aethelbald, King of Mercia, was overlord of the southern English. In Northumbria very debased sceattas or *stycas* continued to be issued until the middle of the ninth century. Though a definitive classification has not yet been developed, the arrangement given below follows the latest work on the series: this list is not exhaustive.

The reference "*B.M.C.*" is to the type given in *British Museum Catalogue: Anglo-Saxon Coins*, and *not* the item number.

North, J. J. *English Hammered Coinage*, Vol. 1, c. 650–1272 (1980).
Metcalf, D. M. "A stylistic analysis of the 'porcupine' sceattas". *Num. Chron.*, 7th ser., Vol. VI (1966).
Rigold, S. E. "The two primary series of sceattas", *B.N.J.*, xxx (1960).
Sutherland, C. H. V. *Anglo-Saxon Gold Coinage in the light of the Crondall Hoard* (1948).

ᚠᚪᚦᚱᚴ·ᚷᛈᚻᚾᛁᛄᛇᛈᛉᛋᛏᛒᛖᛗᛚᛝᛞᚩᚪᚫᛠᚣᚪ
f u t h o r k · z w h n i j ih p x s t b e m l ng d œ a æ ea y
Early Anglo-Saxon Runes

GOLD

A. Anglo-Merovingian types

751 **Thrymsa** (*c.* 1.32 gms). Name and portrait of Bishop Leudard (chaplain to Q. Bertha of Kent). ℞. Cross. *N. 1*. . . . . *Unique*
752 *Canterbury*. Bust r., moneyer's name. ℞. Cross, mint name. *N. 2* . . . . . *Extremely rare*

| 753 | 762 | 763 |

753 No mint name. Bust l. ℞. Cross. *N. 3–5, 7* . . . . *Extremely rare*
754 Bust r. ℞. Cross. *N. 6–9, 12* . . . . *Extremely rare*
755 Cross both sides. *N. 10* . . . . *Extremely rare*
756 Bust r. ℞. Cross, runic letters, *N. 11* . . . . *Extremely rare*

	F	VF
	£	£

B. Roman derivatives

757 **Solidus.** Bust r. copied from 4th cent. solidus. ℞. Various. *N. 13, 14* . . . *Extremely rare*
758 — Runic inscription on reverse. *N. 15* . . . . *Extremely rare*
759 **Thrymsa.** Radiate bust. r. ℞. Clasped hands. *N. 16.* . . . . *Extremely rare*
760 Bust r., hands raised to cross. ℞. Camp gate. *N. 17* . . . . *Extremely rare*
761 Helmeted bust r. ℞. Cross, runic inscription. *N. 18.* . . . . *Extremely rare*
762 Diad. bust r. ℞. "Standard", TOV / XX in centre. *N. 19. M.* — . . . . . *Extremely rare*
763 — Similar. ℞. Victory protecting "two emperors". *N. 20* 1250 2500

C. "London" and derived issues

764   765   767

764 **Thrymsa.** Facing bust, no legend. ℞. Greek cross, LONDVNIV. *N. 21.* . *Extremely rare*
765 Head r. or l. ℞. Plain cross, legend jumbled. *N. 22–24* . . . . *Extremely rare*

D. "Witmen" group

766 **Thrymsa.** Bust r. with trident centre. ℞. Cross with forked limbs,
moneyer's name. *N. 25* . . . . *Extremely rare*
767 — Similar, but blundered legend on reverse, *N. 25 var.* 1700 3500
768 — ℞. Cross potent. *N. 26.* 1700 3500

E. "York" group

769   771   772

769 **Thrymsa.** Three crosses with geometric squared design below. ℞. Small
cross. *N. 27* . . . . *Extremely rare*

F. "Regal" coinages

770 **Solidus** (4.12 gms). Diad.. bust r., moneyer's name around. ℞. Cross potent
on steps. *N. 28.* . . . . *Extremely rare*
771 **Thrymsa.** Diad. bust r., AVDVARLD REGES. ℞. Orb with cross,
moneyer's name. *N. 29* 2350 5500
772 Diad. bust l., moneyer's name around. ℞. Cross and pellets, legend of Xs.
N. 30 . . . . *Extremely rare*
773 Diad. bust r. ℞. Cross botonée, PADA in runes. *N. 31* 1700 3750

	F £	VF £

Miscellaneous issues

774	**Thrymsa.** Crude bust r. ℞. Standing figure with arms outstretched. *N. 33*	*Extremely rare*
775	Crude bust or head r. ℞. Various. *N. 35, 38*	*Extremely rare*
776	Forked cross both sides, and other types. *N. 36, 37, 39*	*Extremely rare*

SILVER

I. Transitional types struck in silver, by thrymsa moneyers, *c.* 675–690

779   780   781

777	**Sceat.** *Kentish.* As 773, diad. bust r. ℞. *Pada* in runes across field. *N. 152*	500	1100
778	— Obv. Similar. ℞. Cross on steps. *B.M.C. type 2*	*Extremely rare*	
778A	As 763. ℞. Victory over two emperors. *B.M.C. 1*	*Extremely rare*	
779	— Diad. bust r., TNC to r. ℞. Cross with annulet in each angle, *Pada* in runes in legend. *B.M.C. 3*	650	1350
780	— *"Varimundus".* As 761, helmeted bust r. with sceptre. ℞. Cross pattée, TmVNVmVC, etc. *Rigold VB, 4–9*	650	1350

II. Primary Sceattas, *c.* 690–725

783   785   786

781	Series A, *Kentish.* Radiate bust r., usually of good style, TIC to r. ℞. "Standard". *B.M.C. 2a*	65	150
782	Series B, *Kentish.* Diad. bust r. ℞. Bird above cross on steps. *B.M.C. 26* .	100	225
783	— Diad. head r. within serpent-circle or bust r. ℞. Bird above cross and two annulets, serpent-circle around. *B.M.C. 27a*	65	150
784	— (Bz.) Diad. head r. of poorer style. ℞. Bird and cross larger and cruder. *B.M.C. 27b* (see also 791).	85	200
785	Series C, *East Anglian (?) Runic.* Radiate bust r. somewhat as 781. *Epa* (etc.) in runes to r. ℞. Neat "Standard" type. *B.M.C. 2b; Rigold R1* (see also 832, and for Frisian copies nos. 839 and 840)	60	100
786	*Early "porcupines".* Porcupine-like figure, body with annulet at one end, triangle at other. ℞. "Standard" with four pellets around central annulet. *Metcalf D*	45	90

787　　　　　　　789　　　　　　　790

	F £	VF £
787 — "Porcupine" has insect-like body with fore-leg. R. "Standard" with four lines and central annulet.. *Metcalf G*	45	90
788 — "Porcupine" with parallel lines in curve of body. R. "Standard" with VOIC-like symbols (and rarely with 5 crosses on *rev.*)	40	80
789 — Figure developed into plumed bird. R. "Standard" has groups of triple pellets. *B.M.C. type 6*	70	150
790 *Slightly later "porcupines" of reduced weight.* As 788 but various symbols in "standard" (some varieties are Frisian imitations—see 841–2 below) .	45	90

SILVER

III. **"Mercian" types,** *c.* 705–730. More than one mint, possibly including London; the fineness dropping from good silver to under .500.

791　　　　　　　792　　　　　　　793

791 Derivative of 784, but bird and cross larger and cruder, no serpent circles. *B.M.C. 27b.*	75	175
792 Two heads face-to-face, cross with trident base between. R. Four birds clockwise around cross. *B.M.C. 37.*	100	250
793 Man holding two crosses. R. Bird and branch. *B.M.C. 23b*	125	300
794 Diad. bust r. with bird or cross. R. Hound and tree. *B.M.C. 42.*	150	400
795 Diad. bust r. with chalice. R. Man standing with cross and bird. *B.M.C. 20.*	135	300
796 Diad. bust r. with cross. R. Wolf curled head to tail. *B.M.C. 32a.*	135	300
797 — Similar, but wolf-headed serpent	135	300
798 — Similar, but wolf-serpent within torque. *B.M.C. 32b*	135	300
799 — Similar, but wolf's head r. or l. with long tongue. *B.M.C. 33.*	175	400
800 — Obv. Similar. R. Celtic cross or shield. *B.M.C. 34*	135	300

IV. **Types of similar style or finess,** *of uncertain political attribution*

800A Kneeling archer r., tree behind. R. Bird on branch r., head turned l. *B.M.C. —*	*Extremely rare*	
801 As 791, but cross before head. R. Large and small bird. *B.M.C. 36.* . . .	150	300
802 Bust r., lettering around or with cable border. R. Bird r. in torque. *B.M.C. 38*	175	350
803 Bust l. within cable border. R. Man with two crosses. *B.M.C. 21*	200	400
804 Facing bust. R. Interlaced cruciform pattern. *B.M.C. 52.*	325	700

797   805   806

		F £	VF £
V.	**South Wessex types,** *c.* 725–750. Found predominantly in excavations at Hamwic (Southampton)		
805	Scutiform design (shield with bosses). R. Bird and branch as 794. *B.M.C. type 39*	120	200
806	Jewel-head, roundels around. R. Bird and branch. *B.M.C. 49*	135	300
807	Scutiform design. R. Wolf-head whorl. *B.M.C. 48*	135	300
VI.	**South Saxon types,** *c.* 720–750		
808	Diad. bust r. cross before. R. "Standard". *B.M.C. 3a*	125	300
809	— Similar but crude style and of very base silver	80	175

808   815   816

VII.	**"Dragon" types,** *c.* 725–735?		
810	Two standing figures, long cross between. R. Monster looking back to r. or l. *B.M.C. type 41b*	175	350
811	One standing figure, cross either side. R. As last. *B.M.C. 23a and 40*	175	350
812	Four interlaced shields. R. As last. *B.M.C. 43*	175	350
813	Bust r., cross before. R. As last. *N. 114*	*Extremely rare*	
814	Wolf's head facing. R. As last. *N. 122*	350	700
815	Wolf and twins. R. Bird in vine. *B.M.C. 7*	200	400
816	Diad. bust r. + LEV. R. "Porcupine" l. *B.M.C. 9*	175	450
817	Facing head. R. Fantastic animal r. or l. *N. 143–146*	250	625
VIII.	**"London issue"** *of around .400 silver content or less, c.* 740–750		
818	Diad. bust r., LVNDONIA (sometimes blundered). R. Man holding two long crosses. *B.M.C. type 12*	350	600
819	— Obv. As last. R. "Porcupine" to l. *B.M.C. 12/15*	350	800
820	— Obv. As last. R. Seated figure r. holding sceptre. *B.M.C. 13*		*Unique*
821	— Obv. As last but bust l. R. Scutiform design. *B.M.C. 14*	300	650
822	Diad. bust r. with cross, no legend. R. As 818. *B.M.C. 15a*	175	350
823	— As last. R. Man standing with branch and cross, or two branches. *B.M.C. 15b*	150	350
824	Diad. bust r. with floral scroll. R. As last	150	350
825	— As last. R. Man with two crosses. *B.M.C. 16*	120	275
826	As 813 but bust l. *B.M.C. 17*	135	325
827	Diad. bust r. with cross. R. Man standing with cross and bird. *B.M.C. 18*	150	300

		F	VF
		£	£
828	Diad. bust l. with cross. R. As last. *B.M.C. 19*	150	350
829	Victory standing with wreath. R. Man with two crosses. *B.M.C. 22* . . .	250	550

818   831

IX. **"Wolf-head whorl"** *types, mostly of about .300 silver or less, c.* 740–750

830	Man standing holding two crosses. R. Wolf-head whorl. *B.M.C. 23e.* . .	100	250
831	Sphinx or female centaur with outstretched wings. R. As above. *B.M.C. 47*	130	275
	See also No. 807.		

832

X. **East Anglian types,** *of about .500 silver or less, c.* 735–750. Struck to a standard of 15 grs./0.97 gm. or less

832	Crude radiate bust l. or r., *Epa, Wigraed,* or *Spi,* etc., in runes. R. "Standard". *Rigold R2* (compare with 785)	75	150
832A	Crude bust r. R. Porcupine modified into profile ½ moon face.	200	400
833	— Similar. R. Cross with each limb ending in annulet. *Rigold R2Z, N. 160.*	110	200
833A	Saltire in square. R. Cross ending in annulets. *B.M.C. 51*	75	150
834	Bird r. looking back. R. "Standard" with four annulets in saltire. *B.M.C. 46.*	125	325
835	"Standard" both sides. *N. 55–57*	*Extremely rare*	
836	Fantastic bird r. or l. R. Fantastic quadruped l. or r. *B.M.C. 44*	100	250
836A	— As above *rev.* on both sides	100	250
836B	— Hd. r. R. As 836 *obv.*	150	350
836C	— Quadruped r. R. Spiral	150	350

836   837   839

XI. **Late sceattas,** *on a restored silver standard, c.* 750–775. These probably include some specimens of 830 and 831 and the following types:

837	"Porcupine". R. *Aethili/raed* in runes in two lines. *B.M.C. 4*	400	850
838	"Porcupine". R. Small cross, S E D E in angles. *N. 47.*	*Extremely rare*	

XII. **Frisian sceattas,** *c.* 700–750. A number of large sceatta hoards have been found in the Netherlands and Lower Rhine area. Some of the coins are now known to have been minted in Frisia but some also circulated in England

839	Crude radiate bust l. or r., as 832, sometimes crude runes. R. Plain cross with pellets or annulets in angles. *Rigold R3. B.M.C. 2c*	35	65
839A	Helmeted head r. R. Cross with annulets	60	120

	F £	VF £
840 "Standard". R. Cross and pellets. *B.M.C. 50*	45	125
840A Very crude facing bust. R. Similar	60	125
841 "Porcupine" with III, XII or XIII in curve. R. "Standard". *Metcalf A, B &* *C*	35	65
842 "Porcupine" has a triangle attached to curve or an outline of pellets. *Metcalf E & F*	40	70

843   844

843 Facing "Wodan" head. R. Monster. *B.M.C. 31*	75	150
843A Similar but "Standard" on *rev.*	175	350
844 — Similar. R. Two men with staves or long cross. *B.M.C. 30a & b*	125	250
844A Good style bust l.; runic inscription. R. Annulet cross and pellets.	—	300

XIII.   Uncertain issues

847

846 **Ealdfrith** (? possibly sub-king of Lindsey, *c.* 790). Now considered to be Northumbria (see 846 below).		
847 **Beonna**, King of East Anglia, *c.* 758. Æ *sceat.* Pellet in centre, Runic inscription. R. EFE in Roman characters around saltire cross.	400	800
847A — Similar. R. Name in Runic	*Extremely rare*	
847B — Similar. R. Interlace pattern.	*Extremely rare*	

KINGS OF NORTHUMBRIA

In the North a series of silver sceats was struck with the king's name on the obverse and a fantastic animal on the reverse.

Towards the end of the eighth century the coinage degenerated to one of base silver and finally to copper or brass; from the second reign of Aethelred I the design becomes standardised with the king's name retained on the obverse but with the moneyer's name on the reverse and in the centre of both sides a cross, pellet or rosette., etc.

A parallel series of ecclesiastical coins was struck by the Archbishops of York. The coinage continued until the conquest of Northumbria by the Danes and the defeat of Osbert in 867, almost a century after introduction of the broad silver penny in Southern England.

846 **Aldfrith** (685–705). Æ *sceat.* Pellet in annulet. R. Fantastic animal l. with trifid tail	1000	2000
852 **Eadberht** (737–758). Æ *sceat.* . Small cross. R. Fantastic quadruped to l. or r.	175	400
Aethelwald Moll (759–765). See Archbishop Ecgberht of York		

853   859   861

		F £	VF £
853	**Alcred** (765–774). Æ *sceat*. As 852.	350	800
854	**Aethelred I,** first reign (774–779). Æ *sceat*. As last	350	800
855	**Aelfwald I** (779–788). Æ *sceat*. As last	400	950
856	— — Small cross. R. With name of moneyer CVDBEVRT	375	900
857	**Aethelred I,** second reign (789–796). Æ *sceat*. Similar. R. SCT CVD (St. Cuthbert), shrine	*Extremely rare*	
858	— Small cross. R. With moneyer's name	225	550

The last and the rest of the sceats, except where otherwise stated, have on the obv. the king's name, and on the rev. the moneyer's name: in the centre on both sides is a cross, a pellet, a rosette, etc. During the following reign the silver sceat becomes debased and later issues are only brass or copper.

		F £	VF £
859	**Eanred** (810–c. 854). Base Æ *sceat*.	30	65
859A	— Æ *penny*. Bust r. R. Cross, part moline part crosslet	*Unique*	
860	— Æ *sceat*	20	40
861	**Aethelred II,** first reign (c. 854–858). Æ *sceat*	20	45
862	— R. Quadruped	200	600
863	**Redwulf** (c. 858). Æ *sceat*..	40	90
864	**Aethelred II,** second reign (c. 858–c. 862). Æ *sceat*, mainly of the moneyer EARDWVLF	20	45
865	**Osbert** (c. 862–867). Æ *sceat*	70	140

Coins with blundered legends are worth less than those with normal readings, and to this series have been relegated those coins previously attributed to Eardwulf and Aelfwald II.

ARCHBISHOPS OF YORK

866   868

		F £	VF £
866	**Ecgberht** (732 *or* 734–766). Æ *sceat*, with king Eadberht. As illustration, or holds cross and crozier	250	550
866A	— — with Aethelwald Moll. Cross each side	*Extremely rare*	
867	— — with Alchred. Cross each side..	*Extremely rare*	
868	**Eanbald II** (796–c. 830). Æ *sceat*. R. With name of moneyer	50	125
869	— Æ *sceat*, as last.	40	90

870   871

	F	VF
	£	£
870 **Wigmund** (837–854). Gold *solidus*. Facing bust. ℞. Cross in wreath. . . .		*Unique*
871 — Æ *sceat*, various	30	60
872 **Wulfhere** (854–900). Æ *sceat*	85	175

MIDDLE ANGLO-SAXON PERIOD, *c.* 780–973

In the kingdom of the Franks a reformed coinage of good quality *deniers* struck on broad flans had been introduced by Pepin in 755 and continued by his son Charlemagne and his descendants. A new coinage of *pennies* of similar size and weighing about 20 grains (1.3 gms) was introduced into England, probably by Offa, the powerful king of Mercia, about 755/780, though early pennies also exist of two little known kings of Kent, Heaberht and Ecgberht, of about the same period.

The silver penny (*Lat.* "denarius", hence the *d.* of our £ *s. d.*) remained virtually the sole denomination of English coinage for almost five centuries, with the rare exception of occasional gold coins and somewhat less rare silver halfpence. The penny reached a weight of 24 grains, i.e., a "pennyweight" during the reign of Aelfred the Great. Silver pennies of this period normally bear the ruler's name, though not always his portrait, and the name of the moneyer responsible for their manufacture.

Pennies were issued by various rulers of the Heptarchy for the kingdoms of Kent, Mercia, East Anglia and Wessex (and possibly Anglian Northumbria), by the Danish settlers in the Danelaw and the Hiberno-Norse kings of York, and also by the Archbishops of Canterbury and a Bishop of London. Under Eadgar, who became the sole ruler of England, a uniform coinage was instituted throughout the country, and it was he who set the pattern for the "reformed" coinage of the later Anglo-Saxon and Norman period.

Halfpence are known from the age of Aelfred to that of Eadgar, but they are rare and were probably never made in large quantities. To provide small change pennies were sometimes cut or broken in half.

Nos. 873–1387 are all silver **pennies** except where stated.

KINGS OF KENT

		F	VF
		£	£
873	**Heaberht** (*c.* 765). Monogram for REX. ℞. Five annulets, each containing a pellet, joined to form a cross		*Unique*
874	**Ecgberht** (*c.* 780). Similar. ℞. Varied. . . . . *from*	1250	3000
875	**Eadberht Praen** (796–798). As illustration. ℞. Varied.	1250	3000

875   877

876	**Cuthred** (798–807). *Canterbury.* Various types without portrait . . . *from*	425	1000
877	— As illustration	475	1100

878   879

878	**Anonymous** (*c.* 822–823). *Canterbury.* As illustration	650	1650
879	**Baldred** (*c.* 823–825). *Canterbury.* Head or bust r. ℞. Varied	750	1850

	F £	VF £
880 — Cross each side	650	1650
881 *Rochester.* Diademed bust r. ℞. Varied	*Extremely rare*	

ARCHBISHOPS OF CANTERBURY

882   885

882 **Jaenberht** (765–792). His name around central ornament or cross and wedges. ℞. OFFA REX in two lines	1750	4500
883 — His name in three lines. ℞. OFFA REX between the limbs of Celtic cross	2250	5500
884 **Aethelheard** (el. 792, cons. 793, d. 805). With Offa as overlord. First issue (792–793), with title *Pontifex*	1600	4000
885 — Second issue (793–796), with title *Archiepiscopus*	1200	3000
886 With Coenwulf as overlord. Third issue (796–805)	1150	2500
887 **Wulfred** (805–832). group I (805–*c.* 810). As illustration. ℞. Crosslet, alpha-omega *from*	800	2000
888 — Group II (*c.* 810). As last. ℞. DOROVERNIA C monogram	550	1350
889 — Group III (pre- 823). Bust extends to edge of coin. ℞. As last	500	1200
890 — Groups IV and V (*c.* 822–823). Anonymous under Ecgberht. Moneyer's name in place of the Archbishop's. ℞. DOROBERNIA CIVITAS in three or five lines	525	1300
891 — Group VI (*c.* 823–825). Baldred type. Crude portrait. ℞. DRVR CITS in two lines	550	2000
892 — Group VII (*c.* 832). Second monogram (Ecgberht) type. Crude portrait r., PLFRED. ℞. DORIB C. Monogram as 1035	550	2000

887   894

893 **Ceolnoth** (833–870). Group I with name CIALNOD. Tonsured bust facing. ℞. Varied *from*	275	750
894 — Group II. Similar but CEOLNOD. ℞. Types of Aethelwulf of Wessex.	300	600
895 — Group III. Diad. bust r. ℞. Moneyer's name in and between lunettes.	400	900

Archbishops of Canterbury *continued*

896

		F £	VF £
896	**Aethered** (870–889). Bust r. ℞. As illustration or with long cross with lozenge panel	1750	4500
897	— Cross pattée. ℞. ELF / STAN		*Unique*

898

898	**Plegmund** (890–914). DORO in circle. ℞. As illustration above, various moneyers . . . . *from*	300	750
899	— Similar, but title EPISC, and XDF in centre	500	1200
900	— Small cross pattée. ℞. Somewhat as last	250	650
901	— Crosses moline and pommée on *obv.*	500	1200

KINGS OF MERCIA

Until 825 Canterbury was the principal mint of the Kings of Mercia and some moneyers also struck coins for the Kings of Kent and Archbishops.

GOLD

902    903

902	**Offa** (757–796). Gold *dinar*. Copy of Arabic dinar of Caliph Al Mansur, dated 157 A.H. (A.D. 774), with OFFA REX added on *rev.*	*Unique*
903	Gold *penny*. Bust r., moneyer's name. ℞. Standing figure, moneyer's name.	*Unique*

SILVER

904 905

		F £	VF £

904 *Canterbury.* Group I (*c.* 784–*c.* 787). Early coins without portraits, small
flans. Various types . . . . *from* 675 1750
905 — Group II (*c* 787–*c.* 792). Various types with portrait, small flans *from* 1000 2300
906 — — — Various types without portraits, small flans. . . . . *from* 550 1300

907 909

907 *Canterbury.* Group III (*c.* 792–796). Various types without portrait, large
flans . . . . *from* 500 1250
908 *East Anglia.* Copies of Group II and III, possibly struck *c.* 790. Ornate,
crude, and sometimes with runic letters 650 1650
909 **Cynethryth** (wife of Offa). Coins as Group II of Offa. As illustration . . . 3000 6000
910 — *O.* As *rev.* of last. R. EOBA on leaves of quatrefoil. 2500 6000
911 **Eadberht** (Bishop of London, died 787/789). EADBERHT EP in three
lines. R. Name of Offa 2000 5000
The attribution to this particular cleric is uncertain.
912 **Coenwulf** (796–821). Group I (796–805). *Canterbury* and *London.* Without
portrait. His name in three lines. R. Varied 450 1100
913 — *Canterbury.* Name around m as illus. below. R. Moneyer's name in two
lines. . . . . *Unique*

914 915

914 — *Both mints.* Tribrach type as illustration 350 750
915 — Group II (*c.* 805–810). *Canterbury.* With portrait. Small flans. R. Varied
but usually cross and wedges. 400 900

		F £	VF £
916	— Groups II and IV (*c.* 810–820). *Canterbury.* Similar but larger flans. R̶. Varied	350	800
917	— *Rochester.* Large diad. bust of coarse style. R̶. Varied. (Moneyers: Dun, Ealhstan)	475	1100
918	— *London.* With portrait generally of Roman style. R̶. Crosslet	450	1000
919	— *E. Anglia.* Crude diad. bust r. R̶. Moneyer's name LVL on leaves in arms of cross	450	1050
920	— — *O.* as last. R̶. Various types . . . . *from*	400	900

921   929

921	**Ceolwulf I** (821–823). *Canterbury.* Group I. Bust r. R̶. Varied. (Moneyers: Oba, Sigestef)	575	1350
922	— — Group II. Crosslet. R̶. Varied	500	1250
923	— — Group III. Tall cross with MERCIORŪ. R̶. Crosslet. SIGESTEF DOROBERNIA		*Unique*
924	— *Rochester.* Group I. Bust r. R̶. Varied	500	1250
925	— — Group IIA. As last but head r.	550	1350
926	— — Group IIB. Ecclesiastical issue by Bp. of Rochester. With mint name, DOROBREBIA, but no moneyer		*Extremely rare*
927	— *East Anglia.* Crude style and lettering with barbarous portrait. R̶. Varied.	500	1250
928	**Beornwulf** (823–825). Bust r. R̶. Moneyer's name in three lines	1350	3500
929	— R̶. Cross crosslet in centre	1100	2500
930	Crude copy of 928 but moneyer's name in two lines with crosses between.		*Extremely rare*

931   933

931	**Ludica** (825–827). Bust r. R̶. Moneyer's name in three lines as 928	*Extremely rare*
932	— Similar. R̶. Moneyer's name around cross crosslet in centre, as 929 . .	*Extremely rare*
933	**Wiglaf,** first reign (827–829). Crude head r. R̶. Crosslet	1750 4500

934

	F £	VF £
934 Second reign (830–840). Cross and pellets. R. Moneyer's name in and between lunettes of pellets	1750	4500

935

		F £	VF £
935	**Berhtwulf** (840–852). Various types with bust . . . . *from*	700	1750
936	— Cross potent over saltire. R. Cross potent	750	1850
937	Berhtwulf with Aethelwulf of Wessex. As before. R. IAETHELWLF REX. cross pommée over cross pattée		*Unique*
938	**Burgred** (852–874). *B.M.C. type A.* Bust r. R. Moneyer's name in and between lunettes	100	175
939	— — B. Similar but lunettes broken in centre of curve.	110	230

938   939   940   941

		F £	VF £
940	— — C. Similar but lunettes broken in angles	110	230
941	— — D. Similar but legend divided by two lines with a crook at each end	100	185
942	— — E. As last, but m above and below	350	900
943	**Ceolwulf II** (874–c. 880). Bust r. R. Two emperors seated. Victory above.		*Unique*

944

	F £	VF £
944 — R. Moneyer's name in angles of long cross with lozenge centre	2000	5000

KINGS OF EAST ANGLIA

946   948

		F	VF
		£	£
	Beonna (*c.* 760). See no. 847		
946	**Aethelberht** (d. 794). As illustration	*Only 3 known*	
947	**Eadwald** (*c.* 798). King's name in three lines. ℞. Moneyer's name in quatrefoil or around cross		5500
948	**Aethelstan I** (*c.* 825–840). Bust r. or l. ℞. Crosslet or star	750	2000
949	Bust r. ℞. Moneyer's name in three or four lines	750	2000
950	Alpha or A. ℞. Varied	400	850
951	*O.* and *rev.* Cross with or without wedges or pellets in angles	400	950
952	— Similar, with king's name both sides	550	1350
952A	Name around ship in centre. ℞. Moneyer Eadgar, pellets in centre. (Possibly the earliest of his coins.)	*Unique*	
953	**Aethelweard** (*c.* 840–*c.* 855), A. Omega or cross and crescents. ℞. Cross with pellets or wedges	700	1500

953   954

954	**Edmund** (855–870). Alpha or A. ℞. Cross with pellets or wedges	350	650
955	— *O.* Varied. ℞. Similar	350	650

For the St. Edmund coins and the Danish issues struck in East Anglia bearing the name of Aethelred I of Wessex, see Danish East Anglia.

VIKING COINAGES
Danish East Anglia, *c.* 885–915

956   957

		F £	VF £
956	**Aethelstan II** (878–890), originally named Guthrum? Cross pattée. ℞. Moneyer's name in two lines	1000	2500
957	**Oswald** (unknown except from his coins). Alpha or A. ℞. Cross pattée.	*Extremely rare*	
958	— Copy of Carolinigian "temple" type. ℞ Cross and pellets	*Unique fragment*	
959	**Aethelred I.** As last, with name of Aethelred I of Wessex. ℞. As last, or cross-crosslet	*Extremely rare*	
960	**St. Edmund**, memorial coinage, Æ *penny*, type as illus. below, various legends of good style	65	125
961	— Similar, but barbarous or semi-barbarous legends.	60	110
962	*Halfpenny.* Similar.	400	1000

961   963

		F	VF
963	**St. Martin of Lincoln**. As illustration	1500	3750
964	**Alfred.** (Viking imitations, usually of very barbarous workmanship.) Bust r. ℞. *Londonia* monogram	400	1200
965	— Similar, but *Lincolla* monogram	*Extremely rare*	

966   970

		F	VF
966	— Small cross, as Alfred group II (*Br. 6*), various legends, some read REX DORO . . . *from*	200	500
967	— Similar. ℞. 'St. Edmund type' A in centre	500	1500
968	— Two emperors seated. ℞. As 964. (Previously attributed to Halfdene.)	*Unique*	

		F	V.
		£	£
969	*Halfpenny.* As 964 and 965 . . . . *from*	500	150
970	— As 966	450	135

Danelaw, *c.* **898–915**

971 **Alfred** (Imitations). ELFRED between ORSNA and FORDA. ℞. Moneyer's name in two lines (occasionally divided by horizontal long cross).   250   55
972 — *Halfpenny.* Similar, of very crude appearance . . . . *Extremely rare*

971   975

973 **Alfred/Plegmund.** *Obv.* ELFRED REX PLEGN . . . . *Extremely rare*
974 **Plegmund.** Danish copy of 900   300   75
975 **Earl Sihtric.** Type as 971. SCELDFOR between GVNDI BERTVS. ℞ SITRIC COMES in two lines . . . . *Extremely rare*

Viking Coinage of York?
References are to "The Classification of Northumbrian Viking Coins in the Cuerdale hoard", by C. S. S. Lyon and B. H. I. H. Stewart, in Numismatic Chronicle, 1964, p. 281ff.

976 **Siefred.** C . SIEFRE DIIS REX in two lines. ℞. EBRAICE CIVITAS (or contractions), small cross. *L. & S. Ia, Ie, Ii*   200   55
977 — Cross on steps between. ℞. As last. *L. & S. If, Ij*   275   75
978 — Long cross. ℞. As last. *L. & S. Ik* . . . . *Extremely rare*
979 SIEFREDVS REX, cross crosslet within legend. ℞. As last. *L. & S. Ih.* . .   130   35
980 SIEVERT REX, cross crosslet to edge of coin. ℞. As last. *L. & S. Ic, Ig, Im*   130   35
981 — Cross on steps between. ℞. As last. *L. & S. Il*   240   65
982 — Patriarchal cross. ℞. DNS DS REX, small cross. *L. & S. Va*   150   40
983 — — ℞. MIRABILIA FECIT, small cross. *L. & S. VIb*   185   50
984 REX, at ends of cross crosslet. ℞. SIEFREDVS, small cross. *L. & S. IIIa, b*   140   38
985 — Long cross. ℞. As last. *L. & S. IIIc.*   120   32
986 *Halfpenny.* Types as 977, *L. & S. Ib*; 980, *Ic*; and 983, *VIb* . . . . *Extremely rare*

980   993

987 **Cnut.** CNVT REX, cross crosslet to edge of coin. ℞. EBRAICE CIVITAS, small cross. *L. & S. Io, Iq.*   70   150
988 — — ℞. CVNNETTI, small cross. *L. & S. IIc*   80   175

		F £	VF £
989	— Long cross. ℞. EBRAICE CIVITAS, small cross. *L. & S. Id, In, Ir* . .	55	110
990	— — ℞. CVNNETTI, small cross. *L. & S. IIa, IId*	55	110
991	— Patriarchal cross. ℞. EBRAICE CIVITAS, small cross. *L. & S. Ip, Is.*	55	110
992	— — ℞.—*Karolus* monogram in centre. *L. & S. It*	400	1000
993	— — ℞. CVNNETTI, small cross. *L. & S. IIb, IIe*	45	90
994	*Halfpenny.* Types as 987, *L. & S. Iq*; 989, *Id*; 991, *Is*; 992, *Iu*; 993, *IIb and e* . . . . *from*	400	850
995	As 992, but CVNNETTI around *Karolus* monogram. *L. & S. IIf*	400	875

995   998

996	**Cnut and/or Siefred**. CNVT REX, patriarchal cross. ℞. SIEFREDVS, small cross. *L. & S. IIId*	110	235
997	— — ℞. DNS DS REX, small cross. *L. & S. Vc.*	150	325
998	— — ℞. MIRABILIA FECIT. *L. & S. VId*	140	200
999	EBRAICE C, patriarchal cross. ℞. DNS DS REX, small cross. *L. & S. Vb.*	120	250
1000	— — ℞. MIRABILIA FECIT. *L. & S. VIc*	140	275
1001	DNS DS REX in two lines. ℞. ALVALDVS, small cross. *L. & S. IVa* .		1500
1002	DNS DS O REX, similar. ℞. MIRABILIA FECIT. *L. & S. VIa*	250	550
1003	*Halfpenny.* As last. *L. & S. VIa*	*Extremely rare*	
1004	**"Cnut"**. Name blundered around cross pattée with extended limbs. ℞. QVENTOVICI around small cross. *L. & S. VII*	300	650
1005	— *Halfpenny.* Similar. *L. & S. VII.*	450	1000

Possibly not Northumbrian; the reverse copied from the Carolingian coins of Quentovic, N. France.

York, early tenth century issues

1006	**St. Peter coinage**. Early issues. SCI PETRI MO in two lines. ℞. Cross pattée.	175	400
1007	— similar. ℞. "Karolus" monogram.	*Extremely rare*	
1008	*Halfpenny.* Similar. ℞. Cross pattée	1000	2250

1006   1009

1009	**Regnald** (blundered types). RAIENALT, head to l. or r. ℞. EARICE CT, "Karolus" monogram.	1250	3000

		F	*VF*
		£	£
1010	— Open hand. ℞. Similar	1000	2500
1011	— Hammer. ℞. Bow and arrow	1250	3000
1012	— Similar. ℞. Sword	*Extremely rare*	

English Coins of the Hiberno-Norse Vikings

Early period, *c.* **919–925**

1013	**Sihtric** (921–927). SITRIC REX, sword. ℞. Cross or T	1500	3750

1015   1016

1014	**St. Peter coinage.** Late issues SCI PETRI MO, sword and hammer. ℞.		
	EBORACEI, cross and pellets	350	850
1015	— Similar. ℞. Voided hammer	450	1000
1016	— Similar. ℞. Solid hammer	700	1600
	St. Peter coins with blundered legends are rather cheaper.		

Later period, 939–954 (after the battle of Brunanburh). Mostly struck at York.

1017	**Anlaf Guthfrithsson,** 939–941. Flower type. Small cross, ANLAF REX TO		
	D. ℞. Flower above moneyer's name	2500	6000
1018	**Olaf Guthfrithsson.** Circumscription type, with small cross each side,		
	ANLAF CVNVNC, M in field on reverse (*Derby*)	2500	6000
1018A	— Two line type. ONLAF REX. Large letter both sides (*Lincoln?*). . . .	2000	5000
1019	— Raven type. As illustration, ANLAF CVNVNC	2000	5000

1019   1020

1020	**Olaf Sihtricsson,** first reign, 941–944. Triquetra type. As illus., CVNVNC.		
	℞. Danish standard	2000	5000
1021	— Circumscription type (a). Small cross each side, CVNVNC	2000	5000
1022	— Cross moline type, CVNVNC. ℞. Small cross	*Extremely rare*	
1023	— Two line type. Small cross. ℞. ONLAF REX. ℞. Name in two lines .	2000	5000
1024	**Regnald Guthfrithsson,** 943–944. Triquetra type. As 1020. REGNALD		
	CVNVNC	3000	7500
1025	— Cross moline type. As 1022, but REGNALD CVNVNC	2500	6000
1026	**Sihtric Sihtricsson,** *c.* 942. Triquetra type. As 1020, SITRIC CVNVNC .	*Unique*	

1025   1030

	F £	VF £
1027 — Circumscription type. Small cross each side		*Unique*
1028 **Eric Blood-axe,** first reign, 948. Two line type. Small cross, ERICVC REX A; ERIC REX AL; or ERIC REX EFOR. R. Name in two lines.	2500	6000
1029 **Olaf Sihtricsson,** second reign, 948–952. Circumscription type (b). Small cross each side. ONLAF REX	2750	6500
1029A — Flower type. small cross ANLAF REX R. Flower above moneyer's name	2500	6000
1029B — Two line type. Small cross, ONLAF REX. R. Moneyer's name in two lines.	2000	5000
1030 **Eric Blood-axe,** second reign, 952–954. Sword type. ERIC REX in two lines, sword between. R. Small cross.	2750	6500

KINGS OF WESSEX

Later, KINGS OF ALL ENGLAND

All are silver pennies unless otherwise stated

BEORHTRIC, 786—802

Beorhtric was dependent on Offa of Mercia and married a daughter of Offa.

1031

1031 As illustration	*Extremely rare*
1032 Alpha and omega in centre. R. Omega in centre	*Extremely rare*

ECGBERHT, 802—839

King of Wessex only, 802–825; then also of Kent, Sussex, Surrey, Essex and East Anglia, 825–839, and of Mercia also, 829–830.

		F	VF
1033 *Canterbury.* Group I. Diad. hd. r. within inner circle. R. Various	*. from*	1450	3500
1034 — II. Non-portrait types. R. Various	*. from*	750	2250

1035

		F £	VF £
1035	— III. Bust r. breaking inner circle. ℞. DORIB C	1250	3500
1036	*London.* Cross potent. ℞. LVN / DONIA / CIVIT		*Unique*
1037	— — ℞. REDMVND MONE around TA	1500	4250
1038	*Rochester,* royal mint. Non-portrait types with king's name ECGBEORHT . . . . *from*	1150	3250
1039	— — Portrait types, ECGBEORHT . . . . *from*	1350	4000
1040	*Rochester,* bishop's mint. Bust r. ℞. SCS ANDREAS (APOSTOLVS) . .	1450	4600
1041	*Winchester.* SAXON monogram or SAXONIORVM in three lines. ℞. Cross.	1150	3250

AETHELWULF, 839—858

Son of Ecgberht; sub-King of Essex, Kent, Surrey and Sussex, 825–839; King of all southern England, 839–855; King of Essex, Kent and Sussex only, 855–858. No coins are known of his son Aethelbald who ruled over Wessex proper, 855–860

1042

1042	*Canterbury.* Phase I (839–*c.* 843). Head within inner circle. ℞. Various. *Br. 3*	225	600
1043	— — Larger bust breaking inner circle. ℞. A. *Br. 1 and 2*	225	600
1044	— — Cross and wedges. ℞. SAXONIORVM in three lines in centre. *BR. 10*	225	550
1045	— — Similar, but OCCINDENTALIVM in place of moneyer. *Br. 11* . .	225	750
1046	— Phase II (*c.* 843–848?). Cross and wedges. ℞. Various, but chiefly a form of cross or a large A. *Br. 4*	225	500
1047	— — New portrait, somewhat as 1043. ℞. As last. *Br. 7*	225	500
1048	— — Smaller portrait. ℞. As last, with *Chi/Rho* monogram. *Br. 7*	250	500
1049	— Phase III (*c.* 848/851–*c.* 855). DORIB in centre. ℞. CANT mon. *Br. 5*	225	500
1050	— — CANT mon. ℞. CAN M in angles of cross. *Br. 6*	250	500

1044 1051

		F £	VF £
1051	— Phase IV (c. 855–859). Type as Aethelberht. New neat style bust R. Large voided long cross. Br. 8	225	450
1052	Winchester. SAXON mon. R. Cross and wedges. Br. 9	350	750

AETHELBERHT, 858–865/866

on of Aethelwulf; sub-King of Kent, Essex and Sussex, 858–860; King of all southern England, 860–865/6

1053	As illustration below	200	400
1054	O. Similar, R. Cross fleury over quatrefoil	700	1500

1053

AETHELRED I, 865/866–871

Son of Aethelwulf; succeeded his brother Aethelberht.

1055	As illustration	250	600
1056	Similar, but moneyer's name in four lines	600	1500

For another coin with the name Aethelred see 959 under Viking coinages.

1055

58

ALFRED THE GREAT, 871—899

Brother and successor to Aethelred, Alfred had to contend with invading Danish armies for much of his reign. In 878 he and Guthrum the Dane divided the country, with Alfred holding all England south and west of Watling Street. Alfred occupied London in 886.

		F £	VF £
Types with portraits			
1057	Bust r. ℞. As Aethelred I. *Br. 1* (*name often* AELBRED)	300	650
1058	— ℞. Long cross with lozenge centre, as 9544, *Br. 5*	1500	4000
1059	— ℞. Two seated figures, as 943. *Br. 2*		*Unique*
1060	— ℞. As Archbp. Aethered; cross within large quatrefoil. *Br. 3*		*Unique*

1057   1062

1061	*London.* Bust. r. ℞. LONDONIA monogram	600	150
1062	— ℞. Similar, but with moneyer's name added	750	170
1063	— *Halfpenny.* Bust r. ℞. LONDONIA monogram as 1061	1000	250
1064	*Gloucester.* ℞. ÆT GLEAPA in angles of three limbed cross		*Unique*

Types without portraits

1065	King's name on limbs of cross, trefoils in angles. ℞. Moneyer's name in quatrefoil. *Br. 4.*		*Unique*

1066   1069

1066	Cross pattée. ℞. Moneyer's name in two lines. *Br. 6*	175	350
1067	— As last, but neater style, as Edw, the Elder	185	375
1068	— *Halfpenny.* As 1066	650	1650
1069	*Canterbury.* As last but DORO added on *obv. Br. 6a*	300	625
	For other pieces bearing the name of Alfred see under the Viking coinages.		
1070	*Exeter?* King name in four lines. ℞. EXA vertical		*Extremely rare*
1071	*Winchester?* Similar to last, but PIN		*Extremely rare*
1072	"Offering penny". Very large and heavy. AELFRED REX SAXORVM in four lines. ℞. ELIMO in two lines i.e. (*Elimosina,* alms)		*Extremely rare*

EDWARD THE ELDER, 899–924

Eadward, the son of Alfred, aided by his sister Aethelflaed 'Lady of the Mercians', annexed all England south of the Humber and built many new fortified boroughs to protect the kingdom.

1074

		F £	VF £
1073	**Rare types**. *Br. 1. Bath?* R. BA.	*Extremely rare*	
1074	— 2. *Canterbury*. Cross moline in pommée. R. Moneyer's name	700	1650
1075	— 3. *Chester?* Small cross. R. Minster.	750	1750
1076	— 4. — Small cross. R. Moneyer's name in single line.	625	1400
1077	— 5. — R. Two stars	850	1800

1078   1082

1078	— 6. — R. Flower above central line, name below	850	1900
1079	— 7. — R. Floral design with name across field	850	1900
1080	— 8. — R. Bird holding twig.	*Extremely rare*	
1081	— 9. — R. Hand of Providence	1000	2250
1082	— 10. — R. City gate of Roman style.	*Extremely rare*	
1083	— 11. — R. Anglo-Saxon burg.	750	1750

1084   1087

1084	**Ordinary types**. *Br. 12*. Bust l. R. Moneyer's name in two lines . . . *from*	400	1000
1085	— — As last, but in *gold*	*Unique*	
1086	— 12a. Similar, but bust r. of crude style	350	850
1087	— 13. Small cross. R. Similar (to 1084)	125	240
1088	*Halfpenny*. Similar to last.	*Extremely rare*	

AETHELSTAN, 924–939

Aethelstan, the eldest son of Eadward, decreed that money should be coined only in a borough, that every borough should have one moneyer and that some of the more important boroughs should have more than one moneyer.

1089   1094

1089	**Main issues.** Small cross. ℞. Moneyer's name in two lines	200	400
1090	Diad. bust r. ℞. As last	650	1500
1091	— ℞. Small cross	550	1350
1092	Small cross both sides	175	375
1093	— Similar, but mint name added	185	400
1094	Crowned bust r. As illustration. ℞. Small cross	450	1000
1095	— Similar, but mint name added	400	850

1100   1104

1096	**Local Issues.** *N. Mercian mints.* Star between two pellets. ℞. As 1089 . . .	550	1250
1097	— Small cross. ℞. Floral ornaments above and below moneyer's name .	550	1250
1098	— Rosette of pellets each side	250	550
1099	— Small cross one side, rosette on the other side	275	650
1100	*N.E. mints.* Small cross. ℞. Tower over moneyer's name	550	1250
1101	— Similar, but mint name added	750	1750
1102	— Bust in high relief r. or l. ℞. Small cross	500	1150
1103	— Bust r. in high relief. ℞. Cross-crosslet	500	1150
1104	"Helmeted" bust r. ℞. As last	600	1500

EADMUND, 939–946

Eadmund, the brother of Aethelstan, extended his realm over the Norse kingdom of York.

1105   1107

	F £	VF £
1105 Small cross or rosette. ℞. Moneyer's name in two lines with crosses or rosettes between . . . . *from*	125	300
1106 Crowned bust r. ℞. Small cross	300	650
1107 Similar, but with mint name	400	850
1108 Small cross either side, or rosette on one side.	175	375
1109 Cross of five pellets. ℞. Moneyer's name in two lines	200	425
1110 Small cross. ℞. Flower above name	750	1750
1111 "Helmeted" bust r. ℞. Cross-crosslet	750	1750

1112

1112 *Halfpenny.* As 1105 . . . . *from*	950	2000

EADRED, 946–955

Eadred was another of the sons of Eadward. He lost the kingdom of York to Eric Bloodaxe.

1113   1115

1113 As illustration. ℞. Moneyer's name in two lines	125	275
1114 — Similar, but mint name after REX	300	750
1115 Crowned bust r. As illustration.	350	850
1116 — ℞. Similar, with mint name added	400	950

	F	VF
	£	£
1117 Rosette. ℞. As 1113.	125	250
1118 Small cross. ℞. Rosette	135	285
1119 — ℞. Flower enclosing moneyer's name. *B.M.C. II*	*Extremely rare*	
1120 *Halfpenny*. Similar to 1113 . . . . *from*	750	1500

HOWEL DDA, d. 949–950

Grandson of Rhodri Mawr, Howel succeeded to the kingdom of Dyfed *c*. 904, to Seisyllog *c*. 920 and became King of Gwynedd and all Wales, 942.

1121

1121 HOPÆL REX, small cross or rosette. ℞. Moneyer's name in two lines. .   *Unique*

EADWIG, 955–959

Elder son of Eadmund, Eadwig lost Mercia and Northumbria to his brother Eadgar in 957.

1122

1122 *Br. 1.* Type as illustration.	175	375
1123 — — Similar, but mint name in place of crosses	350	700
1123A — Similar to 1122, but star in place of cross on *obv*.	*Unique*	
1124 — 2. As 1122, but moneyer's name in one line	600	1350
1125 — 3. Similar. ℞. Floral design	675	1450
1126 — 4. Similar. ℞. Rosette or small cross	250	550
1127 — 5. Bust r. ℞. Small cross (*possibly an altered coin of Eadgar*).	*Extremely rare*	

1128

1128 *Halfpenny*. Small cross. ℞. Flower above moneyer's name . . . .   *Unique*

EADGAR, 959–975

King in Mercia and Northumbria from 957; King of all England 959–975.

It is now possible on the basis of the lettering to divide up the majority of Eadgar's coins into issues from the following regions: N.E. England, N.W. England, York, East Anglia, Midlands, S.E. England, Southern England, and S.W. England. (*See* "Anglo-Saxon Coins", ed. R. H. M. Dolley.)

1129   1135

		F	VF
		£	£
1129	*Br. 1.* Small cross. R. Moneyer's name in two lines, crosses between, trefoils top and bottom	80	175
1130	— — R. Similar, but rosettes top and bottom (a N.W. variety)	80	200
1131	— — R. Similar, but annulets between	80	250
1132	— — R. Similar, but mint name between (a late N.W. type)	125	275
1133	— 2. — R. Floral design	750	1600
1134	— 4. Small cross either side.	80	180
1135	— — Similar, with mint name	250	500
1136	— — Rosette either side	125	240
1137	— — Similar, with mint name	225	475
1138	— 5. Large bust to r. R. Small cross.	400	900
1139	— — Similar, with mint name	600	1500
1140	*Halfpenny.* (8½ grains.) *Br. 3.* Small cross. R. Flower above name.	*Extremely rare*	
	See also 1141 below		
1140A	— — R. Mint name around cross (Chichester)	*Unique*	
1140B	— Bust r. R. 'Londonia' monogram	*Extremely rare*	

LATE ANGLO-SAXON PERIOD

In 973 Eadgar introduced a new coinage. A royal portrait now became a regular feature and the reverses normally have a cruciform pattern with the name of the mint in addition to that of the moneyer. Most fortified towns of burghal status were allowed a mint, the number of moneyers varying according to their size and importance: some royal manors also had a mint and some moneyers were allowed to certain ecclesiastical authorities. In all some seventy mints were active about the middle of the 11th century (see list of mints pp. 65–67).

The control of the currency was retained firmly in the hands of the central government, unlike the situation in France and the Empire where feudal barons and bishops controlled their own coinage. Coinage types were changed at intervals to enable the Exchequer to raise revenue from new dies and periodic demonetization of old coin types helped to maintain the currency in a good state. No halfpence were minted during this period, but pennies were often sheared into two halves.

1141

	F	VF
EADGAR, 959–975 *continued*	£	£
1141 **Penny.** Type 6. Small bust l. R. Small cross, name of moneyer and mint .	450	950

EDWARD THE MARTYR, 975–978

Son of Eadgar and Aethelflaed, Eadward was murdered at Corfe, reputedly on the orders of his stepmother Aelfthryth.

1142

1142 Type as illustration above	650	1300

AETHELRED II, 978–1016

He was the son of Eadgar and Aelfthryth. His reign was greatly disturbed by incursions of Danish fleets and armies which massive payments of money failed to curb. His later by-name 'the Unready' come from *Unrede*, 'no counsel', a play on his given name.

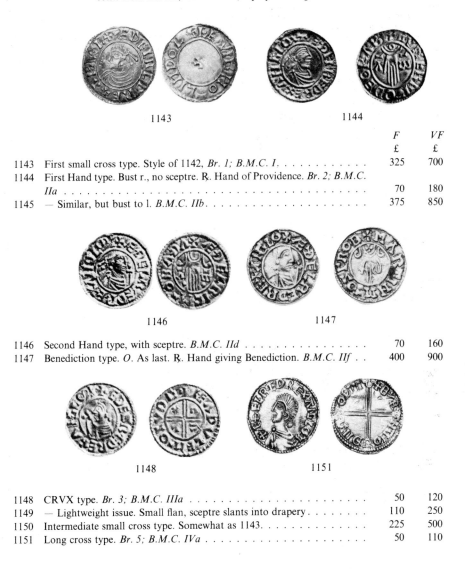

1143   1144

	F £	VF £
1143 First small cross type. Style of 1142, *Br. 1; B.M.C. I*.	325	700
1144 First Hand type. Bust r., no sceptre. ℞. Hand of Providence. *Br. 2; B.M.C. IIa*	70	180
1145 — Similar, but bust to l. *B.M.C. IIb*.	375	850

1146   1147

1146 Second Hand type, with sceptre. *B.M.C. IId*	70	160
1147 Benediction type. *O.* As last. ℞. Hand giving Benediction. *B.M.C. IIf* . .	400	900

1148   1151

1148 CRVX type. *Br. 3; B.M.C. IIIa*	50	120
1149 — Lightweight issue. Small flan, sceptre slants into drapery	110	250
1150 Intermediate small cross type. Somewhat as 1143.	225	500
1151 Long cross type. *Br. 5; B.M.C. IVa*	50	110

1152

		F	VF
		£	£
1152	Helmet type. *Br. 4; B.M.C. VIII*	55	120
1153	— — Similar, but struck in **gold**		Unique
1154	Last small cross type. As 1143, but different style	50	100
1154A	Similar, but bust r.	–	600
1155	— Similar, but bust to edge of coin. *B.M.C. Id*	250	550

1154   1156

1156   Agnus Dei type. *Br. 6; B.M.C. X* . . . .   *Extremely rare*

CNUT, 1016–1035

Son of Swegn Forkbeard, King of Denmark, Cnut was acclaimed King by the Danish fleet in England in 1014 but was forced to leave. He returned in 1015 and in 1016 agreed on a division of the country with Eadmund Ironsides, the son of Aethelred. No coins of Eadmund are known and on his death in November 1016 Cnut secured all England, marrying Emma, widow of Aethelred.

Main types

1157   1158   1159   1160

		F £	VF £
1157	Quatrefoil type. *BR. 2; B.M.C. VIII*	75	145
1158	Helmet type. *Br. 3; B.M.C. XIV*	60	120
1159	Short cross type. *BR. 4; B.M.C. XVI*	60	120
1159A	— Similar, but with banner in place of sceptre.	250	500
1160	Jewel cross type. *Br. 6; B.M.C. XX*. Type as 1163	500	1100

[*This type is now considered to be a posthumus issue struck under the auspices of his widow, Aelgifu Emma.*]

HAROLD I, 1035–1040

Harold, the son of Cnut and Aelgifu of Northampton, initially acted as regent for his half-brother Harthacnut on Cnut's death, was then recognised as King in Mercia and the north, and King throughout England in 1037.

1163   1165

1163	Jewel cross type, as illustration. *Br. 1; B.M.C. 1*	160	325
1164	Long cross and trefoils type. *Br. 2; B.M.C. V.*	160	325
1165	— Similar, but fleur de lis in place of trefoils. *B.M.C. Vc*	150	300

HARTHACNUT, 1035–1042

He was heir to Cnut but lost the throne to his half-brother Harold owing to his absence in Denmark. On Harold's death he recovered his English realm.

1167   1168

1166	**Early period, 1036**. Jewel cross type, as 1163; bust l. *Br. 1; B.M.C. I* . . .	700	1500
1167	— Similar, but bust r. *B.M.C. Ia.*	650	1400
1168	**Restoration, 1040–1042**. Arm and sceptre type, with name Harthacnut. *Br. 2; B.M.C. II* . .	800	1650
1169	— Similar, but with name "Cnut"	500	1100

1169   1170

	F £	VF £
1170 **Danish types**, of various designs, some of English type mostly struck at Lund, Denmark (now Sweden) . . . . *from*	140	300

EDWARD THE CONFESSOR, 1042–1066

Edward was the son of Aethelred II and Emma of Normandy. A number of new mints were opened during his reign.

1171   1173

1171 PACX type, cross extends to edge of coin. *Br. 4; B.M.C. IVa*	150	350
1172 — Similar, but cross ends at legend. *B.M.C. IV*	150	350
1173 Radiate type. *Br. 2; B.M.C. I*	65	135

1174   1175

1174 Trefoil quadrilateral type. *Br. 1; B.M.C. III.*	60	125
1175 Short cross type, small flans. *Br. 3; B.M.C. II*	55	110

1176   1179

1176 Expanding cross type; light issue (18 grs.). *Br. 5; B.M.C. V*	65	135

	F £	VF £
1177 — — Heavy issue (27 grs.)	55	125
1178 — — Similar, but struck in **gold**		*Unique*
1179 Helmet type. *Br. 6; B.M.C. VII*	55	110
1180 — — Similar but bust l.	350	900

1181   1182

1181 Sovereign type. *Br. 7; B.M.C. IX*	75	150
1182 Hammer cross type. *Br. 8; B.M.C. XI*	65	125

1183   1184

1183 Facing bust type. *Br. 9; B.M.C. XIII*	55	125
1184 Pyramids type. *Br. 10; B.M.C. XV*	75	160

1185

1185 Large facing bust with sceptre. ℞. Similar	950	2000

Most York coins of this reign have an annulet in one quarter of the reverse.

HAROLD II, 1066

Harold was the son of Godwin Earl of Wessex. He was the brother-in-law of Edward the Confessor and was recognised as King on Edward's death. He defeated and killed Harald of Norway who invaded the north, but was himself defeated and killed at the Battle of Hastings by William of Normandy.

1186   1187

		F	VF
		£	£
1186	Bust l. with sceptre. R. PAX across centre of *rev. B.M.C. I*	275	500
1187	Similar, but without sceptre. *B.M.C. Ia*	325	700
1188	Bust r. with sceptre	600	1250

ANGLO-SAXON, NORMAN AND EARLY PLANTAGENET MINTS

In Anglo-Saxon times coins were struck at a large number of towns. The place of mintage is normally given on all coins from the last quarter of the 10th century onwards, and generally the name of the person responsible (e.g. BRVNIC ON LVND). Below we give a list of the mints, showing the reigns (Baronial of Stephen's reign omitted), of which coins have been found. After the town names we give one or two of the spellings as found on the coins, although often they appear in an abbreviated or extended form. On the coins the Anglo-Saxon and Norman *w* is like a P or Γ and the *th* is Ð. We have abbreviated the kings' names, etc.:

Alf	—	Alfred the Great	Wi	—	William I
EE	—	Edward the Elder	Wii	—	William II
A'stan	—	Aethelstan	He	—	Henry I
EM	—	Edward the Martyr	St	—	Stephen (regular issues)
Ae	—	Aethelred II	M	—	Matilda
Cn	—	Cnut	HA	—	Henry of Anjou
Hi	—	Harold I	WG	—	William of Gloucester
Htr	—	Harthacnut	T	—	"Tealby" coinage
ECfr	—	Edward the Confessor	SC	—	Short cross coinage
Hii	—	Harold II	LC	—	Long cross coinage

Axbridge (ACXEPO, AGEPOR) Ae, Cn, Ht.
Aylesbury (AEGEL) Ae, Cn, ECfr.
Barnstaple (BEARDA, BARDI), Edwig, Ae-Hi, ECfr, Wi, He.
Bath (BADAN) EE-Edmund, Edwig-ECfr, Wi, He, St.
Bedford (BEDANF, BEDEF) Edwig-T.
Bedwyn (BEDEΓIN) ECfr, Wi.
Berkeley (BEORC) ECfr, Wi.
Bramber ? (BRAN) St.
Bridport (BRIPVT, BRIDI) A'stan, Ae, Cn, Ht, ECfr, Wi.
Bristol (BRICSTO) Ae-T, M. HA, LC.
Bruton (BRIVT) Ae-Cn, ECfr.
Buckingham (BVCIN) EM-Hi̇, ECfr.
Bury St. Edmunds (EDMVN, SEDM, SANTEA) A'stan?, ECfr, Wi, He-LC.
Cadbury CADANB) Ae, Cn.
Caistor (CASTR) EM, Ae, Cn.
Cambridge (GRANTE) Edgar-Wii.
Canterbury (DORO, CAENT, CANTOR, CANTΓAR) Alf, A'stan, Edgar-LC.
Cardiff (CAIRDI, CARDI, CARITI) Wi, He, St, M.
Carlisle (CAR, CARDI, EDEN) He-LC.
Castle Gotha ? (GEOÐA, IOÐA) Ae-Ht.
Castle Rising (RISINGE) St.
Chester (LEIGECES, LEGECE, CESTRE) A'stan, Edgar-T.
Chichester (CISSAN CIV, CICES, CICST) A'stan, Edgar-St, SC.
Chippenham ? (CIPEN) St.
Christchurch, see Twynham.
Cissbury (SIÐEST) Ae, Cn.
Colchester (COLEAC, COLECES) Ae-Hi, ECfr-T.
Crewkerne (CRVCERN) Ae, Cn.
Cricklade (CROCGL, CRIC, CREC) Ae-Wii.
Derby (DEOR, DIORBI, DERBI) A'stan, Edgar-ECfr, Wi-St.
Dorchester (DORCE, DORECES) Ae-ECfr, Wi-He, WG.
Dover (DOFER) A'stan, Edgar-St.
Droitwich (PICC, PICNEH) ECfr. Hii.
Dunwich (DVNE) St.
Durham (DVRE DVRHAN) Wi, St-LC.
Exeter (EAXANC, EXEC, XECST) Alf, A'stan, Edwig-LC.
Eye (EI, EIE) St.
Frome ? (FRO) Cn-ECfr.
Gloucester (GLEAΓEC, GLEΓ, GΓ) Alf, A'stan, Edgar-St, HA, T, LC.
Guildford (GILDEF) EM-Cn, Ht-Wii.

Hastings (HAESTIN) Ae-St.
Hedon, near Hull (HEDVN) St.
Hereford (HEREFOR) A'stan, Ae-St, HA, T, LC.
Hertford (HEORTF) A'stan, Edwig-Hi, ECfr, Wi, Wii.
Horncastle ? (HORN) EM, Ae.
Horndon ? (HORNIDVNE) ECfr.
Huntingdon (HVNTEN) Edwig-St.
Hythe (HIÐEN) ECfr, Wi, Wii.
Ilchester (IVELCE, GIFELCST, GIVELC) Edgar, EM-He, T, LC.
Ipswich (GIPESΓIC) Edgar-SC.
Kings Lynn (LENN, LEÑE) SC.
Langport (LANCPOR) A'stan, Cn, Hi, ECfr.
Launceston (LANSTF, SANCTI STEFANI) Ae, Wi, Wii, St. T.
Leicester (LIGER, LIHER, LEHRE) A'stan, Edgar-T.
Lewes (LAEPES) A'stan, Edgar-T.
Lichfield (LIHFL) SC.
Lincoln (LINCOLNE, NICOLE) Edgar-LC.
London (LVNDENE) Alf-LC.
Louth ? (LVD) Ae.
Lydford (LYDAN) EM-Hi, ECfr.
Lympne (LIMEN) A'stan, Edgar-Cn.
Maldon (MAELDVN, MAELI) A'stan, Ae-Hi, ECfr, Wii.
Malmesbury (MALD, MEALDMES) Ae-Wii, HA.
Marlborough (MAERLEB) Wi, Wii.
Milbourne Port (MYLE) Ae, Cn.
Newark (NEPIR, NIPOR) Edwig, Eadgar, Ae, Cn.
Newcastle (NEWEC, NIVCA) St, T, LC.
Newport (NIPAN, NIPEP) Edgar, ECfr.
Northampton (HAMTVN, NORHANT) Edwig, Edgar-Wi, He-LC.
Norwich (NORPIC) A'stan-LC.
Nottingham (SNOTINC) A'stan, Ae-St.
Oxford (OXNAFOR, OXENEF) A'stan, Edmund, Edred, Edgar-St, M, T-LC.
Pembroke (PAN, PAIN) He-T.
Pershore (PERESC) ECfr.
Peterborough (MEDE, BVR) Ae, Cn, Wi.
Petherton (PEDÐR) ECfr.
Pevensey (PEFNESE, PEVEN) Wi, Wii, St.
Reading (READIN) ECfr.
Rhuddlan (RVDILI, RVLA) Wi, SC.
Rochester (ROFEC) A'stan, Edgar-He, SC.
Romney (RVME, RVMNE) Ae-Hi, ECfr-He.
Rye (RIE) St.
Salisbury (SAEREB, SALEB) Ae-ECfr, Wi- T.
Sandwich (SANPIC) ECfr, Wi-St.
Shaftesbury (SCEFTESB, SCEFITI) A'stan, Ae-St.
Shrewsbury (SCROBES, SALOP) A'stan, Edgar-LC.
Southampton (HAMWIC, HAMTVN) A'stan, Edwig-Cn.
Southwark (SVDGE, SVDΓEEORC) Ae-St.
Stafford (STAFF, STAEF) A'stan, Ae-Hi, ECfr, Wi, Wii, St, T.
Stamford (STANFOR) Edgar-St.
Steyning (STAENIG) Cn-Wii.
Sudbury (SVDBI, SVB) Ae, Cn, ECfr, Wi-St.
Swansea (SWENSEI) HA?
Tamworth (TOMPEARÐGE, TAMPRÐ) A'stan, Edwig-Hi, ECfr, Wi-St.
Taunton (TANTVNE) Ae, Cn, Ht-St.
Thetford (ÐEOTFOR,, TETFOR) Edgar-T.
Torksey (TORC, TVRC) EM-Cn.
Totnes (DARENT VRB, TOTANES, TOTNESE) A'stan, Edwig-Cn, Wii.
Twynham, now Christchurch (TPIN, TVEHAM) Wi, He.
Wallingford (PELING, PALLIG) A'stan, Edgar-He, T, LC.
Wareham (PERHAM) A'stan, Ae, Cn, Ht-St, M, WG.
Warminster (PORIME) Ae-Hi, ECfr.
Warwick (PAERING, PERPIC) A'stan, Edgar-St.
Watchet (PECEDPORT, PICEDI) Ae-ECfr, Wi-St.
Wilton (PILTVNE) Edgar-LC.

Winchcombe (PINCELE, PINCL) Edgar-Cn, Ht-Wi.
Winchester (PINTONIA, PINCEST) Alf-A'stan, Edwig-LC.
Worcester (PIHRAC, PIHREC) Ae-Hi, ECfr-Sc.
York (EBORACI, EOFERPIC) A'stan, Edmund, Edgar-LC.

The location of the following is uncertain.
AESTHE *(? Hastings)* Ae.
BRYGIN *(? Bridgnorth*, but die-links with NIPAN and with *Shaftesbury)* Ae.
DERNE, DYR (E. Anglian mint) ECfr.
DEVITVN *(? Welsh Marches* or *St. Davids)* Wi.
EANBYRIG, Cn.
MAINT, Wi.
ORSNAFORDA *(? Horsforth or Orford)* Alf.
WEARDBYRIG *(? Warborough)* A'stan, Edgar.

EDWARDIAN AND LATER MINTS

London, Tower: Edw. I–GEO. III.
London, Tower Hill: Geo. III–Eliz. II.
London, Durham House: Hen. VIII (posth.)–Edw. VI.
Ashby de la Zouche: Chas. I.
Aberystwyth: Chas. I.
Aberystwyth: -Furnace: Chas. I.
Bridgnorth: Chas. I.
Berwick-on-Tweed: Edw. I–Edw. III.
Birmingham, Heaton: Vic., Geo. V.
Birmingham, King's Norton: Geo. V.
Birmingham, Soho: Geo. III.
Bombay, India (branch mint): Geo. V.
Bristol: Edw. I, Edw. IV, Hen. VI rest., Hen. VIII–Edw. VI, Chas. I, Wm. III.
Bury St. Edmunds: Edw. I–Edw. III.
Calais: Edw. III–Hen. IV, Hen. VI.
Canterbury: Edw. I–Edw. III, Edw. IV, Hen. VII–Edw. VI.
Carlisle: Chas. I.
Chester: Edw. I, Chas. I, Wm. III.
Colchester: Chas. I.
Coventry: Edw. IV.
Durham: Edw. I–Edw. IV, Rich. III–Hen. VIII.
Exeter: Edw. I, Chas. I, Wm. III.
Hartlebury Castle, Worcs.: Chas. I.
Kingston-upon-Hull: Edw. I.
Lincoln: Edw. I.
Llantrisant: Eliz. II (decimal coinage).
Melbourne, Australia (branch mint): Vic.–Geo. V.
Newark: Chas. I.
Newcastle-upon-Tyne: Edw. I.
Norwich: Edw. IV, Wm. III.
Ottowa, Canada (branch mint): Edw. VII–Geo. V.
Oxford: Chas I.
Perth, Australia (branch mint): Vic.–Geo. V.
Pontefract: Chas. I.
Pretoria, South Africa (branch mint): Geo. V.
Reading: Edw. III.
Scarborough: Chas. I.
Shrewsbury: Chas. I.
Southwark: Hen. VIII–Edw. VI.
Sydney, Australia (branch mint): Vic.–Geo. V.
Tournai, Belgium: Hen. VIII.
Truro: Chas. I.
Worcester: Chas I.
York: Edw. I, Edw. III–Edw. IV, Rich. III–Edw. VI, Chas. I, Wm. III.

NORMAN KINGS AND THEIR SUCCESSORS

There were no major changes in the coinages following the Norman conquest. The controls and periodic changes of the type made in the previous reigns were continued. Nearly seventy mints were operating during the reign of William I; these had been reduced to about fifty-five by the middle of the 12th century and, under Henry II, first to thirty and later to eleven. By the second half of the 13th century the issue of coinage had been centralized at London and Canterbury, with the exception of two ecclesiastical mints. Of the thirteen types with the name PILLEMVS, PILLELM, etc. (William), the first eight have been attributed to the Conqueror and the remaining five to his son William Rufus.

From William I to Edward II inclusive all are silver pennies unless otherwise stated.

WILLIAM I, 1066–1087

William Duke of Normandy was the cousin of Edward the Confessor. After securing the throne of England he had to suppress several rebellions.

1250   1251

| 1250 | **Penny**. Profile left type. *Br. I* | 135 | 340 |
| 1251 | Bonnet type. *Br. II* | 125 | 270 |

1252   1253

| 1252 | Canopy type. *Br. III* | 150 | 375 |
| 1253 | Two sceptres type. *Br. IV* | 125 | 300 |

1254   1255

| 1254 | Two stars type. *Br. V* | 90 | 200 |
| 1255 | Sword type. *Br. VI* | 185 | 425 |

1256 1257

		F £	VF £
1256	Profile right type. *Br VII*	250	550
1257	PAXS type. *Br. VIII*	75	125

WILLIAM II, 1087–1100

William Rufus was the second son of William I, his elder brother Robert succeeding to the Dukedom of Normandy. He was killed hunting in the New Forest.

1258 1259

1258	**Penny**. Profile type. *Br. 1*	225	550
1259	Cross in quatrefoil type. *Br. 2*	225	500

1260 1261

1260	Cross voided type. *Br. 3*	225	475
1261	Cross pattée and fleury type. *Br. 4*	250	575

1262

1262	Cross fleury and piles type. *Br. 5*	350	750

HENRY I, 1100–1135

Fifteen types were minted during this reign. In 1108 provision was made for minting round halfpence again, none having been struck since the time of Eadgar, but few can have been made as only one specimen has survived. The standard of coinage manufacture was now beginning to deteriorate badly. Many genuine coins were being cut to see if they were plated counterfeits and there was a reluctance by the public to accept such damaged pieces. About 1112 an extraordinary decision was taken ordering the official mutilation of all new coins by snicking the edges, thus ensuring that cut coins had to be accepted. Pennies of types VII to XII (Nos. 1268–1273) usually have a cut in the flan that sometimes penetrated over a third of the way across the coin.

At Christmas 1124 the famous 'Assize of the Moneyers' was held at Winchester when all the moneyers in England were called to account for their activities and a number are said to have been mutilated for issuing coins of inferior quality.

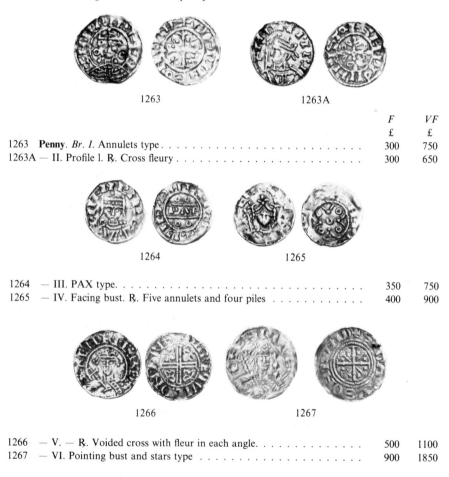

			F	VF
			£	£
1263	**Penny**. *Br. I*. Annulets type		300	750
1263A	— II. Profile l. R. Cross fleury		300	650
1264	— III. PAX type		350	750
1265	— IV. Facing bust. R. Five annulets and four piles		400	900
1266	— V. — R. Voided cross with fleur in each angle		500	1100
1267	— VI. Pointing bust and stars type		900	1850

1263   1263A

1264   1265

1266   1267

1268

		F £	VF £
1268	— VII. Facing bust. R. Quatrefoil with piles	250	500

1269    1270

1269	*Br.* VIII. Large bust l. R. Cross with annulet in each angle	600	1450
1270	— IX. Facing bust. R. Cross in quatrefoil.	450	1000

1271    1272

1271	— X. Small facing bust in circle. R. Cross fleury	225	475
1272	— XI. Very large bust l. R. "Double inscription" around small cross pattée		
		600	1100

1273    1274

1273	— XII. Small bust l. R. Cross with annulet in each angle	350	750
1274	— XIII. Star in lozenge fleury type	250	550

1275   1276

	F	VF
	£	£
1275 — XIV. Pellets in quatrefoil type	120	350
1276 — XV. Quadrilateral on cross fleury type	85	225

1277

1277 *Halfpenny*. Facing head. R. Cross potent with pellets in angles	*Extremely rare*
1277A — As above R. Similar to penny die of type IX	*Unique*

STEPHEN, 1135–1154
and the Civil War and Anarchy, 1138–1153

Stephen of Blois, Count of Boulogne and a nephew of Henry I, hastily crossed the Channel on his uncle's death and secured the throne for himself, despite Henry's wishes that his daughter Matilda should succeed him. She was the widow of the German emperor Henry V, and was then married to Geoffrey, Count of Anjou. Two years later Matilda arrived in England to claim the throne, supported by her half-brother Robert of Gloucester. During the protracted civil war that ensued Matilda and later her son, Henry of Anjou, set up an alternative court at Bristol and held much of the west of England, striking coins at mints under their control. Many irregular coins were struck during this troubled period, some by barons in their own name. Particularly curious are the coins from the Midlands and E. Anglia which have Stephen's head defaced, now believed to have been issued during the Interdict of 1148. In 1153, following the death of Stephen's son, Eustace, a treaty between the two factions allowed for the succession of Matilda's son Henry and a uniform coinage was once more established throughout the kingdom.

    B.M.C.—British Museum Catalogue: *Norman Kings*, 2 vols. (1916). *M.*—Mack, R. P., "Stephen and the Anarchy 1135–54", *BNJ*, XXXV (1966), pp. 38–112.

STEPHEN
Regular regal issues

1278   1280

| | F | VF |
| | £ | £ |

1278 **Penny.** Cross moline (Watford) type. Bust r., with sceptre. R. Cross moline
with lis in angles. *B.M.C. I; M. 3–42* 80 170
1279 — Similar, but obv. reads PERERIC or PERERICM. *M. 43–50* 350 800
1280 Voided cross type. Facing bust with sceptre. R. Voided cross pattée with
mullets in angles. *East and South-east mints only. B.M.C. II; M. 53–66.* . 175 375

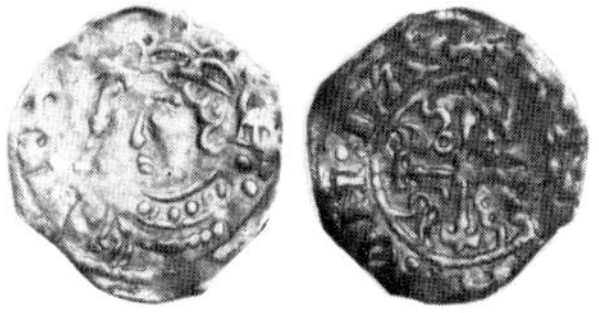

1281 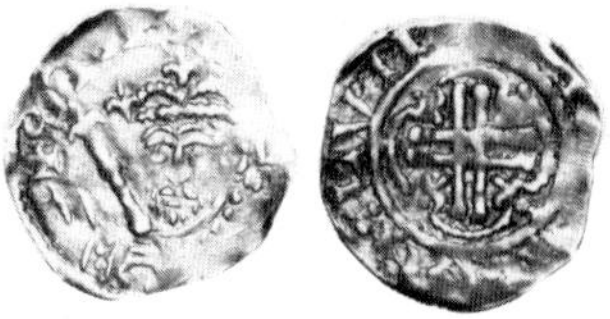   1282

1281 Cross fleury type. Bust l. with sceptre. R. Cross fleury with trefoils in
angles. *East and South-east mints only. B.M.C. VI; M. 77–99* 700 2250
1282 Cross pommée (Awbridge) type. Bust half-left with sceptre. R. Voided
cross pommée with lis in angles. *B.M.C. VII; M. 99z–135b* 175 375

For B.M.C. types III, IV & V, see 1300–1302.

Local and irregular issues of the Civil War
A. Coins struck from erased or defaced dies

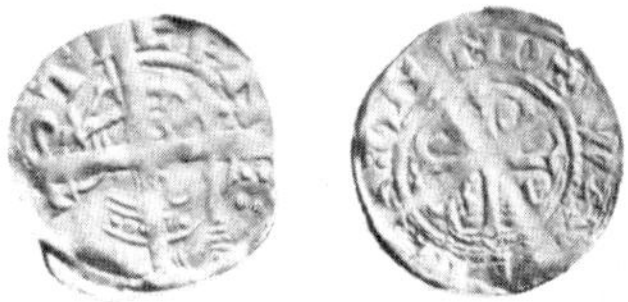

1283 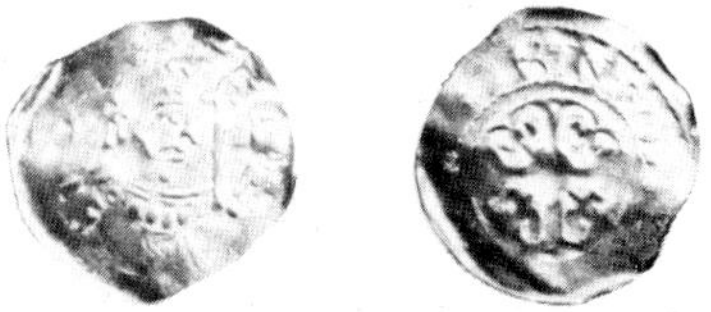   1288

1283 As 1278, with king's bust defaced with long cross. *East Anglian Mints.*
M. 137–147 . . . . 400 900
1284 — Similar, but king's bust defaced with small cross. *Nottingham. M. 149* 500 1100
1285 — Similar, but sceptre defaced with bar or cross. *Nottingham, Lincoln and*
Stamford. M. 148 and 150–154 . . . . 400 900
1286 — Similar, but king's name erased. *Nottingham. M. 157.* 500 1000
1286A — Other defacements . . . . *Extremely rare*

B. South-Eastern variant
1287 As 1278, but king holds mace instead of sceptre. *Canterbury. M. 158.* . . . *Extremely rare*

C. Eastern variants
1288 As 1278, but roundels in centre or on limbs of cross or in angles. *Suffolk*
mints. M. 159–168. . . . . 600 1200
1288A As 1278, but star before sceptre and annulets at tips of fleurs on reverse.
Suffolk mints. M. 188 . . . . 1000 2500

	F	*VF*
	£	£

1289   As 1278, but thick plain cross with pellet at end of limbs, lis in angles. *Lincoln. M. 169–173*. 600   1200

1290   — Similar, but thick plain cross superimposed on cross moline. *M. 174* .   *Extremely rare*

1290A As 1278. ℞. Quadrilateral over voided cross. *M. 176*. . . . .   *Extremely rare*

1290B As 1278. ℞. Long cross to edge of coin, fleurs outwards in angles. *Lincoln*. *M. 186–187* . . . .   *Extremely rare*

D. Southern variants

1291   As 1278, but with large rosette of pellets at end of obverse legend. *M. 184– 185* . . . .   *Extremely rare*

1292   — Similar, but star at end of obverse legend. *M. 187y*. . . . .   *Extremely rare*

1293   Crowned bust r. or l. with rosette of pellets before face in place of sceptre. ℞. As 1280, but plain instead of voided cross. *M. 181–183* . . . .   *Extremely rare*

1295

1295   As 1278, but usually collar of annulets. ℞. Voided cross moline with annulet at centre. *Southampton. M. 207–212* 600   1500

E. Midland variants

1296

1296   As 1278, but cross moline on reverse has fleured extensions into legend. *Leicester. M. 177–178*. 1000   2500

1297   As 1278 but crude work. ℞. Voided cross with lis outwards in angles. *Tutbury. M. 179*. . . . .   *Extremely rare*

1298   Somewhat similar. ℞. Voided cross with martlets in angles. *Derby. M. 175*   1200   3000

1298   1300

	F	VF
	£	£

1299 As 1278. ℞. Plain cross with T-cross in each angle. *M. 180* . . . . *Extremely rare*

1300 Facing bust with three annulets on crown. ℞. Cross pattée, fleurs inwards
in angles. *Northampton or Huntingdon (?). B.M.C. III; M.67–71* 1200 3000

1301

1302

1301 Facing bust with three fleurs on crown. ℞. Lozenge fleury, annulets in
angles. *Lincoln or Nottingham. B.M.C. IV; M. 72–75* 1250 3250

1302 Bust half-right with sceptre. ℞. Lozenge with pellet centre, fleurs inwards
in angles. *Leicester. B.M.C. V; M. 76* 1250 3250

1303 **Robert**, Earl of Leicester(?). As 1280, but reading ROBERTVS. *M. 269* . *Extremely rare*

F. North-east and Scottish border variants

1304 As 1278, but star before sceptre and annulets at tips of fleurs on reverse.
M. 188 . . . . 1000 2500

1305 As 1278, but a voided cross extending to outer circle of reverse. *M. 189–192*

Extremely rare

1306 As 1278, but crude style, with Stephen's name. *M. 276–279 and 281–282.* 700 1750

1307 — Similar. ℞. Cross crosslet with cross-pattée and crescent in angles.
M. 288 . . . . *Extremely rare*

1308 **David I** (K. of Scotland). As 1305, but with name DAVID REX. *M. 280* 1500 —

1309 **Henry** (Earl of Northumberland, son of K. David). hENRIC ERL. As
1278. *M. 283–285* 1200 3000

1310 — Similar. ℞. Cross fleury. *M. 286–287.* 1000 2500

1311 — As 1307, but with name NENCI : COM on obverse. *M. 289.* 1200 2750

G. "Ornamented" series. *So-called 'York Group' but probably minted in Northern France*

1312 As 1278, with obverse inscription NSEPEFETI, STEFINEI or RODBDS.
℞. WISÐ. GNETA, etc., with ornament(s) in legend (sometimes retro-
grade). *M. 215–216 and 227* . . . . *Extremely rare*

1313

1315

1313 Flag type. As 1278, but king holds lance with pennant, star to r. ℞. As
1278, mostly with four ornaments in legend. *M. 217.* 1250 2650

1313A — Similar, but with eight ornaments in reverse inscription. *M. 217.* 1250 2650

	F £	VF £

1314 As 1278, but STIEN and ornaments, sceptre is topped by pellet in lozenge. ℞. Cross fleury over plain cross, ornaments in place of inscription. *M. 218.* *Extremely rare*

1314A King stg. facing, holding sceptre and long standard with triple-tailed pennon. ℞. Cross pattée, crescents and quatrefoils in angles, pellets around, ornaments in legend . . . . *Unique*

1315 **Stephen and Queen Matilda.** Two standing figures holding sceptre, as illustration. ℞. Ornaments in place of inscription. *M. 220* 2500   5000

1316   1320

1316 **Eustace.** EVSTACIVS, knight stg. r. holding sword. ℞. Cross in quatrefoil, EBORACI EDTS (or EBORACI TDEFL). *M. 221–222.* . . . . *Extremely rare*

1317 — Similar, but ThOMHS FILIuS VIF. *M. 223.* . . . . *Extremely rare*

1318 — Similar, but mixed letters and ornaments in rev. legend. *M. 224* . . . . *Extremely rare*

1319 [EVSTA] CII . FII . IOANIS, lion passant r, collonnade (or key?) below. ℞. Cross moline with cross-headed sceptres in angles, mixed letters and ornaments in legend. *M. 225* . . . . *Unique*

1320 Lion rampant r., looped object below, EISTAOhIVS. ℞. Cross fleury with lis in angles, mostly, ornaments in legend. *M. 226* 1400   3250

1321 **Rodbert.** Knight on horse r., RODBERTVS IESTV (?). ℞. As 1314. *M. 228* *Extremely rare*

1321   1322

1322 **Bishop Henry.** Crowned bust r., crozier and star to r., HENRICVS EPC. ℞. Somewhat as last, STEPhANVS REX. *M. 229* . . . . *Extremely rare*

H.   Uncertain issues

1323 Crowned bust r. with sceptre, -NEPΓ:. ℞. Cross pattée with annulets in angles (as Hen. I type XIII). *M. 272.* . . . . *Extremely rare*

1324 Crowned facing bust with sceptre, star to r. (as Hen. I type XIV). ℞. As last. *M. 274* . . . . *Extremely rare*

1325 Other types. . . . . *Extremely rare*

ANGEVINS

1326   1331

1326	**Matilda**, Dowager Empress, Countess of Anjou (in England 1139–1148). As 1278, but cruder style, MATILDI IMP. etc. *M. 230–240*.	900	2000
1326A	Obv. similar. ℞. Cross pattée over cross fleury (Cardiff hoard)	900	2000
1326B	Similar, but triple pellets or plumes at end of cross (Cardiff hoard).	*Extremely rare*	
1327	**Duke Henry**, son of Matilda and Geoffrey of Anjou, Duke of Normandy from 1150 (in England 1147–1149–1150 and 1153–1154). As 1278 but hENRICVS, etc. *M. 241–245*.	2250	5000
1327A	As 1295 but hENRIC. *M. 246*	*Extremely rare*	
1327B	As 1326B, but hENNENNVS R, etc	*Extremely rare*	
1328	Obverse as 1278. ℞. Cross crosslet in quatrefoil. *M. 254*.	*Extremely rare*	
1329	Crowned bust r. with sceptre. ℞. Cross fleury over quadrilateral fleury. *M. 248–253*.	2250	4500
1330	Crowned facing bust, star each side. ℞. Cross botonnée over a quadrilateral pommée. *M. 255–258*	2250	5000
1331	Obverse as 1330. ℞. Voided cross botonnée over a quadrilateral pommée. *M. 259–261*	2250	5000
1332	**William**, Earl of Gloucester (succeeded his father, Earl Robert, in 1147). Type as Henry of Anjou, no. 1329. *M. 262*	*Unique*	
1333	Type as Henry of Anjou, no. 1330. *M. 263*	*Unique*	
1334	Type as Henry of Anjou, no. 1331. *M. 264–268*	2500	5500
1335	**Brian Fitzcount**, Lord of Wallingford (?). Type as Henry of Anjou, no. 1330. *M. 270*.	*Unique*	
1336	**Patrick**, Earl of Salisbury (?). Helmeted bust r. holding sword, star behind. ℞. As Henry of Anjou, no. 1329. *M. 271*	*Extremely rare*	

84

HENRY II, 1154–1189

Cross-and-crosslets ("Tealby") Coinage, 1158–1180

Coins of Stephen's last type continued to be minted until 1158. Then a new coinage bearing Henry's name replaced the currency of the previous reign which contained a high proportion of irregular and sub-standard pennies. The new Cross and Crosslets issue is more commonly referred to as the "Tealby" coinage, as over 5000 of these pennies were discovered at Tealby, Lincolnshire, in 1807. Thirty mints were employed in this re-coinage, but once the re-minting had been completed not more than a dozen mints were kept open. The issue remained virtually unchanged for twenty-two years apart from minor variations in the king's portrait. The coins tend to be poorly struck.

A   B   C

Penny

		Fair £	F £
1337	Class A. No hair.	12	30
1338	— B. Similar but mantle varies.	15	35
1339	— C. Decorated collar, curl of hair	12	30

D   E   F

1340	— D. Decoration continues along shoulder	15	35
1341	— E. Similar bust, but shoulder not decorated	18	40
1342	— F. Hair in long ringlet to r. of bust.	18	40

Mints and classes of the Cross-and-Crosslets coinage

Approximate dates for the various classes are as follows:

A 1158–1161, B and C 1161–1165, D 1165–1168, E 1168–1170 and F 1170–1180.

Bedford . . . . .A – – – – –	Ilchester. . . . . A B C D – F	Pembroke. . . . .A – – – – –
Bristol. . . . . .A B C D E F	Ipswich . . . .– B C D E F	Salisbury . . . . .A – – – – –
Bury St. Edmunds . .A B C D E F	Launceston . . . .A – – – – –	Shrewsbury. . . .A – – – – –
Canterbury . . . . . .A B C D E F	Leichester. . . . .A – – – – –	Stafford. . . . . .A – C – – –
Carlisle . . . . .A – C D E F	Lewes. . . . .– – – – ? F	Thetford . . . . .A – C D – F
Chester . . . . .A – – D – –	Lincoln . . . . . .A B C D E F	Wallingford . . .A – – – – –
Colchester. . . . . .A – C – E –	London. . . . . .A B C D E F	Wilton . . . . . .A – – – – –
Durham. . . . . . . .A B C – – –	Newcastle. . . . .A – C D E F	Winchester . . . .A – C D ? –
Exeter. . . . . .A B C D – –	Northampton . .A – C ? – –	York . . . . .A – C D – –
Gloucester . . . . . .A – – – – –	Norwich . . . . .A B C D – F	
Hereford . . . . . . .A – C – – –	Oxford . . . . . .A – – D E –	

"Short Cross" coinage of Henry II (1180–1189)

In 1180 a coinage of new type, known as the Short Cross coinage, replaced the Tealby issue. The new coinage is remarkable in that it covers not only the latter part of the reign of Henry II, but also the reigns of his sons Richard and John and his grandson Henry III, and the entire issue bears the name "hENRICVS". There are no English coins with names of Richard or John. The Short Cross coins can be divided chronologically into various classes: eleven mints were operating under Henry II and tables of mints, moneyers and classes are given for each reign.

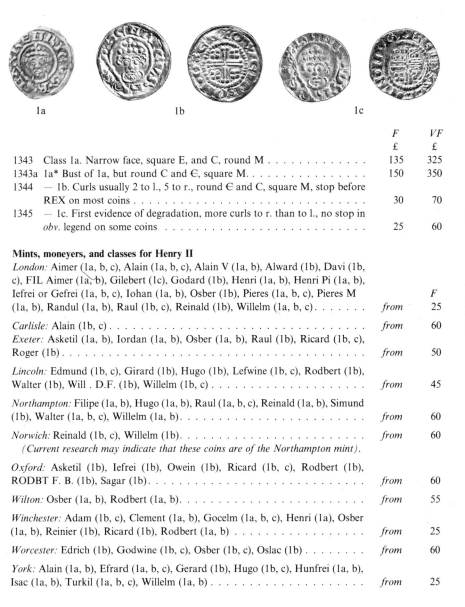

1a   1b   1c

		F	VF
		£	£
1343	Class 1a. Narrow face, square E, and C, round M	135	325
1343a	1a* Bust of 1a, but round C and E, square M.	150	350
1344	— 1b. Curls usually 2 to l., 5 to r., round E and C, square M, stop before REX on most coins	30	70
1345	— 1c. First evidence of degradation, more curls to r. than to l., no stop in *obv.* legend on some coins	25	60

Mints, moneyers, and classes for Henry II

	F
London: Aimer (1a, b, c), Alain (1a, b, c), Alain V (1a, b), Alward (1b), Davi (1b, c), FIL Aimer (1a, b), Gilebert (1c), Godard (1b), Henri (1a, b), Henri Pi (1a, b), Iefrei or Gefrei (1a, b, c), Iohan (1a, b), Osber (1b), Pieres (1a, b, c), Pieres M (1a, b), Randul (1a, b), Raul (1b, c), Reinald (1b), Willelm (1a, b, c). . . . . . . *from*	25
Carlisle: Alain (1b, c). . . . . *from*	60
Exeter: Asketil (1a, b), Iordan (1a, b), Osber (1a, b), Raul (1b), Ricard (1b, c), Roger (1b). . . . . *from*	50
Lincoln: Edmund (1b, c), Girard (1b), Hugo (1b), Lefwine (1b, c), Rodbert (1b), Walter (1b), Will . D.F. (1b), Willelm (1b, c) . . . . *from*	45
Northampton: Filipe (1a, b), Hugo (1a, b), Raul (1a, b, c), Reinald (1a, b), Simund (1b), Walter (1a, b, c), Willelm (1a, b). . . . . *from*	60
Norwich: Reinald (1b, c), Willelm (1b). . . . . *from*	60
(Current research may indicate that these coins are of the Northampton mint).	
Oxford: Asketil (1b), Iefrei (1b), Owein (1b), Ricard (1b, c), Rodbert (1b), RODBT F. B. (1b), Sagar (1b). . . . . *from*	60
Wilton: Osber (1a, b), Rodbert (1a, b). . . . . *from*	55
Winchester: Adam (1b, c), Clement (1a, b), Gocelm (1a, b, c), Henri (1a), Osber (1a, b), Reinier (1b), Ricard (1b), Rodbert (1a, b) . . . . *from*	25
Worcester: Edrich (1b), Godwine (1b, c), Osber (1b, c), Oslac (1b) . . . . *from*	60
York: Alain (1a, b), Efrard (1a, b, c), Gerard (1b), Hugo (1b, c), Hunfrei (1a, b), Isac (1a, b), Turkil (1a, b, c), Willelm (1a, b) . . . . *from*	25

RICHARD I, 1189–1199

Pennies of Short Cross type continued to be issued throughout the reign, all bearing the name hЄNRICVS. The coins of class 4, which have very crude portraits, continued to be issued in the early years of the next reign. The only coins bearing Richard's name are from his territories of Aquitaine and Poitou in western France.

2	3a	3b	4a	4b

	F	VF
	£	£

"Short Cross" coinage (reading HЄNRICVS)

		F	VF
1346	Class 2. Round face; 5 or more pearls in crown; mass of small curls at both sides of head	60	150
1347	— 3a. Large face; 7 or more pearls in crown; 3 or 4 curls at either side of head; beard of small curls, large pellet eyes	55	120
1347A	— 3b. Similar, but smaller face.	40	100
1348	— 4a. Similar, but beard of pellets.	30	70
1348A	— 4b. Very crude bust, hair represented by only one or two crescents each side	30	65
1348B	— 4a*. As 4a, but colon stops on reverse	35	80

Mints, moneyers, and classes for Richard I

		F
London: Aimer (2–4b), Fulke (4a, b), Goldwine (4a), Henri (4a–4b), Raul (2), Ricard (2–4b), Stivene (2–4b), Willelm (2–4b)	*from*	30
Canterbury: Goldwine (2–4b), Hernaud (4b), Io(h)an (4b), Meinir (2–4b), Reinald (2–4a), Reinaud (4b), Roberd (2–4b), Samuel (4b), Ulard (2–4b)	*from*	30
Carlisle: Alein (3–4b)	*from*	110
Durham: Adam (4a), Alein (4a–b)	*from*	125
Exeter: Ricard (3b)	*from*	90
Lichfield: Ioan (2)	*Extremely rare*	
Lincoln: Edmund (2), Lefwine (2), Willelm (2)	*from*	45
Northampton: Geferi (4a), Roberd (3), Waltir (3).	*from*	90
Norwich: Randul (4a–b), Willelm (4a–b)	*from*	90
Shrewsbury: Ive (4b), Reinald (4a, 4b), Willelm (4a)	*from*	150
Winchester: Adam (3a), Gocelm (2–3), Osbern (3–4a), Pires (4a), Willelm (2–4).	*from*	50
Worcester: Osbern (2).	*Extremely rare*	
York: Davi (4b?), Everard (2–4b), Hue (2–4a), Nicole (4b), Turkil (2–4b)	*from*	35

JOHN, 1199–1216

"Short Cross" coinage *continued.* All with name hЄNRICVS

The Short Cross coins of class 4 will have continued during the early years of John's reign, but in 1205 a re-coinage was initiated and new Short Cross coins of better style replaced the older issues. Coins of classes 5a and 5b were issued in the re-coinage in which sixteen mints were employed. Only ten of these mints were still working by the end of class 5. The only coins to bear John's name are the pennies, halfpence and farthings issues for Ireland.

| 4c | 5a | 5b | 5c | 6a1 | 6a2 |

	F	VF
	£	£
1349 Class 4c. Somewhat as 4b, but letter S is reversed	30	70
1350 — 5a. New coinage of neat style and execution; realistic face; 5 or more pearls to crown; letter S is reversed; *mm* cross pommée	30	65
1350A — — with ornamented letters	35	110
1350B — 5a/5b or 5b/5a mules	35	80
1351 — 5b. Similar, but S normal and *mm* reverts to cross pattée.	20	45
1352 — 5c. Similar, but letter X composed of 4 strokes in the form of a St. Andrew's cross.	20	45
1353 — 6a1. Coarser style; letter X composed of 2 wedges in the form of a St. Andrew's cross.	15	40
1353A — 6a2. Similar, but letter X has arms at right angles and with rounded ends	15	40

Mints, moneyers and classes for John   *F*

London: Abel (5c–6a), Adam (5b–c), Arnaud (5b), Beneit (5b–c), Fulke (4c–5a), Henri (4c–5b), Ilger (5b–6a), Iohan (5b), Rauf (5c–6a), Rener (5b–c), Ricard (4c–5b), Ricard B (5b–c), Ricard T (5b), Walter (5c–6a), Willelm (4c–5c), Willelm B (5b–c), Willelm L (5b–c), Willelm T (5b–c) . . . .   *from*   15

Bury St. Edmunds: Fulke (5b–c) . . . .   *from*   50

Canterbury: Arnaud (5a–c), Coldwine (4c–5c), (H)ernaud (5a), Hue (4c–5c), Io(h)an (4c–5c), Iohan B (5b–c), Iohan M (5b–c), Rauf (Vc?), Roberd (4c–5c), Samuel (4c–5c), Simon (5a or c), Simun (4c–5b) . . . .   *from*   15

Carlisle: Tomas (5b) . . . .   *from*   90

Chichester: Pieres (5b), Rauf (5a–b), Simon (5a–b), Willelm (5b) . . . .   *from*   50

Durham: Pieres (4c–6a) . . . .   *from*   70

Exeter: Gilebert (5a–b), Iohan (5a–b), Ricard (5a–b) . . . .   *from*   45

Ipswich: Alisandre (5b, c), Iohan (5b–c) . . . .   *from*   50

Kings Lynn: Iohan (5b), Nicole (5b), Willelm (5b) . . . .   *from*   135

Lincoln: Alain (5a), Andreu (5a–c), Hue (5b–c), Iohan (5a), Rauf (5a–b), Ricard (5a), Tomas (5a, b) . . . .   *from*   40

Northampton: Adam (5b–c), Randul (4c), Roberd (5b), Roberd T (5b). . . . . .   *from*   45

		F
		£

Norwich: Gifrei (5a–c), Iohan (5a–c), Renald (5a), Renaud (5a–c) . . . . *from* 45

Oxford: Ailwine (5b), Henri (5b), Miles (5b) . . . . *from* 50

Rhuddlan: An irregular issue probably struck during this reign. Halli, Henricus, Tomas, Simond . . . . *from* 80

Rochester: Alisandre (5b), Hunfrei (5b) . . . . *from* 120

Winchester: Adam (5a–c), Andreu (5b–c), Bartelme (5b–c), Henri (5a), Iohan (5a–c), Lukas (5b, c), Miles (5a–c), Rauf (5b–c), Ricard (5a, b) . . . . *from* 25

York: Davi (4c–5b), Nicole (4c–5c), Renaud (5b), Tomas (5b) . . . . *from* 30

HENRY III, 1216–72

"Short Cross" coinage *continued* (1216–47)

The Short Cross coinage continued for a further thirty years during which time the style of portraiture and workmanship deteriorated. By the 1220s minting had been concentrated at London and Canterbury, one exception being the mint of the Abbot of Bury St. Edmunds.

| 6b | 6c | 7 early | 7 middle | 7 late |

	F	VF
	£	£

"Short Cross" coinage, 1216–47

1354	Class 6b. Very tall lettering; early coins have a head similar to 6a, but later issues have a long thin face.	15	35
1355	— 6c. Pointed face	15	35
1355A	— — Ornamental lettering	50	135
1355B	— 6x. Large face, two curls each side of hd., pellet on chin, letter X only by sceptre	—	—
1355C	— Tall, straight-sided letter, pellet on crossbar of N on most coins. . . .	—	—
1356	— 7. No stops between words in rev. legend; no neck	12	30

| 8a | 8b1 | 8b2 | 8b3 |

1357	— 8a. New style; *mm* cross pattée; letter X curule shaped	*Extremely rare*	
1357A	— 8b1. Similar; *mm* cross pommée.	20	100
1357B	— 8b2. Cruder version; wedge-shaped letter X	20	100
1357C	— 8b3. Very crude version; letter X is cross pommée	20	100
1357D	**Halfpenny**. (**See end of* Henry III)		

Mints, moneyers, and classes for Henry III "Short Cross" coinage F

London: Abel (6b–7), Adam (7), (H)elis (7), Giffrei (7), Ilger (6b–7), Ledulf (7), Nichole (7–8), Rau(l)f (6b–7), Ricard (7), Terri (7), Walter (6b–6c). . . . . *from* 12

	F
	£

Bury St. Edmunds: Io(h)an (7–8), Norman (7), Rauf (6b–7), Simund (7), Willelm (7). . . . . *from* 30

Canterbury: Arnold (6x), Henri (6b–7), Hiun (6b–7), Iun (7), Io(h)an (6b–8), Ioan Chic (7), Ioan F. R. (7), Nicole (7–8), Norman (7), Osmund (7), Roberd (6b), Robert (7), Robert Vi (7), Roger (6b–7), Roger of R (7), Salemun (6x, 7), Samuel (6b–7), Simon (7), Simun (6b–7), Tomas' (6d, 7), Walter (6b–7), Willem (7–8), Willem Ta (7) . . . . *from* 12

Durham: Pieres (7) . . . . *from* 75

Winchester: Henri (6c) . . . . *from* 20

York: Iohan (6c), Peres (6c), Tomas (6c), Wilam (6c) . . . . *from* 120

"Long Cross" coinage (1247–72)

By the middle of Henry's reign the coinage in circulation was in a poor state, being worn and clipped. In 1247 a fresh coinage was ordered, the new pennies having the reverse cross extended to the edge of the coin to help safeguard the coins against clipping. The earliest of these coins have no mint or moneyers' names. A number of provincial mints were opened for producing sufficient of the Long Cross coins, but these were closed again in 1250, only the royal mints of London and Canterbury and the ecclesiastical mints of Durham and Bury St. Edmunds remaining open.

In 1257, following the introduction of new gold coinages by the Italian cities of Brindisi (1232), Florence (1252) and Genoa (1253), Henry III issued a gold coinage in England. This was a gold "Penny" valued at 20 silver pence and twice the weight of the silver penny. The coinage was not a success, being undervalued, and coinage ceased after a few years—few have survived.

Without sceptre

Ia   Ib

		F	VF
		£	£
1358	Class Ia. hENRICVS: REX. ℞. ANGLIE TERCI.	75	150
1359	Ib. hENRICVS REX. ANG. ℞. LIE TERCI LON *(London)*, CAN *(Canterbury)* or AED *(Bury St. Edmunds)* . . . . *from*	40	65
1360	— — I/II mule	45	75
1361	— II. hENRICVS REX TERCI. ℞. Moneyer and mint.	25	50

II   IIIa   IIIb   IIIc

1362	— IIIa. hENRICVS REX · III, thin face as class II	10	25
1363	— IIIb. Smaller, rounder face	10	25
1364	— IIIc. Face with pointed chin, neck indicated by two lines, usually REX : III.	10	25

With sceptre

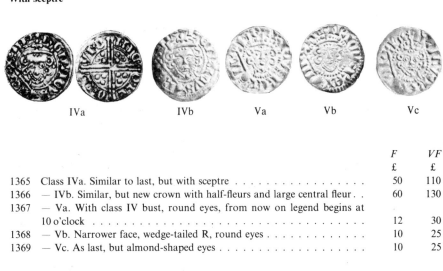

IVa   IVb   Va   Vb   Vc

		F	VF
		£	£
1365	Class IVa. Similar to last, but with sceptre	50	110
1366	— IVb. Similar, but new crown with half-fleurs and large central fleur ..	60	130
1367	— Va. With class IV bust, round eyes, from now on legend begins at 10 o'clock	12	30
1368	— Vb. Narrower face, wedge-tailed R, round eyes	10	25
1369	— Vc. As last, but almond-shaped eyes	10	25

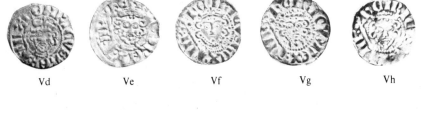

Vd   Ve   Vf   Vg   Vh

1370	— Vd. Portrait of quite different style; new crown with true-shaped fleur	35	85
1371	— Ve. Similar, with jewelled or beaded crown	90	225
1372	— Vf. New style larger face, double-banded crown.	15	40
1373	— Vg. Single band to crown, low central fleur, curule chair shaped X ..	13	35
1374	— Vh. Crude copy of Vg, with pellets in lieu of fleur	20	50
1375	— Vi. Similar to last, but triple line of pellets for beard	*Extremely rare*	

Vi   1376

1376	**Gold penny** of 20d. As illustration	*Extremely rare*

A very fine specimen sold at auction in June 1985 for £65,000.

F
£

Mints, Moneyers, and classes for Henry III "Long Cross" coinage

London: Davi or David (IIIc–Vf), Henri (IIIa–Vd, f, g), Ion, Ioh, Iohs or Iohan (Vc–g), Nicole (Ib/II mule, II–Vc), Renaud (Vg–i), Ricard (IIIc–Vg), Robert (Vg), Thomas (Vg), Walter (Vc–g), Willem (Vc–g and gold penny) . . . . *from* 10

Bristol: Elis (IIIa, b, c), Henri (IIIb), Iacob (IIIa, b, c), Roger (IIIa, b, c), Walter (IIIb, c). . . . . *from* 22

Bury St. Edmunds: Ion or Iohs (II–Va, Vg, h, i), Randulf (Va–f), Renaud (Vg), Stephane (Vg) . . . . *from* 17

Canterbury: Alein (Vg, h), Ambroci (Vg), Gilbert (II–Vd/c mule, Vf, g), Ion, Ioh, Iohs, or Iohanes (IIIe–Vd, f, g), Nicole or Nichole (Ib/II mule, II–Vh), Ricard (Vg, h), Robert (Vc–h), Walter (Vc–h), Willem or Willeme (Ib/II mule, II–Vd, f, g) *from* 10

Carlisle: Adam (IIIa, b), Ion (IIIa, b), Robert (IIIa, b), Willem (IIIa, b) . . . . . *from* 50

Durham: Philip (IIIb), Ricard (V, b, c), Roger (Vg), Willem (Vg). . . . . *from* 60

Exeter: Ion (II–IIIc), Philip (II–IIIc), Robert (II–IIIc), Walter (II–IIIb) . . . . . *from* 35

F

Gloucester: Ion (II–IIIc), Lucas (II–IIIc), Ricard (II–IIIc), Roger (II–IIIc). . . . *from* 25

Hereford: Henri (IIIa, b), Ricard (IIIa, b, c), Roger (IIIa, b, c), Walter (IIIa, b, c). *from* 40

Ilchester: Huge (IIIa, b, c), Ierveis (IIIa, b, c), Randulf (IIIa, b, c), Stephe (IIIa, b, c) . . . . *from* 60

Lincoln: Ion (II–IIIc), Ricard (II–IIIc), Walter (II–IIIc), Willem (II–IIIc) . . . . *from* 25

Newcastle: Adam (IIIa, b), Henri (IIIa, b, c), Ion (IIIa, b, c), Roger (IIIa, b, c) . *from* 22

Northampton: Lucas (II–IIIb), Philip (II–IIIc), Tomas (II–IIIc), Willem (II–IIIc) *from* 25

Norwich: Huge (II–IIIc), Iacob (II–IIIc), Ion (II–IIIc), Willem (II–IIIc) . . . . . *from* 35

Oxford: Adam (II–IIIc), Gefrei (II–IIIc), Henri (II–IIIc), Willem (II–IIIc) . . . . *from* 35

Shrewsbury: Lorens (IIIa, b, c), Nicole (IIIa, b, c), Peris (IIIa, b, c), Ricard (IIIa, b, c) . . . . *from* 45

Wallingford: Alisandre (IIIa, b), Clement (IIIa, b), Ricard (IIIa, b), Robert (IIIa, b). . . . . *from* 35

Wilton: Huge (IIIb, c), Ion (IIIa, b, c), Willem (IIIa, b, c). . . . . *from* 40

Winchester: Huge (II–IIIc), Iordan (II–IIIc), Nicole (II–IIIc), Willem (II–IIIc) . *from* 22

York: Alain (II–IIIb), Ieremie (II–IIIb), Ion (II–IIIc), Rener (II–IIIc), Tomas (IIIb, c). . . . . *from* 25

1357D

1357D **"Short Cross" coinage.** (*c.* 1122–40). Ch. VII. Halfpenny. hЄNRICVS REX. Ŗ. TER.RI ON LUND (London) . . . . *Unique*

EDWARD I, 1272–1307

"Long Cross" coinage *continued* (1272–79). With name hЄNRICVS

The earliest group of Edward's Long Cross coins are of very crude style and known only of Durham and Bury St. Edmunds. Then, for the last class of the type, pennies of much improved style were issued at London, Durham and Bury, but in 1279 the Long Cross coinage was abandoned and a completely new coinage substituted.

VI   VII

		F	VF
		£	£
1377	Class VI. Crude face with new realistic curls, Є and N ligate	15	45
1378	— VII. Similar, but of improved style, usually with Lombardic U	70	125

Mints, moneyers, and classes for Edward I "Long Cross" coinage		F
London: Phelip, Renaud (VII)	*from*	85
Bury St. Edmunds: Ioce (VII), Ion or Ioh (VI, VII)	*from*	15
Durham: Roberd (VI), Robert (VII)	*from*	100

New Coinage (from 1279).

A major re-coinage was embarked upon in 1279 which introduced new denominations. In addition to the penny, halfpence and farthings were also minted and, for the first time, a fourpenny piece called a "Groat" (from the French *Gros*).

As mint administration was now very much centralized, the practice of including the moneyer's name in the coinage was abandoned (except for a few years at Bury St. Edmunds). Several provincial mints assisted with the re-coinage during 1279–81, then minting was again restricted to London, Canterbury, Durham and Bury.

The provincial mints were again employed for a subsidiary re-coinage in 1299–1302 in order to re-mint lightweight coins and the many illegal *esterlings* (foreign copies of the English pennies or *Sterlings*, mainly from the Low Countries, are usually poorer quality than the English coins).

1379

		F	VF
		£	£
1379	**Groat**. (= 4d.; wt. 89 grs.). Type as illustration but several minor varieties.	1000	2350
	Most extant specimens show traces of having been mounted on the obverse and gilded on the reverse; unmounted coins are worth more.		

la   lb   lc

		F	VF
		£	£
1380	**Penny**. *London*. Class 1a. Crown with plain band, ЄDW RЄX; Lombardic N on obv.	300	650
1381	— 1b. — ЄD RЄX; no drapery on bust, Roman N	350	750
1382	— Ic. — ЄDW RЄX; Roman N, normal or reversed; small lettering . . .	14	35
1383	— Id. — ЄDW R;—; large lettering and face	12	30
1384	— — — Annulet below bust (for the Abbot of Reading)	135	325

1d (1384)   2a   2b

1385	— 2a. Crown with band shaped to ornaments; large face and short neck similar to 1d; usually broken left petal to central fleur of crown.	16	40
1386	— 2b. — tall bust; long neck; N reversed	12	33

3a   3b   3c

1387	— 3a. Crescent-shaped contraction marks; pearls in crown, drapery is foreshortened circle	40	80
1388	— 3b. — — drapery is segment of a circle	25	45
1389	— 3c. — normal crown; drapery in one piece, hollowed in centre.	8	25

3e   3f   3g

		F	VF
		£	£
1390	— 3d. — — drapery in two pieces, broad face	10	30
1391	— 3e. — long narrow face (mostly Northern mints)	12	32
1392	— 3f. — broad face, large nose, rougher work, late S first used	25	60
1393	— 3g. — small neat bust, narrow face	7	25

4a   4b   4c   4d   4e

		F	VF
		£	£
1394	— 4a. Comma-shaped contraction mark, late S always used, C and Є open	10	30
1395	— 4b. Similar, but face and hair shorter.	7	25
1396	— 4c. Larger face with more copious hair; unbarred A first used	7	25
1397	— 4d. Pellet at beginning of *obv.* and/or *rev.* inscription	10	30
1398	— 4e. Three pellets on breast; pellet in *rev.* legend	12	32

5a   5b

		F	VF
1399	— 5a. Well spread coins, pellet on breast, A normally unbarred	35	85
1400	— 5b. Coins more spread, tall lettering, long narrow face, pellet on breast.	35	95

6a   6b   7a

	F	VF
	£	£

1401 — 6a. Smaller coins, initial cross almost plain, crown with wide fleurs . . | 90 | 200

1402 — 6b. Initial cross well pattée; lettering of good style; closed Є (from now on) . . . . | 35 | 85

1403 — 7a. Rose on breast; almond-shaped eyes, double barred N . . . . | 40 | 100

| 7b | 8a | 8b | 9a | 9b |

1404 — 7b. — — longer hair, new crown . . . . | 40 | 100

1404A Type as 7, but no rose | *Extremely rare* |

1405 — 8a. Smaller crown; top-tilted S; longer neck . . . . | 25 | 60

1406 — 8b. Not unlike 9a, but top-tilted S . . . . | 25 | 60

1407 — 9a. Narrow face, flatter crown, star on breast . . . . | 14 | 35

1408 — 9b. Small coins; Roman N, normal, un-barred, or usually of pot-hook form; often star or pellet on breast. . . . . | 8 | 23

| 10ab | 11a | 10cf | 10cf |
| | (see p. 98) | | |

1409⎤
1410⎦ 10ab. Read ЄDWARR, ЄDWARD, ЄDWR'R'. Ornate Rs. Usually bi-foliate crown from now on . . . . | 15 | 35

1411⎤
1412⎥ 10cf. Read ЄDWA. Plain Rs . . . . | 7 | 15
1413⎥
1414⎦

For further classification of Class 10, see "Sylloge of British Coins, 39, The J. J. North Collection, Edwardian English Silver Coins 1279–1351", Chapter 10, Class 10, c. 1301–10, by C. Wood.

Prices are for full flan, well struck coins.

The prices for the above types are for London. For coins of the following mints (see over page); types struck in brackets. Prices are for the commonest type of each mint.

Berwick type I	Type II	Type III	Type IV

		F	*	VF
		£		£
1415	*Berwick-on-Tweed.* (Blunt types I–IV) . . . . *from*	20		55
1416	*Bristol.* (2; 3b; c, d; 3f, g; 9b) . . . . *from*	18		40
1417	*Bury St. Edmunds.* Robert de Hadelie (3c, d, g; 4a, b, c) . . . . . . *from*	50		120
1418	— Villa Sci Edmundi (4e; 5b; 6b; 7a; 8a–10f) . . . . *from*	20		50
1419	*Canterbury.* (2; 3b–g; 4; 5; 7a; 9;10) . . . . *from*	8		25
1420	*Chester.* (3g; 9b) . . . . *from*	35		70
1421	*Durham.* King's Receiver (9b; 10a, b, e, f) . . . . *from*	16		35
1422	— Bishop de Insula (2; 3b, c, e, g; 4a) . . . . *from*	18		40
1423	— Bishop Bec (4b, c, d; 5b; 6b; 7a; 8b; 9; 10b–f) mostly with *mm.* cross moline . . . . *from*	18		40
1424	— — (4b) cross moline in one angle of *rev.* . . . . *from*	120		250
1425	*Exeter.* (9b)	40		110
1426	*Kingston-upon-Hull.* (9b)	40		110
1427	*Lincoln.* (3c, d, f, g) . . . . *from*	16		34
1428	*Newcastle-upon-Tyne.* (3e; 9b; 10) . . . . *from*	25		50
1429	*York.* Royal mint (2; 3b, c, d, f; 9b) . . . . *from*	15		40
1430	— Archbishop's mint (3e, f; 9b). ℞. Quatrefoil in centre . . . . . . *from*	25		70

1431　　　　　　　　　　1436

1431	**Halfpenny**, *London.* Class IIIb. Drapery as segment of circle	30	75
1432	—IIIc. Normal drapery as two wedges	30	75
1433	— IIIg. Similar, larger letters, wider crown	25	65
1433A	— — IV c. Comma abbreviation mark, thick waisted s.	30	75
1433B	— — Pellet before LON	35	85
1434	IVe. Usually three pellets on breast, one on *rev.*	30	75
1434A	— VI. Double barred N, small lettering	35	85
1435	— VII. Double barred N, large lettering.	32	80
1436	IX. Pot-hook N, usually no star on breast, crown band curved at fleurs .	20	55
1437	— X.ЄDWAR R ANGL DNS hYB, thick waisted letters	20	55

The above prices are for London; halfpence of the mints given below were also struck.

1438	*Berwick-on-Tweed.* (Blunt types II and III) . . . . *from*	80	250
1439	*Bristol.* (IIIc; IIIg)	50	175

		F £	VF £
1440	*Lincoln.* (IIIc)	70	175
1441	*Newcastle.* (IIIe). With single pellet in each angle of *rev.*	135	360
1442	*York.* (IIIb)	75	200

1443    1445    1446

		F £	VF £
1443	**Farthing**, *London.* Class I. Heavy weight (6.85 grains), ЄDWARDVS REX. R. LONDONIЄNSIS, bifoliate crown	25	100
1443A	— — — trifoliate crown	30	100
1444	— II. Similar, but reversed N's	20	80
1445	— IIIc. As class I, but different bust	—	70
1446	— IIIg. Lighter weight (5.5 grs.) Є R ANGLIЄ, no inner circle on *obv.*	ˇ20	80
1446A	— — Reads CIVITAS LONDON, narrow crown	45	120
1446B	— — — Wider crown	45	120
1447	— VII. Similar, double barred N, pellet eyes	70	160
1448	VIII. Є R ANGL DN, closed Є	50	120
1449	— IX. Pot-hook N	45	110
1450	— X or XI. (Edward II) ЄDWARDVS REX A or AN inner circle both sides	25	70

The above prices are for London; farthings of the mints given below were also struck.

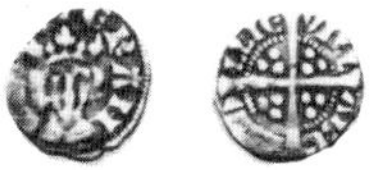

1452

			F £	VF £
1451	*Berwick-on-Tweed.* (Blunt type III)		150	350
1452	*Bristol.* (II; III as illustration)	*from*	85	225
1453	*Lincoln.* (III)	*from*	120	300
1453A	*Newcastle* (IIIe), triple pellet in *rev.* quarters		Extremely rare	
1454	*York.* (II; III)	*from*	125	300

For further information on the pennies of Edward I and II see the articles by K. A. Jacob in "Notes on English Silver Coins, 1066–1648", and for the mint of Berwick-on-Tweed, see the article by C. E. Blunt, in the Num. Chron., 1931.

EDWARD II, 1307–27

The coinage of this reign differs only in minor details from that of Edward I. No groats were issued in the years *c.* 1282–1351.

11a 12 13 14

15a 15b 15c

		F	VF
		£	£
1455	**Penny,** *London.* Class 11a. Broken spear-head or pearl on l. side of crown; long narrow face, straight-sided N	10	30
1456	— 11b. — Є with angular back (till 15b), N with well-marked serifs . . .	10	30
1457	— 11c. — — A of special form.	30	65
1458	— 12. Central fleur of crown formed of three wedges	20	45
1459	— 13. Central fleur of crown as Greek double axe	16	40
1460	— 14. Crown with tall central fleur; large smiling face with leering eyes .	12	35
1461	— 15a. Small flat crown with both spear-heads usually bent to l.; face of 14.	16	40
1462	— 15b. — very similar, but smaller face.	16	40
1463	— 15c. — large face, large Є	18	45

The prices of the above types are for London. We can sometimes supply coins of the following mints; types struck in brackets.

Type V Type VI Type VII

1464	*Berwick-on-Tweed.* (Blunt types V, VI and VII). . . . . *from*	50	95
1465	*Bury St. Edmunds.* (11; 12; 13; 14; 15) . . . . *from*	16	40
1466	*Canterbury.* (11; 12; 13; 14; 15). . . . . *from*	16	40
1467	*Durham.* King's Receiver (11a), *mm.* plain cross . . . . *from*	25	55
1468	— Bishop Bec. (11a), *mm.* cross moline	25	60
1469	— Bishop Kellawe (11; 12; 13), crozier on *rev.* . . . . *from*	25	55
1470	— Bishop Beaumont (13; 14; 15), *mm.* lion with lis. . . . . *from*	30	70
1471	Sede Vacante (15c); *mm.* plain cross	55	135

*Prices are for full flan, well struck coins.

			F	VF
			£	£
1472	**Halfpenny** of *London*. ЄDWARDVS REX A(NG)		55	135
1473	— — *Berwick-on-Tweed*. (Blunt type V)		80	200
1474	**Farthing** of *London*. ЄDWARDVS REX (AN)G		65	160
1475	—*Berwick-on-Tweed*. (Blunt type V)		*Extremely rare*	

EDWARD III, 1327-77

During Edward's early years small quantities of silver coin were minted following the standard of the previous two reigns, but in 1335 halfpence and farthings were produced which were well below the .925 Sterling silver standard. In 1344 an impressive gold coinage was introduced comprising the Florin or Double Leopard valued at six shillings, and its half and quarter, the Leopard and the Helm. The design of the Florin was based on the contemporary gold of Philip de Valois of France. The first gold coinage was not successful and it was replaced later the same year by a heavier coinage, the Noble, valued at 6s. 8d, i.e., 80 pence, half a mark or one third of a pound, together with its fractions. The Noble was lowered in weight in two stages over the next few years, being stabilized at 120 grains in 1351. With the signing of the Treaty of Bretigni in 1360 Edward's title to the Kingdom of France was omitted from the coinage, but it was resumed again in 1369.

In 1344 the silver coinage had been re-established at the old sterling standard, but the penny was reduced in weight to just over 20 grains and in 1351 to 18 grains. Groats were minted again in 1351 and were issued regularly henceforth until the reign of Elizabeth.

Subsequent to the treaty with France which gave England a cross-channel trading base at Calais, a mint was opened there in 1363 for minting gold and silver coins of English type. In addition to coins of the regular English mints, the Abbot of Reading also minted silver pence and a halfpence with a scallop shell badge while coins from Berwick display one or two boars' heads.

Mintmarks

| 6 | 1 | 2 | 3 | 74 | 4 | 5 | 7a |

1334–51	Cross pattée (6)	1356	Crown (74)
1351–2	Cross 1 (1)	1356–61	Cross 3 (4)
1351–7	Crozier on cross end (76a, *Durham*)	1361–9	Cross potent (5)
1352–3	Cross 1 broken (2)	1369–77	Cross pattée (6)
1354–5	Cross 2 (3)		Plain cross (7a)
			Cross potent and four pellets

The figures in brackets refer to the plate of mintmarks on page 350.

GOLD

Third coinage, 1344–51
First period, 1344

| 1476 | 1477 | 1478 |

	F	VF
	£	£

1476 **Florin** or **Double Leopard**. (= 6s.; wt. 108 grs.). King enthroned beneath canopy; crowned leopard's head each side. ℞. Cross in quatrefoil. . . . . *Extremely rare*

1477 **Half-florin** or **Leopard**. Leopard sejant with banner l. ℞. Somewhat as last. *Extremely rare*

1478 **Quarter-florin** or **Helm**. Helmet on fleured field. ℞. Floriate cross. . . . . *Extremely rare*

Second period, 1344–46

1479 **Noble** (= 6s. 8d., wt. $138\frac{6}{13}$ grs.). King stg. facing in ship with sword and shield. ℞. L in centre of royal cross in tressure . . . . *Extremely rare*

1480 **Quarter-noble**. Shield in tressure. ℞. As last.   600   1350

Third period, 1346–51

1481 **Noble** (wt. $128\frac{4}{7}$ grs.). As 1479, but Є in centre; large letters   500   1200

1482 **Half-noble**. Similar 6000

1483 **Quarter-noble**. As 1480, but Є in centre   200   400

Fourth coinage, 1351–77
   Reference: L. A. Lawrence, The Coinage of Edward III from 1351.
Pre-treaty period, 1351–61. With French title.

| 1488 | 1498 |

1484 **Noble** (wt. 120 grs.), series B (1351). Open Є and C, Roman M; *mm.* cross 1 (1).   325   600

1485 — — *rev.* of series A (1351). Round lettering, Lombardic M and N; closed inverted Є in centre   350   675

		F	VF
		£	£
1486	C (1351–1352). Closed Є and C, Lombardic M; *mm*. cross 1 (1)	275	500
1487	D (1352–1353). *O*. of series C. Ꝗ. *Mm*. cross 1 broken (2)	400	700
1488	E (1354–1355). Broken letters, V often has a nick in r. limb; *mm*. cross 2 (3).	250	475
1489	F (1356). *Mm*. crown (74)	325	600
1490	G (1356–1361). *Mm*. cross 3 (4). Many varieties	250	450
1491	**Half-noble**, B. As noble with *rev*. of series A, but closed Є in centre not		
	inverted.	175	425
1492	C. *O*. as noble. *Rev*. as last	200	450
1493	E. As noble	450	800
1494	G. As noble. Many varieties	175	375
1495	**Quarter-noble**, B. Pellet below shield. Ꝗ. Closed Є in centre	125	225
1496	C. *O*. of series B. *Rev*. details as noble.	130	275
1497	E. *O*. as last. *Rev*. details as noble, pellet in centre	150	300
1498	G. *Mm*. cross 3 (4). Many varieties	100	200

Transitional treaty period, 1361. Aquitaine title added and FRANC omitted on the noble and, rarely, the half-noble; irregular sized letters; *mm*. cross potent (5).

1499	**Noble**. Ꝗ. Pellets or annulets at corners of central panel	325	625
1500	**Half-noble**. Similar	165	400
1501	**Quarter-noble**. Similar. Many varieties.	140	250

1499   1503

Treaty period, 1361–69. Omits FRANC, new letters, usually curule-shaped X; *mm*. cross potent (5).

1502	**Noble**. *London*. Saltire before ЄDWARD	235	500
1503	— Annulet before ЄDWARD	235	500
1504	*Calais*. C in centre of *rev*., flag at stern of ship	275	620
1505	— — without flag	265	600

1506   1508

		F	*VF*
		£	£
1506	**Half-noble**. *London*. Saltire before €DWARD	175	325
1507	— Annulet before €DWARD	175	350
1508	*Calais*. C in centre of *rev*., flag at stern of ship	275	575
1509	— — without flag	275	575
1510	**Quarter-noble**. *London*. As 1498. R. Lis in centre	100	225
1511	— — annulet before €DWARD	100	225
1512	*Calais*. R. Annulet in centre	125	250
1513	— — cross in circle over shield	135	275
1514	— R. Quatrefoil in centre; cross over shield	135	275
1515	— — crescent over shield	225	475

Post-treaty period, 1369–1377. French title resumed.

1516	**Noble**. *London*. Annulet before €D. R. Treaty period die	275	525
1517	— — — crescent on forecastle	300	575
1518	— — post-treaty letters. R. € and pellet in centre	250	500
1519	— — — R. € and saltire in centre	325	600
1520	*Calais*. Flag at stern. R. € in centre	275	550

1521

1521	— — *Rev*. as 1518, with € and pellet in centre	235	500
1522	— As 1520, but without flag. R. C in centre	250	575
1523	**Half-noble**. *London*. O. Treaty die. *Rev*. as 1518	*Extremely rare*	
1524	*Calais*. Without AQT, flag at stern. R. € in centre	325	700
1525	— — R. Treaty die with C in centre	350	725

SILVER

rst coinage, 1327–35 (.925 fineness)

1526   1530   1535

		F £	VF £
1526	**Penny**. *London*. As Edw. II; class XVd with Lombardic n's	275	650
1527	*Bury St. Edmunds*. Similar	Extremely rare	
1528	*Canterbury; mm.* cross pattée with pellet centre	160	350
1529	— — three extra pellets in one quarter	160	375
1530	*Durham*. Ŗ. Small crown in centre	400	850
1531	*York*. As 1526, but quatrefoil in centre of *rev.*	125	300
1532	— — — pellet in each quarter of *mm.*	125	300
1533	— — — three extra pellets in one quarter	125	300
1534	— — — Roman N on *obv.*	125	300
1535	*Berwick* (1333–1342, Blunt type VIII). Bear's head in one quarter of *rev.*.	250	600
1536	**Halfpenny**. *London*. ЄDWARDVS RЄX AII(G)*, neat work, flat crown .	100	225
1537	*Berwick* (Bl. VIII). Bear's head in one or two quarters	75	170
1538	**Farthing**. *London*. ЄDWARDVS RЄX A*, flat crown	85	175
1539	*Berwick* (Bl. VIII). As 1537	150	325

1537   1540

Second coinage, 1335–43 (.833 fineness)

1540	**Halfpenny**. *London*. ЄDWARDVS RЄX A(NG)*, rough work, tall crown.	20	55
1541	*Reading*. Escallop in one quarter	300	550
1542	**Farthing**. *London*. As halfpenny	85	175

Third or florin coinage, 1344–51. Bust with bushy hair. (.925 fine, 18 grs.)

1543   1555

		F	VF
		£	£
1543	**Penny**. *London*. Class 1. ЄDW, Lombardic n's	13	45
1544	— 2, ЄDWA, n's, but sometimes N's on *rev.*	10	35
1545	— 3, ЄDW, N's, sometimes reversed or n's on *rev.*	10	35
1546	— 4, ЄDW, no stops, reversed N's, but on *rev.* sometimes n's, N's or double-barred N's	10	35
1547	*Canterbury*. ЄDWA, n's	45	95
1548	— ЄDW, reversed N's	40	85
1549	*Durham*, Sede Vacante (1345). A, ЄDW R. ℞. No marks	75	175
1550	— — B, similar, ЄDWAR R	125	275
1551	— Bp. Hatfield. C, similar, but pellet in centre of *rev.*	75	175
1552	— — — Crozier on *rev.*	75	200
1553	— — — — with pellet in centre of *rev.*	75	200
1554	— — — D, ЄDWARDVS RЄX AIn, crozier on *rev.*	175	400
1555	*Reading*. *O*. as 1546. ℞. Escallop in one quarter	200	400
1556	*York*. *O*. as 1546. ℞. Quatrefoil in centre	50	110
1557	**Halfpenny**. *London*. ЄDWARDVS RЄX(An).	25	50
1558	— — pellet either side of crown	30	60
1559	— — saltire either side of crown and in one quarter of *rev.*	28	55
1560	*Reading*. *O*. Similar. ℞. Escallop in one quarter	275	500
1561	*Continental imitation*. Mostly reading ЄDWARDIENSIS	18	45
1562	**Farthing**. *London*. ЄDWARDVS REX	75	175
1562A	*Reading*. As last. ℞. As halfpenny		*Unique*

Fourth coinage, 1351–77
    Reference: L. A. Lawrence, *The Coinage of Edward III from 1351*.
    Pre-treaty period, 1351–61. With French title.

1567   1570

		F	VF
		£	£
1563	**Groat** (=4d., 72 grs.). *London*, series B (1351). Roman M, open C and Є; *mm.* cross 1	100	250
1564	— — — crown in each quarter		*Unique*
1565	— C (1351–2). Lombardic m, closed C and Є, R with wedge-shaped tail; *mm.* cross 1	20	70
1566	— D (1352–3). R with normal tail; *mm.* cross 1 or cross 1 broken (2)	25	90
1567	— E (1354–5). Broken letters, V often with nick in r. limb; *mm.* cross 2 (3)	18	60
1568	— — — lis on breast	20	70
1569	— F (1356). *Mm.* crown (74)	25	90
1570	— G (1356–61). Usually with annulet in one quarter and sometimes under bust, *mm.* cross 3 (4). Many varieties	20	70
1571	*York*, series D. As London	50	130
1572	— E. As London	45	115

1573   1574

1573	**Halfgroat.** *London*, series B. As groat	50	140
1574	— C. As groat	15	50
1575	— D. As groat	17	55
1576	— E. As groat	15	50
1577	— F. As groat	20	60
1578	— G. As groat	17	55
1579	— — — annulet below bust	20	60
1580	*York*, series D. As groat	30	75
1581	— E. As groat	25	65
1582	— — — lis on breast	35	90

1584   1587   1591

1583	**Penny.** *London.* Series A (1351). Round letters, Lombardic m and n, annulet in each quarter; *mm.* cross pattée	40	80
1584	— C. Details as groat, but annulet in each quarter	10	30
1585	— D. Details as groat, but annulet in each quarter	10	30
1586	— E. Sometimes annulet in each quarter	10	30
1587	— F. Details as groat	12	35

		F	*VF*
		£	£
1588	— G. Details as groat.	10	30
1589	— — — annulet below bust	10	35
1590	— — — saltire in one quarter	25	50
1591	*Durham*, Bp. Hatfield. Series A. As 1583, but extra pellet in each quarter, VIL LA crozier DVRRЄM	150	350
1592	— C. Details as groat. ℞. Crozier, CIVITAS DVNЄLMIЄ	30	70
1593	— D — — —	30	77
1594	— E — — —	25	55
1595	— F — Є. Crozier, CIVITAS DVRЄMЄ	30	65
1596	— G — — —	18	40
1597	— — — — annulet below bust	20	45
1598	— — — — saltire in one quarter	20	45
1599	— — — — annulet on each shoulder	20	45
1600	— — — — trefoil of pellets on breast	25	55
1601	— — — ℞. Crozier, CIVITAS DVRЄLMIЄ	30	65
1602	*York*, Royal Mint. Series D.	30	55
1603	— — E.	15	30
1604	— Archb. Thorsby. Series D. ℞. Quatrefoil in centre.	25	45
1605	— — G —	15	30
1606	— — — annulet or saltire on breast.	15	30
1607	**Halfpenny**. *London*. Series E. ЄDWARDVS RЄX An	75	200
1608	— G, but with *obv*. of F (*mm.* crown). Annulet in one quarter	*Extremely rare*	
1609	**Farthing**. *London*. Series E. ЄDWARDVS RЄX	150	300
1609A	— — Series G. Annulet in one quarter	*Extremely rare*	

Transitional treaty period, 1361. French title omitted, irregular sized letters; *mm.* cross potent (5).

		F	*VF*
1610	**Groat**. *London*. Annulet each side of crown	100	325
1611	**Halfgroat**. Similar, but only seven arches to tressure	90	225

1611   1612

		F	*VF*
1612	**Penny**, *London*. Omits RЄX, annulet in two upper qtrs. of *mm*	40	110
1613	**York**, Archb. Thoresby. Similar, but quatrefoil enclosing pellet in centre of *rev*.	40	110
1614	*Durham*. Bp. Hatfield. Similar. ℞. Crozier, CIVITAS DORЄLMЄ	55	125
1615	**Halfpenny**. Two pellets over *mm*., ЄDWARDVS RЄX An	75	150

Treaty period, 1361–69. French title omitted, new letters, usually "Treaty" X; *mm.* cross potent (5).

		F	*VF*
1616	**Groat**, *London*. Many varieties	25	90
1617	— Annulet before ЄDWARD	30	100
1618	— Annulet on breast	60	175
1619	*Calais*. As last	85	225

1621   1635

		F	VF
		£	£
1620	**Halfgroat**, *London*. As groat	20	50
1621	— — Annulet before ЄDWARDVS	15	40
1622	— — Annulet on breast	45	120
1623	*Calais*. As last	90	200
61624	**Penny**, *London*. ЄDWARD AnGL R, etc	15	35
61625	— — — pellet before ЄDWARD	20	45
61626	*Calais*. Ŗ. VILLA CALЄSIE	55	135
61627	*Durham*. Ŗ. DIVITAS DVNЄLMIS	35	80
61628	— Ŗ. Crozier, CIVITAS DVRЄMЄ	25	65
1629	*York*, Archb. Thoresby. Quatrefoil in centre of *rev.*, ЄDWARDVS DЄI G RЄX An	30	65
1630	— — — ЄDWARDVS RЄX ANGLI	12	35
1631	— — — — quatrefoil before ЄD and on breast	15	40
1632	— — — — annulet before ЄD	20	45
1633	— — — ЄDWARD AnGL R DnS HYB	27	60
1634	**Halfpenny**. ЄDWARDVS RЄX An, pellet stops	20	45
1635	— Pellet before ЄD, annulet stops	22	60
1636	**Farthing**. ЄDWARDVS RЄX, pellet stops	80	180

Post-treaty period, 1369–77. French title resumed, X like St. Andrew's cross; *mm.* 5, 6, 7a.

1637   1638

1637	**Groat**. Various readings, *mm.* cross pattée	85	250
1638	— — row of pellets across breast (chain mail)	165	500
1639	— row of annulets below bust (chain mail); *mm.* cross potent with four pellets	190	600
1640	**Halfgroat**. Various readings	85	225
1640A	— Thin portrait of Richard II		*Rare*
1641	— row of pellets one side of breast (chain mail)	165	525
1642	**Penny**, *London*. No marks on breast	33	85
1643	— Pellet or annulet on breast	45	110
1644	— Cross or quatrefoil on breast	38	100
1645	*Durham*, Bp. Hatfield. *Mm.* 7a, CIVITAS DVnOLM, crozier	38	100

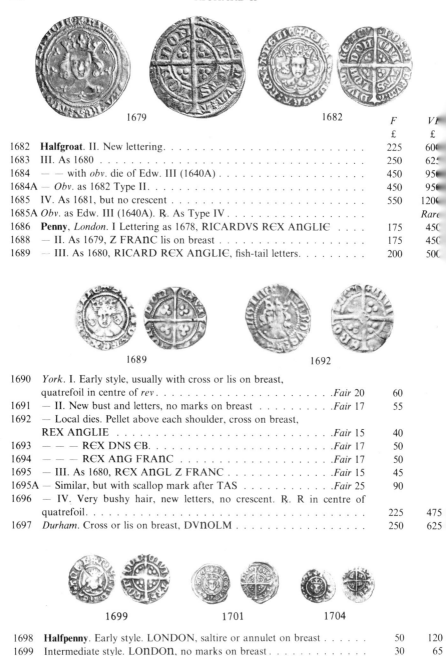

1679   1682

		F	V[
		£	£
1682	**Halfgroat**. II. New lettering.	225	60(
1683	III. As 1680	250	62:
1684	— — with *obv.* die of Edw. III (1640A).	450	95(
1684A	— *Obv.* as 1682 Type II.	450	95(
1685	IV. As 1681, but no crescent	550	120(
1685A	*Obv.* as Edw. III (1640A). R̸. As Type IV		*Rar(*
1686	**Penny**, *London*. I Lettering as 1678, RICARDVS RЄX AПGLIЄ	175	45(
1688	— II. As 1679, Z FRAПC lis on breast	175	45(
1689	— III. As 1680, RICARD RЄX AПGLIЄ, fish-tail letters.	200	50(

1689   1692

1690	*York*. I. Early style, usually with cross or lis on breast, quatrefoil in centre of *rev*. . . . .*Fair* 20	60	
1691	— II. New bust and letters, no marks on breast . . . .*Fair* 17	55	
1692	— Local dies. Pellet above each shoulder, cross on breast, REX AПGLIE . . . .*Fair* 15	40	
1693	— — — RЄX DNS ЄB. . . . .*Fair* 17	50	
1694	— — — RЄX AПG FRAПC . . . .*Fair* 17	50	
1695	— III. As 1680, RЄX AПGL Z FRANC . . . .*Fair* 15	45	
1695A	— Similar, but with scallop mark after TAS . . . .*Fair* 25	90	
1696	— IV. Very bushy hair, new letters, no crescent. R̸. R in centre of quatrefoil.	225	475
1697	*Durham*. Cross or lis on breast, DVПOLM	250	625

1699   1701   1704

1698	**Halfpenny**. Early style. LONDON, saltire or annulet on breast	50	120
1699	Intermediate style. LOПDOП, no marks on breast	30	65
1700	Type III. Late style. Similar, but fishtail letters	40	95
1700A	Type IV. Short, stubby lettering	. 35	85
1701	**Farthing**. Small bust and letters	200	375

		F	VF
		£	£
1702	— — rose after RЄX	225	450
1703	Large head, no bust	250	500
1704	Rose in each angle of *rev.* instead of pellets	450	800

HENRY IV, 1399–1413

In 1412 the standard weights of the coinage were reduced, the noble by 12 grains and the penny by 3 grains, partly because there was a scarcity of bullion and partly to provide revenue for the king, as Parliament had not renewed the royal subsidies. As in France, the royal arms were altered, three fleur-de-lis taking the place of the four or more lis previously displayed.

Mintmark: cross pattée (6)

Heavy coinage, 1399–1412   GOLD

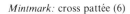

1707   1708

		F	VF
		£	£
1705	**Noble** (120 grs.), *London.* Old arms with four lis in French quarters; crescent or annulet on rudder	—	6000
1706	— New arms with three lis; crescent, pellet or no marks on rudder	—	6000
1707	*Calais.* Flag at stern, old arms; crown on or to l. of rudder	*Extremely rare*	
1708	— — new arms; crown or star on rudder	*Extremely rare*	
1709	**Half-noble**, *London.* Old arms	*Extremely rare*	
1710	— new arms	*Extremely rare*	
1711	*Calais.* New arms	*Extremely rare*	
1712	**Quarter-noble**, *London.* Crescent over old arms	750	1500
1713	— — — new arms	650	1300
1714	*Calais.* New arms. R. *Mm.* crown	850	1750

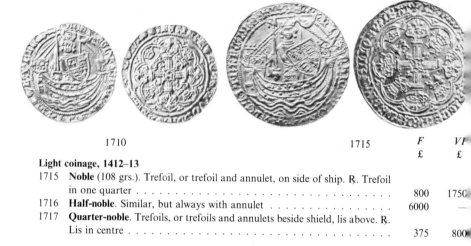

1710   1715

	F	VF
	£	£

Light coinage, 1412–13

1715	**Noble** (108 grs.). Trefoil, or trefoil and annulet, on side of ship. ℞. Trefoil in one quarter	800	1750
1716	**Half-noble**. Similar, but always with annulet	6000	—
1717	**Quarter-noble**. Trefoils, or trefoils and annulets beside shield, lis above. ℞. Lis in centre	375	800

SILVER

Heavy coinage, 1399–1412

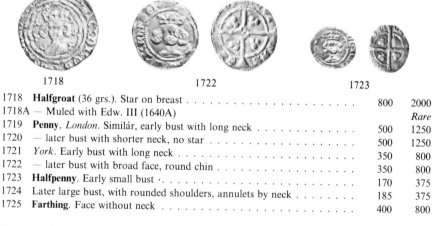

1718   1722   1723

1718	**Halfgroat** (36 grs.). Star on breast	800	2000
1718A	— Muled with Edw. III (1640A)		*Rare*
1719	**Penny**, *London*. Similar, early bust with long neck	500	1250
1720	— later bust with shorter neck, no star	500	1250
1721	*York*. Early bust with long neck	350	800
1722	— later bust with broad face, round chin	350	800
1723	**Halfpenny**. Early small bust	170	375
1724	Later large bust, with rounded shoulders, annulets by neck	185	375
1725	**Farthing**. Face without neck	400	800

Light coinage, 1412–13

1728   1731   1737

		F £	VF £
1726	**Groat** (60 grs.). I. Pellet to l., annulet to r. of crown; altered die of Richard II	1500	3500
1727	New dies; II. Annulet to l., pellet to r. of crown, 8 or 10 arches to tressure	1250	3000
1728	— III. Similar but 9 arches to tressure.	1250	3000
1729	**Halfgroat**. Pellet to l., annulet to r. of crown	*Extremely rare*	
1730	Annulet to l., pellet to r. of crown	650	1500
1731	**Penny**, *London*. Annulet and pellet by crown; trefoil on breast and before CIVI	450	1050
1732	— — annulet or slipped trefoil before LON.	450	1050
1733	— Pellet and annulet by crown.		*Unique*
1734	*York*. Annulet on breast. R̟. Quatrefoil in centre	400	900
1735	*Durham*. Trefoil on breast, DVnOLM.	450	950
1736	**Halfpenny**. Struck from heavy dies.	160	350
1737	New dies; annulet either side of crown or none	160	350
1738	**Farthing**. Face, no bust; slipped trefoil after REX	475	950

HENRY V, 1413–22

There was no change of importance in the coinage of this reign. There was, however, a considerable development in the use of privy marks which distinguished various issues, except for the last issue of the reign when most marks were removed. The Calais mint, which had closed in 1411, did not reopen until early in the next reign.

Mintmarks

Cross pattée (4, but with pellet centre). Pierced cross (18).

GOLD

1756

1744

		F	VF
		£	£
1739	**Noble**. A. Quatrefoil over sail and in second quarter of *rev.* Short broad letters, no other marks	*Extremely rare*	
1740	— B. Ordinary letters; similar, or with annulet on rudder	500	900
1741	— C. Mullet by sword arm, annulet on rudder	450	750
1742	— — broken annulet on side of ship	300	525
1743	—D. Mullet and annulet by sword arm, trefoil by shield, broken annulet on ship	325	575
1744	— E. Mullet, or mullet and annulet by sword arm, trefoil by shield, pellet by sword point and in one quarter, annulet on side of ship	350	650
1745	— — Similar, but trefoil on ship instead of by shield	400	700
1746	— F. Similar, but no pellet at sword point, trefoil in one quarter	350	700
1747	— G. No marks; annulet stops, except for mullet after first word	575	1050
1748	**Half-noble**. B. As noble; Hen. IV *rev.* die	*Extremely rare*	
1749	— C. Broken annulet on ship, quatrefoil below sail	375	800
1750	— — Mullet over shield, broken annulet on *rev.*	350	700
1751	— F. Similar, but no annulet on ship, usually trefoil by shield	400	850
1752	— F/E. As last, but pellet in 1st and annulet in 2nd quarter.	450	1000
1753	— G. As noble, but quatrefoil over sail, mullet sometimes omitted after first word of *rev.*	500	1150
1754	**Quarter-noble**. A. Lis over shield and in centre of *rev.* Short broad letters; quatrefoil and annulet beside shield, stars at corners of centre on rev.	225	425
1755	— C. Ordinary letters; quatrefoil to l., quat. and mullet to r. of shield	140	275
1756	— — — annulet to l., mullet to r. of shield	125	250

		F £	VF £
1757	**Quarter-noble**. F. Ordinary letters; trefoil to l., mullet to r. of shield . . .	175	350
1758	— G. — no marks, except mullet after first word.	175	350

SILVER

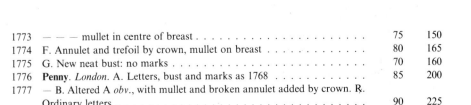

1759   1762

		F	VF
1759	**Groat**. A. Short broad letters; "emaciated" bust	450	950
1760	— — muled with Hen. IV *obv.* or *rev*	450	950
1761	— — muled with later *rev.* of Hen. V	400	850
1762	B. Ordinary letters; 'scowling' bust.	250	500
1762A	— — mullet in centre of breast.	200	450
1763	— — muled with Hen. IV or later Hen. V	275	600
1764	C. Normal bust	60	140
1765	— — mullet on r. shoulder.	50	120
1767	G. Normal bust; no marks	100	200
1768	**Halfgroat**. A. As groat, but usually with annulet and pellet by crown . .	375	800
1769	B. Ordinary letters; no marks.	120	250
1770	— — muled with Hen. IV or class D (HV) *obv.*	160	325
1771	C. Tall neck, broken annulet to l. of crown	70	140
1772	— — — mullet on r. shoulder	70	160

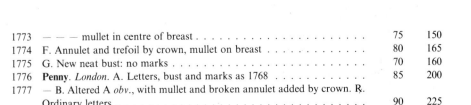

1773   1774

		F	VF
1773	— — — mullet in centre of breast	75	150
1774	F. Annulet and trefoil by crown, mullet on breast	80	165
1775	G. New neat bust: no marks	70	160
1776	**Penny**. *London*. A. Letters, bust and marks as 1768	85	200
1777	— B. Altered A *obv.*, with mullet and broken annulet added by crown. R̹.		
	Ordinary letters	90	225

1778   1791

		F £	VF £
1778	— C. Tall neck, mullet and broken annulet by crown	20	55
1779	— D. Similar, but whole annulet.	25	75
1780	— F. Mullet and trefoil by crown	27	80
1781	— G. New neat bust, no marks, DI GRA.	25	75
1782	*Durham*. C. As 1778 but quatrefoil at end of legend	45	135
1783	— D. As 1779	40	125
1784	— G. Similar, but new bust. ℞. Annulet in one qtr.	50	160
1785	*York*. C. As 1778, but quatrefoil in centre of *rev.*.	20	55
1786	— D. Similar, but whole annulet by crown	20	55
1787	— E. As last, but pellet above mullet	40	110
1788	— F. Mullet and trefoil by crown	27	75
1789	— — Trefoil over mullet to l., annulet to r. of crown	22	60
1790	— G. Mullet and trefoil by crown (London dies).	22	60
1791	— — Mullet and lis by crown, annulet in one qtr. (usually local dies and muled with Henry VI).	22	70

1796   1798

		F £	VF £
1792	**Halfpenny**. A. Emaciated bust, annulets by crown	28	70
1793	— altered dies of Hen. IV	38	100
1794	C. Ordinary bust, broken annulets by crown	18	40
1795	D. Annulets, sometimes broken, by hair.	18	40
1796	F. Annulet and trefoil by crown	20	45
1797	G. New bust; no marks, usually muled with Henry VI.	75	175
1798	**Farthing**. G. Small face with neck	175	400

HENRY VI, First Reign, 1422–61

The supply of gold began to dwindle early in the reign, which accounts for the rarity of gold after 1426. The Calais mint was reopened in 1424 and for some years a large amount of coin was struck there. It soon stopped minting gold; the mint was finally closed in 1440. A royal mint at York was opened for a short time in 1423/4.

Marks used to denote various issues become more prominent in this reign and can be used to date coins to within a year or so.

Reference: *Heavy Coinage of Henry VI*, by C. A. Whitton (B.N.J. 1938–41).

Mintmarks

| 7a | 105 | 18 | — | 8 | 9 | 15 |

1422–60	Plain cross (7a, intermittently)	1427–34	Cross patonce (8)
	Lis (105, on gold)		Cross fleurée (9)
1422–27	Pierced cross (18)	1434–35	Voided cross (15)
1422–34	Cross pommée	1435–60	Cross fleury (9)
		1460	Lis (105, on *rev.* of some groats)

For Restoration marks see p. 121.

GOLD

Annulet issue, 1422–7

1799

		F £	VF £
1799	**Noble**. *London*. Annulet by sword arm, and in one spandrel on *rev.*; trefoil stops on *obv.* with lis after hЄNRIC, annulets on *rev.*, with mullet after IhC.	300	550
1800	— Similar, but *obv.* from Henry V die.	600	1200
1801	— As 1799, but Flemish imitative coinage	200	425
1802	*Calais*. As 1799, but flag at stern and C in centre of *rev*	425	850
1803	— — with h in centre of *rev.*	400	725
1804	*York*. As London, but with lis over stern	400	700
1805	**Half-noble**. *London*. As 1799	250	400
1806	— Similar, but *obv.* from Henry V die.	350	675
1807	*Calais*. As noble, with C in centre of *rev.*	625	1100
1808	— — with h in centre of *rev.*	325	675
1809	*York*. As noble.	375	850

	F	VF
	£	£
1810 **Quarter-noble.** *London.* Lis over shield; *mm.* large lis	125	225
1811 — — — trefoil below shield	175	400
1812 — — — pellet below shield.	*Extremely rare*	
1813 *Calais.* Three lis over shield; *mm.* large lis.	200	400
1814 — Similar but three lis around shield	225	450
1815 — As 1810, but much smaller *mm..*	175	375
1816 *York.* Two lis over shield	225	400

1814   1819

Rosette-mascle issue, 1427–30

	F	VF
1817 **Noble.** *London.* Lis by sword arm and in *rev.* field; stops, rosettes, or rosettes and mascles.	525	1150
1818 *Calais.* Similar, with flag at stern.	530	1350
1819 **Half-noble.** *London.* Lis in *rev.* field; stops, rosettes and mascles.	500	1100
1820 *Calais.* Similar, flag at stern; stops, rosettes	600	1400
1821 **Quarter-noble.** *London.* As 1810; stops, as noble	225	475
1822 — without lis over shield	200	450
1823 *Calais.* Lis over shield, rosettes r. and l., and rosette stops.	325	500

Pinecone-mascle issue, 1430–4

	F	VF
1824 **Noble.** *London.* Stops, pinecones and mascles	600	1200
1825 **Half-noble.** *London. O.* Rosette-mascle die. ℞. As last	*Extremely rare*	
1826 **Quarter-noble.** As 1810, but pinecone and mascle stops	*Unique*	

Leaf-mascle issue, 1434–5

	F	VF
1827 **Noble.** Leaf in waves; stops, saltires with two mascles and one leaf	1000	2500
1828 **Half-noble.** (Fishpool Hoard).	*Unique*	
1829 **Quarter-noble.** As 1810; stops, saltire and mascle; leaf on inner circle of *rev.* .	1350	2750

Leaf-trefoil issue, 1435–8

	F	VF
1830 **Noble.** Stops, leaves and trefoils	*Extremely rare*	
1830A **Half-noble.** Mule with Annulet Issue reverse die	*Unique*	
1831 **Quarter-noble.** Similar.	*Unique*	

Trefoil issue, 1438–43

	F	VF
1832 **Noble.** Trefoil below shield and in *rev.* legend.	1000	2500

Leaf-pellet issue, 1445–54

	F	VF
1833 **Noble.** Annulet, lis and leaf below shield	1000	2500

Cross-pellet issue, 1454–60

	F	VF
1834 **Noble.** Mascle at end of *obv.* legend	*Unique*	

SILVER

Annulet issue, 1422–7

1835   1840

		F £	VF £
1835	**Groat**. *London*. Annulet in two quarters of *rev.*	20	55
1836	*Calais*. Annulets at neck. R̨. Similar	17	35
1837	— — no annulets on *rev.*	20	45
1838	*York*. Lis either side of neck. R̨. As 1835	500	950
1839	**Halfgroat**. *London*. As groat	20	50
1840	*Calais*. As 1836	15	35
1841	— — no annulets on *rev.*	20	45
1842	— — only one annulet on *rev.* (mule with annulet-trefoil *rev.*)	22	55
1843	*York*. As groat	500	1000
1844	**Penny**. *London*. Annulets in two qtrs.	20	50
1845	*Calais*. Annulets at neck. R̨. As above	18	35
1846	— — only one annulet on *rev.*	22	50
1847	*York*. As London, but lis at neck	500	950
1848	**Halfpenny**. *London*. As penny	20	45
1849	*Calais*. Similar, but annulets at neck	20	45
1850	*York*. Similar, but lis at neck	350	700
1851	**Farthing**. *London*. As penny, but *mm.* cross pommée	175	350
1852	*Calais*. Similar, but annulets at neck	275	550

1843   1849   1852

Annulet-trefoil sub-issue

1853	**Groat**. *London*. As 1835, but trefoil of pellets to l. of crown (*North*)	50	125
1854	*Calais*. Similar, but annulets by neck also	40	105
1855	**Halfgroat**. *Calais*. Similar, but usually with ann. or ros.-mas. *rev.*	50	125
1856	**Penny**. *Calais*. Similar	60	150
1857	— — only one annulet on *rev*	75	185

Rosette-mascle issue, 1427–30. All with rosettes (early) or rosettes and mascles somewhere in the legends.

		F	VF
		£	£
1858	**Groat**. *London*.	35	75
1859	*Calais*.	20	50
1860	— mascle in two spandrels (as illus. 1863).	40	100

| 1861 | 1863 | 1872 |

1861	**Halfgroat**. *London*.	30	70
1862	*Calais*.	20	40
1863	— mascle in two spandrels, as illustrated	35	90
1864	**Penny**. *London*.	50	100
1865	*Calais*.	25	60
1866	*York*. Archb. Kemp. Crosses by hair, no rosette	25	70
1867	— — Saltires by hair, no rosette	25	70
1868	— — Mullets by crown	25	70
1869	*Durham*, Bp. Langley. Large star to l. of crown, no rosette, DVnOLMI.	60	160
1870	**Halfpenny**, *London*	25	45
1871	*Calais*.	20	40
1872	**Farthing**, *London*	110	225
1873	*Calais*. *Mm*. cross pommée	120	250

| 1879 | 1884 |

Pinecone-mascle issue, 1430–4. All with pinecones and mascles in legends.

1874	**Groat**, *London*	30	65
1875	*Calais*.	25	55
1876	**Halfgroat**, *London*.	25	60
1877	*Calais*.	22	45
1878	**Penny**, *London*.	50	100
1879	*Calais*.	24	55
1880	*York*, Archb. Kemp. Mullet by crown, quatrefoil in centre of *rev*.	20	42
1881	— — rosette on breast, no quatrefoil	18	40
1882	— — mullet on breast, no quatrefoil	40	85
1883	*Durham*, Bp. Langley. DVnOLMI.	75	200
1884	**Halfpenny**, *London*	25	45
1885	*Calais*.	25	45

Full flan coins are difficult to find in the smaller denominations.

	F	VF
	£	£
1886 **Farthing**, *London*	100	225
1887 *Calais. Mm.* cross pommée	150	325

Leaf-mascle issue, 1434–5. Usually with a mascle in the legend and a leaf somewhere in the design.

1888 **Groat**. *London*. Leaf below bust	40	100
1889 — — *rev*. of last or next coinage	35	90
1890 *Calais*. Leaf below bust, and usually below MЄVM	28	75
1891 **Halfgroat**. *London*. Leaf under bust, pellet under TAS and DON.	30	70
1892 *Calais*. Leaf below bust, and sometimes on *rev*..	32	75
1893 **Penny**. *London*. Leaf on breast, no stops on *rev*.	24	55
1894 *Calais*. Leaf on breast and below SIЄ	20	45
1895 **Halfpenny**. *London*. Leaf on breast and on *rev*..	20	40
1896 *Calais*. Leaf on breast and below SIЄ	45	100

1892   1897   1912

Leaf-trefoil issue, 1435–8. Mostly with leaves and trefoil of pellets in the legends.

1897 **Groat**. *London*. Leaf on breast	37	80
1898 — without leaf on breast	30	70
1899 *Calais*. Leaf on breast	*Extremely rare*	
1900 **Halfgroat**. *London*. Leaf on breast; *mm*. plain cross	25	55
1901 — *O. mm*. cross fleury; leaf on breast	25	55
1902 — — without leaf on breast	25	55
1903 **Penny**. *London*. Leaf on breast	25	50
1903A *Calais*. Similar	*Unique*	
1904 *Durham*, Bp. Neville. Leaf on breast. Ŗ. Rings in centre, no stops, DVnOLM	80	200
1905 **Halfpenny**. *London*. Leaf on breast.	17	40
1906 — without leaf on breast	22	45
1907 **Farthing**. *London*. Leaf on breast; stops, trefoil and saltire on *obv*.	100	250

Trefoil issue, 1438–43. Trefoil of pellets either side of neck and in legend, leaf on breast.

1908 **Groat**. *London*. Sometimes a leaf before LON	40	100
1909 — Fleurs in spandrels, sometimes extra pellet in two qtrs..	50	115
1910 — Trefoils in place of fleurs at shoulders, none by neck, sometimes extra pellets.	40	100
1911 *Calais*.	100	250
1911A **Halfgroat**. Similar, but trefoil after DEUM. Mule only with leaf trefoil *obv*.	*Extremely rare*	
1912 **Halfpenny**, *London*	35	85

Trefoil pellet issue, 1443–5

1913 **Groat**. Trefoils by neck, pellets by crown, small leaf on breast; sometimes extra pellet in two quarters	50	125

		F	VF
		£	£

Leaf-pellet issue, 1445–54. Leaf on breast, pellet each side of crown, except where stated.

1914	**Groat.** ANGL; extra pellet in two quarters	35	85
1915	Similar, but ANGLI.	25	65
1916	— — trefoil in *obv.* legend	35	85
1917	Leaf on neck, fleur on breast, often extra pellet in two quarters.	30	75
1918	As last, but two extra pellets by hair.	55	150
1919	**Halfgroat.** As 1914 *mm.*8	25	60
1920	Similar, but *mm.* plain cross, sometimes no leaf on breast, no stops	25	60
1921	**Penny.** *London.* Usually extra pellets in two quarters.	24	65
1922	— — pellets by crown omitted	24	65
1923	— — trefoil in legend	30	80
1924	*York,* Archb. Booth. ℞. Quatrefoil and pellet in centre	24	60
1925	— — two extra pellets by hair (local dies).	18	55
1926	*Durham,* Bp. Neville. Trefoil in *obv.* legend. B. Two rings in centre of cross.	75	225
1927	— — Similar, but without trefoil.	75	225
1928	**Halfpenny.** Usually extra pellet in two quarters.	25	55
1929	— *mm.* plain cross.	25	55
1930	**Farthing.** As last.	120	250

1915   1927   1935

Unmarked issue, 1453–4

1931	**Groat.** No marks on *obv.*; two extra pellets on *rev.*	120	275
1932	— four extra pellets on *rev.*	130	300
1933	**Halfgroat.** As 1931	130	300

Cross-pellet issue, 1454–60

1934	**Groat.** Saltire either side of neck, pellets by crown, leaf and fleur on breast, extra pellets on *rev.*	70	175
1935	Saltire on neck, no leaf, pellets by crown, usually mullets in legend; extra pellets on *rev.*	35	105
1936	— Similar, but mascles in place of mullets on *obv.*	35	105
1937	— — pellets by hair instead of by crown	45	125

Full flan coins are difficult to find in the smaller denominations.

		F £	VF £
1938	**Halfgroat**. Saltire on neck, pellets by crown and on *rev.*, mullets in legend.	90	225
1939	**Penny**. *London*. Saltire on neck, pellets by crown and on *rev.*, mascle(s), or mullet and mascle in legend	75	175
1940	*York*, Archb. Wm. Booth. Saltires by neck, usually leaf on breast, pellets by crown. ℞. Cross in quatrefoil in centre. Illustrated below	40	90
1941	*Durham*, Bp. Laurence Booth. Saltire and B at neck, pellets by crown. ℞. Rings in centre.	100	250
1942	**Halfpenny**. Saltires by neck, usually two extra pellets on *rev.*	50	110
1943	Similar, but saltire on neck, sometimes mullet after hℰnRIC	100	225
1944	**Farthing**. Saltire on neck, pellets by crown and on *rev.*.	120	250

1940   1945

Lis-pellet issue, 1456–60

| 1945 | **Groat**. Lis on neck; pellets by crown. ℞. Extra pellets . . . . | 150 | 325 |

EDWARD IV, First Reign, 1461–70

In order to increase the supply of bullion to the mint the weight of the penny was reduced to 12 grains in 1464, and the current value of the noble was raised to 8s. 4d. Later, in 1465, a new gold coin was issued, the Ryal or "Rose Noble", weighing 120 grains and having a value of 10s. However, as 6s. 8d. had become the standard professional fee the old noble was missed, and a new coin was issued to take its place, the Angel of 80 grains.

Royal mints were opened at Canterbury and York to help with the re-coinage, and other mints were set up at Bristol, Coventry and Norwich, though they were not open for long.

Reference: C. E. Blunt and C. A Whitton, *The Coinage of Edward IV and Henry VI (Restored)*, B.N.J. 1945–7.

Mintmarks

105	9	7a	33	99	28	74	11

1461–4	Lis (105)	1467–70	Lis (105, *York*)	
	Cross fleury (9)	1467–8	Crown (74)	often
	Plain cross (7a)		Sun (28)	combined
1464–5	Rose (33 and 34)	1468–9	Crown (74)	sometimes
1464–7	Pall (99, *Canterbury*)		Rose (33)	combined
1465–6	Sun (28)	1469–70	Long cross	often
1466–7	Crown (74)		fitchée (11)	combined
			Sun (28) ·	

GOLD

Heavy coinage, 1461–4	*F*	*VF*
	£	£
1946 **Noble** (= 6s. 8d., wt. 108 grs.). Normal type, but *obv.* legend commences at top left, lis below shield; *mm.* -/lis	4000	8000
1947 — Quatrefoil below sword arm; *mm.* rose/lis	*Extremely rare*	
1948 — R. Roses in two spandrels; *mm.* rose	*Extremely rare*	
1949 **Quarter-noble**	*Unique*	

1946   1950

Light coinage, 1464–70		
1950 **Ryal** or rose-noble (= 10s., wt. 120 grs.), *London*. Type as next illus. Large fleurs in spandrels; *mm.* 33–74	325	525
1951 — — Small trefoils in spandrels; *mm.* 74–11	300	500
1952 — Flemish imitative coinage (mostly 16th cent.)	225	475

Light coinage, *continued.*

		F	VF
		£	£
1953	*Bristol.* B in waves, large fleurs; *mm.* 28, 74	350	750
1954	— — small fleurs in spandrels; *mm.* 74, 28	350	750
1955	*Coventry.* C in waves; *mm.* sun	650	1400
1956	*Norwich.* N in waves; *mm.* sun, rose?	800	1750
1957	*York.* Є in waves, large fleurs in spandrels, *mm.* 28, 105	375	800
1958	— — small fleurs, *mm.* 105, 28	375	800
1959	**Half-ryal.** *London.* As 1950	250	435
1960	*Bristol.* B in waves; *mm.* 28–28/74	350	850
1961	*Coventry.* C in waves; *mm.* sun	*Extremely rare*	
1962	*Norwich..* N in waves; *mm.* rose	1000	2250

1963   1965

1963	*York.* Є in waves; *mm.* 28, 105, 33/105	275	525
1964	**Quarter-ryal.** Shield in tressure of eight arcs, rose above. ℞. Somewhat as		
	half ryal; *mm.* 28/33	*Unique?*	
1965	Shield in quatrefoil, ℞. Є above, rose on l., sun on r.; *mm.* 33/28–74/33 .	175	425
1966	— — sun on l., rose on r.; *mm.* 74–11	190	475

1967

1967	**Angel** (= 6s. 8d., wt. 80 grs.). St. Michael spearing dragon. ℞. Ship, rays of		
	sun at masthead, large rose and sun beside mast; *mm.* -/33	*Extremely rare*	
1968	— — small rose and sun at mast; *mm.* -/74	*Extremely rare*	

First reign SILVER

1978

1972

1985

Heavy coinage, 1461–4

		F £	VF £
1969	**Groat** (60 grs.). Group I, lis on neck, pellets by crown; *mm.* 9, 7a, 105, 9/105	55	150
1970	— Lis on breast, no pellets; *mm.* plain cross, 7a/105	55	140
1971	— — with pellets at crown; *mm.* plain cross	55	140
1972	II, quatrefoils by neck, crescent on breast; *mm.* rose	55	140
1973	III, similar but trefoil on breast; *mm.* rose	55	140
1974	— — — eye in *rev.* inner legend, *mm.* rose	50	125
1975	— Similar, but no quatrefoils by bust	65	150
1976	— — Similar, but no trefoil on breast	65	150
1977	IV, annulets by neck, eye after TAS; *mm.* rose	80	175
1978	**Halfgroat.** I, lis on breast, pellets by crown and extra pellets in two qtrs.; *mm.* 9, 7a	140	300
1979	II, quatrefoils at neck, crescent on breast; *mm.* rose	160	350
1980	III, similar, but trefoil on breast, eye on *rev.*; *mm.* rose	160	350
1981	— Similar, but no mark on breast	150	325
1982	IV, annulets by neck, sometimes eye on *rev.*; *mm.* rose	140	300
1983	**Penny** (15 grs.), *London.* I, marks as 1978, but mascle after RЄX; *mm.* plain cross	135	300
1984	— II, quatrefoils by neck; *mm.* rose	125	275
1985	— III, similar, but eye after TAS; *mm.* rose	120	260
1986	— IV, annulets by neck; *mm.* rose	150	375
1987	*York,* Archb. Booth. Quatrefoils by bust, voided quatrefoil in centre of *rev.*; *mm.* rose	120	250
1988	*Durham. O.* of Hen. VI. R. DVnOLIn	160	350
	Some of the Durham pennies from local dies may belong to the heavy coinage period, but if so they are indistinguishable from the light coins.		
1989	**Halfpenny.** I, as 1983, but no mascle	100	200
1990	II, quatrefoils by bust; *mm.* rose	60	140
1991	— saltires by bust; *mm.* rose	80	160
1992	III, no marks by bust; *mm.* rose	65	150
1993	IV, annulets by bust; *mm* rose	65	160
1994	**Farthing.** I, as 1989	*2 known*	

Light coinage, 1464–70. There is a great variety of groats and we give only a selection. Some have pellets in one quarter of the reverse, or trefoils over the crown; early coins have fleurs on the cusps of the tressure, then trefoils or no marks on the cusps, while the late coins have only trefoils.

		F	VF
		£	£
1995	**Groat** (48 grs.), *London*. Annulets at neck, eye after TAS; *mm*. 33 (struck from heavy dies, IV)	45	120
1996	– – – Similar, but new dies, eye after TAS or DOn	40	105
1997	– Quatrefoils at neck, eye; *mm*. 33 (heavy dies, III)	45	115
1998	– – – Similar, but new dies, eye in *rev*. legend	35	100
1999	– No marks at neck, eye; *mm*. 33	60	140

2000   2002

2000	– Quatrefoils at neck, no eye; *mm*. 33, 74, 28, 74/28, 74/33, 11/28	20	45
2001	– – – rose or quatrefoil on breast; *mm*. 33, 74/28	22	60
2002	– No marks at neck; *mm*. 28, 74, 11/28, 11	22	60
2003	– Trefoils or crosses at neck; *mm*. 11/33, 11/28, 11	22	60
2004	*Bristol*. B on breast, quatrefoils at neck; *mm*. 28/33, 28, 28/74, 74, 74/28	25	65
2005	– – trefoils at neck; *mm*. 28	30	80
2006	– – no marks at neck; *mm*. 28	35	90
2007	– Without B, quatrefoils at neck; *mm*. 28	28	75
	Bristol is variously rendered as BRESTOLL, BRISTOLL, BRESTOW, BRISTOW.		
2008	*Coventry*. C on breast, quatrefoils at neck, COVETRE; *mm*. 28/33, 28	65	160
2009	– – Local dies, similar; *mm*. rose	65	160
2010	– – – as last, but no C or quatrefoils	70	200
2011	*Norwich*. n on breast, quatrefoils at neck, nORWIC or nORVIC, *mm*. 28/33, 28	50	135
2012	*York*. Є on breast, quatrefoils at neck, ЄBORACI; *mm*. 28, 105/74, 105, 105/28	30	75
2013	– Similar, but without Є on breast, *mm*. 105	40	90
2014	– Є on breast, trefoils at neck; *mm*. 105/28, 105	30	80
2015	**Halfgroat**. *London*. Annulets by neck (heavy dies); *mm*. 33		*Unique*
2016	– Quatrefoils by neck; *mm*. 33/-, 28/-, 74, 74/28	40	95
2017	– Saltires by neck; *mm*. 74, 74/28	40	95
2018	– Trefoils by neck; *mm*. 74, 74/28, 11/28	35	85
2019	– No marks by neck; *mm*. 11/28	80	180
2020	– *Bristol*. Saltires or crosses by neck; *mm*. 33/28, 28, 74, 74/-	80	170
2021	– Quatrefoils by neck; *mm*. 28/-, 74, 74/-	80	160

Light coinage, silver, *continued.*

		F	VF
		£	£
2022	— Trefoils by neck; *mm.* 74	95	200
2023	— No marks by neck; *mm.* 74/28	95	200
2024	*Canterbury*, Archb. Bourchier (1464–7). Knot below bust; quatrefoils by neck; *mm.* 99/-, 99, 99/33, 99/28	15	40
2025	— — — quatrefoils omitted *mm.* 99	15	40
2026	— — — saltires by neck; *mm.* 99/-, 99/28	20	45
2026A	— — — trefoils by neck; *mm.* 99	*Extremely rare*	

2027   2030

2027	— — — wedges by hair and/or neck; *mm.* 99, 99/33, 99/28	20	50
2028	— — As 2024 or 2025, but no knot	25	60
2029	— Royal mint (1467–9). Quatrefoils by neck; *mm.* 74, 74/-	15	40
2030	— — Saltires by neck; *mm.* 74/-, 74	20	45
2031	— — Trefoils by neck; *mm.* 74, 74/-, 74/28, 33	20	45
2032	— No marks by neck; *mm.* 28	50	125
2033	*Coventry*. Crosses by neck; *mm.* sun		*Unique*
2034	*Norwich*. Saltires by neck; *mm.* sun	*Extremely rare*	
2035	*York*. Quatrefoils by neck; *mm.* sun, lis, lis/-	45	130
2036	— Saltires by neck; *mm.* lis	40	100
2037	— Trefoils by neck; *mm.* lis, lis/-	40	100
2038	— Є on breast, quatrefoils by neck; *mm.* lis/-	45	105
2039	**Penny** (12 grs.), *London*. Annulets by neck (heavy dies); *mm.* 33	70	160
2040	— Quatrefoils by neck; *mm.* 28, 74	30	60
2041	— Trefoil and quatrefoil by neck; *mm.* 74	35	75
2042	— Saltires by neck; *mm.* 74	35	75
2043	— Trefoils by neck; *mm.* 74, 11	25	50
2044	— No marks by neck; *mm.* 11	*Extremely rare*	
2045	*Bristol*. Crosses, quatrefoils or saltires by neck, BRISTOW; *mm.* crown	60	150
2046	— Quatrefoils by neck; BRI(trefoil)STOLL	75	185
2047	— Trefoil to r. of neck BRISTOLL	100	250
2048	*Canterbury*, Archb. Bourchier. Quatrefoils or saltires by neck, knot on breast; *mm.* pall	45	110
2049	— — Similar, but no marks by neck	55	125
2050	— — As 2048, but no knot	50	120
2051	— — Crosses by neck, no knot	50	120
2052	— Royal mint. Quatrefoils by neck; *mm.* crown	90	200
2053	— *Durham*, King's Receiver (1462–4). Local dies, mostly with rose in centre of *rev.*; *mm.* 7a, 33	20	60
2054	— Bp. Lawrence Booth (1465–70). B and D by neck, B on *rev.*; *mm.* 33	22	65
2055	— — Quatrefoil and B by neck; *mm.* 28	24	70
2056	— — B and quatrefoil by neck; *mm.* 74	*Extremely rare*	

Light coinage, silver, *continued.*

		F £	VF £
2057	— — D and quatrefoil by neck; *mm.* 74	26	75
2058	— — Quatrefoils by neck; *mm.* crown	30	90
2059	— — Trefoils by neck; *mm.* crown	30	90
2060	— — Lis by neck; *mm.* crown	30	90
2061	*York,* Sede Vacante (1464–5). Quatrefoils at neck, no quatrefoil in centre of *rev.; mm.* 28, 33	50	125
2062	— Archb. Neville (1465–70). Local dies, G and key by neck, quatrefoil on *rev.; mm.* 33, 7a	25	65

2063   2068

2063	— — London-made dies, similar; *mm.* 28, 105, 11	20	70
2064	— — Similar, but no marks by neck; *mm.* large lis	*Extremely rare*	
2065	— — — Quatrefoils by neck; *mm.* large ljs	15	50
2066	— — — Trefoils by neck; *mm.* large lis	30	65
2067	**Halfpenny,** *London.* Saltires by neck; *mm.* 34, 28, 74	30	70
2068	— Trefoils by neck; *mm.* 28, 74, 11	25	55
2069	— No marks by neck; *mm.* 11	*Unique?*	
2070	*Bristol.* Crosses by neck; *mm.* 74	110	250
2071	— Trefoils by neck; *mm.* 74	90	200
2072	*Canterbury,* Archb. Bourchier. No marks; *mm.* pall	100	225
2072A	— — — Trefoils by neck, *mm.* pall	100	225
2073	— Royal mint. Saltires by neck; *mm.* crown	65	140
2074	— — Trefoils by neck; *mm.* crown	60	125
2075	*York,* Royal mint. Saltires by neck; *mm.* lis/-, sun/-	65	140
2076	— — Trefoils by neck; *mm.* lis/-	60	125
2077	**Farthing,** *London.* ЄDWARD DI GRA RЄX, no marks at neck, *mm.* 33	*Extremely rare*	
2077A	— Trefoils by neck, *mm.* 74	*Extremely rare*	

Full flan coins are difficult to find in the smaller denominations.

HENRY VI RESTORED, Oct. 1470–Apr. 1471

The coinage of this short restoration follows closely that of the previous reign. Only angel gold was issued, the ryal being discontinued. Many of the coins have the king's name reading hЄnRICV—a distinguishing feature.

Mintmarks

| 6 | 13 | 44 | 33 | 105 | 12 |

Cross pattée (6)
Restoration cross (13)
Trefoil (44 and 45)

Rose (33, Bristol)
Lis (105
Short cross fitchée (12)

GOLD

2079

			F	VF
			£	£
2078	**Angel**, *London*. As illus. but no B; *mm*. -/6, 13, -/105, none		450	1000
2079	*Bristol*. B in waves; *mm*. -/13, none		650	1500
2080	**Half-angel**, *London*. As 2078; *mm*. -/6, -/13, -/105.		1250	2750
2081	*Bristol*. B in waves; *mm*. -/13			*Unique*

SILVER

2082   2084

2082	**Groat**, *London*. Usual type; *mm*. 6, 6/13, 6/105, 13, 13/6, 13/105, 13/12. .	110	200
2083	*Bristol*. B on breast; *mm*. 13, 13/33, 13/44, 44, 44/13, 44/33, 44/12	140	325
2084	*York*. Є on breast; *mm*. lis, lis/sun	125	265
2085	**Halfgroat**, *London*. As 2082; *mm*. 13, 13/-	200	450
2086	*York*. Є on breast; *mm*. lis		*Extremely rare*
2087	**Penny**, *London*. Usual type; *mm*. 6, 13, 12.	250	550

	F £	VF £
2087A *Bristol.* Similar; *mm.* 12		Unique?
2088 *York.* G and key by neck; *mm.* lis	175	350
2089 **Halfpenny,** *London.* As 2087; *mm.* 12	200	450
2090 *Bristol.* Similar; *mm.* cross		Unique?

EDWARD IV, Second Reign, 1471–83

The Angel and its half were the only gold denominations issued during this reign. The main types
and weight standards remained the same as those of the light coinage of Edward's first reign. The
use of the "initial mark" as a mintmark to denote the date of issue was now firmly established.

Mintmarks

33	12	55	44	55	28	56	17

37	6	18	19	20	31	11	38

1471–83	Rose (33, *York &*	1473–7	Cross pattée (6)
	Durham)		Pierced cross 1 (18)
1471	Short cross fitchée (12)	1477–80	Pierced cross and
1471–2	Annulet (large, 55)		pellet (19)
	Trefoil (44)		Pierced cross 2 (18)
	Rose (33, *Bristol*)		Pierced cross, central
1471–3	Pansy (30, *Durham*)		pellet (20)
1472–3	Annulet (small, 55)	1480–3	Rose (33, *Canterbury*)
	Sun (28, *Bristol*)		Heraldic cinquefoil (31)
1473–7	Pellet in annulet (56)		Long cross fitchée
	Cross and four pellets (17)		(11, *Canterbury*)
	Cross in circle (37)		Halved sun and rose (38)?

GOLD

2091   2093

	F £	VF £
2091	**Angel.** *London.* Type as illus.; *mm.* 12, 55, 56, 17, 18, 19, 31	235	450
2092	*Bristol.* B in waves; *mm.* 55	650	1400
2093	**Half-angel.** As illus.; *mm.* 55, cross in circle, 19, 20/19, 31	250	425
2094	King's name and title on *rev.*; *mm.* 12/-	375	750
2095	King's name and the title both sides; *mm.* 55/-	300	600

SILVER

2101   2106

		F	VF
		£	£
2096	**Groat**, *London*. Trefoils on cusps, no marks by bust; *mm.* 12–37	25	70
2097	— — roses by bust; *mm.* 56	35	95
2098	— Fleurs on cusps; no marks by bust; *mm.* 18–20	25	65
2099	— — pellets by bust; *mm.* 18 (2)	60	175
2100	— — rose on breast; *mm.* 31	25	60
2101	*Bristol*. B on breast; *mm.* 33, 33/55, 28/55, 55, 55/-, 28	60	165
2102	*York*. Є on breast; *mm.* lis	65	175
2103	**Halfgroat**, *London*. As 2096; *mm.* 12–31	30	80
2104	*Bristol*. B on breast; *mm.* 33/12	*Extremely rare*
2105	*Canterbury* (Royal mint). As 2103; *mm.* 33, 11, 11/31, 31	25	55
2106	— C on breast; *mm.* rose	18	40
2107	— — R. C in centre; *mm.* rose	18	40
2108	— — R. Rose in centre; *mm.* rose	20	45
2109	*York*. No. Є on breast; *mm.* lis	75	200
2110	**Penny**, *London*. No marks by bust; *mm.* 12–31	30	70
2111	*Bristol*. Similar; *mm.* rose	*Unique?*
2112	*Canterbury* (Royal). Similar; *mm.* 33, 11	65	140
2113	— C on breast; *mm.* 33	80	175

2115   2116   2123

2114	*Durham*, Bp. Booth (1471–6). No marks by neck; *mm.* 12, 44	18	60
2115	— — D in centre of *rev.*; B and trefoil by neck; *mm.* 44, 33, 56	18	65
2116	— — — two lis at neck; *mm.* 33	18	60
2117	— — — crosses over crown, and on breast; *mm.* 33	15	55
2118	— — — crosses over crown, V under CIVI; *mm.* 33, 30	15	55
2119	— — — B to l. of crown, V on breast and under CIVI	15	55
2120	— — — As last but crosses at shoulders	15	55
2121	— Sede Vacante (1476). R. D in centre; *mm.* 33	35	125
2122	— Bp. Dudley (1476–83). V to r. of neck; as last	18	60
2123	— — D and V by neck; as last, but *mm.* 31	15	55

Nos. 2117–2123 are from locally-made dies.

2125   2134

		F £	VF £
2124	*York*, Archb. Neville (1471–2). Quatrefoils by neck. ℞. Quatrefoil; *mm.* 12 (over lis)	*Extremely rare*	
2125	— — Similar, but G and key by neck; *mm.* 12 (over lis)	13	35
2126	— Neville suspended (1472–5). As last, but no quatrefoil in centre of *rev.*.	15	37
2126A	— — no marks by bust, similar	90	225
2127	— — No marks by neck, quatrefoil on *rev.*; *mm.* 55, cross in circle, 33. .	15	40
2128	— — Similar but Є and rose by neck; *mm.* 33	15	40
2129	— Archb. Neville restored (1475–6). As last, but G and rose	18	45
2130	— — Similar, but G and key by bust	15	40
2131	— Sede Vacante (1476). As 2127, but rose on breast; *mm.* 33	18	45
2132	— Archb. Lawrence Booth (1476–80). B and key by bust, quatrefoil on *rev.*; *mm.* 33, 31	13	35
2133	— Sede Vacante (1480). Similar, but no quatrefoil on *rev.*; *mm.* 33	15	37
2134	— Archb. Rotherham (1480–3). T and slanting key by neck, quatrefoil on *rev.*; *mm.* 33	13	35
2135	— — — Similar, but star on breast	150	350
2136	— — — Star on breast and to r. of crown	70	150
2137	**Halfpenny**, *London*. No marks by neck; *mm.* 12-31	15	50
2138	— Pellets at neck; *mm.* 18	20	55
2139	*Canterbury* (Royal). C on breast and in centre of *rev.*; *mm.* rose	70	150
2140	— C on breast only; *mm.* rose	60	130
2141	— Without C either side; *mm.* 11	70	160
2142	*Durham*, Bp. Booth. No marks by neck. ℞. DERAM, D in centre; *mm.* rose	90	200
2142A	— — Lis either side of neck. ℞. D or no mark in centre	*Extremely rare*	
2143	— — — Similar, but V to l. of neck	90	200

Full flan coins are very difficult to find in the small denominations.

EDWARD IV or V

Mintmark: Halved sun and rose.

The consensus of opinion now favours the last year of Edward IV for the introduction of the halved-sun-&-rose mintmark, but it is suggested that the earliest coins of Edward V's reign were struck from these Edw. IV dies. The coins are very rare.

	GOLD	F	VF
		£	£
2144	**Angel**. As 2091	700	1750
2145	**Half-angel**. As 2093	*Extremely rare*	

2145   2146

SILVER

2146	**Groat**. As 2098	300	750
2147	**Penny**. As 2110	400	900
2148	**Halfpenny**. As 2137	300	700

EDWARD V, 1483

On the death of Edward IV, 9th April, 1483, the 12-year-old Prince Edward was placed under the guardianship of his uncle, Richard, Duke of Gloucester, but within eleven weeks Richard usurped the throne and Edward and his younger brother were confined to the Tower and were never seen alive again. The boar's head was a personal badge of Richard, Edward's 'Protector'.

Recent research indicates that the mint marks previously thought to be for this reign are now attributable to Edward IV, Edward IV or V, or Richard III. On the publication of this research paper in the near future, it is expected we will remove coins of specifically Edward V.

Mintmarks: Boar's head on *obv.*, halved sun and rose on *rev.*

GOLD

2149	**Angel**. As 2091	*Extremely rare*
	A fine specimen sold at auction in June 1985 for £11,200.	
2150	**Half-angel**. Similar	*Unique*

SILVER

2151

		F	VF
		£	£
2151	**Groat**. As 2098.		*Extremely rare*
2152	**Halfgroat**. As 2103		*Unique*
2153	**Penny**. As 2110		*Unknown?*

RICHARD III, 1483–5

Richard's brief and violent reign was brought to an end on the field of Bosworth. His coinage follows the pattern of the previous reigns. The smaller denominations of the London mint are all rare.

Mintmarks

38	62	63	105	33

Halved sun and rose, 3 styles (38, 39 and another with the sun more solid, see *North*).
Boar's head, narrow (62) wide (63).
Lis (105, *Durham*)
Rose only (33).

GOLD

2154	**Angel**. Reading ЄDWARD but with R and rose by mast; *mm.* sun and rose.		*Unique*
2155	— Similar, but boar's head *mm.* on *obv*		*Unique*

2156   2158

2156	Reading RICARD or RICAD. Ŗ. R and rose by mast; *mm.* various combinations.	550	1050
2157	— Similar, but R by mast over rose (?)	600	1100
2158	**Half-angel**. Ŗ. R and rose by mast; *mm.* boar's head.		*Extremely rare*

SILVER

2159   2160

		F	VF
		£	£
2159	**Groat**, *London. Mm.* various combinations	200	400
2160	— Pellet below bust	200	400
2161	*York. Mm.* Sun and rose (*obv.*)	350	800
2162	**Halfgroat.** *Mm.* sun and rose on *obv.* only	750	1500
2163	Pellet below bust; *mm.* sun and rose		Unique
2164	— *mm.* boar's head (*obv.*)	850	1750
2165	**Penny.** *London. mm.* boar's head (*obv.*)		Unique

This was the R. Carlyon-Britton specimen. It was stolen from our premises
Feb. 1962.

2168   2169

		F	VF
2166	*York*, Archb. Rotherham. ℞. Quatrefoil in centre; *mm.* sun and rose	300	550
2167	— — T and upright key at neck; *mm.* rose	170	375
2168	— — — *mm.* boar's head	170	375
2169	*Durham*, Bp. Sherwood. S on breast. ℞. D in centre; *mm.* lis	130	325
2170	**Halfpenny**, *London. Mm.* sun and rose	325	600
2171	— *Mm.* boar's head	500	—

Most small denomination coins are short of flan and unevenly struck.

HENRY VII, 1485–1509

For the first four years of his reign Henry's coins differ only in name and mintmark from those of his predecessors, but in 1489 radical changes were made in the coinage. Though the pound sterling had been a denomination of account for centuries, a pound coin had never been minted. Now a magnificent gold pound was issued, and, from the design of the king enthroned in majesty, was called a 'Sovereign'. The reverse had the royal arms set in the centre of a Tudor rose. A few years later the angel was restyled and St. Michael, who is depicted about to thrust Satan into the Pit with a cross-topped lance, is no longer a feathered figure but is clad in armour of Renaissance style. A gold ryal of ten shillings was also minted again for a brief period.

The other major innovation was the introduction of the Shilling in the opening years of the 16th century. It is remarkable for the very fine profile portrait of the King which replaces the representational image of a monarch that had served on the coinage for the past couple of centuries. This new portrait was also used on groats and halfgroats but not on the smaller denominations.

Mintmarks

39	41	40	42	33	11	7a	123

105	76b	31	78	30	91	43	57

85	94	118	21	33	53

1485–7	Halved sun and rose (39)	1495–8	Pansy (30)
	Lis upon sun and rose (41)		Tun (123, *Canterbury*)
	Lis upon half rose (40)		Lis (105, *York*)
	Lis-rose dimidiated (42)	1498–9	Crowned leopard's head (91)
	Rose (33, *York*)		Lis issuant from rose (43)
1487	Lis (105)		Tun (123, *Canterbury*)
	Cross fitchy (11)	1499–1502	Anchor (57)
1487–8	Rose (33)	1502–4	Greyhound's head (85)
	Plain cross (7a, *Durham*)		Lis (105, profile issue only)
1488–9	No marks		Martlet (94, *York*)
1489–93	Cinquefoil (31)	1504–5	Cross-crosslet (21)
	Crozier (76b, *Durham*)	1504–9	Martlet (94, *York* and
1492	Cross fitchy (11, gold only)		*Canterbury*)
1493–5	Escallop (78)		Rose (33, *York* and
	Dragon (118, gold only)		*Canterbury*)
	Lis (105, *Canterbury* and *York*	1505–9	Pheon (53)
	Tun (123, *Canterbury*)		

The coins are placed in groups, as in Brooke, *English Coins*, to correspond to the classification of the groats.

GOLD

		F	VF
		£	£
2173	**Sovereign** (20s; wt. 240 grs.). Group I. Large figure of king sitting on backless throne. ℞. Large shield crowned on large Tudor rose. *mm.* 31. .		*Unique*
2172	— Group II. Somewhat similar but throne has narrow back, lis in background. ℞. Large Tudor rose bearing small shield. *mm.* -/11		*Extremely rare*

Gold

2174

	F £	VF £
2174　**Sovereign** III. King on high-backed very ornamental throne, with greyhound and dragon on side pillars. R. Shield on Tudor rose; *mm.* 118. . .	5550	12,000
2175　IV. Similar but throne with high canopy breaking legend and broad seat, *mm.* 105/118, (also with no *obv.* i.c. *mm.* 105/118, very rare).	5000	11,000
2176　— Narrow throne with a portcullis below the king's feet (like Henry VIII); *mm.* 105/21, 105/53	5250	11,000
2177　**Double-sovereign** and **Treble-sovereign** from same dies as 2176. These *piedforts* were probably intended as presentation pieces *mm.* 105/21, 105/53. .	*Extremely rare*	

2178

2178　**Ryal** (10s.). As illustration: *mm.* -/11.	6500	15,000

		F	VF
2181	2183	£	£

2179 **Angel** (6s. 8d). I. Angel of old type with one foot on dragon. R. PЄR
CRVCЄM. etc., *mm.* 39, 40, (also muled both ways) 235 700
2179A — With Irish title, and legend over angel head. *mm.* 33/– *Extremely rare*
2180 — — Name altered from RICARD? and h on *rev.* from R. *mm.* 41/39,
41/40, 41/– 500 1100
2181 II. As 2179, but *mm.* none. 31/-. 200 500
2181A II/III mule. *mm.* 31/78. . . . . 275 575
2182 As 2181. R. Ihc AVTЄM TRAnSIЄnS etc.; *mm.* none, 31/-. 275 575
2183 III. New dies, angel with both feet on dragon; (large straight lettering) *mm.*
78–85 except 91 (many mules exist) 200 400
2183A — Angel with very small wings. *mm.* 78 *Rare*
2184 — — R. Ihc AVTEM TRAnSIЄnS, etc.; *mm.* 78 . . . . 250 550
2185 IV. Small square lettering; *mm.* 85 (also muled with 2183). 200 475
2186 — Tall thin lettering; *mm.* 21 (also muled with 2185 *obv.*) 200 400
2187 V. Large crook-shaped abbreviation after hЄNRIC; *mm.* 21 and 53
(combinations and mules exist). 200 400
2188 **Half-angel or angelet.** I. *Mm.* 39, 41, (old dies RIII altered) 250 700
2189 III. Angel with both feet on dragon: *mm.* 30, 57/30, –/85 . . . . 165 350
2190 IV. Small square lettering; *mm.* 33 . . . . *Extremely rare*
2191 — *Obv.* as last. R. Tall thin lettering; *mm.* 33/21 . . . . *Extremely rare*
2192 V. As angel; *mm.* pheon. 165 350

SILVER

Facing bust issues. Including "Sovereign" type pennies.

	2194	2195	

2193 **Groat.** I. Open crown; *mm.* 40 (rose on bust), 39–42 and none (combinations) 70 140
2194 — — crosses or saltires by neck, 41, 40, 105–33 and none (combinations) 80 165
2195 IIa. Large bust with out-turned hair, crown with two plain arches; *mm.*
none, 31, 31/-, 31/78. . . . . 30 65
2196 — — similar but crosses by neck; *mm.* none, –/105 . . . . 35 90
2197 — — R. Portcullis over long cross; *mm.* –/lis . . . . *Extremely rare*

		F	VF
		£	£
2236	**Penny.** — — single pillar	25	55
2237	— — — ornate lettering, rosette or no stops, single pillar	25	55
2238	— — — — — two pillars sometimes with crosses between legs of throne.	25	55

          2245   2248   2249

* 2239	**Halfpenny,** *London.* I. Open crown; *mm.* 40, 42	50	120
2240	— — — trefoils at neck; no *mm.*, rose.	50	120
2241	— — — crosses at neck; *mm.* 33	35	90
2242	— II. Double arched crown; *mm.* cinquefoil, none	25	60
2243	— — — saltires at neck; no *mm.*	22	55
2244	— III. Crown with single arch, ornate lettering; no *mm.*	25	60
2245	— V. Much smaller portrait; *mm.* pheon, lis, none	35	75
2246	*Canterbury,* Archb. Morton. I. Open crown. R̃. m in centre	*Extremely rare*	
2247	— — II. Similar, but arched crown, saltires by bust; *mm.* profile eye (82)	*Extremely rare*	
2248	— King and Archb. III. Arched crown; *mm.* 105, none	55	150
2249	*York,* Archb. Savage. Arched crown, key below bust.	55	175
2250	**Farthing,** *London.* hᴇnRIC DI GRA RᴇX (A), arched crown	150	300

*No.s 2239–49 have *mm.* on *obv.* only.

Profile issue

                    2253

2251	**Testoon** (ls.). Type as groat. hᴇnRIC (VS); *mm.* lis	3200	7500
2252	— hᴇnRIC VII; *mm.* lis	3500	9000
2253	— hᴇnRIC SᴇPTIM; *mm.* lis	4500	10,000

          2254   2258

		F	VF
		£	£
2254	**Groat**, *Tentative issue* (contemporary with full-face groats). Double band to crown, hⒺnRIC VII; *mm.* none, 105/-, -/105: 105/85, 105, 85, 21 . . .	110	220
2255	— — — tressure on *obv.*; *mm.* 21	2000	4500
2256	— — hⒺnRIC (VS); *mm.* 105, -/105, 105/85, none	300	700
2257	— — hⒺnRIC SⒺPTIM; *mm.* -/105	2250	5500
2258	*Regular issue.* Triple band to crown; *mm.* 21, 21 and 53/21, 21/21 and 53, 53 (both *mm.*s may occur on some *obv.* and *rev.*).	45	120

2261   2263

2259	**Halfgroat**, *London.* As last; *mm.* 105, 53/105, 105/53, 53	40	90
2260	— — no numeral after King's name, no *mm.*, -/lis	*Extremely rare*	
2261	*Canterbury*, King and Archb. As London, but *mm.* 94, 33, 94/33	30	55
2262	*York*, Archb. Bainbridge. As London, but two keys below shield; *mm.* 94, 33, 33/94	25	55
2262A	— Similar but no keys; *mm.* 94, 33/94	30	60
2263	— — XB beside shield; *mm.* 33/94	*Extremely rare*	

HENRY VIII, 1509–47

Henry VIII is held in ill-regard by numismatists as being the author of the debasement of England's gold and silver coinage; but there were also other important numismatic innovations during his reign. For the first sixteen years of the reign of the coinage closely followed the pattern of the previous issues, even to the extent of retaining the portrait of Henry VII on the larger silver coins. In 1526, in an effort to prevent the drain of gold to continental Europe, the value of English gold was cried up by 10%, the sovereign to 22s. 0d. and the angel to 7s. 4d., and a new coin valued at 4s. 6d.—the Crown of the Rose—was introduced as a competitor to the French *écu au soleil*. The new crown was not a success and within a few months it was replaced by the Crown of the Double Rose valued at 5 shillings but made of gold of only 22 carat fineness, the first time gold had been minted below the standard 23¾ carat. At the same time the sovereign was again revalued to 22s. 6d. and the angel to 7s. 6d., with a new coin, the George Noble, valued at 6s. 8d. (one-third pound).

The royal cyphers on some of the gold crowns and half-crowns combine the initial of Henry with those of his queens: Katherine of Aragon, Anne Boleyn and Jane Seymour. The architect of this coinage reform was the Chancellor, Cardinal Thomas Wolsey, but besides his other changes he had minted at York a groat bearing his initials and cardinal's hat in addition to the other denominations normally authorized for the ecclesiastical mints.

In view of Henry's final break with Rome in 1534, followed by the Act of Supremacy of 1535, it was hardly surprising that the Church's coining privileges in England were finally terminated and the mints of Durham and York (ecclesiastical) were closed.

In 1544, to help finance the king's inordinate extravagances, it was decided to extend the process of debasement. Initially all the "fine" gold coins were reduced in quality to 23 carat, then in the following year gold was issued of 22 carat and later of 20 carat fineness. Concurrently the silver coins were reduced from the sterling standard fineness of 11 oz. 2 dwt. (i.e. .925 silver) to 9 oz. (.750), and later to 6 oz. (.500) and eventually 4 oz. (.333) fineness. Henry's nickname of "Old Coppernose" was earned not through his own personal characteristics but by his last poor 'silver' coins which soon displayed their two-thirds copper content once they became slightly worn.

Mintmarks

53	69	70	108	33	94	73	11

105	22	23	30	78	15	24	110

1509–26	Pheon (53)		Lis (105, *Canterbury, Durham*)
	Castle (69)		
	Castle with H (70, gold)	1509–14	Martlet (94, *York*)
	Portcullis crowned (108)	1509–23	Radiant star (22, *Durham & York*)
	Rose (33, *Canterbury*)	1513–18	Crowned T
	Martlet (94, *Canterbury*)	1514–26	Star (23, *York & Durham*)
	Pomegranate (73, but		Pansy (30, *York*)
	broader, *Cant.*)		Escallop (78, *York*)
	Cross fitchée (11, *Cant.*)		Voided cross (15, *York*)
		1523–26	Spur rowel (24, *Durham*)

52	72a	44	8	65a	114	121	90

36	106	56	S	Є	116

1526–44	Rose (33)
	Lis (105)
	Sunburst (110)
	Arrow (52)
	Pheon (53)
	Lis (106)
	Star (23, *Durham*)
1526–9	Crescent (72a, *Durham*)
	Trefoil (44 variety, *Durham*)
	Flower of eight petals and circle centre (*Durham*)
1526–30	Cross (7a, sometimes slightly voided, *York*)
	Acorn (65a, *York*)

1526–32	Cross patonce (8, *Cant.*)
	T (114, *Canterbury*)
	Uncertain mark (121, *Canterbury*)
1529–44	Radiant star (22, *Durham*)
1530–44	Key (90, *York*)
1533–44	Catherine wheel (36, *Canterbury*)
1544–7	Lis (105 and 106)
	Pellet in annulet (56)
	S
	Є or E
1546–7	WS monogram (116, *Bristol*)

GOLD

First coinage, 1509–26

		F	VF
		£	£
2264	**Sovereign** (20s.). Similar to last sov. of Hen. VII; *mm.* 108.	3000	7000
2264A	**Ryal** (10s.) King in ship holding sword and shield. ℞. Similar to 1950, *mm.* -/108		*Unique*
2265	**Angel** (6s. 8d.). As Hen. VIII, but hЄnRIC? VIII DI GRA RЄX, etc.; *mm.* 53, 69, 70, 70/69, 108, ℞. May omit h and rose, or rose only; *mm.* 69, 108.	200	400
2266	**Half-angel**. Similar (sometimes without VIII), *mm.* 69, 70, 108/33, 108	210	400

Second coinage, 1526–44

2267

2267	**Sovereign** (22s. 6d.). As 2264, ℞. single or double tressure *mm.* 110, 105, 105/52	2500	5500
2268	**Angel** (7s. 6d.). As 2265, hЄnRIC VIII D(I) G(RA) R(EX) etc.; *mm.* 110, 105	250	600
2269	**Half-angel**. Similar; *mm.* 105	400	900

Second coinage gold

2270   2272

		F	VF
		£	£
2270	**George-noble** (6s. 8d.). As illustration; *mm.* rose	2250	5000
2270A	— Similar, but more modern ship with three masts, without initials hR. R.		
	St. George brandishing sword behind head.		*Unique*
2271	**Half-George-noble**. Similar to 2270.		*Unique*
2272	**Crown of the rose** (4s. 6d., 23 ct). As illustration; *mm.* rose	*Extremely rare*	

2279   2285

2279   2285

2273	**Crown of the double-rose** (5s., 22 ct). Double-rose crowned, hK (Henry and		
	Katherine of Aragon) both crowned in field. R. Shield crowned; *mm.* rose.	165	350
2274	— hK both sides; *mm.* rose/lis, lis, arrow	180	350
2275*	— hK / hA or hA / hK; *mm.* arrow	200	550
2276*	— hR / hK or hI / hR; *mm.* arrow	*Extremely rare*	
2277	— hA (Anne Boleyn); *mm.* arrow	225	575
2278	— hA / hR; *mm.* arrow	—	2250
2279	— hI (Jane Seymour); *mm.* arrow	200	450
2280*	— hK / hI; *mm.* arrow	225	650
2281	— hR / hI; *mm.* arrow	225	675
2282	— hR (Rex); *mm.* arrow	180	375
2283	— — but with hIBERIE REX; *mm.* pheon.	400	1000
2284	**Halfcrown**. Similar but king's name henric 8 on *rev.*, no initials; *mm.* rose	155	375
2285	— hK uncrowned on *obv.*; *mm.* rose	140	350
2286	— hK uncrowned both sides; *mm.* rose/lis, lis, arrow	150	360
2287	— hI uncrowned both sides; *mm.* arrow	210	450
2288	— hR uncrowned both sides; hIBREX; *mm.* pheon.	325	750

*The hK initials may on later coins refer to Katherine Howard (Henry's fifth wife).

Third coinage, 1544–7

2291

		F £	VF £
2289	**Sovereign**, I (20s., Wt. 200 grs., 23 ct.). As illustration but king with larger face and larger design; *mm.* lis	4000	9500
2290	II (20s., wt. 200 or 192 grs., 23, 22 or 20 ct.). *Tower.* As illustration; *mm.* lis, pellet in annulet/lis	1250	3050
2291	— *Southwark.* Similar; *mm.* S, Є/S	1200	2950
2292	— — Similar but Є below shield; *mm.* S/Є	*Extremely rare*	
2293	— *Bristol.* As London but *mm.* WS/-	2750	5000
2294	**Half-sovereign** (wt. 100 or 96 grs.), *Tower.* As illus.; *mm.* lis, pellet in annulet	200	525
2295	— Similar, but with annulet on inner circle (either or both sides)	225	600
2296	*Southwark. Mm.* S.	225	600
2297	— Є below shield; *mm.* S, Є, S/Є, Є/S, (known without sceptre; *mm.* S) .	200	550
2298	*Bristol.* Lombardic lettering; *mm.* WS/-	350	900

2303   2304

2299	**Angel** (8s., 23 ct). Annulet by angel's head and on ship, hЄnRIC' 8; *mm.* lis.	185	400
2300	— Similar, but annulet one side only or none	200	425
2301	**Half-angel.** Annulet on ship; *mm.* lis	175	425
2302	— No annulet on ship; *mm.* lis	200	475
2303	— Three annulets on ship; *mm.* lis	250	500
2304	**Quarter-angel** Angel wears armour; *mm.* lis	175	400
2304A	— Angel wears tunic; *mm.* lis.	200	450

Third coinage gold

		F	VF
		£	£
2305	**Crown**, *London*. Similar to 2283, but henRIC' 8; Lombardic lettering; *mm.* 56	160	350
2306	— without RVTILAnS; *mm.* 56	170	375
2307	— — — with annulet on inner circle	180	400
2307A	— King's name omitted. DEI GRA both sides, *mm.* 56	*Extremely rare*	
2308	— *Southwark*. As 2306; *mm.* S, Є, E/S, Є/-, E/Є	180	400
2309	*Bristol*. henRIC VIII. ROSA etc. ℞. D G, etc.; *mm.*-/WS	165	375
2310	— Similar but henRIC(VS) 8 ℞. D(EI) G(RA); *mm.* -/WS, WS	165	375
2311	**Halfcrown**, *London*. Similar to 2288; *mm.* 56, -/56	125	300
2312	— — with annulet on inner circle *mm.* 56	135	310
2313	*Southwark*. As 2311; *mm.* S	160	375
2314	— *O.* henRIC 8 ROSA SINE SPIn. ℞. DEI GRA, etc.; *mm.* Є	175	400
2315	*Bristol. O.* RVTILAnS, etc. ℞. henRIC 8; *mm.* WS/-	250	450

For other gold coins in Henry's name see page 152.

SILVER

First coinage, 1509–26

2316   2327

2316	**Groat**. Portrait of Hen. VII. *London mm.* 53, 69, 108	45	125
2317	— *Tournai; mm.* crowned T. ℞. CIVITAS TORnACEn *	200	600
2318	**Halfgroat**. Portrait of Hen. VII. *London; mm.* 108, 108/-	80	175
2319	— *Canterbury*, Archb. Warham. POSVI *rev.; mm.* rose	70	180
2320	— — — WA above shield; *mm.* martlet	30	100
2321	— — — WA beside shield; *mm.* cross fitchée	40	120
2322	— — CIVITAS CAnTOR *rev.*, similar; *mm.* 73, 105, 11/105	30	80
2323	— *York*, POSVI *rev.*, Archb. Bainbridge (1508–14). Keys below shield; *mm.* martlet	30	90
2324	— — — XB beside shield no keys; *mm.* martlet	45	125
2325	— — — Archb. Wolsey (1514–30). Keys and cardinal's hat below shield; *mm.* 94, 22	70	170
2326	— — CIVITAS ЄBORACI *rev.* Similar; *mm.* 22, 23, 30, 78, 15, 15/78	25	60
2327	— — As last with TW beside shield; *mm.* voided cross	27	70
2327A	— *Tournai*. As 2317	*Unique*	

*Other non-portrait groats and half-groats exist of this mint, captured during an invasion of France in 1513. (Restored to France in 1518.)

2332   2335   2336

	F	VF
	£	£
2328 **Penny**, "Sovereign" type, *London; mm.* 69, 108/-	17	55
2329 — *Canterbury.* WA above shield; *mm.* martlet	*Extremely rare*	
2330 — — — WA beside shield; *mm.* 73/-.	30	70
2331 — *Durham,* Bp. Ruthall (1509–23). TD above shield; *mm.* lis	17	45
2332 — — — TD beside shield; *mm.* lis, radiant star.	25	55
2333 — — Bp. Wolsey (1523–9). DW beside shield, cardinal's hat below; spur rowel	80	200
2334 **Halfpenny**. Facing bust, hЄnRIC DI GRA RЄX (AGL). *London; mm.* 69, 108/-	35	75
2335 — *Canterbury.* WA beside bust; *mm.* 73/-, 11	45	120
2336 **Farthing**. *O. Mm.* 108/-, hЄnRIC DI GRA RЄX, a portcullis as type. R̸. CIVITAS LOnDON, rose in centre of long cross	900	1500

Second coinage, 1526–44

2337   2337D   2337E

2337 **Groat**. His own young portrait. *London;* bust r., with heavy jowls; mainly *mm.* rose, Roman letters, both sides, roses in cross ends	85	260
2337A *Obv.* as last. R̸. Lombardic letters, saltires in cross ends; *mm.* rose	50	150
2337B Bust as 2337 but Lombardic letters. R̸. Lombardic letters but roses in cross ends; *mm.* rose.	45	90
2337C *Obv.* as last. R̸. As 2337A; *mm.* rose	45	90
2337D Second bust, Greek profile, longer hair, less heavy jowls; *mm.* rose	30	60
2337E Third bust, stereotyped as ill. 2337E; *mm.* 33–53 (muling occurs)	25	50
2338 — — with Irish title HIB; larger flan, saltires in cross ends; *mm.* 53, 105 (also muled), 53/105, 105/53, 105.	300	750
2339 — *York,* Archb. Wolsey. TW beside shield, cardinal's hat below; *mm.* voided cross, acorn, muled (both ways)	50	130
2340 — — — omits TW; *mm.* voided cross	175	500

Second coinage silver

2342   2343   2348

	F	VF
	£	£

2341 **Halfgroat.** Type as groats, Lombardic lettering both sides. *London; mm.* rose to arrow (*obv.*) or none (sometimes muled) . . . . | 35 | 80
2341A *Obv.* Similar to 2337, *mm.* rose, ℞ Lombardic letters. . . . . | | Rare
2342 — — with Irish title HIB; *mm.* pheon . . . . | 350 | 800
2343 — *Canterbury*, Archb. Warham (—1532). ℞. CIVITAS CAnTOR, WA beside shield; *mm.* 121, 121/-, 121/33, 8, 8/T, T . . . . | 15 | 40
2344 — — — nothing by shield; *mm.* 121/- . . . . | 30 | 70
2345 — — Archb. Cranmer (1533—). TC beside shield; *mm.* 36, 36/-. . . . . . | 20 | 60
2346 — *York*, Archb. Wolsey (—1530). ℞. CIVITAS ЄBORACI, TW beside shield, hat below; *mm.* 15/-, 15 . . . . | 20 | 60
2347 — — Sede Vacante (1530/1). No marks; *mm.* key . . . . | 30 | 65
2348 — — Archb. Lee (1531–44). EL or LE beside shield; *mm.* key . . . . . . | 20 | 45

2350   2354   2359

2349 **Penny.** "Sovereign" type h . D . G . ROSA SInЄ SPInA, *London; mm.* rose to arrow (*obv.* only). . . . . | 20 | 60
2350 — *Canterbury*. WA beside shield; *mm.* 121/-, 8/-, T/-. . . . . | 60 | 150
2351 — — TC beside shield; *mm.* 36/-. . . . . | 50 | 135
2352 — *Durham*, Bp. Wolsey (—1529). TW beside shield, hat below; *mm.* 23, 23/44, 23/-, 72a/-, 44, 44/-, 72a/44 (muled with 2333 *obv.*, *mm.* 24/44) . . | 25 | 70
2353 — — Sede Vacante (1529–30). No marks; *mm.* 23/-, 22/- . . . . | 25 | 75
2354 — — Bp. Tunstall (1530—). CD beside shield; *mm.* 23, 23/-, 22/-, 22. . . | 20 | 60
2355 — *York*. EL beside shield; *mm.* key/- . . . . | 65 | 150
2356 **Halfpenny.** Facing bust, h D G ROSA SIЄ SPIA. *London; mm.* rose to arrow (*obv.* only) . . . . | 30 | 65
2357 — *Canterbury*. WA beside bust; *mm.* 8/-, T/-. . . . . | 28 | 60
2358 — — TC beside bust; *mm.* 36/-. . . . . | 45 | 100
2359 — *York*. TW beside bust; *mm.* 15/-, acorn/-. . . . . | 55 | 125
2360 — — Sede Vacante. Key below bust; *mm.* 15/- . . . . | 50 | 110
2361 — — EL or LE beside bust; *mm.* key/- . . . . | 45 | 90
2362 **Farthing.** *O.* RVTILANS ROSA, portcullis; *mm.* 33/-, 105/-, 110/-. ℞. DEO GRACIAS...., long cross with pellet in each angle. . . . . | 1000 | 1600
2363 — — *mm.* arrow/- ℞. DEO GRACIAS, rose on long cross . . . . | Extremely rare
2363A — *Canterbury*. *O.* Similar. ℞. Similar. *mm.* 36/- . . . . | Extremely rare

Third coinage, 1544–7 (Silver progressively debased. 9oz (.750), 6oz (.500) 4oz (.333).)

2384

2364

		Fair £	Fine £	VF £
2364	**Testoon.** *Tower.* hℭnRIC'. VIII, etc. ℞. Crowned rose between h and R.POSVI, etc.; *mm.* lis, lis, lis and 56, lis/two lis	90	275	
2365	— hℭnRIC 8, *mm.* 105 and 56, 105/56, 105 and 56/56, 56 . . .	80	250	750
2366	— — annulet on inner circle of rev. or both sides; *mm.* pellet in annulet	95	300	
2367	*Southwark.* As 2365. ℞. CIVITAS LOnDOn; *mm.* S, ℭ, S/ℭ, ℭ/S	90	250	
2368	*Bristol.* Mm. -/WS monogram. (Tower or local dies.).	100	350	

Bust 1	Bust 2	Bust 3

		F £	VF £
2369	**Groat.** *Tower.* As ill. above, busts 1, 2, 3; *mm.* lis/-, lis	25	135
2369A	Bust I, ℞. As second coinage; i.e. saltires in forks; *mm.* lis	50	175
2370	Bust 2 or 3 annulet on inner circle, both sides or rev. only.	35	165
2371	*Southwark.* As 2367, busts 1, 2, 3, 4; no *mm.* or lis/-; S or S and ℭ or ℭ in forks	30	150
2372	*Bristol. Mm.* -/WS monogram, Bristol bust and Tower bust 2 or 3	35	160
2373	*Canterbury.* Busts 1, 2, (2 var); no *mm.* 105/-	35	140
2374	*York.* Busts 1 var., 2, 3, no *mm.*	35	140
2375	**Halfgroat.** *Tower.* As 2365, bust 1; *mm.* lis, none	55	150
2376	*Southwark.* As 2367, bust 1; no *mm.*; S or ℭ and S in forks	*Extremely rare*	
2377	*Bristol. Mm.* -/WS monogram	35	135
2378	*Canterbury.* Bust 1; no *mm.*	25	110
2379	*York.* Bust 1; no *mm.*	35	135
2380	**Penny.** *Tower.* Facing bust; no *mm.* or lis/-	30	110
2381	*Southwark.* Facing bust; *mm.* S/-, ℭ/-, -/ℭ	*Extremely rare*	
2382	*Bristol.* Facing bust; no *mm.* (Tower dies or local but truncated at neck).	35	120
2383	*Canterbury.* Facing bust; no *mm.*.	35	125
2384	*York.* Facing bust; no *mm.*	35	120
2385	**Halfpenny.** *Tower.* Facing bust; no *mm.* or lis/-, pellet in annulet in *rev.* centre.	40	125
2386	*Bristol.* Facing bust; no *mm.*	70	185
2387	*Canterbury.* Facing bust; no *mm.*, (some read H 8).	40	135
2388	*York.* Facing bust; no *mm.*	40	135

HENRY VIII POSTHUMOUS COINAGE, 1547–51

These coins were struck during the reign of Edward VI but bear the name and portrait of Henry VIII, except in the case of the half-sovereigns which bear the youthful head of Edward.

Mintmarks

◎	✠	⚓	**K**	**E**	**W**
56	105	52	K	E	116

(	**Ⱦ**	✿	ᘓ	**t**	🕊
66	115	33	122	t	94

1547	Annulet and pellet (56)	1549	TC monogram (115, *Bristol*)
1547–8	Lis (105)		Lis (105, *Canterbury*)
1547–9	Arrow (52)		Rose (33, *Canterbury*)
	K		Grapple (122)
	Roman E (*Southwark*)	1549/50	t (*Canterbury*)
	WS monogram (116, *Bristol*)	1550/1	Martlet (94)
1548–9	Bow (66, *Durham House*)		

GOLD

		F £	VF £
2389	**Sovereign** (20 ct), *London*. As no. 2290, but Roman lettering; *mm.* lis. . .	1550	3750
2390	— *Bristol*. Similar but *mm.* WS	1700	4250

2391A   2395

2391	**Half-sovereign.** As 2294, but with youthful portrait with sceptre. *Tower;* *mm.* 52, 105, 94 (various combinations)	250	600
2391A	— Similar but no sceptre; *mm.* 52/56	300	650
2392	— — — K below shield; *mm.* -/K, none,. E/-	275	625
2393	— — — grapple below shield; *mm.* 122, none, 122/-, -/122. ·	300	650
2394	— *Southwark*. *Mm*. E, E/-, -/E, Є/E. Usually Є or E (sometimes retrograde) below shield (sceptre omitted; *mm.* -/E)	250	600
2394A	— — — Ɽ. As 2296; *mm*.-/S	250	650
2395	**Crown.** Similar to 2305. *London; mm.* 52, 52/-, -/K, 122, 94, K	350	750

		F	VF
		£	£
2396	— Similar but transposed legends without numeral; *mm.* -/arrow	375	775
2396A	— As 2395, but omitting RVTILANS; *mm.* arrow	*Extremely rare*	
2396B	Similar, but RVTILANS both sides; *mm.* arrow	*Extremely rare*	
2397	— *Southwark*. Similar to 2396; *mm.* E	*Extremely rare*	
2398	— — King's name on *obv.*; *mm.* E/-, E, -/E	400	
2399	**Halfcrown**. Similar to 2311. *London; mm.* 52, K/-, 122/-, 94, -/52	225	550
2399A	As last but E over h on *rev.*, *mm.* 56/52	*Extremely rare*	
2399B	As 2399 but RUTILANS etc. on both sides, *mm.* arrow	*Extremely rare*	
2400	— *Southwark. Mm.* E, E/-, -/E	225	550

SILVER

AR (4oz .333)

		Fair	Fine
2401	**Testoon**. *Tower*. As 2365 with lozenge stops one side; -/56, 56	75	275
2402	*Southwark*. As 2367; *mm.* S/E	115	375

Some of the Bristol testoons, groats and halfgroats with **WS** *monogram were struck after the death of Henry VIII but cannot be distinguished from those struck during his reign.*

Bust 4   Bust 5   Bust 6

		F	VF
		£	£
2403	**Groat**. *Tower*. Busts 4, 5, 6 (and, rarely, 2). ℞. POSVI, etc.; *mm.* 105–94 and none (frequently muled)	35	150
2404	*Southwark*. Busts 4, 5, 6. ℞. CIVITAS LONDON; no *mm.* -/E; lis/-, -/lis, K/E; roses or crescents or S and Є in forks	40	160
2405	*Durham House*. Bust 6. ℞. REDDE CVIQUE QVOD SVVM EST; *mm.* bow	110	300
2406	*Bristol. Mm.* WS on *rev.* Bristol busts A and B, Tower bust 2 and 3	50	185
2407	— — *Mm.* TC on *rev.* Similar, Bristol bust B.	75	300
2408	*Canterbury*. Busts 5, 6; no *mm.* or rose/-	35	140
2409	*York*. Busts 4, 5, 6; no *mm.* or lis/-, -/lis	35	150
2410	**Halfgroat**. Bust 1. *Tower*. POSVI, etc.; *mm.* 52, 52/-, 52/K, -/K, 52/122, 122, -/122	25	110
2411	— *Southwark*. CIVITAS LONDON; *mm.* E, -/E, none, 52/E, K/E	23	100
2412	— *Durham House*. ℞. REDD, etc.; *mm.* bow, -/bow	135	300
2413	— *Bristol. Mm.* WS on *rev.*	30	120
2414	— — *mm.* TC on *rev.*	40	135
2415	— *Canterbury*. No *mm.* or t/-, -/t	23	100
2416	— *York*. No *mm.*, bust 1 and three quarter facing	25	110

2422   2418   2427

		F £	VF £
2417	**Penny**. *Tower*. CIVITAS LONDON. Facing bust; *mm*. 52/-, -/52, -/K, 122/-, -/122, none	25	100
2418	— — three-quarter bust; no *mm*.	25	100
2419	*Southwark*. As 2417; *mm*. E, -/E	*Extremely rare*	
2420	*Durham House*. As groat but shorter legend; *mm*. -/bow	135	400
2421	*Bristol*. Facing busts, as 2382, no *mm*.	30	120
2422	*Canterbury*. Similar	25	100
2423	— three-quarters facing bust; no *mm*.	25	100
2424	*York*. Facing bust; no *mm*.	25	100
2425	— three-quarters facing bust; no *mm*.	30	120
2426	**Halfpenny**. *Tower*. 52?, none	42	150
2427	*Canterbury*. No *mm*., sometimes reads H8.	32	110
2428	*York*. No *mm*.	45	150

EDWARD VI, 1547–53

Coinage in his own name

While base coins continued to be issued bearing the name of Henry VIII, plans were made early in Edward's reign to reform the coinage. As a first step, in 1549, the standard of the gold was raised to 22 carat and "silver" was increased to 50% silver content. Baser shillings were issued in 1550, but finally, in 1551, it was decided to resume the coinage of some "fine" gold and a new silver coinage was ordered of 11 oz. 1 dwt. Fineness, i.e. almost up to the ancient standard. At the same time four new denominations were added to the coinage—the silver crown, halfcrown, sixpence and threepence. Pennies continued to be struck in base silver.

The first dates on English coinage appear in Roman numerals during this reign; MDXLVIII = 1548; MDXLIX = 1549; MDL = 1550; MDLI = 1551.

66	52	35	115	E	53	122
t	T	111	Y	126	94	91A
92	105	y	97	123	78	26

Mintmarks

1548–9	Bow (66, *Durham House*)	1549–50	6 (126 gold only)
1549	Arrow (52)	1550	Martlet (94)
	Grapple (122)	1550	Leopard's head (91A)
	Rose (35, *Canterbury*)	1550–1	Lion (92)
	TC monogram (115, *Bristol*)		Lis (105)
	Roman E (*Southwark*)		Rose (33)
	Pheon (53)	1551	Yor y (117)
	t or T (*Canterbury*)		Ostrich's head (97, gold only)
1549–50	Swan (111)	1551–3	Tun (123)
	Roman Y (*Southwark*)		Escallop (78)
		1552–3	Pierced mullet (26, *York*)

GOLD

First period, Apr. 1547–Jan. 1549

2429   2431

		F	VF
First period gold, *continued*		£	£

2429 **Half-sovereign** (20 ct). As 2391, but reading EDWARD 6. *Tower; mm.*
    arrow.   400   850

2430   — *Southwark* (Sometimes with E or Є below shield); *mm.* E   350   750

2431 **Crown.** RVTILANS, etc., crowned rose between E R both crowned. ℞.
    EDWARD 6, etc., crowned shield between ER both crowned; *mm.* arrow,
    E over arrow/-. . . . .   *Extremely rare*

2431A — *Obv.* as last. ℞. As 2305, *mm.* 52/56 . . . .   *Extremely rare*

2432 **Halfcrown.** Similar to 2431, but initials not crowned; *mm.* arrow . . . . .   *Extremely rare*

Second period, Jan. 1549–Apr. 1550

2433

2433 **Sovereign** (22 ct). As illustration; *mm.* arrow, Y, -/52.   1600   3400

2435   2438

2434 **Half-sovereign.** Uncrowned bust. *London.* TIMOR etc., MDXLIX on *obv.*;
    mm. arrow . . . .   *Extremely rare*

2435   — — SCVTVM, etc., as illustration; *mm.* arrow, **6**, Y   400   1000

2436   — *Durham House.* Uncrowned, ½ length bust with MDXLVIII at end of
    obv. legend; *mm.* bow; SCVTVM etc.   *Extremely rare*

2437   — Normal, uncrowned bust. LVCERNA, etc., on *obv.*; *mm.* bow. . . . .   *Extremely rare*

2438 **Crowned bust.** *London.* EDWARD VI, etc. ℞. SCVTVM, etc.; *mm.* 52,
    122, 111/52, 111, Y, 94   375   850

2439   — *Durham House.* Crowned, half-length bust; *mm.* bow . . . .   *Unique*

2440   — — King's name on *obv.* and *rev.*; *mm.* bow (mule of 2439/37)   4000   7500

2441   2444

* *Small denominations often occur creased or straightened.*

		F	VF
		£	£
2441	**Crown**. Uncrowned bust, as 2435; *mm*. **6**, Y, 52/-, Y/-	700	1300
2442	Crowned bust, as 2438; *mm*. 52, 122, 111, Y (usually *obv*. only).	475	1000
2443	**Halfcrown**. Uncrowned bust; ℞. As 2441, *mm*. arrow, Y, Y/-, 52/-	550	1300
2444	Crowned bust, as illus. above; *mm*. 52, 52/111, 111, 122, Y, Y/-.	450	1100
2445	Similar, but king's name on *rev*., *mm*. 52, 122.	550	1200

Third period, 1550–3

2446	**"Fine" sovereign** (= 30s.). King on throne; *mm*. 97, 123	8000	20,000
2447	**Double sovereign**. From the same dies, *mm*. 97	*Extremely rare*	

2448   2451

2448	**Angel** (= 10s.). As illustration; *mm*. 97, 123	4000	8000
2449	**Half-angel**. Similar, *mm*. 97.		*Unique*
2450	**Sovereign**. (= 20s.). Half-length figure of king r., crowned and holding		
	sword and orb. ℞. Crowned shield with supporters; *mm*. y, tun	700	1650
2451	**Half-sovereign**. As illustration above; *mm*. y, tun	500	950
2452	**Crown**. Similar, but *rev*. SCVTVM etc., *mm*. y, tun	800	2000
2453	**Halfcrown**. Similar, *mm*. tun, y.	800	2000

SILVER

First period, Apr. 1547–Jan. 1549

2459   2460

		F	VF
		£	£
2454	**Groat**. Cr. bust r. *Tower*. ℞. Shield over cross, POSVI, etc.; *mm*. arrow .	225	650
2455	— As last, but EDOARD 6, *mm*. arrow.	*Extremely rare*	
2456	— *Southwark*. *Obv*. as 2454. ℞. CIVITAS LONDON; *mm*.-/E or none, S in forks	300	700
2457	**Halfgroat**. *Tower*. *Obv*. as 2454; *mm*. arrow.	300	700
2458	*Southwark*. As 2456; *mm*. arrow, E	350	800
2459	*Canterbury*. Similar. No *mm*., also reads EDOARD (as ill.)	175	450
2460	**Penny**. *Tower*. As halfgroat, but E.D.G. etc. ℞. CIVITAS LONDON; *mm*. arrow.	225	700
2461	— *Southwark*. As last, but *mm*. -/E.	225	700
2462	*Bristol*. Similar, but reads ED6DG or E6DG no *mm*.	200	575
2463	**Halfpenny**. *Tower*. *O*. As 2460, *mm*. E (?). ℞. Cross and pellets	*Extremely rare*	
2464	— *Bristol*. Similar, no *mm*. but reads E6DG or EDG	275	600

Second period, Jan. 1549–Apr. 1550

At all mints except Bristol, the earliest shillings of 1549 were issued at only 60 grains wt., but of 8 oz. standard. This weight and size were soon increased to 80 grains wt., but the fineness was reduced to 6 oz. so the silver content remained the same.

2472   *Fair*   *Fine*

		Fair	Fine
		£	£
2465	**Shilling**. *Tower*. Broad bust with large crown. *Obv*. TIMOR ·etc. MDXLIX. ℞. Small, oval garnished shield (dividing ER). EDWARD VI etc., *mm*. 52, -/52, no *mm*.	25	60
2465A	*Southwark*. As last, *mm*. Y, EY/Y	30	75
2465B	*Canterbury*. As last, *mm*. -/rose.		*Rare*
2466	*Tower*. Tall, narrow bust with small crown. *Obv*. EDWARD VI etc. MDXLIX or MDL. ℞. As 2465 but TIMOR etc., *mm*. 52–91a (frequently muled)	25	60
2466A	— *Obv*. as last, MDXLIX. ℞. Heavily garnished shield, Durham House style. *mm*. 122		*Rare*

The prices and rarity of nos. 2465–2473A are very much estimates, as they have not previously been divided thus.

		Fair	Fine
2466B	*Southwark.* As 2466, *mm.* Y, Y/swan	30	75
2466C	— — — ℞. as 2466A. *mm.* Y	30	75
2467	*Bristol. Obv.* similar to 2466. ℞. Shield with heavy curved garniture or as 2466, *mm.* TC/rose TC, rose TC		Rare
2468	*Canterbury.* As 2466, *mm.* T, t, t/T.	40	110
2469	*Durham House.* Bust with elaborate tunic and collar TIMOR etc. MDXLIX. ℞. Oval shield, very heavily garnished in different style.	Fine	VF
	EDWARD VI etc., *mm.* bow	150	500
2470	— Bust as last. INIMICOS etc., no date. ℞. As last	125	400
2471	— — As last, but legends transposed	100	350
2472	— Bust similar to 2466. EDWARD VI etc. ℞. INIMICOS etc.	125	400
2472A	As last but legends transposed	125	400
2472B	*Tower.* Elegant bust with extremely thin neck. ℞. As 2466, *mm.* 94	90	200
2472C	*Southwark.* As last, *mm.* Y	90	200

For coins of Edward VI countermarked, see p. 154.

Third period, 1550–3
Very base issue 1550–1 (.250 fine)

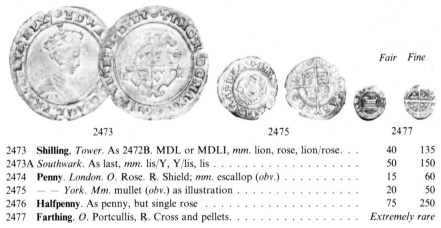

		Fair	Fine

| | 2473 | 2475 | 2477 |

2473	**Shilling,** *Tower.* As 2472B. MDL or MDLI, *mm.* lion, rose, lion/rose. . .	40	135
2473A	*Southwark.* As last, *mm.* lis/Y, Y/lis, lis	50	150
2474	**Penny.** *London. O.* Rose. ℞. Shield; *mm.* escallop (*obv.*)	15	60
2475	— — *York. Mm.* mullet (*obv.*) as illustration	20	50
2476	**Halfpenny.** As penny, but single rose	75	250
2477	**Farthing.** *O.* Portcullis, ℞. Cross and pellets	*Extremely rare*	

The prices and rarity of nos. 2465–2473A are very much estimates, as they have not previously been divided thus.

Fine silver issue, (1551–3)

2478

2479

	F £	VF £
2478 **Crown**. King on horseback with date below horse. ℞. Shield on cross; *mm.* y. 1551; tun, 1551–3 (1553, wire line inner circle may be missing)	100	400
2479 **Halfcrown**. Walking horse with plume; *mm.* y, 1551	135	350
2480 Galloping horse without plume; *mm.* tun, 1551–3	175	450
2481 Large walking horse without plume; *mm.* tun, 1553	375	1000
2482 **Shilling**. Facing bust, rose l., value XII r. *mm.* y, tun (bust varieties) . . .	35	100

2482   2483   2486

2483 **Sixpence**. *London*. Similar, as illustration; *mm.* y/-, -/y, y, tun (bust		
varieties)	40	125
2484 *York*. As last, but CIVITAS ЄBORACI; *mm.* mullet.	165	400
2485 **Threepence**. *London*. As sixpence, but III; *mm.* tun	110	350
2486 *York*. As 2484, but III by bust	175	550
2487 **Penny**. "Sovereign" type; *mm.* tun	*Extremely rare*	

MARY, 1553–4

All Mary's gold coin was struck in 23 carat 3½ grain gold, the "crown" gold denominations being temporarily discontinued. The mintmarks appear at the end of the first or second word of the legends.

Pomegranate Half-rose (or half-rose and castle)

GOLD

2488

		F	VF
		£	£
2488	**"Fine" Sovereign** (= 30s.). Queen enthroned. ℞. Shield on rose, MDLIII, MDLIIII and undated, *mm.* pomegranate, half-rose (or mule)	1400	2750
2489	**Ryal** (= 15s.). As illus, MDLIII. ℞. As 1950 but ADNO etc. *mm.* pomegranate/-	*Extremely rare*	
	A very fine specimen sold at auction in November 1985 for £13,000.		
2490	**Angel** (= 10s.). Usual type; *mm.* pomegranate, half-rose, none? (Known with rose and M transposed)	450	1000
2491	**Half-angel.** Similar; *mm.* pomegranate, pomegranate/-	2300	6000

2489   2492

2492	**Groat.** Crowned bust l. ℞. VERITAS, etc.; *mm.* pomegranate, pomegranate/-	45	120
2493	**Halfgroat.** Similar	300	750
2494	**Penny.** Similar, but M . D. G. ROSA, etc.	400	900
2495	— As last. ℞. CIVITAS LONDON; no *mm.*	250	650
2495A	— Base penny. Similar to 2474 but M.D.G. etc.	*All late 19th cent. copies*	

PHILIP AND MARY, 1554–8

The groats and smaller silver coins of this period have Mary's portrait only, but the shillings and sixpences show the bust of the queen's husband, Philip of Spain.

Mintmarks

Lis (105)   🌸   Half-rose and castle   ⛫

GOLD

2496

		F £	VF £
2496	**Angel**. As illustration; wire line inner circles, calm sea, *mm.* lis	1200	2500
2496A	— — New-style, large wings, wire line i.c.	1400	2700
2496B	— — As above but beaded i.c.	1400	2700
2497	**Half-angel**. Similar to 2496	*Extremely rare*	

SILVER

2505   2510

2498	**Shilling**. Busts face-to-face, full titles, undated, no *mm.*	90	270
2499	— — — also without mark of value	165	450
2500	— — 1554	80	250
2501	— English titles only 1554, 1555	80	275
2502	— — without mark of value, 1554, 1555 (rare)	175	550
		Fair	
2503	— — date below bust, 1554, 1555	£125	
2504	— — As last, but without ANG., 1555	£150	
2505	**Sixpence**. Similar. Full titles, 1554	100	325
2506	— English titles only, 1555 (no *mm.*, rare), 1557 (*mm.* lis, 1557 only)	90	325
2506A	— As last but heavy beaded i.c. on obv. 1555. (? Irish 4d. obv. mule)	*Extremely rare*	
2507	— — date below bust, 1554, 1557	*Fair* £125	
2508	**Groat**. Crowned bust of Mary l. R. POSIMVS etc.; *mm.* lis	45	120
2509	**Halfgroat**. Similar, but POSVIM, *mm.* lis	350	900
2510	**Penny**. Similar to 2495, but P . Z . M . etc.; *mm.* lis	300	750
2510A	**Base penny**. Similar to 2495A, but P . Z . M . etc.; *mm.* halved rose and H (or castle)/-	40	125

Similar pence of the York mint were made for currency in Ireland (see Coins and Tokens of Ireland, no. 6502).

ELIZABETH I, 1558–1603

Elizabeth's coinage is particularly interesting on account of the large number of different denominations issued. 'Crown' gold coins were again issued as well as the 'fine' gold denominations. In 1559 the base shillings of Edward VI's second and third coinages were called in and countermarked for recirculation at reduced values. The normal silver coinage was initially struck at .916 fineness as in the previous reign but between 1560 and 1577 and after 1582 the old sterling standard of .925 was restored. Between 1578 and 1582 the standard was slightly reduced and the weights were reduced by 1/32nd in 1601. Gold was similarly reduced slightly in quality 1578–82, and there was a slight weight reduction in 1601.

To help alleviate the shortage of small change, and to avoid the expense of minting an impossibly small silver farthing, a threefarthing piece was introduced to provide change if a penny was tendered for a farthing purchase. The sixpence, threepence, threehalfpence and threefarthings were marked with a rose behind the queen's head to distinguish them from the shilling, groat, half-groat and penny.

Coins of exceedingly fine workmanship were produced in a screw press introduced by Eloye Mestrelle, a French moneyer, in 1561. With parts of the machinery powered by a horse-drawn mill, the coins produced came to be known as "mill money". Despite the superior quality of the coins produced, the machinery was slow and inefficient compared to striking by hand. Mestrelle's dismissal was engineered in 1572 and six years later he was hanged for counterfeiting.

Mintmarks

106	21	94	23	53	33	107	92
74	71	26	77	65b	27	7	14
113	60	54	79	72b	86	123	124
		90	57	0	1	2	

1558–60	Lis (106)		1578–9	Greek cross (7)
1560–1	Cross crosslet (21)		1580–1	Latin cross (14)
	Martlet (94)		1582	Sword (113)
1560–6	Star (23, milled)		1582–3	Bell (60)
1561–5	Pheon (53)		1582–4	A (54)
1565	Rose (33)		1584–6	Escallop (79)
1566	Portcullis (107)		1587–9	Crescent (72b)
1566–7	Lion (92)		1590–2	Hand (86)
1567–70	Coronet (74)		1591–5	Tun (123)
	Lis (105, milled)		1594–6	Woolpack (124)
1569–71	Castle (71)		1595–8	Key (90)
1570	Pierced mullet (26, milled)		1597–1600	Anchor (57)
1572–3	Ermine (77)		1600	0
1573–4	Acorn (65b)		1601–2	1
1573–7	Eglantine (27)		1602	2

N.B. *The dates for* mms *sometimes overlap. This is a result of using up old dies, onto which the new mark was punched.*

GOLD

Hammered Coinage
First to Third issues, 1559–78. ('Fine' gold of .979. 'Crown' gold of .916 fineness. Sovereigns of 240 grs. wt.). Mintmarks; lis to eglantine.

2512

		F £	VF £
2511	**'Fine' Sovereign** of 30 sh. Queen enthroned, tressure broken by throne, reads Z not ET, no chains to portcullis. R. Arms on rose; *mm.* lis.	1500	3000
2512	—— Similar but ET, chains on portcullis; *mm.* crosslet	1400	2750
2513	**Angel**. St. Michael. R. Ship. Wire line inner circles; *mm.* lis.	300	600
2513A	— Similar, but beaded i.c. on *obv.*, *mm.* lis	300	600
2514	—— Similar, but beaded inner circles; ship to r.; *mm.* 106, 21, 74, 77–27.	250	450
2515	——— Similar, but ship to l.; *mm.* 77–27	275	500
2516	**Half Angel**. As 2513, wire line inner circles; *mm.* lis		*? Exists*
2516A	— As last, but beaded i.c.s, legend ends. Z.HIB		*Extremely rare*
2517	— As 2514, beaded inner circles; *mm.* 106, 21, 74, 77–27	180	400
2518	**Quarter Angel**. Similar; *mm.* 106, 74, 77–27.	175	400

2513   2520A

2519	**Half Pound** of 10 sh. Young crowned bust l. R. Arms. Wire line inner circles; *mm.* lis.	400	900
2520	— Similar, but beaded inner circles; *mm.* 21, 33–107	325	650
2520A	—— Smaller bust; *mm.* 92.	400	750
2520B	—— Broad bust, ear visible; *mm.* 74, 71	400	750
2521	**Crown**. As 2519; *mm.* lis		*Extremely rare*
2522	— Similar to 2520; *mm.* 21, 33–107	250	575

	F	VF
	£	£
2522A — Similar to 2520A; *mm.* 92	275	650
2522B — Similar to 2520B; *mm.* 74, 71	275	650
2523 **Half Crown**. As 2519; *mm.* lis.	*Extremely rare*	
2524 — As 2520; *mm.* 21, 33–107	275	650
2524A — Similar to 2520A; *mm.* 92	*Extremely rare*	
2524B — Similar to 2520B; *mm.* 74, 71	300	700

Fourth Issue, 1578–82 ('Fine' gold only of .976). Mintmarks: Greek cross, Latin cross and sword.

2525	**Angel**. As 2514; *mm.* 7, 14, 113.	250	475
2526	**Half Angel**. As 2517; *mm.* 7, 14, 113.	180	425
2527	— Similar, but without E and rose above ship; *mm.* 14	375	800
2528	**Quarter Angel**. As last; *mm.* 7, 14, 113.	175	400

Fifth Issue, 1583–1600 ('Fine' gold of .979, 'crown' gold of .916; pound of 174.5 grs. wt.). Mintmarks: bell to **O**.

2529   2534

2529	**Sovereign** (30 sh.). As 2512, but tressure not normally broken by back of throne; *mm.* 54–123	1250	2250
2530	**Ryal** (15 sh.). Queen in ship. ℞. Similar to 2489; *mm.* 54–86 (*rev.* only). .	2250	6000
2531	**Angel**. As 2514; *mm.* 60–123, 90–**O**	250	450
2532	**Half Angel**. As 2517; *mm.* 60–57	200	425
2533	**Quarter Angel**. As 2518; *mm.* 60–57	175	400
2534	**Pound** (20 sh.). Old bust l., with elaborate dress and profusion of hair; *mm.*, lion and tun/tun, 123–**O**	650	1300
2535	**Half Pound**. Similar; *mm.* 123	450	750
2535A	— Similar but smaller bust with less hair; *mm.* 124–**O**	450	750
2536	**Crown**. Similar to 2534; *mm.* 123–90. **O**	275	600
2537	**Half Crown**. Similar; *mm.* -/123, 123–90, **0**	250	600

Sixth Issue, 1601–3 ('Fine' gold of .979, 'crown' gold of .916; Pound of 172 grs. wt.). Mintmarks: **1** and **2**

		F £	VF £
2538	**Angel**. As 2531; *mm.* **1, 2**	300	650
2539	**Pound**. As 2534; *mm.* **1, 2**	800	1800
2540	**Half Pound**. As 2535A; *mm.* **1, 2**	600	1150

2541

| 2541 | **Crown**. As 2536; *mm.* **1, 2** .... | *Rare* |
| 2542 | **Half Crown**. As 2537; *mm.* **1, 2** .... | *Rare* |

Milled Coinage, 1561–70

2543	**Half Pound**. Crowned bust l.; *mm.* star, lis	650	1600
2544	**Crown**. Similar; *mm.* star, lis	800	2000
2545	**Half Crown**. Similar; *mm.* star, lis	1400	3000

For further details on both AV and AR milled coinage, *see* D. G. Borden 'An introduction to the Mill coinage of Elizabeth I'.

SILVER

Hammered Coinage

   Countermarked Edward VI base shillings (1559)

2546   2547

| 2546 | **Fourpence-halfpenny**. Edward VI 2nd period 6 oz shillings countermarked on obverse with a portcullis; *mm.* 66, 52, t, 111, Y and 122 .... | *Extremely rare* |
| 2547 | **Twopence-farthing**. Edward VI 3rd period 3 oz shillings countermarked on obverse with a seated greyhound; *mm.* 92. 105 and 35 .... | *Extremely rare* |

N.B. *Occasionally the wrong cmk. was used*

First Issue, 1559–60 (.916 fine, shillings of 96 grs.)

2548

		F £	*VF* £
2548	**Shilling**. Without rose or date. ELIZABET(H), wire line inner circles, pearls on bodice; *mm.* lis. (Minor bust varieties exist)	175	500
2549	Similar but reads ELIZABETH, no pearls; *mm.* lis (several bust varieties). Wire line and beaded inner circles	100	350

2551

2550	**Groat**. Without rose or date, wire line inner circles, ornate bust, *mm.* lis .	110	250
2550A	— Similar bust, pearls on dress; *mm.* lis . . . . :	100	250
2550B	— Similar bust, plain dress; *mm.* lis	110	250
2551	— Similar, but large bust, wire line and beaded circles; *mm.* lis	50	125
2551A	Similar, with small bust and shield, ? from half groat punch; *mm.* lis . . .	100	250
2552	**Halfgroat**. Without rose or date, wire line inner circles; *mm.* lis	150	350
2553	**Penny**. Without rose or date, wire line inner circles; *mm.* lis	115	275
2554	Similar, but dated 1558 on *obv.*	*Extremely rare*	

Second Issue, 1560–1 (.925 fineness, shilling of 96 grs.)

2555	**Shilling**. Without rose or date, beaded circles. ET instead of Z, large ornate bust; *mm.* cross crosslet, 94	75	200
2555A	— Similar, but tall bust, plain bodice with pearls, *mm.* 21, 94	60	175
2555B	Similar to 2549, but much larger bust; *mm.* 21, 94	50	150
2556	**Groat**. As last. *mm.* cross crosslet, martlet.	35	90
2557	**Halfgroat**. As last. *mm.* cross crosslet, martlet	25	70
2558	**Penny**. As last. *mm.* cross crosslet. martlet, (minor bust varieties)	15	35

Third Issue, 1561–77 (Same fineness and weight as last)

2562a   2567   2571

		F £	VF £
2559	**Sixpence.** With rose and date 1561, large flan (27 mm. or more), large bust with hair swept back; *mm.* pheon	150	325
2560	— Large flan, small bust; *mm.* pheon	40	115
2561	— Very small bust; *mm.* pheon	35	110
2561A	Smaller flan (26.5 *mm.*). Very large bust, 1564–5; *mm.* pheon	20	55
2562	Without rose, 1561; *mm.* pheon	*Extremely rare*	
2562A	Small regular bust, 1561–6; *mm.* 53–107	20	55
2562B	Middle bust, 1566–74; *mm.* 92–65 b, ear shows, (also *mm.* 71/74, 1567)	20	55
2562C	Larger bust, 1573–7; *mm.* 77–27	20	55
2563	Without date; *mm.* lion, coronet, ermine	*Extremely rare*	
2564	**Threepence.** With rose and date 1561, large flan (21 mm.); *mm.* pheon	25	75
2565	— 1561–66, regular (19 mm.); *mm.* pheon to lion	15	45
2565A	— Thin bust, 1563/2; *mm.* pheon	30	90
2565B	— Taller bust, pointed trunc, ear shows, 1566–77; *mm.* 92–27, 27/-, 27/65b	15	45
2566	Without rose. 1568; *mm.* coronet	*Unique*	
2567	**Halfgroat.** Without rose or date; *mm.* portcullis to castle	20	60
2568	**Threehalfpence.** With rose and date 1561, large flan (17 mm.) *mm.* pheon	40	100
2569	Regular flan (16 mm.); 1561–2, 1564–70, 1572–7; *mm.* 53–107, 74–27	20	55
2570	**Penny.** Without rose or date; *mm.* 33–71, 27, 33/107	15	45
2571	**Threefarthings.** With rose and date 1561–2, 1568, 1572–7; *mm.* 53, 74, 77–27	50	150

Fourth Issue, 1578–82 (.921 fineness, shilling of 95.6 grs.)

2572	**Sixpence.** As 2562C, 1578–82; *mm.* 7–113, 14/113, 14/7	20	60
2573	**Threepence.** As 2565, 1578–82; *mm.* 7–113	20	65

2573   2577   2581

		F	VF
		£	£
2574	**Threehalfpence**. As 2569, 1578–9, 1581–2; *mm.* 7–113	20	55
2575	**Penny**. As 2570; *mm.* 7–113, 7/14, 14/7	20	50
2576	**Threefarthings**. As 2571, 1578–9, 1581–2; *mm.* 7–113.	60	175

Fifth Issue, 1582–1600 (.925 fineness, shilling of 96 grs.)

2577	**Shilling**. Without rose and date, ELIZAB; ruff covers ear, minor bust varieties, *mm.* bell–72b, ear shows. *mm.* 72b–0 (several mule *mm.*s)	30	85
2577A	New tall thin bust, with bodice differently ornamented FRA; *mm.* 79 . .	*Extremely rare*	
2577B	— Plain bodice; *mm.* tun	40	90
2578	**Sixpence**. As 2572; *mm.* bell, 1582	25	55
2578A	Similar, but reads ELIZAB; *mm.* 60–**O**, 1582–1600, (later *mm.*s have larger crown); also *mm.* 79/54, 1583	20	50
2579	**Halfgroat**. Without rose and date. E. D. G. ROSA etc., two pellets behind bust. ℞. CIVITAS LONDON; bell to **O** (occasionally, bell without pellets).	12	45
2580	**Penny**. As last, but no marks behind bust; *mm.* bell to 57 (*mm.* 90, 57, **O**, also exist *obv.* only)	12	40
2581	**Halfpenny**. Portcullis. ℞. Cross and pellets; *mm.* none, A to **O**	35	90

Sixth Issue, 1601–2 (.925 fineness, shilling of 93 grs.)

| 2582 | **Crown**. Similar to illustration below; *mm.* **1, 2** . . . . | 225 | 600 |

2583

2583	**Halfcrown**. Similar, *mm.* **1, 2**	175	425
2584	**Shilling**. As 2577, *mm.* **1, 2**	35	110
2585	**Sixpence**. With rose and date 1601–2; *mm.* **1, 2**.	25	75
2586	**Halfgroat**. As 2579, *mm.* **1, 2, 2/-**	15	40
2587	**Penny**. As 2580, *mm.* **1, 2, 2/-**	15	40
2588	**Halfpenny**. .As 2581, *mm.* **1, 2**	25	85

Milled coinage

2592

		F	VF
		£	£
2589	**Shilling**. Without rose or date; *mm*. star. Plain dress, large size	250	700
2590	— decorated dress, large size (over 31 mm.).	110	375
2591	— — intermediate size (30–31 mm.)	70	225
2592	— — small size (under 30 mm.)	75	275
2593	**Sixpence**. Small bust, large rose. ℞. Cross fourchée, 1561–2; *mm*. star . .	30	85

2594   2601

		F	VF
2594	Tall narrow bust with plain dress, large rose, 1561–2; *mm*. star . . . *from*	30	85
2595	— similar, but decorated dress, 1561? 1562	30	85
2596	Large broad bust, elaborately decorated dress, small rose, 1562; *mm*. star	25	75
2597	— — cross pattée on *rev*., 1562–4; *mm*. star.	35	110
2598	— similar, pellet border, 1563–4	50	165
2598A	Bust with low ruff, raised rim, 1566 (over 4/3/2)	75	150
2599	Small bust, 1567–8, ℞. As 2593; *mm*. lis	40	115
2600	Large crude bust breaking legend; 1570, *mm*. lis; 1571/0, *mm*. castle (over lis)	90	250
2601	**Groat**. As illustration	75	275
2602	**Threepence**. With rose, small bust with plain dress, 1561.	65	190
2603	Tall narrow decorated bust with medium rose, 1562	60	165
2604	Broad bust with very small rose, 1562	80	210
2605	Cross pattée on *rev*., 1564/3	150	400
2606	**Halfgroat**. As groat	90	300
2607	**Threefarthings**. E . D . G . ROSA, etc., with rose. ℞. CIVITAS LONDON, shield with 1563 above	*Extremely rare*	

2607C

Portcullis money
Trade coins of 8, 4, 2, and 1 Testerns were coined at the Tower Mint in 1600/1 for the first voyage of the incorporated "Company of Merchants of London Trading into the East Indies". The coins bear the royal arms on the obverse and a portcullis on the reverse and have the *mm.* **O**. They were struck to the weights of the equivalent Spanish silver 8, 4, 2 and 1 reales.

2607A Eight testerns	700	1700
2607B Four testerns.	350	800
2607C Two testerns	425	900
2607D One testern.	275	700

JAMES I, 1603–25

With the accession of James VI of Scotland to the English throne, the royal titles and coat of arms are altered on the coinage; on the latter the Scottish rampant lion and the Irish harp now appear in the second and third quarters. In 1604 the weight of the gold pound was reduced and the new coin became known as the 'Unite'. Fine gold coins of 23½ carat and crown gold of 22 carat were both issued, and a gold four-shilling piece was struck 1604–19. In 1612 all the gold coins had their values raised by 10%; but in 1619 the Unite was replaced by a new, lighter 20s. piece, the 'Laurel', and a lighter rose-ryal, spur-ryal and angel were minted.

In 1613 the King granted Lord Harrington a licence to coin farthings of copper as a result of repeated public demands for a low value coinage; this was later taken over by the Duke of Lennox. Towards the end of the reign coins made from silver sent to the mint from the Welsh mines had the Prince of Wales's plumes inserted over the royal arms.

Mintmarks

125	105	33	79	84	74	90
60	25	71	45	32	123	132
72b	7a	16	24	125	105	46

First coinage
1603–4   Thistle (125)
1604–5   Lis (105)
Second coinage
1604–5   Lis (105)
1605–6   Rose (33)
1606–7   Escallop (79)
1607   Grapes (84)
1607–9   Coronet (74)
1609–10   Key (90)
1610–11   Bell (60)
1611–12   Mullet (25)
1612–13   Tower (71)
1613   Trefoil (45)

1613–15   Cinquefoil (32)
1615–16   Tun (123)
1616–17   Closed book (132)
1617–18   Crescent (72b, gold)
1618–19   Plain cross (7a)
1619   Saltire cross (16)

Third coinage
1619–20   Spur rowel (24)
1620–1   Rose (33)
1621–3   Thistle (125)
1623–4   Lis (105)
1624   Trefoil (46)

GOLD

First coinage, 1603–4 (Obverse legend reads D' . G' . ANG : SCO : etc.)

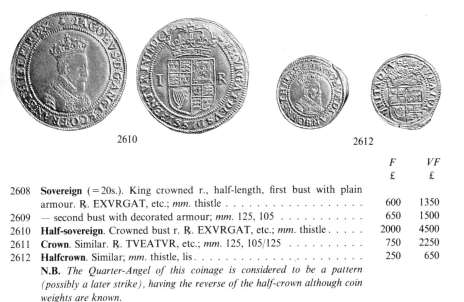

2610   2612

		F	VF
		£	£
2608	**Sovereign** (= 20s.). King crowned r., half-length, first bust with plain armour. ℞. EXVRGAT, etc.; *mm.* thistle	600	1350
2609	— second bust with decorated armour; *mm.* 125, 105	650	1500
2610	**Half-sovereign.** Crowned bust r. ℞. EXVRGAT, etc.; *mm.* thistle	2000	4500
2611	**Crown.** Similar. ℞. TVEATVR, etc.; *mm.* 125, 105/125	750	2250
2612	**Halfcrown.** Similar; *mm.* thistle, lis	250	650

N.B. *The Quarter-Angel of this coinage is considered to be a pattern (possibly a later strike), having the reverse of the half-crown although coin weights are known.*

Second coinage, 1604–19 (Obverse legend reads D' G' MAG : BRIT : etc.)

2613   2614

		F	VF
2613	**Rose-ryal** (= 30s., 33s. from 1612). King enthroned. ℞. Shield on rose; *mm.* 33–90, 25–132	700	1400
2614	**Spur ryal** (= 15s., 16s. 6d. from 1612). King in ship; *mm.* 33, 79, 74, 25–32, 132	1700	3500
2615	**Angel** (= 10s., 11s. from 1612). Old type but larger shield; *mm.* 33–74, 60–16.	350	700
2616	—— pierced for use as touch-piece	150	350
2617	**Half-angel** (= 5s., 5s. 6d. from 1612). Similar; *mm.* 71–132, 7a, 16	1300	3000

Second coinage gold

2620   2627

		F	VF
		£	£
2618	**Unite** (= 20s., 22s. from 1612). Half-length second bust r. R. FACIAM etc.; *mm.* lis or rose	250	450
2619	— fourth bust; *mm.* rose to cinquefoil	220	400
2620	— fifth bust; *mm.* cinquefoil to saltire	200	375
2621	**Double-crown.** Third bust r. R. HENRICVS, etc.; *mm.* lis or rose	160	350
2622	Fourth bust; *mm.* rose to bell	160	350
2623	Fifth bust; *mm.* mullet to saltire, key	175	365
2624	**Britain crown.** First bust r.; *mm.* lis to coronet	135	265
2625	Third bust; *mm.* key to cinquefoil	135	265
2626	Fifth bust; *mm.* cinquefoil to saltire	125	235
2627	**Thistle crown** (= 4s.). As illus.; *mm.* lis to plain cross	125	250
2628	— IR on only one side	140	275
2629	**Halfcrown.** I' D' G' ROSA SINE SPINA. First bust; *mm.* lis to coronet	115	225
2630	Third bust; *mm.* key to trefoil	120	250
2631	Fifth bust; *mm.* cinquefoil to plain cross	110	200

Third coinage, 1619–25

2632	**Rose-ryal** (= 30s.; 196½ grs.). King enthroned. R. XXX above shield; lis, lion and rose emblems around; *mm.* 24–105	1000	2000
2633	Similar but plain back to throne; *mm.* 46	1100	2500

2634   2635

2634	**Spur-ryal** (= 15s.). As illus. R. Somewhat like 2530, but lis are also crowned. *mm.* 24–125, 46	1600	3250
2635	**Angel** (= 10s.) of new type; *mm.* 24–46	450	950
2636	— pierced for use as touch-piece	200	400

	F	VF
	£	£
2637 **Laurel** (= 20s.; 140½ grs.). First (large) laur, bust l.; *mm.* 24	225	485
2638 Second, medium, square headed bust, 'SS' tie ends; *mm.* 24, 33	200	375
2638A Third, small rounded head, ties wider apart; *mm.* 33, 125	200	375
2638B Fourth head, very small ties; *mm.* 105, 46.	200	375
2638C Fourth head variety, tie ends form a bracket to **XX**; *mm.* lis	200	375
2639 Fifth, small rather crude bust; *mm.* trefoil.	1250	2750

2641   2642

2640 **Half-laurel.** First bust; *mm.* spur rowel	200	400
2641 — As 2638A; *mm.* rose	175	330
2641A — As 2638B; *mm.* 33–46	175	330
2642 **Quarter-laurel.** Bust with two loose tie ends; *mm.* 24–105	120	175
2642A Bust as 2638C; *mm.* 105, 46.	120	175
2642B As last but no rev. inner circle; *mm.* 46	130	200

Rev. mm. on ½ and ¼ laurels normally follows REGNA.

SILVER

2643

First coinage, 1603–4

2643 **Crown.** King on horseback. ℞. EXVRGAT, etc., shield; *mm.* thistle, lis .	275	750
2644 **Halfcrown.** Similar.	225	650
2645 **Shilling.** First bust, square-cut beard. ℞. EXVRGAT, etc.; *mm.* thistle . .	50	160
2646 — Second bust, beard merges with collar; *mm.* thistle, lis	30	125

First coinage silver

		2647		2648		

		F	VF
		£	£
2647	**Sixpence.** First bust; 1603; *mm.* thistle	30	13:
2648	Second bust; 1603–4; *mm.* thistle, lis	25	12(
2649	**Halfgroat.** As illustration 2648 but II; *mm.* thistle, lis	25	7(
2650	**Penny.** First bust I behind head; *mm.* thistle, lis	25	6(
2650A	— Second bust; *mm.* thistle	*Extremely rare*

	2650		2651	

| 2651 | **Halfpenny.** As illustration; *mm.* thistle, lis . . . . | 20 | 50 |

Second coinage, 1604–19

2652	**Crown.** King on horseback. R. QVAE DEVS, etc. *rev.* stops; *mm.* 105–84.	275	625:
2653	**Halfcrown.** Similar; *mm.* 105, 79, 123, 33	300	850
2654	**Shilling.** Third bust, beard cut square and stands out (*cf.* illus. 2657); *mm.*		
	lis, rose	25	100
2655	— Fourth bust, armour plainer (*cf.* 2658); *mm.* 33–74	20	90
2656	— Fifth bust, similar, but hair longer; *mm.* 74–7a	20	95

	2657		2658	

2657	**Sixpence.** Third bust; 1604–6; *mm.* lis, rose	25	95
2658	— Fourth bust; 1605–15; *mm.* rose to tun, 90/60	20	100
2658A	— Fifth bust, 1618; *mm.* plain cross	*Unique*

	2660		2663	

	F	VF
	£	£
2659 **Halfgroat**. As illus. but larger crown on *obv.*; *mm.* lis to coronet	10	30
2660 — — Similar, but smaller crown on *obv.*; *mm.* coronet to plain cross . . .	15	40
2660A As before, but TVEATVR legend both sides; *mm.* 7a, rose	40	75
2661 **Penny**. As halfgroat but no crowns; *mm.* 105–32,7a and none, -/84	10	30
2661A — Similar, but without i.c. on one or both sides	10	30
2662 — As before but TVEATVR legend both sides; *mm.* mullet	100	—
2663 **Halfpenny**. As illus.; *mm.* lis to mullet (except 90) cinquefoil on *rev.* only	15	30

Third coinage, 1619–25

	F	VF
2664 **Crown**. As 2652, with plain or grass ground line, colon stops on *obv.*, no stops on *rev.*; *mm.* 33–46	160	375
2665 — — plume over shield; *mm.* 125–46	180	425

2666   2667

	F	VF
2666 **Halfcrown**. As 2664 but normally plain ground line only; all have bird-headed harp; *mm.* 125–46.	100	235
2666A — — Similar but no ground line; *mm.* rose	120	275
2667 — — Plume over shield; groundline *mm.* 125–46	110	325
2668 **Shilling**. Sixth (large) bust, hair longer and very curly; *mm.* 24–46	25	85
2669 — — plume over shield; *mm.* 125–46	40	115

2670   2672

	F	VF
2670 **Sixpence**. Sixth bust; 1621–4; *mm.* 33–46	25	110
2671 **Halfgroat**. As 2660 but no stops on *rev.*; *mm.* 24–46 and none, 105 and 46; *mm.* 24 with *rev.* stops known	10	25
2671A Similar but no inner circles; *mm.* lis	40	110
2672 **Penny**. As illus.; *mm.* 24, 105, 46 and none, two pellets, 105/··	10	25
2672A — Similar but without inner circles on one or both sides; *mm.* lis, two pellets.	10	25
2673 **Halfpenny**. As 2663, but no *mm.*	15	30

178

COPPER

For mintmarks see *English Copper, Tin and Bronze Coins in the British Museum, 1558–1958, by C. Wilson Peck.*

2675   2676   2679

		F £	VF £
2674	**Farthing**. "Harington", small size. 1a, letter or other mark below crown (originally tinned surface)........................*from*	15	40
2675	— — 1b, central jewel on circlet of crown with *mm.* below or crown unmodified.....................................	20	45
2676	— 2, normal size of coin; *mm.* on *rev.*....................	10	20
2677	"Lennox". 3a; *mm. rev.* only.........................	5	16
2678	— 3b; *mm.* both sides.............................	4	14
2679	— — 3c; *mm. obv.* only............................	4	14
2680	— — 3d; larger crown	4	14
2681	— 4; oval type, legend starts at bottom l.................	15	40

CHARLES I, 1625–49

Numismatically, this reign is one of the most interesting of all the English monarchs. Some outstanding machine-made coins were produced by Nicholas Briot, a French die-sinker, but they could not be struck at sufficient speed to supplant hand-hammering methods. In 1637 a branch mint was set up at Aberystwyth to coin silver extracted from the Welsh mines. After the king's final breach with Parliament the parliamentary government continued to issue coins at London with Charles's name and portrait until the king's trial and execution. The coinage of copper farthings continued to be manufactured privately under licences held first by the Duchess of Richmond, then by Lord Maltravers and later by various other persons. The licence was finally revoked by Parliament in 1644.

During the Civil War coins were struck at a number of towns to supply coinage for those areas of the country under Royalist control. Many of these coins have an abbreviated form of the 'Declaration" made at Wellington, Shropshire, Sept., 1642, in which Charles promised to uphold the Protestant Religion, the Laws of England and the Liberty of Parliament. Amongst the more spectacular pieces are the gold triple unites and the silver pounds and half-pounds struck at Shrewsbury and Oxford, and the emergency coins made from odd-shaped pieces of silver plate during the sieges of Newark, Scarborough, Carlisle and Pontefract.

Mintmarks

105	10	96	71	57	88	101	35

87	107	60	75	123	57	119a	23

119b	98	112	81	120	109

Tower Mint under Charles I

1625	Lis (105)
1625–6	Cross Cavalry (10)
1626–7	Negro's head (96)
1627–8	Castle (71)
1628–9	Anchor (57)
1629–30	Heart (88)
1630–1	Plume (101)
1631–2	Rose (35)
1632–3	Harp (87)
1633–4	Portcullis (107)
1634–5	Bell (60)

1635–6	Crown (75)
1636–8	Tun (123)
1638–9	Anchor (57)
1639–40	Triangle (119a)
1640–1	Star (23)
1641–3	Triangle in circle (119b)

Tower Mint under Parliament

1643–4	P in brackets (98)
1644–5	R in brackets (112)
1645	Eye (81)
1645–6	Sun (120)
1646–8	Sceptre (109)

59	B	58 *var*	58

Briot's Mint

1631–2	Flower and B (59)	1638–9	Anchor and B (58)
1632	B		Anchor and mullet

On mint mark no. 58 the 'B' below the anchor is sometimes shown as ꓭ

61	104	35	92	103	6	65b
89	91 *var.*	131	84	94 *var.*	64	93	3
102	67	127	128	129	25	83

134	71	A	B	75

Provincial Mints

1638–42 Book (61, *Aberystwyth*)
1642 Plume (104, *Shrewsbury*)
      Pellets or pellet (*Shrewsbury*)
1642–3 Rose (35, *Truro*)
      Bugle (134, *Truro?*)
1642–4 Lion (92, *York*)
1642–6 Plume (103, *Oxford*)
      Pellet or pellets (*Oxford*)
      Lis (105, *Oxford*)
1643 Cross pattée (6, *Bristol*)
      Acorn (65b, *Bristol*)
      Castle (71, *Worcester* or
        Shrewsbury)
      Helmet (89, *Worcester*
        and *Shrewsbury*)
1643–4 Leopard's head (91 var.
        Worcester)
      Two lions (131, *Worcester*)
      Lis (105, *Worcs.* or *Shrews.*)
      Bunch of grapes (84, *Worcs.*
        or *Shrews.*)
      Bird (94 var., *Worcs.* or *Shrews.*)

1643–4 Boar's head (*Worcs.* or *Shrews.*
      Lion rampant (93, *Worcs.* or *S*
      Rosette (34, *Worcs.* or *Shrews.*)
1643–5 Plume (102, *Bristol*)
      Br. (67, *Bristol*)
      Pellets (*Bristol*)
      Rose (35, *Exeter*)
      Rosette (34, *Oxford*)
1643–6 Floriated cross (127, *Oxford*)
1644 Cross pattée (6, *Oxford*)
      Lozenge (128, *Oxford*)
      Billet (129, *Oxford*)
      Mullet (25, *Oxford*)
1644–6 Gerb (83, *Chester*)
      Pear (100, *Worcester*)
      Lis (105, *Hereford?*)
      Castle (71, *Exeter*)
      A   (Ditto)
1646 B   (Ditto)
      Crown (75, *Aberystwyth-*
1648–9 (*Furnace*)

GOLD

Tower mint, under the King, 1625–42

2687

	F £	VF £
2682 **Angel**. As for James I last issue, but *rev.* reads AMOR POPULI etc; without mark of value; *mm.* lis and cross calvary.	550	1400
2683 — — pierced for use as touch-piece	200	350

Tower Gold

2684 — X in field to r.; *mm.* 96–88, 71 and 96/71, 57 and 71/57.	450	1200
2685 — — — pierced for use as touch-piece	200	350
2686 — X in field to l.; *mm.* 96, 88, 35–119b	425	1100
2687 — — — pierced for use as touch-piece	200	350

2688   2697

2688 **Unite** (= 20s.). First bust with ruff and collar of order, high double-crown. R. Square-topped shield; *mm.* 105.	200	375
2688A — Similar, but extra garnishing to shield; *mm.* lis	225	450
2689 — Similar, but flat single-arched crown; *mm.* 105, 10	200	400
2689A R. As 2688A. *mm.* 105	200	425
2690 Second bust with ruff and armour nearly concealed with scarf; R. Square-topped shield with slight garnishing *mm.* 10–88.	175	375
2690A Similar but more elongated bust, usually dividing legend. *mm.* 57–101, 88/101	175	375
2691 — As 2690A but *mm.* anchor below bust	275	550
2691A *Obv.* as 2690A. R. As next: *mm.* plume	200	400
2692 Third bust, more armour visible. R. Oval shield with CR at sides; *mm.* 101, 35. .	185	425
2692A *Obv.* as next. R. As last, *mm.* plume	185	425
2693 Fourth bust, small lace collar with large high crown usually breaking i.c., long hair. Garter ribbon on breast. R. Oval shield with crowned CR at sides; *mm.* 87, 107	200	440
2693A Similar, but unjewelled crown, within or touching i.c.; *mm.* 107–23	200	425
2694 Sixth (Briot's) bust, large lace collar. R. Similar; *mm.* 119a–119b	225	475
2695 Briot's hammered issue, (square-topped shield); *mm.* 57	*Extremely rare*	
Note. *An extremely fine example of this coin sold at auction for £4500 in 1986.*		
2696 **Double-crown**. First bust. As 2688. R. Square-topped shield; *mm.* 105 . .	175	375
2696A Similar to last but wider flatter double-arched crown; *mm.* 105, 10	175	375
2697 Second bust. R. Similar to 2690; *mm.* 10–57	160	350
2697A Similar to 2690A: *mm.* 57–101	175	365
2697B *Obv.* as last. R. As next: *mm.* plume	200	385

* For these coins inner circles are sometimes omitted on *obv.*, *rev.*, or both. *See also 2704, 2704A and 2707.*

Tower Gold

		F	V
		£	£
2698	**Double-crown.** Third bust. Flat or domed crown. ℞. Oval shield with CR at sides; *mm.* 101, 35	210	45C
2699	Fourth bust, large head, high wide crown. ℞. Oval shield with crowned CR at sides; *mm.* 87	*Extremely rare*	
2699A	Similar to last, but flat crown, jewelled outer arch: *mm.* 87–123	175	375
2699B	Similar, but smaller head, unjewelled crown: *mm.* 60–57	175	375
2699C	Sim. to 2699, but bust within i.c.; *mm.* 60	*Extremely rare*	
2700	Fifth bust (Early Aberystwyth style). ℞. Similar; *mm.* 57	*Extremely rare*	
2700A	— (Late Aberystwyth style). ℞. *mm.* 57, 119a	250	50C
2701	Sixth bust. ℞. Normal; *mm.* 119a–119b	235	475
2702	— ℞. Briot's square-topped shield; *mm.* 57	*Extremely rare*	
2703	**Crown.** First bust with small round crown. ℞. Square-topped shield; *mm.* 105, 10	125	225
2703A	As 2696A. *mm.* 10	125	225
* 2704	Second bust as 2690. ℞. Similar; *mm.* 10–71	115	225
* 2704A	As 2690A. *mm.* 57–101, 88/-, 57/-, 101/-	115	225
2704B	As 2691. Wire line i.c.s on *rev.*	*Rare*	
2705	*Obv.* as 2690A. ℞. As next; 101, 35, 101/-	135	250
2706	Third bust. ℞. Oval shield with CR at sides; *mm.* 101	*Extremely rare*	
* 2707	Fourth bust. ℞. Oval shield with crowned CR at sides; *mm.* -/87, 87–119b, 23/119a, 107/60	125	225
2708	Fifth (Aberystwyth style) bust. ℞. Similar; *mm.* 57	165	350
2709	Sixth (Briot's) bust. ℞. Similar; *mm.* 57	*Unique*	

2703   2714

Tower mint, under Parliament, 1642–9. All Charles I types

2710	**Unite.** Fourth bust, as 2693A; *mm.* (P), (P)/-	250	600
2711	Sixth bust, as 2694 but crude style; *mm.* (P), (R), 119b	325	700
2712	Seventh bust, cruder style; *mm.* 81–109	350	775
2713	**Double-crown.** Fourth bust, as 2699B; *mm.* eye	*Extremely rare*	
2714	Fifth bust, as 2700A; *mm.* sun, sceptre	325	750
2715	Sixth bust, as 2701; *mm.* (P)	400	925
2716	Eighth, dumpy bust with single flat-arched crown; *mm.* sun	*Unique*	
2717	**Crown.** Fourth bust, as 2707 jewelled crown; *mm.* -/98, 98/-, 98–120	150	375
2717A	Sim. but unjewelled crown. ℞. Small crude shield; *mm.* 81–109	150	375

Nicholas Briot's coinage, 1631–2

2718	**Angel.** Type somewhat as Tower but smaller and neater; *mm.* -/B	*Extremely rare*	
2719	**Unite.** As illustration. ℞. FLORENT etc.; *mm.* flower and B/B	750	1750
2720	**Double-crown.** Similar but X. ℞. CVLTORES, etc. *mm.* flower and B/B	600	1500
2720A	Similar but King's crown unjewelled: *mm.* flower and B/B, B	650	1600
2721	**Crown.** Similar; *mm.* B	*Extremely rare*	

* *Inner circles sometimes omitted on obv. or rev. or both.*
BRIOTS HAMMERED GOLD: See No. 2695.

2719

	F	VF
	£	£

Provincial issues, 1638–49
Chester mint
2722 **Unite**. As Tower. Somewhat like a crude Tower sixth bust. ℞. Crowned,
  oval shield, crowned CR, *mm*. plume . . . . *Extremely rare*
Shrewsbury mint, 1642 (See also 2749)
2723 **Triple unite**, 1642. Half-length figure 1 holding sword and olive-branch;
  mm. : ℞. EXVRGAT, etc., around RELIG PROT, etc., in two wavy lines.
  III and three plumes above, date below . . . . *Extremely rare*

Oxford mint, 1642–6

2724

		F	VF
2724	**Triple unite**. As last, but *mm*. plume, tall narrow bust, 1642	1750	3500
2725	Similar, but "Declaration" on continuous scroll, 1642–3.	1850	3750
2725A	Large bust of fine style. King holds short olive branch; *mm*. small lis. . .	*Extremely rare*	
2726	As last, but taller bust, with scarf behind shoulder, 1643, *mm*. plume. . .	2050	4000
2727	Similar, but without scarf, longer olive branch, 1643.	1750	3400
2728	Similar, but OXON below 1643, rosette stops.	*Extremely rare*	
2729	Smaller size, olive branch varies, bust size varies, 1644 OXON	1850	3750
2730	— Obv. as 2729, 1644 / OX	2050	4000

Gold

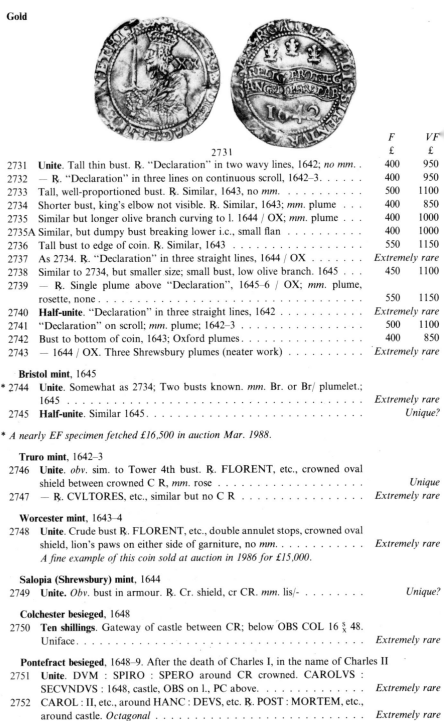

2731

		F £	VF £
2731	**Unite**. Tall thin bust. ℞. "Declaration" in two wavy lines, 1642; *no mm*. .	400	950
2732	— ℞. "Declaration" in three lines on continuous scroll, 1642–3.	400	950
2733	Tall, well-proportioned bust. ℞. Similar, 1643, no *mm*.	500	1100
2734	Shorter bust, king's elbow not visible. ℞. Similar, 1643; *mm*. plume . . .	400	850
2735	Similar but longer olive branch curving to l. 1644 / OX; *mm*. plume . . .	400	1000
2735A	Similar, but dumpy bust breaking lower i.c., small flan	400	1000
2736	Tall bust to edge of coin. ℞. Similar, 1643	550	1150
2737	As 2734. ℞. "Declaration" in three straight lines, 1644 / OX	*Extremely rare*	
2738	Similar to 2734, but smaller size; small bust, low olive branch. 1645 . . .	450	1100
2739	— ℞. Single plume above "Declaration", 1645–6 / OX; *mm*. plume, rosette, none	550	1150
2740	**Half-unite**. "Declaration" in three straight lines, 1642	*Extremely rare*	
2741	"Declaration" on scroll; *mm*. plume; 1642–3	500	1100
2742	Bust to bottom of coin, 1643; Oxford plumes.	400	850
2743	— 1644 / OX. Three Shrewsbury plumes (neater work)	*Extremely rare*	

Bristol mint, 1645

* 2744	**Unite**. Somewhat as 2734; Two busts known. *mm*. Br. or Br/ plumelet.; 1645	*Extremely rare*	
2745	**Half-unite**. Similar 1645.	*Unique?*	

* A nearly EF specimen fetched £16,500 in auction Mar. 1988.

Truro mint, 1642–3

2746	**Unite**. *obv*. sim. to Tower 4th bust. ℞. FLORENT, etc., crowned oval shield between crowned C R, *mm*. rose	*Unique*	
2747	— ℞. CVLTORES, etc., similar but no C R	*Extremely rare*	

Worcester mint, 1643–4

2748	**Unite**. Crude bust ℞. FLORENT, etc., double annulet stops, crowned oval shield, lion's paws on either side of garniture, no *mm*.	*Extremely rare*	
	A fine example of this coin sold at auction in 1986 for £15,000.		

Salopia (Shrewsbury) mint, 1644

2749	**Unite**. *Obv*. bust in armour. ℞. Cr. shield, cr CR. *mm*. lis/-	*Unique?*	

Colchester besieged, 1648

2750	**Ten shillings**. Gateway of castle between CR; below OBS COL 16 $\frac{S}{X}$ 48. Uniface.	*Extremely rare*	

Pontefract besieged, 1648–9. After the death of Charles I, in the name of Charles II

2751	**Unite**. DVM : SPIRO : SPERO around CR crowned. CAROLVS : SECVNDVS : 1648, castle, OBS on l., PC above.	*Extremely rare*	
2752	CAROL : II, etc., around HANC : DEVS, etc. ℞. POST : MORTEM, etc., around castle. *Octagonal*	*Extremely rare*	

SILVER

Tower mint, under the King, 1625–42

2759

		F	VF
		£	£
2753	**Crown**. King on horseback with raised sword. 1a. Horse caparisoned with plume on head and crupper. ℞. Square-topped shield over long cross fourchée; *mm.* 105, 10.	175	500
2754	— 1b. Similar, but plume over shield, no cross; *mm.* 105, 10, 71	500	1000
2755	— 2a. Smaller horse, plume on hd. only, cross on housings, king holds sword on shoulder. ℞. Oval garnished shield over cross fourchée, CR above; *mm.* harp.	150	400
2756	— 2b¹. — — plume divides CR, no cross; *mm.* 101, 35.	200	450
2757	— 2b². — — — with cross; *mm.* harp	250	650
2758	— 3a. Horse without caparisons. ℞. Oval shield without CR; *mm.* 60–23.	175	350
2759	— 3b. — — plume over shield; *mm.* 107, 75, 123.	175	450
2760	"Briot" horse with ground-line; *mm.* 119b	*Three known?*	

2762

2761	**Halfcrown**. As 2753. 1a¹. Rose on housings, ground-line; *mm.* lis	90	260
2761A	— Similar, but no rose on housings; *mm.* lis	*Very rare*	
2762	— 1a². Similar, but no rose or ground-line; *mm.* lis (and rarely 10 over 105)	110	300

Tower Silver

		F £	VF £
2763	— 1a³. As last but clumsier horse and shield not over cross; *mm.* 10–71 .	75	175
2763A	— Sim. but only slight garnishing to shield; *mm.* 10	75	175
2764	— 1a⁴. — — with ground-line; *mm.* lis.	450	1000
2765	— 1b. — — plume over shield; *mm.* lis to anchor	300	600
2765A	— Sim. but only slight garnishing; *mm.* 96–57	300	600
2767	— 2a. As 2755. ℞. Flattened oval garnished shield without cross; *mm.* 101/35 plume, rose, (CR above, divided by rose (rare), lis over rose, lis) . . .	60	135
2768	— 2b. Similar, but large plume between the CR; *mm.* 101, 35.	115	275
2769	— 2c. As 2a, but differently garnished oval shield with CR at sides; *mm.* harp, portcullis, 107/87	50	125
2770	— 2d. Similar, but with plume over shield; *mm.* harp	225	550

2771   2775

2771	— 3a¹. No caparisons on horse, upright sword, scarf flies out from waist. ℞. Round garnished shield, no CR; *mm.* 57, 60–57.	35	125
2772	— 3b. — — plume over shield; *mm.* 107–123	85	200
2773	— 3a². — cloak flies from king's shoulder; ℞. Shields vary; *mm.* 123–23 .	35	110
2774	— — — — rough ground beneath horse; ℞. Shields vary; *mm.* 119a, 23 .	35	110

Note. *(2771–4) See* Brooker *Coins of Charles I 340–52.*

2775	— 4. Foreshortened horse, mane before chest, tail between legs; *mm.* 23, 119b	30	115

Most late Tower halfcrowns have irregular flans.

2776A

2776	**Shilling**. 1. Bust in ruff, high crown, jewelled arches. ℞. Square-topped shield over cross fourchée; *mm.* lis, cross Calvary (normal weight 92¾ grs.).	35	110
2776A	— Sim. but larger crown, plain inner arch; *mm.* 105, 10	35	110

		F £	VF £
2777	— — — light weight (81$\frac{33}{47}$ grs.); *mm.* 10	75	200
2778	— 1b^1. As 2776A, but plume over shield, no cross; *mm.* 105, 10.	80	230
2779	— 1a. Bust in ruff and armour concealed by scarf. ℞. As 2776; 10–71 . .	30	90
2780	— — — — light weight; *mm.* cross Calvary (mostly extremely small XII)	75	210
2781	— 1b^2. As 2779, but plume over shield, no cross; *mm.* 10–101.	50	150
2782	— 1b^3, — — — cross; *mm.* negro's head (crowns and armour dress vary)	350	750
2783	— 2a. More armour visible. ℞. Oval shield, CR above; *mm.* plume, rose.	25	85
2784	— 2b. — — plume over shield; *mm.* 101, 35, 101 over 88/101	100	300
2785	— 3^1. Bust with lace collar, (size and crowns vary). ℞. Flattish oval shield, CR at sides; *mm.* harp, portcullis.	25	80
2786	— 3^2. — — plume over shield; *mm.* harp	200	400
* 2787	— 3a. — no inner circles, rounder shield without CR; *mm.* 60–123	20	70
2788	— 3b. — — plume over shield; *mm.* 60–123.	55	115

* *This type contains at least four varieties of bust, ranging from 3' style to the 4' Aberystwyth type.*

2789	— 4^1. Large Aberystwyth bust, medium or small XII. ℞. Square-topped shield over cross fleury; *mm.* tun, small neat cross ends	30	95
2790	— 4^1. var. Similar, but rounder shoulders, large XII; *mm.* 123-, 119a, (cross ends vary)	20	65
2791	— 4^2. Smaller Aberystwyth bust with small double-arched crown, small XII; *mm.* tun, small neat cross ends	20	65
2792	— 4^3. — single-arches, large XII; *mm.* 123, 57, 119a, 119b (cross ends vary).	20	65
2793	— 4^4. Older (Briot's style) bust, very pointed beard; *mm.* 57–119b	20	60
2793A	— *Obv.* as last. ℞. As Briots hammered issue; lozenge stops; *mm.* △ . . .		*Rare*

2797   2799

2794	**Sixpence.** 1. As 2776, but dated 1625–6; *mm.* 105, 10 (large bust *mm.* 10 noted, lightweight?)	45	175
2795	— 1a^1. As 2779, but dated 1625–9; *mm.* 10–88 (busts vary)	50	190
2796	— 1a^2. — no cross, 1629–30; *mm.* 88, 101.	55	200
2797	— 2a. As 2783, no date; *mm.* plume, rose	40	135
2798	— 2b. — plume dividing CR; *mm.* plume, rose	75	230
2799	— 3. As 2785; *mm.* harp, portcullis (busts and crowns vary).	40	150

Tower Silver

		F	VF
		£	£
2800	**Sixpence.**— 3a. — no inner circles; *mm.* 60–123 (busts and crowns vary).	25	100
2801	— 4¹. As first Aberystwyth sixpence, double-arch crown, small VI. ℞. Square-topped shield over cross; *mm.* tun	30	100
2802	— 4¹. var. — similar, but large VI; *mm.* tun, anchor	35	120
2803	— 4². Second Aberystwyth bust, single-arched crown; *mm.* 57, 119a . . .	25	90
2804	— 4². larger bust, *mm.* 119a	35	115
2805	— 4³. Older (Briot's style) bust; *mm.* 119a–119b (moline cross ends) . . .	25	95

2806   2808   2818

2806	**Halfgroat.** 1. Crowned rose type; *mm.* 105–96, 105/-	10	25
2807	— 1a. —— without inner circles on one or both sides; *mm.* 96–101, 105, 105/-	10	25
2808	— 2a. King's 2nd bust in ruff and mantle. ℞. Oval shield; *mm.* plume, rose.	10	30
2809	— 2b. Similar, but with plume over shield; *mm.* plume, rose.	22	55
2809A	—— 2a Var. 3rd bust, with more armour. ℞. As last; *mm.* plume, rose .	10	25
2809B	—— Sim. but plume over shield; *mm.* 101	25	50
2810	— 3¹. Bust with lace collar. ℞. Oval shield between CR; no inner circles; *mm.* rose harp, crown, portcullis	10	30
2811	— 3². —— inner circles sometimes only on one side; *mm.* harp, portcullis.	10	30
2814	— 3⁵. —— no CR, inner circles; *mm.* portcullis	10	30
2815	— 3⁶. — — — inner circles on *obv.*; *mm.* portcullis.	10	30
2816	— 3a¹. — ℞. Rounder shield, different garniture, no i.cs.; *mm.* 60–119a .	10	30
2817	— 3a². — — inner circles on *obv.*; *mm.* triangle.	10	30
2818	— 3a³. — — inner circles both sides; *mm.* 119a–119b	10	30
2819	— 3a⁴. Aberystwyth bust, no inner circles; *mm.* anchor	15	40
2820	— 3a⁵. — inner circle on *rev.*; *mm.* anchor	15	40
2821	— 3a⁶. Very small bust, no inner circles; *mm.* anchor.	15	40

2822   2828   2837

2822	**Penny.** 1. Rose each side; i.cs.; *mm.* 96, :/lis, lis/:, one or two pellets, lis .	10	30
2823	— 1a. — no i.cs.; *mm.* lis, one or two pellets, anchor.	10	30
2824	— 1b. — i.c. on *rev.*; *mm.* negro's head/two pellets.	12	35
2825	— 2. Bust in ruff and mantle. ℞. Oval shield; i.cs.; *mm.* plume	12	35
2826	— 2¹. — — no i.cs.; *mm.* plume	15	40
2827	— 2a¹. More armour visible; no i.cs.; *mm.* plume, rose.	12	30
2828	— 2a². — i.c. on *obv.*; *mm.* plume, rose	15	40
2829	— 2a³. — i.cs. both sides; *mm.* plume, rose	12	35

		F	VF
		£	£
2830	— 2a⁴. — i.c. on rev.; *mm.* rose/plume	20	55
2831	— 3¹. Bust in lace collar. ℞. CR at sides of shield; no i.cs.; *mm.* harp, one or two pellets. ¨/harp (also *obv.* i.c. *mm.* harp)	12	30
2832	— 3². — similar but no CR; *mm.* 87, 107, 107/¨, none	12	35
2833	— 3³. — — i.c. on *obv.*; *mm.* harp,¨,	12	35
2834	— 3⁴. — — i.c. on *rev.*; *mm.* harp	12	35
2835	— 3a¹. — similar, but shield almost round and with scroll garniture; no i.cs.; *mm.* bell, triangle, one to four pellets, none, bell/¨	10	25
2835A	— 3a¹ variety — i.c. on *obv.*, *rev.* or both sides only; *mm.* triangle/two pellets, △,¨,	15	35
2836	— 3a³. Aberystwyth bust; i.c. on *obv.* or none; *mm.* one or two pellets or none, △/¨	10	· 25
2837	**Halfpenny.** Rose each side; no legend or *mm.*	15	35

Many small denominations have uneven irregular flans.

Tower mint, under Parliament, 1642–8. All Charles I type

		F	VF
2838	**Crown.** 4. Foreshortened horse; *mm.* (P) to sun	200	450
2839	— 5. Tall spirited horse; *mm.* sun	225	550
2840	**Halfcrown.** 3a³. As 2773, but coarse work; *mm.* (P) to sun, 81/120	35	105
2841	— 4. Foreshortened horse; *mm.* (P)	120	250
2842	— 5. Tall horse; *mm.* sun, sceptre	40	125
2843	**Shilling.** 4⁴. Briot style bust, *mm,* (P) (R), coarse work; *mm.* eye, sun	35	110
2843A	— — *Rev.* from 2/6 die. *mm.* (P)?		*Rare*

2844   2845

		F	VF
2844	— 4⁵. Long narrow coarse bust; *mm.* sun, sceptre	30	80
2845	— 4⁶. Short broad bust; As illus. *mm.* sceptre	35	115
2845A	Short bust with much narrower crown.	35	115
2846	**Sixpence.** 4³. Briot style bust; *mm.* (P) to sun	40	115
2847	— 4⁴. Late Aberystwyth bust modified; *mm.* (R) to sceptre	45	110
2848	— 4⁵. Squat bust of crude style; *mm.* eye and sun	150	350
2849	**Halfgroat.** 3a³. Sim. to 2818; *mm.* (P) to eye, sceptre, 98/119b	20	55
2850	— 3a⁷. Older, shorter bust, pointed beard; *mm.* eye to sceptre	20	55
2851	**Penny.** 3a². Older bust; *mm.* pellets, i.c. on *obv.* only	18	50

Nicholas Briot's coinage, 1631–9

First milled issue, 1631–2

		F	VF
2852	**Crown.** King on horseback. ℞. Crowned shield between C R crowned; *mm.* flower and B / B	300	650

		F £	VF £
2853	**Halfcrown**. Similar.	175	450
2854	**Shilling**. Briot's early bust with falling lace collar. ℞. Square-topped shield over long cross fourchée; ℞. Legend starts at top or bottom *mm*. flower and B/B, B	110	300
2855	**Sixpence**. Similar, but VI behind bust; *mm*. flower and B/B, flower and B/-	60	150

2855   2856

2856	**Halfgroat**. Briot's bust, B below, II behind. ℞. IVSTITIA, etc., square-topped shield over long cross fourchée	35	80
2856A	Pattern halfgroat. Uncrowned bust in ruff r. ℞. crowned, interlocked Cs. (North 2687). (Included because of its relatively regular appearance.) . .	60	150
2857	**Penny**. Similar, but I behind bust, no B; position of legend may vary. . . .	25	50

Second milled issue, 1638–9

2858

2858	**Halfcrown**. As 2853, but *mm*. anchor and B.	150	400
2859	**Shilling**. Briot's late bust, the falling lace collar is plain with broad lace border, no scarf. ℞. As 2854 but cross only to inner circle; *mm*. anchor and B, anchor.	50	140
2860	**Sixpence**. Similar, but VI; *mm*. 57, anchor and mullet/anchor	30	80

The two last often exhibit flan reduction marks.

Briot's hammered issue, 1638–9

* 2861	**Halfcrown**. King on Briot's style horse with ground line. ℞. Square-topped shield; *mm*. anchor, triangle over anchor	600	1200
* 2862	**Shilling**. Sim. to 2859; *mm*. anchor, triangle. ℞. Square-topped shield over short cross fleury	400	850

* *There occur muled with Tower obv. and rev. dies; mm. △, or △/anchor. Rare*

Provincial and Civil War issues, 1638–49   *F*   *VF*

York mint, 1643–4. *Mm.* lion   £   £

2863 **Halfcrown**. 1. Ground-line below horse. ℞. Square-topped shield between
CR   140   375

2864 — 2. — ℞. Oval shield as Tower 3a, groundline grass or dotted   150   475

2865 — 3. No ground-line. ℞. Similar   125   350

2866 *— 4. As last, but EBOR below horse with head held low. Base metal,
often very base.   110   300

2867 — 5. Tall horse, mane in front of chest, EBOR below. ℞. Crowned square-
topped shield between CR, floral spray in legend   90   250

2868 — 6. As last, but shield is oval, garnished (*rev.* detail variations)   80   235

2868   2872

2869 — 7. Similar, but horse's tail shows between legs. ℞. Shield as last, but with
lion's skin garniture, no CR or floral spray   70   200

2870 **Shilling**. 1. Bust in scalloped lace collar 3[1]. ℞. EBOR above square-topped
shield over cross fleury   50   135

2871 — 2. Similar, but bust in plain armour, mantle; coarse work   65   175

2872 — 3. *Obv.* as 2870. — ℞. EBOR below oval shield   65   175

2873 — 4. — Similar, but crowned oval shield (*obv.* finer style)   50   135

2874 — 5. — As last, but lion's skin garniture   50   135

2876   2877

2875 **Sixpence**. *Obv.* Sim. to 2870. Crowned oval shield   145   375

2876 — — C R at sides   135   300

2877 **Threepence**. As type 4 shilling, but III behind bust. ℞. As 2870   30   70

These pieces are contemporary forgeries (BNJ1984).

Aberystwyth mint, 1638/9–42. *Mm*. book.
Plume 1 = with coronet and band. Plume 2 = with coronet only

		F	VF
		£	£
2878	**Halfcrown**. Horseman similar to 2773, but plume 2 behind. ℞. Oval garnished shield with large plume above. *Obv*. plume 2, *rev*. plume 1. . .	300	750
2879	— Similar to 2774, plume 1 behind King, ground below horse. *Obv*. squat plume 1, *rev*. plume 1	350	850
2880	As 2773A. More spirited horse, no ground. FRAN ET HIB, plume 2/1 .	400	950
2881	**Shilling**. Bust with large square lace collar, plume 2 before, small XII. ℞. As before. No inner circles	125	375
2882	— inner circle on *rev*.	135	425
2883	As 2881, but large plume 1 or 2, large XII, inner circles	125	375
2884	As last, but small narrow head, square lace collar, large or square plume	135	425
2885	Small Briot style bust with round collar, plume 2.	165	450

2886

2886	**Sixpence**. Somewhat as 2881, but double-arched crown, small VI; no inner circles.	130	325
2887	Similar to 2886, but single arched crown, plume 2, inner circle *obv*. Large VI.	165	375
2888	Similar, but with inner circles both sides	130	325
2889	— — *Rev*. with small squat-shaped plume above, sometimes no *rev. mm*.	135	325
2890	Bust as the first Oxford sixpence; with crown cutting inner circle	165	375
2891	**Groat**. Large bust, lace collar, no armour on shoulder. Crown breaks or touches inner circle. ℞. Shield, plume 1 or 2	20	45
2892	— Similar, armour on shoulder, shorter collar. ℞. Similar.	25	55
2893	— Smaller, neater bust well within circle. ℞. Similar	20	45

2891 2894 2895–9

2894	**Threepence**. Small bust, large or small plume 2 before. ℞. Shield, plume 1 or 2 above, *obv*. legend variations	18	45
2895	— Similar, but squat pl. on *obv*., crown cuts i.c. ℞. Pl. 2, *Obv*. legend variations.	20	50

Aberystwyth, *continued*

		F £	VF £
2900	**Halfgroat**. Bust as Tower type 3. ℞. Large plume. No i.cs, *mm*. pellet/book, book	70	140
2900A	Bust as 2886. ℞. As last, no i.c.	60	150
2901	Bust with round lace collar; single arch crown, inner circles, colon stops .	50	125
2902	After Briot's bust, square lace collar: inner circles	50	125

2905   2907

2903	**Penny**. As 2901; CARO; no inner circles	45	135
2904	As 2901; CARO; inner circles	45	135
2905	As last but reads CAROLVS; inner circles	43	120
2906	*Obv*. similar to 2890, tall narrow bust, crown touches inner circle.	55	150
2907	**Halfpenny**. No legend. *O*. Rose. ℞. Plume.	100	250

Aberystwyth-Furnace mint, 1648/9. *Mm*. crown

2908	**Halfcrown**. King on horseback. ℞. Sim. to 2878	800	1750
2909	**Shilling**. Aberystwyth type, but *mm*. crown	*Extremely rare*	
2910	**Sixpence**. Similar	*Extremely rare*	

2911   2913

2911	**Groat**. Similar	135	275
2912	**Threepence**. Similar	175	350
2913	**Halfgroat**. Similar. ℞. Large plume	185	375
2914	**Penny**. Similar	450	900

Uncertain mint (? Hereford)

2915

		Fair	Fine
2915	**Halfcrown**. As illustration, dated 1645 or undated	600	1500
2915A	— Scarf with long sash ends. CH below horse. ℞. Oval shield 1644 . . .		Rare
2915B	— ℞. Crowned oval shield, lion paws		Rare

Shrewsbury mint, 1642. *Mm.* plume without band

		F £	VF £
2917	**Pound**. King on horseback, plume behind, similar to Tower grp. 3 crowns. ℞. Declaration between two straight lines, XX and three Shrewsbury plumes above, 1642 below; *mm.* pellets, pellets/-	900	2500
2918	Similar, but Shrewsbury horse walking over pile of arms	850	2000
2919	As last, but cannon amongst arms and only single plume and XX above Declaration, no *mm.*.	1150	3000
2920	**Half-pound**. As 2917, but X; *mm.* pellets.	350	950
2921	Similar, but only two plumes on *rev.*.	400	1000
2922	Shrewsbury horseman with ground-line, three plumes on *rev.*.	325	900
2923	— with cannon and arms below horse; *mm.* pellets/-.	300	850
2924	— no cannon in arms, no plume in *obv.* field; *mm.* plume/pellets	300	850

2926

2925	**Crown**. Aberystwyth horseman	*Extremely rare*	
2926	Shrewsbury horseman with ground-line; *mm.* -/pellets	300	800
2927	**Halfcrown**. *O*. From Aberystwyth die; (S2880); *mm.* book. ℞. Single plume above Declaration, 1642	250	625

		F	VF
		£	£
2928	Sim. to Aberystwyth die, fat plume behind. ℞. Three plumes above		
	Declaration; *mm.* pellets, pellets/-	165	400
2929	Shrewsbury horseman. ℞. As 2927, single plume, no *mm.*	185	475
2930	— ℞. 2: plume; 6, above Declaration	300	750
2931	— with ground-line. ℞. Similar.	275	650
2932	— — ℞. As 2927, single plume.	175	450
2933	— — ℞. Three plumes above Declaration; *mm.* none or pellets	110	330
2933A	*Obv.* as last. ℞. Aberystwyth die, plume over shield; *mm.* -/book		*Rare*
2934	— — — no plume behind king; *mm.* plume/pellets.	125	350
2935	**Shilling.** *O.* From Aberystwyth die; S2885 *mm.* book. ℞. Declaration type.	300	750
2936	*O.* From Shrewsbury die. ℞. Similar.	325	800

Oxford mint, 1642/3–6. *Mm.* usually plume with band, except on the smaller denominations when it is lis or pellets. There were so many dies used at this mint that we can give only a selection of the more easily identifiable varieties.

2937	**Pound.** Large horseman over arms, no exergual line, fine workmanship. ℞.		
	Three Shrewsbury plumes and XX above Declaration, 1642 below	1050	3450

2937

2938	— Similar, but three Oxford plumes, 1643	1050	3450
2939	Shrewsbury horseman trampling on arms, exergual line. ℞. As last, 1642.	650	2100
2940	— — cannon amongst arms, 1642–3.	600	1950
2941	— as last but exergue is chequered, 1642	750	2450
2942	Briot's horseman, 1643	1150	3700
2943	*O.* As 2937. ℞. Declaration in cartouche, single large plume above, 1644		
	OX below	1500	4500
2944	**Half-pound.** As next. ℞. Shrewsbury die, 1642	250	600
2945	Oxford dies both sides, 1642–3	210	425
2946	**Crown.** *O.* Shrewsbury die with ground-line. ℞. As last but V	225	550
2947	Oxford horseman with grass below, 1643	400	1100
2948	By Rawlins. King riding over a view of the city. ℞. Floral scrolls above and		
	below Declaration, 1644 / OXON below (Beware forgeries!).	*Extremely rare*	
	An extremely fine specimen sold at auction in 1978 for £25,000.		

Oxford Silver, *continued*

		F	VF
		£	£
2949	**Halfcrown**. *O*. From Shrewsbury die S2931 or 2934. R. 3 Ox plumes over 'Dec' 1642	135	375
2950	Ox plume, Shrewsbury horse. R. From Shrewsbury die, 1642	105	275
2951	Both Oxford dies, but Shrewsbury type horse, ground-line, 1642	70	200
2952	— — without ground-line, 1642	90	250
2953	Oxford type horse, ground-line, 1643	75	225

2954

2954	— without ground-line, 1643	70	200
2954A	— — R. 3 Shrewsbury plumes, 1642	100	300
2955	Briot's horse, grass below, 1643, 1643 / OX	80	225
2956	— — large central plume, 1643, 1643 / OX, 1644 / OX	90	275
2957	— lumpy ground, 1643, 1643 / OX	80	210
2958	— — large central plume, 1643–4 / OX	80	225
2959	— plain ground, 1644–5 / OX	80	225
2960	— — large central plume, 1644 / OX	80	225
2960A	Sim. but 2 very small Shrewsbury plumes at sides	100	300
2961	— — — Similar, but large date in script	105	325
2962	Rocky ground, two small plumes at date, 1644 / OX	225	500
2963	Large horse (as Briot's, but clumsier), plain ground, 1644–5 / OX	90	275
2964	— lumpy ground, 1644–5 / OX	90	275
2965	— — large central plume, 1644 / OX	90	275
2966	— pebbly ground, 1645–6 / OX	90	275
2967	— — pellets or annulets by plumes and at date, 1645–6 / OX	90	275
2968	— grass below, 1645–6 / OX	90	325
2969	— — rosettes by plumes and at date, 1645 / OX	110	400
2970	**Shilling**. *O*. From Shrewsbury die. R. Declaration type, 1642	90	225
2971	Both Oxford dies. Small bust, 1642–3	65	170
2972	Similar, but coarser work, 1643	65	170
2973	Large bust of fine work, 1643	65	170
2974	— 1644–6 / OX	75	200
2975	Bust with bent crown, 1643	75	200
2976	— 1644 / OX	75	200
2977	Rawlins' dies. Fine bust with R on truncation, 1644	100	265
2978	— — 1644 / OX	110	300
2979	Small size, 1646, annulets or pellets at date	125	325

2980

	F	VF
	£	£

2980 **Sixpence**. *O*. Aberystwyth die S2890. ℞. With three Oxford plumes, 1642–3; *mm*. book/- 120 285

2981 — ℞. With three Shrewsbury plumes, 1643; *mm*. book/- 120 275

2982 — ℞. With Shrewsbury plume and two lis, 1644 / OX; *mm*. book/-. ... 135 325

2985 2991

2983 **Groat**. *O*. Aberystwyth die S2892. ℞. As 2985 .... 35 110

2984 As last but three plumes above Declaration. 75 200

2985 As illustration, with lion's head on shoulder 50 120

2895A *Obv*. as last ℞. 3 Shrewsbury plumes, 1644 / OX 75 150

2986 Large bust reaching to top of coin. ℞. As 2985. .... 50 120

2987 Large bust to bottom of coin, lion's head on shoulder, legend starts at bottom l. ℞. As last. 60 140

2988 Rawlins' die; similar, but no i.c., and with R on shoulder. ℞. As last. .. 60 140

2989 *O*. As 2985. ℞. Large single plume and scroll above Declaration, 1645. . 60 140

2990 *O*. As 2987. ℞. As last 60 140

2991 *O*. As 2988. ℞. Large single plume above Declaration, which is in cartouche, 1645-6 .... 80 200

2992 **Threepence**. *O*. Aberystwyth die; *mm*. book ℞. Declaration type, 1644 / OX 50 135

2993 Rawlins' die, R below shoulder; *mm*. lis. ℞. Aberystwyth die with oval shield; *mm*. book 45 135

2994 — ℞. Declaration type, three lis above, 1644 below; *mm*. lis/-. 40 125

2995 — Similar, without the R, 1646 (over 1644); no *mm*. 40 125

2996 **Halfgroat**. ℞. Aberystwyth type with large plume 65 175

2997 — ℞. Declaration type, 1644 / OX; *mm*. cross 90 200

2995 2999

Oxford Silver, *continued.*

		F	VF
		£	£
2998	**Penny**. *O*. Aberystwyth die S2904; *mm.* book. ℞. Type, small plume . . .	85	200
2999	As 2906 ℞. Type, large plume	85	200
3000	— Rawlins' die with R. ℞. Type, small plume	85	200
3001	— Wider bust similar to the halfgroat. ℞. Similar	100	275
3002	— — ℞. Declaration type, 1644	200	550

Bristol mint, 1643–5. *Mm.* usually plume or Br., except on small denominations

3003	**Halfcrown**. *O*. Oxford die with or without ground-line. ℞. Declaration, three Bristol plumes above, 1643 below	80	250
3004	— — Br. *mm.* on *rev.*, 1643.	70	240
3005	King wears unusual flat crown, *obv. mm.* acorn? between four pellets. ℞. As 3003, 1643	85	260
3006	— Br. *mm.* on *rev.*, 1643–4.	85	240
3007	Shrewsbury plume behind king. ℞. As last	65	165
3008	— Br. below date, 1644.	70	220
3009	Br. below horse and below date, 1644–5.	75	210
3010	Br. also *mm.* on *rev.*, 1644–5	75	210

3009   3024

3011	**Shilling**. *O*. Oxford die. ℞. Declaration, 1643	80	225
3012	— — Similar, but Br. as *rev. mm.*, 1643–4.	80	225
3013	Coarse bust. ℞. As 3011, 1643	80	225
3014	— — Similar, but Br. as *rev. mm.*, 1644	80	225
3015	Bust of good style, plumelet before. ℞. As last, 1644–5	80	225
3016	— — Similar, but Br. below date instead of as *mm.*, 1644	85	240
3016A	— — — Plume and two plumelets 1644.	90	225
3016B	Taller bust with high crown, no plumelets before. ℞. As last 1645	90	225
3017	Bust with round collar, *mm.* Br. on its side. ℞. As 3016, 1644–5	85	240
3018	Bust with square collar. ℞. Br. as *mm.*, 1645	80	215
3019	**Sixpence**. Small bust, nothing before. ℞. Declaration, 1643; *mm.* ·/Br. . .	140	500
3020	Fine style bust. Plumelet before face, 1644; *mm.* ·/Br. (on its side)	125	400
3021	**Groat**. Bust l. ℞. Declaration, 1644	80	240
3022	— Plumelet before face, 1644.	110	300
3023	— Br. below date, 1644.	100	260
3024	**Threepence**. *O*. As 2992. Aberystwyth die; *mm.* book. ℞. Declaration, 1644.	100	350
3025	Bristol die, plume before face, no *mm.*, 1644	90	300
3026	**Halfgroat**. Br. in place of date below Declaration	150	425
3027	**Penny**. Similar bust, I behind. ℞. Large plume with bands.	200	550

Late 'Declaration' issues, 1645–6
(Previously given as Lundy Island and/or Appledore and Barnstaple/Bideford, it seems likely that coins marked A, 1645 may be Ashby de la Zouch and the coins marked B or with plumes may be Bridgnorth on Severn. A West Country provenance, or any association with Thomas Bushell now seems unlikely.)

		F	VF
		£	£
3028	**Halfcrown**. A below horse and date and as *rev. mm.* 1645	700	2000
3029	Similar but *rev.* from altered Bristol die (i.e. the A's are over Br.).	525	1500
3030	As 3028 but without A below date 1645.	475	1450
3031	A below horse and as *rev. mm.* Scroll above Declaration, B below 1646 .	*Extremely rare*	
3032	Plumelet below horse struck over A. ℞. *Mm.* Shrewsbury plumes; scroll above Declaration, 1646	300	850
3033	— Similar, but plumelet below date	350	1000
3034	**Shilling**. Crowned bust l., *mm.* plume. ℞. Declaration type; *mm.* A and A below 1645.	300	650
3035	— Similar, but plumelet before face	300	650
3036	— — ℞. Scroll above Declaration. 1646, *mm.* plume/plumelet	135	285
3037	Shrewsbury plume before face. ℞. As last but *mm.* pellet	135	325

3039   3044

3038	**Sixpence**. *O.* Plumelet before face; *mm.* ➤ ; ℞. 1645, 3 plumelets over 'Dec'	165	350
3039	*O.* Large Shrewsbury plume before face; *mm.* B. ℞. Scroll above Declaration, 1646, Shrewsbury plume and two plumelets	90	200
3040	**Groat**. As 3038.	*Extremely rare*	
3041	Somewhat similar, but *obv. mm.* plumelet; 1646.	100	235
3042	**Threepence**. Somewhat as last but only single plumelet above Declaration, no line below, 1645; no *mm.*	80	210
3043	— Scroll in place of line above, 1646 below.	65	150
3044	**Halfgroat**. Bust l., II behind. ℞. Large plume with bands dividing 1646; no *mm.*.	200	450

The penny listed under Bristol may belong to this series.

Truro mint, 1642–3. *Mm.* rose

3045	**Half-pound**. King on horseback, face turned frontwards, sash in large bow. ℞. CHRISTO, etc., round garnished shield. Struck from crown dies on thick flan.	*Extremely rare*	
3046	**Crown**. Similar type	135	350
3047	— Shield garnished with twelve even scrolls.	160	425
3048	King's face in profile, sash flies out in 2 ends, well-shaped flan, finer workmanship	185	450

Truro Silver, *continued.*

3049

		F	*VF*
		£	£
3049	**Halfcrown**. King on spirited horse galloping over arms. ℞. Oval garnished shield, 1642 in cartouche below	900	3000
3050	Similar, but no arms. ℞. Oblong shield, CR at sides	700	2500
3051	Galloping horse, king holds sword. ℞. Similar	650	2300
3052	— ℞. Similar, but CR above	600	1900
3053	Trotting horse. ℞. Similar, but CR at sides	300	750
3054	Walking horse, king's head in profile. ℞. Similar	275	725
3055	— ℞. Similar, but CR above	325	850
3055A	Similar, but groundline below horse. ℞. Similar, *mm*. bugle/-	*Extremely rare*	
3056	**Shilling**. Small bust of good style. ℞. Oblong shield	*Extremely rare*	
3057	Larger bust with longer hair. ℞. Round shield with eight even scrolls . .	550	1400
3058	— ℞. Oval shield with CR at sides.	250	700
3059	Normal bust with lank hair. ℞. As last	150	450
3060	— ℞. As 3057	450	1300
3061	— ℞. Round shield with six scrolls	150	450

Truro or Exeter mint. *Mm.* rose

3064   3067-9

3062	**Halfcrown**. King on horseback, sash tied in bow. ℞. Oblong shield with CR at sides.	110	300
3063	— ℞. Round shield with eight even scrolls	70	190
3064	— ℞. Round shield with six scrolls	75	200
3064A	— Angular garnish of triple lines to oblong shield	*Extremely rare*	
3065	King's sash flies out behind. ℞. As 3063.	105	275
3066	— ℞. As 3064A	*Extremely rare*	
3067	Briot's horse with ground-line. ℞. As 3063	105	275
3068	— ℞. As 3066	*Unique*	
3069	— ℞. As 3064	105	275

	F £	VF £

Exeter mint, 1643–6. *Mm.* rose except where stated

3070	**Crown.** As 3046, but 1644 divided by *rev. mm.*	125	300
3071	Similar, but 1644 to l. of *mm.*	110	260
3072	Similar, but 1645 and *rev. mm.* EX.	125	300
3073	King's sash in two loose ends; *mm.* castle/rose, 1645	110	260
3074	— *mm.* castle/EX, 1645	150	350
3075	— *mm.* castle, 1645	110	260
3076	**Halfcrown.** As 3049, but 1644–5 in legend	*Extremely rare*	
3077	Similar, but *rev. mm.* castle, 1645	*Unique*	
3078	Short portly figure, leaning backwards on ill-proportioned horse, 1644, 16 rose 44	175	450
3079	Briot's horse and lumpy ground; 1644	125	350

Larger denominations often have irregular flans.

3080

3080	Horse with twisted tail; 1644–5	120	350
3081	— R. *Mm.* castle, 1645	160	450
3082	— R. *Mm.* EX, 1645	160	450
3083	— R. Declaration type; *mm.* EX. 1644–5	750	2100
3084	— — — EX also below 1644	550	1650
3085	**Shilling.** As 3061. 1644, 1645, *mm.* rose (may be before, after or middle of date)	125	265
3086	— R. Declaration type, 1645	350	1250
3087	**Sixpence.** Sim. to 3085, 1644, 16 rose 44	150	400
3088	**Groat.** Somewhat similar but 1644 at beginning of *obv.* legend	60	140

3089   3091

3089	**Threepence.** As illustration, 1644	65	160
3090	**Halfgroat.** Similar, but II. R. Oval shield, 1644	80	240
3091	— R. Large rose, 1644	100	300
3092	**Penny.** As last but I behind head	135	400

Worcester mint, 1643–4

3096

		F	VF
		£	£
3093	**Halfcrown**. King on horseback l., W below; *mm.* two lions. ℞. Declaration type 1644; *mm.* pellets.	300	850
3094	— ℞. Square-topped shield; *mm.* helmet, castle	225	850
3095	— ℞. Oval shield; *mm.* helmet	225	700
3096	Similar but grass indicated; *mm.* castle. ℞. Square-topped shield; *mm.* helmet or pellets. (Illustrated above)	225	700
3097	— ℞. Oval draped shield, lis or lions in legend	250	775
3098	— ℞. Oval shield CR at sides, roses in legend	275	850
3099	— ℞. FLORENT etc., oval garnished shield with lion's paws each side	350	950
3100	Tall king, no W or *mm.* ℞. Oval shield, lis, roses, lions or stars in legend.	225	700
3101	— ℞. Square-topped shield; *mm.* helmet.	275	900
3102	— ℞. FLORENT, etc., oval shield; no *mm.*.	350	950
3103	Briot type horse, sword slopes forward, ground-line. ℞. Oval shield, roses in legend; *mm.* 91v, 105, none (combinations).	225	850
3104	— Similar, but CR at sides, 91v/-	275	850
3105	Dumpy, portly king, crude horse. ℞. As 3100; *mm.* 91v, 105, none	225	700

3106

3106	Thin king and horse. ℞. Oval shield, stars in legend; *mm.* 91v, none	225	700

Worcester or Salopia (Shrewsbury)

3106A	**Shilling**. Bust of good style r. ℞. Cr. dr. oblong shield. Cr. at sides; *mm.* pear/-	400	1250
3106B	— — ℞. Cr. draped oval shield, no Cr.; *mm.* pear/lis	400	1250
3107	Bust of king l., adequately rendered. ℞. Square-topped shield; *mm.* castle.	400	1250
3108	— ℞. CR above shield; *mm.* helmet and lion	400	1250
3109	— ℞. Oval shield; *mm.* lion, pear	375	1150

3111   3117

	F	VF
	£	£

3110 **Shilling**. Bust a somewhat crude copy of last; *mm.* bird, lis. ℞. Square-
topped shield with lion's paws above and at sides; *mm.* boar's head, helmet. · 400 · 1250

3111 — — CR above . . . . · 400 · 1250

3112 — ℞. Oval shield, lis in legend; *mm.* lis . . . . · 350 · 1000

3113 — ℞. Round shield; *mm.* lis, 3 lis . . . . · 375 · 1050

3114 Bust r.; *mm.* pear. ℞. Oval shield, rose and lis in legend . . . . *Extremely rare*

3115 **Sixpence**. As 3110; *mm.* castle, castle/boar's hd . . . . · 500 · 1250

3116 **Groat**. As 3112; *mm.* lis/helmet, rose/helmet. . . . . · 375 · 750

3117 **Threepence**. Similar; *mm.* lis *obv*. . . . . · 250 · 550

3118 **Halfgroat**. Similar; *mm.* lis (*O*.) various (℞.) . . . . · 350 · 750

Salopia (Shrewsbury) mint, 1644

3119 **Halfcrown**. King on horseback l. SA below; *mm.* lis. ℞. (*mm*.s lis, helmet,
lion rampant, none). Cr. oval shield; *mm.* helmet . . . . *Extremely rare*

3120 — ℞. FLORENT, etc., crowned oval shield, no *mm.* . . . . *Extremely rare*

3121 — SA erased or replaced by large pellet or cannon ball; *mm.* lis in legend,
helmet. ℞. As last . . . . · 1200 · 2750

3122 Tall horse and king, nothing below; *mm.* lis. ℞. Large round shield with
crude garniture; *mm.* helmet . . . . · 525 · 1250

3123 — ℞. Uncrowned square-topped shield with lion's paw above and at sides;
mm. helmet. . . . . · 575 · 1400

3124 — ℞. Small crowned oval shield; *mm.* various . . . . · 525 · 1250

3125 — ℞. As 3120 . . . . · 600 · 1500

3126 Finer work with little or no mane before horse. ℞. Cr. round or oval shield · 525 · 1250

3127 Grass beneath horse. ℞. Similar; *mm.* lis or rose . . . . · 525 · 1250

3128 Ground below horse. ℞. As 3120 . . . . · 575 · 1400

Hartlebury Castle (Worcs.) mint, 1646

3129

	F	VF
	£	£

3129 **Halfcrown**. *O. Mm.* pear. ℞. HC (Hartlebury Castle) in garniture below shield; *mm.* three pears 1100 3000

Chester mint, 1644

3130

		F	VF
3130	**Halfcrown.** As illus. ℞. Oval shield; *mm.* three gerbs and sword	375	850
3131	— Similar, but without plume or CHST; ℞. Cr. oval shield with lion skin; *mm.* prostrate gerb; -/cinquefoil, -/∴	450	950
3132	— ℞. Crowned square-topped shield with CR at sides both crowned *rev.*; *mm.* cinquefoil	475	1200
3133	As 3130, but without plume or CHST. ℞. Declaration type, 1644 *rev.*; *mm.* plume.	425	1050
3133A	**Shilling.** Bust l. ℞. Oval garnished shield; *mm.* ∴ (obv. only)	*Extremely rare*	
3133B	— ℞. Square-topped shield; *mm.* as last	*Extremely rare*	
3133C	— ℞. Shield over long cross.	*Extremely rare*	
3134	**Threepence.** ℞. Square-topped shield; *mm.*-/ prostrate gerb	300	650

Coventry (or Corfe Castle) mint? *Mm.* two interlocked C's
3135 **Halfcrown.** King on horseback l. ℞. Oval shield. *(Now considered to be probably a contemporary forgery) . . . . *Extremely rare*

Carlisle besieged, 1644–5
3136	**Three shillings.** Large crown above C . R / . III . S . ℞. OBS . CARL / · 1645.	1500	3000
3137	Similar but : OBS :/-: CARL ::/·1645	1500	3500

3138

	F	*VF*
	£	£
3138 **Shilling**. As illustration	850	2250
3139 ℞. Legend and date in two lines	900	2500

Note. *(3136–39) Round or Octagonal pieces exist.*

Newark besieged, several times 1645–6, surrendered May 1646

3140

3140 **Halfcrown**. Large crown between CR ; below, XXX. ℞. OBS / NEWARK / 1645 or 1646.	175	400
3141 **Shilling**. Similar but curious flat shaped crown, NEWARKE, 1645. . . .	140	275
3142 Similar but high arched crown, 1645.	110	250
3143 — NEWARK, 1645 or 1646	100	230
3144 **Ninepence**. As halfcrown but IX, 1645 or 1646	120	285
3145 — NEWARKE, 1645.	115	265
3146 **Sixpence**. As halfcrown but VI, 1646	125	325

Pontefract besieged, June 1648–March 1648–9
Pontefract besieged, *continued*

3147 **Two shillings** (lozenge shaped). DVM : SPIRO : SPERO around CR crowned. ℞. Castle surrounded by OBS, PC, sword and 1648.	*Extremely rare*	
3148 **Shilling** (lozenge shaped, octagonal or round). Similar	275	575
3149 — Similar but XII or r. dividing PC.	270	550

After the death of Charles I (30 Jan. 1648/9), in the name of Charles II

Pontefract besieged, *continued*

3149   3150

		F	VF
		£	£

3150 **Shilling** (octagonal). *O.* As last. ℞. CAROLVS : SECVNDVS : 1648, castle
gateway with flag dividing PC, OBS on l., cannon protrudes on r. 275 575
3151 CAROL : II : etc., around HANC : DE / VS : DEDIT 1648. ℞. POST :
MORTEM : PATRIS : PRO : FILIO around gateway etc. as last 275 575

Scarborough besieged, July 1644–July 1645

3165   3168

£

Type I. Castle with gateway to left, value punched below or to side

		£
3152	**Five shillings and eightpence**.	*Extremely rare*
3153	**Crown**. Similar but SC also punched.	*Extremely rare*
3154	**Three shillings and fourpence**. As 3152	*Extremely rare*
3155	**Three shillings**. Similar	*Extremely rare*
3156	**Two shillings and tenpence**. Similar.	4500
3157	**Halfcrown**. Similar.	3750
3158	**Two shillings and fourpence**. Similar	*Extremely rare*
3159	**Two shillings and twopence**. Similar	*Extremely rare*
3160	**Two shillings**. Similar	*Extremely rare*
3161	**One shilling and ninepence**. Similar.	*Extremely rare*
3162	**One shilling and sixpence**. Similar	*Extremely rare*
3163	**One shilling and fourpence**. Similar.	*Extremely rare*

£

3164	**One shilling and threepence**. Similar	*Extremely rare*
3165	**Shilling**. As illustration	*Extremely rare*
3166	**Sixpence**. Similar	*Extremely rare*
3167	**Groat**. Similar	*Extremely rare*

Type II. Castle with two turrets, value punched below

3168	**Two shillings**. Two castles.	*Extremely rare*
3170	**One shilling and sixpence**. Single castle.	*Extremely rare*
3171	**One shilling and fourpence**. Similar.	3000
3172	**One shilling and threepence**. Similar	*Extremely rare*
3173	**One shilling and twopence**. Similar	*Extremely rare*
3174	**One shilling and one penny**. Similar.	*Extremely rare*
3175	**Shilling**. Similar	4000
3176	**Elevenpence**. Similar.	*Extremely rare*
3177	**Tenpence**. Similar	*Extremely rare*
3178	**Ninepence**. Similar.	*Extremely rare*
3179	**Sevenpence**. Similar	*Extremely rare*
3180	**Sixpence**. Similar	*Extremely rare*

COPPER

For mintmarks see *English Copper, Tin and Bronze Coins in the British Museum, 1558–1958*, by C. Wilson Peck.

3185   3191   3194

		F	VF
		£	£
3181	**Royal farthing**. "Richmond" round, colon stops, 1a. CARO over IACO; *mm.* on *obv.*	6	18
3182	— — 1b. CARA; *mm.* on *obv.*	60	125
3183	— — 1c. CARO; *mm.* on *obv.*	4	12
3184	— apostrophe stops. 1d. Eagle-headed harp.	6	18
3185	— 1e. Beaded harp	5	15
3186	— 1f. Scroll-fronted harp, 5 jewels on circlet	10	30
3187	— 1g. — — 7 jewels on circlet	5	15
3188	Transitional issue, double-arched crowns	15	45
3189	"Maltravers" round, 3a; *mm.* on *obv. only*	8	20
3190	— 3b. *Mm.* both sides.	4	12
3191	— 3c. Different *mm.* either side.	5	16
3192	"Richmond" oval. 4a. CARO over IACO; *mm.* both sides	15	40
3193	— — — *mm.* on *obv.*	15	40
3194	— 4b. CARO, colon stops; *mm.* on *obv..*	12	35
3195	— — — — *mm.* on *rev..*	12	35
3196	— — — — *mm.* both sides	12	35

		F £	VF £
3197	**Royal farthing.** — 4c. apostrophe stops; *mm.* rose on *obv.*..	15	40
3198	— — — — *mm.* rose both sides	15	40
3199	— — — — *mm.* rose (*obv.*); scroll (*rev.*).	15	40
3200	"Maltravers" oval. 5. CAROLVS; *mm.* lis both sides	22	45

3201   3207

		F £	VF £
3201	**Rose farthing.** 1a. Double-arched crowns; double rose; sceptres within inner circle, **BRIT**; *mm.* on *obv.* or *rev.* or both sides, or different each side	7	20
3202	— 1b. — — sceptres just break circle, **BRIT**; *mm.* on *obv.* or both sides or no *mm.*.	6	18
3203	— 1c. — — sceptres almost to outer circle, **BRIT**; *mm.*s as 3201	4	14
3204	— 1d. — — — **BRI**; *mm.* on *obv.* or both sides, or different each side . .	4	14
3205	Transitional mules of types 1d/2, with double and single arched crowns; *mm.* as 3204	7	20
3206	— 2. Single-arched crowns; single rose; *mm.* as 3204	3	9
3207	— 3. Sceptres below crown; *mm.* mullet	10	30

COMMONWEALTH, 1649–60

The coins struck during the Commonwealth have inscriptions in English instead of Latin which was considered to savour too much of papacy. St. George's cross and the Irish harp take the place of the royal arms. The silver halfpenny was issued for the last time.

Coins with *mm.* anchor were struck during the protectorship of Richard Cromwell.

Mintmarks

1649–57 Sun   1658–60 Anchor

GOLD

3208   3213

		F	VF
		£	£
3208	**Unite.** As illustration; *mm.* sun, 1649–57	450	850
3209	— *mm.* anchor, 1658, 1660	1000	3000
3210	**Double-crown.** As illus., but *X*; *mm.* sun, 1649–57	350	675
3211	— *mm.* anchor, 1660	1100	2500
3212	**Crown.** As illus., but *V*; *mm.* sun, 1649–57	250	500
3213	—*mm.* anchor, 1658, 60	900	2000

SILVER

3214	**Crown.** Same type; *mm.* sun, 1649, 51–4, 56		200	400
3215	**Halfcrown.** Similar; *mm.* sun, 1649, 1651–6		95	200
3216	— *mm.* anchor, 1658–1660 . . . . *Fair*	135	350	750
3217	**Shilling.** Similar; *mm.* sun, 1649, 1651–7		60	135
3218	— *mm.* anchor, 1658–60 . . . . *Fair*	110	275	550
3219	**Sixpence.** Similar; *mm.* sun, 1649, 1651–7		50	130
3220	— *mm.* anchor, 1658–60 . . . . *Fair*	75	225	550

3221   3223

3221	**Halfgroat.** As illustration	20	45
3222	**Penny.** Similar, but *I* above shields.	15	35
3223	**Halfpenny.** As illustration.	15	35

Oliver Cromwell. All said to be only patterns, but some circulated, especially the 1656 halfcrown and the shillings. Half broads exist, but are not contemporary.

GOLD

3224**Fifty shillings.** Head l. ℞. Shield, 1656. Inscribed edge . . . . *Extremely rare*

A very fine specimen sold at auction in November 1985 for £10,500.

3225

	F	VF	EF
	£	£	£
3225 **Broad.** (= 20s.). Similar, but grained edge		1800	3750

SILVER

3227

		F	VF	EF
3226	**Crown.** Bust l. ℞. Shield, 1658. Inscribed edge	475	900	1650
3227	**Halfcrown.** Similar, 1656, 1658	225	450	800
3228	**Shilling.** Similar, but grained edge, 1658	175	350	600
3229	**Sixpence.** Similar	*Extremely rare*		

COPPER

3230

	F	VF	EF
	£	£	£
3230 **Farthing.** Dr. bust l. ℞. CHARITIE AND CHANGE, shield . .	1200	2250	—

There are also other reverses.

SEVENTEENTH-CENTURY TOKENS

As there was no authorized copper coinage under the Commonwealth, towns and traders took it into their own hands to issue small change. Between 1648 and 1672 there was an enormous and very varied issue of these tokens. They were mostly farthings and halfpennies, but there were also some pennies. No collection is truly representative unless it contains at least a few. Many collectors specialize in those of their own town or county.

	F
	£
Price of commoner pennies.	28
— — — round halfpennies.	8
— — — octagonal halfpennies.	18
— — — heart-shaped halfpennies	100
— — — square or lozenge-shaped halfpennies	75
— — — round farthings	5

For further details of seventeenth-century tokens, see *Trade Tokens issued in the Seventeenth Century* by G. C. Williamson, also Seaby's *British Tokens and their Values*, and *Seventeenth Century Tokens of the British Isles and their Values* by Michael Dickinson, 1986.

212

CHARLES II, 1660–85

For the first two years after the Restoration the same denominations, apart from the silver crown, were struck as were issued during the Commonwealth. In 1662 the hand hammering of coins was abandoned in favour of manufacture by the Roettiers improved mill and screw presses. As a prevention against clipping the larger coins were made with the edge inscribed DECVS ET TVTAMEN and the regnal year and the medium-sized coins were given a grained edge.

The new gold coins were current for 100s., 20s. and 10s., and they came to be called "guineas" as the gold from which some of them were made was imported from Guinea by the Africa Company (whose badge was the Elephant and Castle). It was not until some years later that the guinea increased in value to 21s. and more. The Africa Co. badge is also found on some silver, and so is the plume symbol indicating silver from the Welsh mines. The four smallest silver denominations, though known today as "Maundy Money", were actually issued for general circulation: at this period the silver penny was probably the only coin distributed at the royal Maundy ceremonies. The smaller "machine"-made coins were perhaps minted later than 1662.

A good regal copper coinage was issued for the first time in 1672, but later in the reign, farthings were struck in tin (with a copper plug) in order to help the Cornish tin industry.

For the emergency issues struck in the name of Charles II in 1648/9, see the siege pieces of Pontefract listed under Charles I, nos. 3150–1.

Mintmark: Crown.

GOLD

Hammered coinage, 1660–2
First issue. Without mark of value

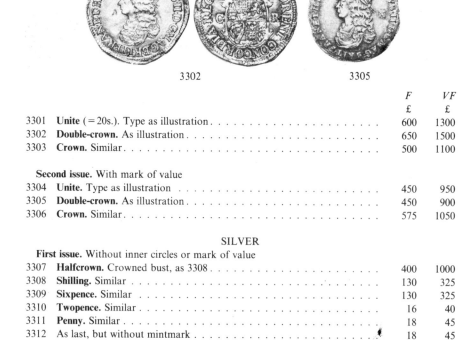

3302   3305

		F	VF
		£	£
3301	**Unite** (= 20s.). Type as illustration	600	1300
3302	**Double-crown.** As illustration	650	1500
3303	**Crown.** Similar	500	1100
	Second issue. With mark of value		
3304	**Unite.** Type as illustration	450	950
3305	**Double-crown.** As illustration	450	900
3306	**Crown.** Similar	575	1050

SILVER
First issue. Without inner circles or mark of value

3307	**Halfcrown.** Crowned bust, as 3308	400	1000
3308	**Shilling.** Similar	130	325
3309	**Sixpence.** Similar	130	325
3310	**Twopence.** Similar	16	40
3311	**Penny.** Similar	18	45
3312	As last, but without mintmark	18	45

3308   3313   3322

	F	VF
	£	£

Second issue. Without inner circles, but with mark of value

			F	VF
3313	Halfcrown. Crowned bust		550	1500
3314	Shilling. Similar		250	650
3315	Sixpence. Similar		450	1150
3316	Twopence. Similar, but *mm.* on *obv.* only		75	175
3317	Similar, but *mm.* both sides (machine made)		10	25
3318	Bust to edge of coin, legend starts at bottom l. (machine made, single arch crown)		10	25
3319	Penny. As 3317		12	30
3320	As 3318 (single arch crown)		10	25

3310   3317   3326

Third issue. With inner circles and mark of value

			F	VF
3321	Halfcrown. Crowned bust to i.c. (and rarely to edge of coin)		60	225
3322	Shilling. Similar		50	160
3323	Sixpence. Similar		50	150
3324	Fourpence. Similar		15	35
3325	Threepence. Similar		15	30
3326	Twopence. Similar		10	20
3327	Penny. Similar		20	35

GOLD

Milled coinage

3328   3335

3328   Five guineas. First bust, pointed truncation

	F	VF	EF		F	VF	EF
	£	£	£		£	£	£
1668	700	1550	3600	1674	800	1700	3750
1669	750	1600	3600	1675	750	1600	3500
1670	700	1400	3400	1676	800	1700	3750
1671	800	1750	3750	1677	750	1600	3600
1672	700	1550	3600	1678	700	1500	3600
1673	700	1550	3600				

3329   — with elephant below bust

	F	VF	EF		F	VF	EF
1668	700	1400	3400	1675	950	2200	4500
1669	950	2200	4500	1677/5	*Extremely rare*		

3330   — with elephant and castle below

	F	VF	EF		F	VF	EF
1675	*Extremely rare*			1677	800	1700	3750
1676	750	1600	3600	1678	850	1900	4000

3331   Second bust, rounded truncation

	F	VF	EF		F	VF	EF
1678/7	850	1900	4000	1682	700	1400	3400
1679	700	1400	3400	1683	700	1550	3600
1680	750	1600	3600	1684	700	1400	3400
1681	700	1400	3400				

3332   — with elephant and castle below

	F	VF	EF		F	VF	EF
1680	*Extremely rare*						
1681	850	1900	4000	1683	850	1900	4000
1682	750	1600	3600	1684	700	1400	3400

3333   Two guineas. First bust, pointed truncation

	F	VF	EF		F	VF	EF
1664	350	800	3250	1669	*Extremely rare*		
1665	*Extremely rare*			1671	400	900	3500

3334   — with elephant below

	F	VF	EF
1664	275	650	2750

3335   Second bust, rounded truncation

	F	VF	EF		F	VF	EF
1675	375	800	3250	1680	400	900	3500
1676	300	650	2750	1681	250	650	2750
1677	250	650	2750	1682	250	650	2750
1678/7	250	600	2500 .	1683	250	600	2500
1679	300	650	2750	1684	375	750	3000

3336 — with elephant and castle below

	F	VF	EF		F	VF	EF
	£	£	£		£	£	£
1676	275	650	2750	1682	250	600	2500
1677		*Extremely rare*		1683	400	900	3500
1678	300	650	2750	1684	400	900	3500

3337 — with elephant only below, 1678 . . . .   *Extremely rare*

Overstruck dates are listed only if commoner than the normal date or if no normal date is known.

3343   3345

3338	**Guinea.** First bust, 1663	500	1450	3250
3339	— with elephant below, 1663	400	1150	2750
3340	Second bust, 1664	350	950	2500
3341	— with elephant below, 1664		*Extremely rare*	

3342 Third bust, normal portrait

1664	200	600	1950	1669	250	750	2250
1665	200	600	1950	1670	200	600	1950
1666	200	600	1950	1671	200	600	1950
1667	200	600	1950	1672	250	750	2250
1668	200	600	1950	1673	350	950	2500

3343 — with elephant below

1664	250	750	2250	1668		*Extremely rare*	
1665	250	750	2250				

3344 Fourth bust, rounded truncation

1672	175	500	1750	1679	150	450	1650
1673	175	500	1750	1680	150	450	1650
1674	250	750	2250	1681	175	500	1750
1675	200	600	1950	1682	175	500	1750
1676	150	450	1650	1683	150	450	1650
1677	150	450	1650	1684	175	500	1750
1678	150	450	1650				

3345 — with elephant and castle below

1674		*Extremely rare*		1680	400	1200	3000
1675	250	750	2250	1681	250	750	2250
1676	175	500	1750	1682	275	800	2250
1677	175	500	1750	1683	400	1200	3000
1678	350	950	2500	1684	275	800	2250
1679	250	750	2250				

	F £	*VF* £	*EF* £		*F* £	*VF* £	*EF* £

3346 Guinea. Fourth bust, with elephant below

1677		*Extremely rare*		1678		*Extremely rare*	

3347 Half-guinea. First bust, pointed truncation

| 1669 . . . . . . | 175 | 500 | 1800 | 1671 . . . . | 225 | 650 | 2000 |
| 1670 . . . . . . | 150 | 350 | 1500 | 1672 . . . . | 225 | 650 | 2000 |

3348 Second bust, rounded truncation

1672	175	400	1600	1679	135	350	1500
1673	300	750	2250	1680	300	750	2250
1674	300	750	2250	1681	300	750	2250
1675		*Extremely rare*		1682	200	600	2000
1676	175	375	1500	1683	175	400	1600
1677	175	400	1600	1684	135	325	1500
1678	175	400	1600				

3349 with elephant and castle below

1676	350	850	—	1682	300	800	2400
1677	300	800	2400	1683		*Extremely rare*	
1678/7	225	650	2000	1684	175	400	1600
1680		*Extremely rare*					

SILVER

Milled coinage

3350

		F	*VF*	*EF*
3350	**Crown.** First bust, rose below, edge undated, 1662	35	175	800
3351	— — edge dated, 1662.	45	225	950
3352	— no rose, edge dated, 1662	50	275	1000
3353	— — edge not dated, 1662	45	225	950
3354	— — new reverse, shields altered, 1663, regnal year on edge in Roman figures ANNO REGNI XV	40	200	950

3355

3355 Second bust, regnal year on edge in Roman figures

	F	VF	EF		F	VF	EF
	£	£	£		£	£	£
1664	45	200	950	1666	45	225	950
1665	150	600	—				

3356 — — elephant below bust, 1666 130   450   —

3357 — regnal year on edge in words (e.g. 1667 = DECIMO NONO)

	F	VF	EF		F	VF	EF
1667	35	165	800	1670	45	200	950
1668	35	165	800	1671	35	165	800
1669	100	400	—				

3358 Third bust

	F	VF	EF		F	VF	EF
1671	35	165	800	1676	35	165	800
1672	35	165	800	1677	35	165	800
1673	35	165	800	1678/7	100	400	—
1674		*Extremely rare*		1679	35	165	800
1675/3	165	600	—	1680/79	50	200	950

3359 Fourth bust

	F	VF	EF		F	VF	EF
1679	35	165	800	1682/1	45	200	950
1680	35	165	800	1683	110	450	—
1681	40	200	950	1684	70	350	—

3360 — elephant and castle below bust, 1681   950   2250   —

3367   3369   3370

	F	VF	EF
	£	£	£
3361 **Halfcrown.** First bust, regnal year on edge in Roman figures, 1663	40	175	750
3362 Second bust, 1664	60	275	950
3363 Third bust, 1666	500	1750	—
3364 — elephant below bust, 1666	225	550	—

3365 — regnal date on edge in words

	F	VF	EF			F	VF	EF
	£	£	£			£	£	£
1667/4		*Extremely rare*		1669/4	110	350	—
1668/4	90	300	—	1670	25	125	650

3366 — Third bust variety

| 1671 . . . . | 25 | 100 | 550 | 1672 . . . . | 30 | 125 | 650 |

3367 Fourth bust

1672	40	150	600	1679	25	100	550
1673	25	100	550	1680	100	300	—
1674	75	250	950	1681	35	175	750
1675	35	175	750	1682	50	225	850
1676	25	90	475	1683	30	125	650
1677	25	100	550	1684/3	90	350	—
1678	100	300	—				

3368 — plume below bust

| 1673 . . . . | | *Extremely rare* | | 1683 . . . . | | *Extremely rare* | |

3371   3376   3380

3369 — plume below bust and in centre of *rev.*, 1673 . . . .   *Extremely rare*

3370 — elephant and castle below bust, 1681 . . . . *fair* 350   —   —   —

3371   3376   3380

| **3371** **Shilling.** First bust, 1663 . . . . | 20 | 60 | 225 |

3372 Shilling. First bust variety

	F £	VF £	EF £		F £	VF £	EF £
1663	20	60	225	1668	160	400	—
1666		*Extremely rare*		1669/6		*Extremely rare*	

3373 — elephant below bust, 1666 . . . . | 140 | 500 | —

3374 Guinea head, elephant below bust, 1666 . . . . | 350 | 1000 | —

3375 Second bust

	F	VF	EF		F	VF	EF
1666		*Extremely rare*		1676	30	90	400
1668	20	60	225	1677	30	90	400
1669		*Extremely rare*		1678	45	175	600
1670	45	175	600	1679	30	100	400
1671	50	225	700	1680		*Extremely rare*	
1672	30	120	450	1681	50	225	700
1673	45	175	700	1682/1	225	500	—
1674	45	175	700	1683		*Extremely rare*	
1675	90	300	—				

3376 — plume below bust and in centre of *rev.*

	F	VF	EF		F	VF	EF
1671	80	350	—	1676	80	350	—
1673	80	400	—	1679	100	450	—
1674	80	350	—	1680	150	550	—
1675	80	400	—				

3377 — plume *rev.* only, 1674 . . . . | 125 | 450 | —

3378 — plume *obv.* only

	F	VF	EF		F	VF	EF
1677	125	500	—	1679	90	400	—

3379 — elephant and castle below bust, 1681/0 . . . . | 1550 | — | —

3380 Third (large) bust

	F	VF	EF		F	VF	EF
1674	125	475	—	1675	75	275	950

3381 Fourth (large) bust, older features

	F	VF	EF		F	VF	EF
1683	75	200	800	1684	60	175	700

3382 Sixpence

	F	VF	EF		F	VF	EF
1674	15	45	150	1680	25	90	300
1675	15	45	150	1681	15	45	150
1676	20	90	300	1682/1	18	65	200
1677	15	45	150	1683	15	45	150
1678/7	18	65	200	1684	15	50	180
1679	18	65	200				

3383 Fourpence. Undated. Crowned bust l. to edge of coin, value behind. R. Shield . . . . | 7 | 15 | 30

3384 Dated. *O*. As illustration on p.220. R. Four C's

	F	VF	EF		F	VF	EF
1670	4	10	30	1678	4	9	27
1671	4	10	30	1679	3	9	27
1672/1	4	10	30	1680	3	9	27
1673	4	10	30	1681	3	9	27
1674	4	10	30	1682	4	9	27
1675	4	10	30	1683	3	9	27
1676	4	10	30	1684/3	3	9	27
1677	4	9	27				

3385 Threepence. Undated. As 3383 . . . . | 8 | 18 | 40

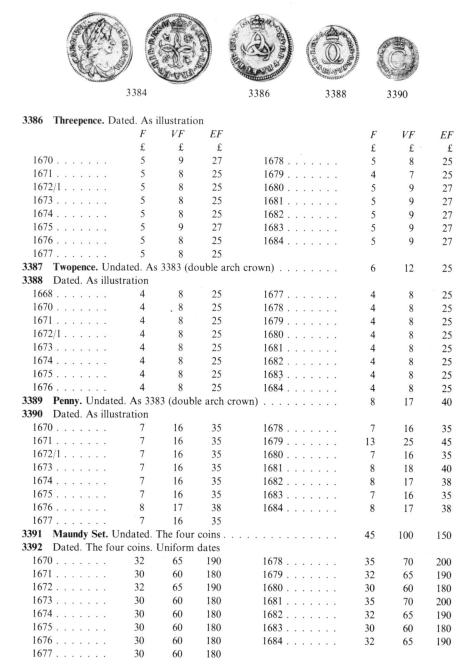

3384 3386 3388 3390

3386 Threepence. Dated. As illustration

	F	VF	EF		F	VF	EF
	£	£	£		£	£	£
1670	5	9	27	1678	5	8	25
1671	5	8	25	1679	4	7	25
1672/1	5	8	25	1680	5	9	27
1673	5	8	25	1681	5	9	27
1674	5	8	25	1682	5	9	27
1675	5	9	27	1683	5	9	27
1676	5	8	25	1684	5	9	27
1677	5	8	25				

3387 Twopence. Undated. As 3383 (double arch crown) 6 12 25

3388 Dated. As illustration

	F	VF	EF		F	VF	EF
1668	4	8	25	1677	4	8	25
1670	4	8	25	1678	4	8	25
1671	4	8	25	1679	4	8	25
1672/1	4	8	25	1680	4	8	25
1673	4	8	25	1681	4	8	25
1674	4	8	25	1682	4	8	25
1675	4	8	25	1683	4	8	25
1676	4	8	25	1684	4	8	25

3389 Penny. Undated. As 3383 (double arch crown) 8 17 40

3390 Dated. As illustration

	F	VF	EF		F	VF	EF
1670	7	16	35	1678	7	16	35
1671	7	16	35	1679	13	25	45
1672/1	7	16	35	1680	7	16	35
1673	7	16	35	1681	8	18	40
1674	7	16	35	1682	8	17	38
1675	7	16	35	1683	7	16	35
1676	8	17	38	1684	8	17	38
1677	7	16	35				

3391 Maundy Set. Undated. The four coins 45 100 150

3392 Dated. The four coins. Uniform dates

	F	VF	EF		F	VF	EF
1670	32	65	190	1678	35	70	200
1671	30	60	180	1679	32	65	190
1672	32	65	190	1680	30	60	180
1673	30	60	180	1681	35	70	200
1674	30	60	180	1682	32	65	190
1675	30	60	180	1683	30	60	180
1676	30	60	180	1684	32	65	190
1677	30	60	180				

COPPER AND TIN

3393   3394

3393 Copper **halfpenny**

	F	VF	EF			F	VF	EF
	£	£	£			£	£	£
1672	20	60	225		1675	20	60	225
1673	20	60	225					

3394 Copper **farthing**. As illustration

	F	VF	EF			F	VF	EF
1672	12	30	175		1675	18	40	175
1673	12	30	175		1679	20	50	225
1674	15	35	175					

3395 Tin **farthing**. Somewhat similar, but with copper plug, edge inscribed NUMMORVM FAMVLVS, and date on edge only

	Fair	F	VF	EF
	£	£	£	£
1684	20	45	125	450
1685		*Extremely rare*		

JAMES II, 1685–8

Tin halfpence and farthings provided the only base metal coinage during this short reign. All genuine tin coins of this period have a copper plug.

GOLD

		F	VF	EF
		£	£	£
3396	**Five guineas.** First bust l., sceptres misplaced, 1686	950	1750	3800
3397	Sceptres normal. First bust			

	F	VF	EF		F	VF	EF
	£	£	£		£	£	£
1687	900	1650	3600	1688	850	1600	3600
3397a — second bust							
1687	900	1650	3600	1688	850	1600	3600
3398 — first bust. Elephant and castle below bust							
1687	1000	1800	4000	1688	1000	1800	4000
3399 Two guineas. Similar							
1687	450	1300	3000	1688/7	500	1400	3250

3403   3404

3400 Guinea. First bust							
1685	180	450	1550	1686	225	600	1900
3401 — elephant and castle below							
1685	225	650	2150	1686		*Extremely rare*	
3402 Second bust							
1686	180	450	1550	1688	180	450	1550
1687	180	450	1550				
3403 Elephant and castle below							
1686	300	950	—	1688	200	500	1700
1687	200	500	1700				
3404 Half-guinea							
1686	175	450	1350	1688	200	500	1500
1687	250	600	1800				
3405 Elephant and castle below, 1686	450	1500	—				

SILVER

3406 Crown. First bust, 1686	60	250	600				
3407 Second bust							
1687	45	175	400	1688	50	200	450

3408   1st bust   2nd bust

3408 Halfcrown. First bust

	F	VF	EF			F	VF	EF
	£	£	£			£	£	£
1685	35	120	450	1687		35	120	450
1686	35	120	450					

3409 Second bust

| 1687 . . . . | 50 | 200 | 600 | 1688 . . . . | | 45 | 155 | 525 |

3410 Shilling

| 1685 . . . . | 35 | 120 | 350 | 1687/6 . . . . . . | | 40 | 155 | 450 |
| 1686 . . . . | 35 | 120 | 350 | 1688 . . . . | | 40 | 155 | 450 |

3411 Plume in centre of *rev.*, 1685 . . . .   *Extremely rare*

3412 Sixpence. Early type shields

	F	VF	EF			F	VF	EF
	£	£	£			£	£	£
1686	25	80	250	1687		30	90	275

3413 Late type shields

| 1687 . . . . | 25 | 80 | 250 | 1688 . . . . | | 30 | 90 | 275 |

3414   3415   3416   3417

3414 Fourpence. *O*. As illus. R. IIII crowned

| 1686 . . . . | 6 | 14 | 30 | 1688 . . . . | | 6 | 14 | 30 |
| 1687/6 . . . . . . | 6 | 13 | 28 | | | | | |

3415 Threepence. As illustration

1685	6	13	27					
1686	6	13	27	1687/6		6	13	27
				1688		6	13	27

3416 Twopence. As illustration

| 1686 . . . . | 6 | 13 | 25 | 1688 . . . . | | 7 | 13 | 25 |
| 1687 . . . . | 6 | 13 | 25 | | | | | |

3417 Penny. As illustration | | | | 1687 . . . . | | 10 | 20 | 30 |

| 1685 . . . . | 10 | 20 | 30 | | | | | |
| 1686 . . . . | 10 | 20 | 30 | 1688 . . . . | | 10 | 20 | 30 |

3418 Maundy Set. As last four. Uniform dates

| 1686 . . . . | 35 | 70 | 150 | 1688 . . . . | | 35 | 70 | 150 |
| 1687 . . . . | 35 | 70 | 150 | | | | | |

TIN

3419

3419 **Halfpenny**	*Fair*	*F*	*VF*	*EF*
1685	20	40	125	400
1686	22	45	150	450
1687	20	40	125	400
3420 **Farthing.** Cuirassed bust				
1684			*Extremely rare*	
1685	20	40	125	400
1686	22	45	150	450
1687			*Extremely rare*	
3421 Draped bust, 1687	30	55	175	500

WILLIAM AND MARY, 1688–94

Due to the poor state of the silver coinage, much of it worn hammered coin, the guinea, which was valued at 21s. 6d. at the beginning of the reign, circulated for as much as 30s. by 1694. The tin halfpennies and farthings were replaced by copper coins in 1694. The rampant lion of Orange is now placed as an inescutcheon on the centre of the royal arms.

GOLD

3422 Five guineas. Conjoined heads r.

	F £	VF £	EF £		F £	VF £	EF £
1691	750	1750	3800	1693	750	1750	3800
1692	750	1750	3800	1694	800	2000	4000

3423 — elephant and castle below

	F	VF	EF		F	VF	EF
1691	850	1950	4500	1693	1100	2350	5000
1692	900	2000	4500	1694	1000	2250	4750

3424 Two guineas. Conjoined heads r.

	F	VF	EF		F	VF	EF
1693	400	900	3000	1694/3	400	900	3000

3425 — elephant and castle below

	F	VF	EF		F	VF	EF
1691		Extremely rare		1694/3	650	1400	4000
1693	650	1400	4000				

3427

3426 Guinea. Conjoined heads r.

	F	VF	EF		F	VF	EF
1689	180	450	1350	1692	225	650	1800
1690	200	550	1650	1693	225	600	1650
1691	225	600	1650	1694	180	500	1450

3427 — elephant and castle below

	F	VF	EF		F	VF	EF
1689	200	500	1450	1692	250	600	1650
1690	270	750	2100	1693		Extremely rare	
1691	225	550	1650	1694	250	600	1700

3428 — elephant only below

	F	VF	EF		F	VF	EF
1692	270	750	2100	1693		Extremely rare	

3429   3430

3429 Half-guinea. First heads, 1689   175   450   1500

Overstruck dates are listed only if commoner than the normal date or if no normal date is known.

3430 Half-guinea. Second head, normal portraits

	F	VF	EF		F	VF	EF
	£	£	£		£	£	£
1690	180	450	1600	1693		*Extremely rare*	
1691	225	550	1800	1694	125	350	1250
1692	180	450	1600				

3431 — — elephant and castle below

1691	155	450	1350	1692	125	350	1250

3432 — — elephant only below, 1692 . . . . *Extremely rare*

SILVER

3433 Crown. Conjoined busts, as 3436 below

1691	120	300	900	1692	120	300	900

3434

3435

3434 Halfcrown. First busts and first shields, 1689 . . . . 25 70 300

3435 — and second shield

1689	30	80	375	1690	35	120	450

3436 Second busts. R. As illustration below

1691	32	110	400	1693	30	90	375
1692	35	120	450				

3436

3438

3437 Shilling. Similar

1692	30	95	350	1693	22	80	300

3438 Sixpence. Similar

1693	20	65	250	1694	40	140	400

3439	**Fourpence.** First busts, no tie to wreath							
		F	VF	EF		F	VF	EF
		£	£	£		£	£	£
	1689	6	16	30	1691	8	19	40
	1690	7	16	35	1694	8	17	38
3440	Second busts, tie to wreath							
	1691	8	20	45	1693	10	21	45
	1692	7	18	40	1694	10	21	45
3441	**Threepence.** First busts, no tie							
	1689	6	14	28				
	1690	7	14	30	1691	12	28	45
3442	Second busts, tie to wreath							
	1691	7	19	40	1693	7	17	38
	1692	7	19	40	1694	7	16	37
3443	**Twopence**							
	1689	5	13	30	1693	7	14	35
	1691	7	14	35	1694	8	15	38
	1692	7	14	35				
3444	**Penny.** Legend continuous over heads, 1689.					90	200	375
3445	— legend broken by heads							
	1690	12	23	50	1693	12	23	50
	1691	12	23	50	1694	12	23	50
	1692	12	23	50				

3446

3446	**Maundy Set.** As last pieces. Uniform dates							
	1689	130	275	500	1693	60	120	210
	1691	50	110	200	1694	50	110	200
	1692	50	110	200				

TIN AND COPPER

		Fair	F	VF	EF
		£	£	£	£
3447	**Tin Halfpenny.** Small draped busts, 1689.	175	350	900	—
3448	Large cuirassed busts; date only on edge				
	1690	20	40	110	400
3449	— — date in exergue and on edge				
	1691	20	40	110	400
	1692	20	40	110	400
3450	**Tin Farthing.** Small draped busts				
	1689	90	175	500	—
	1689, edge 1690			*Extremely rare*	

3451 **Tin Farthing.** Large cuirassed busts

	Fair	*F*	*VF*	*EF*
	£	£	£	£
1690, edge 1689			*Extremely rare*	
1690	20	40	115	425
1691	20	40	115	425
1692	22	45	120	475

3453

3452	Copper **Halfpenny**, 1694.	15	35	300
3453	Copper **Farthing**, 1694.	20	40	350

WILLIAM III, 1694–1702

In 1696 a great re-coinage was undertaken to replace the hammered silver that made up most of the coinage in circulation, much of it being clipped and badly worn. Branch mints were set up at Bristol, Chester, Exeter, Norwich and York to help with the re-coinage. For a short time before they were finally demonetized, unclipped hammered coins were allowed to circulate freely provided they were officially pierced in the centre. Silver coins with roses between the coats of arms were made from silver obtained from the West of England mines.

GOLD

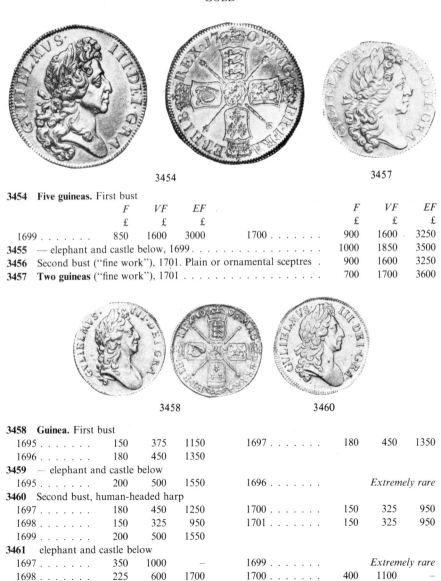

3454   3457

3454	**Five guineas.** First bust	F	VF	EF		F	VF	EF
		£	£	£		£	£	£
	1699	850	1600	3000	1700	900	1600	3250
3455	— elephant and castle below, 1699.					1000	1850	3500
3456	Second bust ("fine work"), 1701. Plain or ornamental sceptres .					900	1600	3250
3457	**Two guineas** ("fine work"), 1701					700	1700	3600

3458   3460

3458	**Guinea.** First bust							
	1695	150	375	1150	1697	180	450	1350
	1696	180	450	1350				
3459	— elephant and castle below							
	1695	200	500	1550	1696		*Extremely rare*	
3460	Second bust, human-headed harp							
	1697	180	450	1250	1700	150	325	950
	1698	150	325	950	1701	150	325	950
	1699	200	500	1550				
3461	elephant and castle below							
	1697	350	1000	—	1699		*Extremely rare*	
	1698	225	600	1700	1700	400	1100	—

			F	VF	EF
			£	£	£
3462	**Guinea.** — R. Large lettering and large date, 1698		150	375	1150
3463	— R. Scrolled harp, 1701		150	375	1150
3464	— — elephant and castle, 1701			*Extremely rare*	
3465	Third bust ("fine work"), 1701		300	700	2500
3466	**Half-guinea.** R. With early harp, 1695		100	250	700
3467	**Half-guinea.** Elephant and castle. R. With early harp				

	F	VF	EF			
	£	£	£			
1695	225	550	1600	1696	115	300	900
3468	R. With late harp					
1697	160	400	1200	1700	110	250	675
1698	110	250	675	1701	110	250	675
1699		*Extremely rare*				
3469 — elephant and castle, 1698					180	450	1400

SILVER

3470	**Crown.** First bust, first harp					
1695	25	95	275	1696	25	95	250
3471	Second bust (hair across breast), 1696					*Unique*
3472	Third bust, first harp, 1696			30	100	275
3473	— second harp, 1697			250	800	—
3474	Third bust variety, third harp, 1700			30	115	300

3490

			F	VF	EF
3475	**Halfcrown.** Small shields, 1696		15	50	175
3476	— B (*Bristol*) below bust, 1696		20	70	225
3477	— C (*Chester*) below bust, 1696		30	125	375
3478	— E (*Exeter*) below bust, 1696		45	175	500
3479	— N (*Norwich*) below bust, 1696		25	90	275
3480	— y (*York*) below bust, 1696		30	125	375
3481	Large shield, early harp, 1696		15	50	175
3482	— — B (*Bristol*) below bust, 1696		20	70	225
3483	— — C (*Chester*) below bust, 1696		25	90	275
3484	— — E (*Exeter*) below bust, 1696		30	125	375
3485	— — N (*Norwich*) below bust, 1696		45	175	500
3486	— — y (*York*) below bust, 1696		25	90	275
3487	Large shields, ordinary harp				

1696	35	135	400	1697	15	50	175
3488 — — B (*Bristol*) below bust, 1697					20	80	250

3489 ——C(*Chester*) below bust

	F	VF	EF		F	VF	EF
	£	£	£		£	£	£
1696	35	135	400	1697	20	70	225

3490 —— E (*Exeter*) below bust

1696	35	135	400	1697	20	55	195

3491 —— N (*Norwich*) below bust

1696	45	175	500	1697	20	70	225

3492 —— y (*York*) below bust, 1696. . . . . | 20 | 55 | 195 |

3493 Second bust (hair across breast), 1696 . . . . *Unique*

3494 Half-crown. Modified large shields

1698	15	55	200	1700	20	60	225
1699	30	90	300	1701	25	65	250

3495 Elephant and castle below bust, 1701 . . . . *Fair* 250

3496 Plumes in angles on *rev.*, 1701 . . . . | 30 | 100 | 300 |

1st bust   2nd bust   3rd bust   3507

3rd bust var.   4th bust   5th bust

3497 Shilling. First bust

1695	18	50	150	1697	9	25	80
1696	9	25	80				

3498 — B (*Bristol*) below bust

1696	18	45	135	1697	20	50	150

3499 — C (*Chester*) below bust

1696	20	50	150	1697	20	50	150

3500 — E (*Exeter*) below bust

1696	20	50	150	1697	20	50	150

3501 — (*Norwich*) below bust

1696	20	50	150	1697	20	50	150

3502 — y (*York*) below bust

1696	20	50	150	1697	20	50	150

3503 — Y (*York*) below bust

1696	22	60	175	1697	22	60	175

	F	VF	EF		F	VF	EF
	£	£	£		£	£	£
3504 **Shilling.** Second bust (hair across breast), 1696							*Unique*
3505 Third bust, 1697					9	25	80
3506 — B (*Bristol*) below bust, 1697					22	60	175
3507 — C (*Chester*) below bust							
1696	45	150	450	1697	20	50	150
3508 — E (*Exeter*) below bust, 1697					22	60	175
3509 — N (*Norwich*) below bust, 1697					20	60	175
3510 — y (*York*) below bust							
1696		*Extremely rare*		1697	22	60	175
3511 Third bust variety							
1697	9	25	85	1698	18	50	150
3512 — B (*Bristol*) below bust, 1697					22	60	175
3513 Third bust variety C (*Chester*) below bust, 1697					50	150	450
3514 — R. Plumes in angles, 1698					55	175	525
3515 Fourth bust ("flaming hair")							
1698	30	70	250	1699	30	70	250
3516 Fifth bust (hair high)							
1699	22	60	200	1701	22	60	200
1700	15	35	100				
3517 R. Plumes in angles							
1699	40	115	350	1701	40	115	350
3518 — R. Roses in angles, 1699					55	150	450
3519 — plume below bust, 1700					750	—	—

3520   3542

	F	VF	EF		F	VF	EF
3520 **Sixpence.** First bust, early harp							
1695	20	60	175	1696	5	18	50
3521 — — B below bust, 1696					8	22	65
3522 — — C below bust, 1696					15	45	135
3523 — — E below bust, 1696					20	60	175
3524 — — N below bust, 1696					12	40	120
3525 — — y below bust, 1696					10	30	90
3526 — — Y below bust, 1696					20	60	175
3527 — later harp, large crowns, 1696					25	75	225
3528 — — — B below bust							
1696	25	75	225	1697	20	60	175
3529 — — — C below bust, 1697					25	75	225
3530 — — — E below bust, 1697					22	70	225
3531 — — small crowns							
1696	20	65	190	1697	8	22	65
3532 — — — B below bust							
1696	18	55	160	1697	12	40	120

	F £	VF £	EF £		F £	VF £	EF £
3533 — — — C below bust							
1696	35	10	300	1697	12	40	120
3534 — — — E below bust, 1697					15	45	135
3535 — — — N below bust							
1696	30	90	275	1697	10	30	90
3536 — — — y below bust, 1697					25	75	225
3537 Second bust							
1696	150	300	—	1697	35	120	350
3538 Third bust, large crowns							
1697	5	18	50	1700	8	22	65
1698	8	22	65	1701	11	35	90
1699	27	80	240				
3539 — — E below bust, 1697					15	45	135
3540 — — C below bust, 1697					25	70	200
3541 — — E below bust, 1697					30	90	275
3542 Third bust small crowns, 1697					10	30	90
3543 — — C below bust, 1697					22	65	180
3544 — — E below bust, 1697					16	50	150
3545 — — Y below bust, 1697					25	80	240
3546 — R. Plumes in angles							
1698	10	30	90	1699	14	40	120
3547 — R. Roses in angles, 1699					25	75	225
3548* — plume below bust, 1700					*Extremely rare*		

* An extremely fine specimen sold at auction in October 1985 for £3500.

3549   3550   3551   3552

3549 Fourpence. R. 4 crowned							
1697			*Unique*	1700	11	20	45
1698	12	22	50	1701	12	24	55
1699	11	22	50	1702	11	20	45
3550 Threepence. R. 3 crowned							
1698	11	20	45	1700	11	20	45
1699	12	22	48	1701	11	20	45
3551 Twopence. R. 2 crowned							
1698	11	19	38	1700	10	19	38
1699	10	18	36	1701	9	18	38
3552 Penny. R. 1 crowned							
1698	11	19	38	1700	12	20	40
1699	12	20	40	1701	11	19	38
3553 Maundy Set. As last four. Uniform dates							
1698	50	105	180	1700	60	115	190
1699	60	115	190	1701	50	105	180

COPPER

3554 Halfpenny. First issue. Britannia with r. hand raised

	F	VF	EF			F	VF	EF
	£	£	£			£	£	£
1695	8	30	175		1697	7	25	175
1696	7	25	175		1698	9	40	200

3555 Second issue. R. Date in legend

1698	8	30	175		1699	7	25	175

3556 Third issue. R. Britannia with r. hand on knee

1699	7	25	175		1701	8	30	175
1700	7	25	175					

3557

3558

3557 Farthing. First issue

	F	VF	EF			F	VF	EF
1695	10	35	225		1698	60	175	—
1696	9	30	200		1699	9	30	200
1697	9	30	200		1700	9	30	200

3558 Second issue. R. Date at end of legend

1698	25	75	400					
1699	14	45	275					

ANNE, 1702–14

The Act of Union of 1707, which effected the unification of the ancient kingdoms of England and Scotland into a single realm, resulted in a change in the royal arms—on the after-Union coinage the English leopards and Scottish lion are emblazoned per pale on the top and bottom shields. After the Union the rose in the centre of the reverse of the gold coins is replaced by the Garter star.

Following a successful Anglo–Dutch expedition against Spain, bullion seized in Vigo Bay was sent to be minted into coin, and the coins made from this metal had the word VIGO placed below the queen's bust.

GOLD

Before Union with Scotland

3560 **Five guineas**	F	VF	EF		F	VF	EF
	£	£	£		£	£	£
1705	1000	2250	6000	1706	950	2000	5500
3561 VIGO below bust, 1703					6000	15,000	—
3562 **Guinea**							
1702	175	550	1750	1706	275	700	2250
1705	275	675	2150	1707	325	800	2500
3563 VIGO below bust, 1703					3000	7000	—
3564 **Half-guinea**							
1702	225	550	1750	1705	225	550	1750
3565 VIGO below bust, 1703					2250	5000	—

3562   3574

After Union with Scotland. The shields on the reverse are changed

	F	VF	EF		F	VF	EF
3566 Five guineas. Ordinary bust, 1706.					850	1900	5000
3567 Narrower shields, tall narrow crowns, larger rev. letters, 1709 . .					950	2000	5500
3568 Broader shields							
1711	850	1900	5000	1714/3	850	1900	5000
1713	950	2000	5500				
3569 Two guineas							
1709	400	950	2750	1713	400	950	2750
1711	400	950	2750	1714	450	1000	3000
3570 Guinea. First bust							
1707	200	400	1300	1708		*Extremely rare*	
3571 — elephant and castle below, 1707.					400	950	2750
3572 Second bust							
1707		*Extremely rare*		1709	200	425	1400
1708	180	375	1200				
3573 — elephant and castle below							
1708	350	900	2750	1709	325	800	2500

3574 Guinea. Third bust

	F	VF	EF		F	VF	EF
	£	£	£		£	£	£
1710	150	300	850	1713	150	275	800
1711	150	300	850	1714	150	275	800
1712	200	400	1200				

3575 Half-guinea

1707	160	325	900	1711	135	260	700
1708	200	450	1200	1712	160	325	900
1709	135	275	750	1713	135	275	750
1710	120	260	700	1714	135	275	750

SILVER

Before Union with Scotland

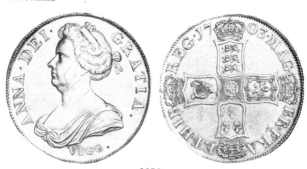

3576

3576	**Crown.** VIGO below bust, 1703			90	275	750
3577	R. Plumes in angles, 1705			150	450	1350
3578	R. Roses and plumes in angles					
1706	70	225	600	1707	65	200	600
3579	**Halfcrown.** No marks below bust or on *rev.* (i.e. plain), 1703			275	750	—
3580	VIGO below bust, 1703			25	80	250
3581	R. Plumes in angles					
1704	45	150	400	1705	30	95	275
3582	R. Roses and plumes in angles					
1706	25	80	250	1707	20	70	200

3583   3589

3583	**Shilling.** First bust, 1702			30	90	225
3584	— R. Plumes in angles, 1702			30	100	275
3585	— VIGO below bust, 1702			30	95	250

		F £	VF £	EF £		F £	VF £	EF £
3586	Second bust, VIGO below, 1703	20	60	150				
3587	— plain							
	1704	165	400	—	1705	40	100	275
3588	— R. Plumes in angles							
	1704	40	120	300	1705	30	90	250
3589	— R. Roses and plumes in angles							
	1705	25	75	200	1707	30	85	225

3593   3594   Early Shield   Late Shield

		F £	VF £	EF £		F £	VF £	EF £
3590	Sixpence. VIGO below bust, 1703	12	35	95				
3591	Plain, 1705	20	70	200				
3592	R. Early shields, plumes in angles, 1705	16	50	150				
3593	R. Late shields, plumes in angles, 1705	20	60	175				
3594	R. Roses and plumes in angles							
	1705	18	60	200	1707	16	45	125
3595	Fourpence. R. Crowned 4							
	1703	7	15	30	1708	6	14	28
	1704	6	14	28	1709	6	14	28
	1705	7	15	30	1710	6	14	28
	1706	6	14	28	1713	6	14	28
3596	Threepence. R. Crowned 3							
	1703	7	15	35	1708	6	14	28
	1704	6	12	26	1709	6	14	28
	1705	6	12	26	1710	6	14	28
	1706	6	14	28	1713	6	14	28
	1707	6	14	28				
3597	Twopence. R. Crowned 2							
	1703	6	13	27	1708	6	12	26
	1704	6	12	26	1709	7	13	27
	1705	6	12	26	1710	6	12	26
	1706	6	13	27	1713	6	12	26
	1707	6	13	27				
3598	Penny. R. Crowned 1							
	1703	11	21	35	1709	10	19	32
	1705	10	19	32	1710	14	30	40
	1706	10	19	32	1713	11	21	35
	1708	11	21	35				

3599

	F	VF	EF			F	VF	EF
	£	£	£			£	£	£

3599 Maundy Set. As last four. Uniform dates

1703	45	75	175	1709	45	75	175
1705	45	75	175	1710	50	80	180
1706	40	70	165	1713	45	75	125
1708	45	75	175				

After Union with Scotland

The shields on reverse are changed. The Edinburgh coins have been included here as they are now coins of Great Britain.

3600 Crown. Second bust, E (Edinburgh) below

1707	40	125	450	1708	45	145	500

3601 — plain

1707	45	125	450	1708	45	125	450

3602 R. Plumes in angles, 1708. . . . . 55 225 675

3603 Third bust. R. Roses and plumes, 1713 . . . . 40 125 450

3604

3604 Halfcrown. Plain

1707	20	65	175	1709	20	65	175
1708	20	60	175	1713	25	75	200

3605 Halfcrown. E below bust

1707	18	55	150	1709	65	225	675
1708	18	55	150				

3606 R. Plumes in angles, 1708. 30 90 250

3607 R. Roses and plumes in angles

1710	25	80	225	1713	25	80	225
1712	22	70	200	1714	22	70	200

3609

	F £	VF £	EF £		F £	VF £	EF £
3608 **Shilling.** Second bust, E below							
1707	18	50	150	1708	30	95	300
3609 — E* below							
1707	35	110	350	1708	20	60	175
3610 Third bust, plain							
1707	12	35	90	1709	12	35	90
1708	8	25	75	1711	40	150	450
3611 — R. Plumes in angles							
1707	22	60	175	1708	15	45	135
3612 — E below							
1707	15	40	120	1708	25	80	250
3613 **Shilling.** Second bust. R. Roses and plumes, 1708.					50	150	450
3614 Third bust. R. Roses and plumes							
1708	25	70	200	1710	12	35	90
3615 "Edinburgh" bust, E* below							
1707		*Extremely rare*		1709	30	95	275
1708	25	80	250				
3616 — E below, 1709.						*Extremely rare*	
3617 Fourth bust. R. Roses and plumes							
1710	25	80	250	1713/2	15	50	150
1712	12	35	90	1714	12	35	90
3618 — plain, 1711					8	20	60

3620   3623

	F £	VF £	EF £		F £	VF £	EF £
3619 **Sixpence.** Normal bust. R. Plain							
1707	9	22	65	1711	5	15	45
1708	10	30	90				
3620 — E below bust							
1707	10	30	90	1708	12	40	120
3621 — E* below bust, 1708					12	50	150
3622 "Edinburgh" bust, E* below, 1708.					15	55	165

Overstruck dates are listed only if commoner than normal date or if no normal date is known.

3623 **Sixpence.** Normal bust. ℞. Plumes in angles

	F	VF	EF			F	VF	E
	£	£	£			£	£	
1707	11	35	95	1708		12	40	12•

3624 ℞. Roses and plumes in angles, 1710. . . . . 15 50 15•

COPPER

3625

3625 **Farthing,** 1714 . . . . 75 150 30(

241

GEORGE I, 1714–27

The coins of the first of the Hanoverian kings have the arms of the Duchy of Brunswick and Luneberg on one of the four shields, the object in the centre of the shield being the crown of Charlemagne. The king's German titles also appear, in abbreviated form, and name him "Duke of Brunswick and Luneberg. Arch-treasurer of the Holy Roman Empire, and Elector", and on the guinea of 1714, "Prince Elector". A quarter-guinea was struck for the first time in 1718, but it was an inconvenient size and the issue was discontinued.

Silver coined from bullion supplied to the mint by the South Sea Company in 1723 shows the company's initials S.S.C.; similarly Welsh Copper Company bullion has the letters W.C.C. below the king's bust and plumes and an interlinked CC on the reverse. Roses and plumes together on the reverse indicate silver supplied by the Company for Smelting Pit Coale and Sea Coale.

GOLD

3626 Five guineas

	F	VF	EF		F	VF	EF
	£	£	£		£	£	£
1716	1000	2250	4750	1720	1250	2550	5000
1717	1250	2550	5000	1726	1000	2250	4750

3627 Two guineas

	F	VF	EF		F	VF	EF
1717	575	1200	3000	1726	475	1100	2800
1720	575	1200	3000				

3627   3628

		F	VF	EF
3628	**Guinea.** First head. R. Legend ends ET PR . EL (Prince Elector), 1714.	300	750	2000
3629	Second head, tie with two ends, 1715	175	375	900

3630 Third head, no hair below truncation

	F	VF	EF		F	VF	EF
1715	150	300	850	1716	200	450	1000

3631 Fourth head, tie with loop at one end

	F	VF	EF		F	VF	EF
1716	150	300	850	1720	150	300	850
1717	175	350	1000	1721	175	400	1000
1718		Extremely rare		1722	150	300	850
1719	150	300	850	1723	175	400	1000

3632 — elephant and castle below

	F	VF	EF		F	VF	EF
1721		Extremely rare		1722		Extremely rare	

3633   3638

	F	VF	EF		F	VF	EF
	£	£	£		£	£	£

3633 Guinea. Fifth (older) head, tie with two ends

1723	200	400	1000	1726	150	350	900
1724	200	400	1000	1727	225	500	1350
1725	200	400	1000				

3634 — elephant and castle below, 1726 . . . . 500 1200 —

3635 Half-guinea. First head

1715	150	300	700	1721		*Extremely rare*	
1717	125	300	700	1722	125	300	700
1718	100	250	650	1723		*Extremely rare*	
1719	100	250	650	1724	175	400	775
1720	175	450	850				

3636 — elephant and castle below, 1721 . . . . *Extremely rare*

3637 Second (older) bust

1725	90	225	600	1727	100	300	700
1726	100	300	700				

3638 Quarter-guinea, 1718 . . . . 35 85 165

SILVER

3639 Crown. R. Roses and plumes in angles

1716	115	250	850	1720/18	175	350	1100
1718/6	175	350	1100	1726	125	300	950

3640 R. SSC (South Sea Company) in angles, 1723 . . . . 125 300 950

3641 Halfcrown. Plain (proof only), 1715 *FDC* £4000

3642 R. Roses and plumes in angles

1715	45	130	500	1720/17	45	130	500
1717	45	130	500				

3643 R. SSC in angles, 1723 . . . . 45 125 450

3644 R. Small roses and plumes, 1726 . . . . 600 1400 —

3645 Shilling. First bust. **R.** Roses and plumes

1715	15	45	140	1720	15	45	140
1716	30	120	325	1721/0	18	55	175
1717	15	45	140	1722	15	45	140
1718	15	40	135	1723	15	45	140
1719	30	120	325				

3646 — plain (i.e. no marks either side)

1720	15	45	140	1721	55	200	500

3647 R. SSC in angles, 1723 . . . . 9 25 75

3648 Second bust, bow to tie. **R.** Similar, 1723 . . . . 10 35 90

3647   3650

3649 ℞. Roses and plumes

	F	VF	EF		F	VF	EF
	£	£	£		£	£	£
1723	18	50	150	1726	110	350	1100
1724	18	50	150	1727	90	300	850
1725	18	50	150				

3650 — W.C.C. (Welsh Copper Company) below

1723	90	300	850	1725	90	325	900
1724	90	325	900	1726	90	325	900

3651 **Sixpence.** ℞. Roses and plumes in angles

1717	25	75	250	1720/17	25	75	250

3652 ℞. SSC in angles, 1723 . . . . 5 20 65

3653 ℞. Small roses and plumes, 1726 . . . . 20 50 150

3654   3655   3656   3657

3654 **Fourpence**

1717	8	18	36	1723	9	18	36
1721	8	18	36	1727	10	19	38

3655 **Threepence**

1717	8	19	33	1723	10	20	35
1721	9	20	35	1727	10	20	35

3656 **Twopence**

1717	5	10	22	1726	5	9	20
1721	5	9	20	1727	5	10	22
1723	6	10	22				

3657 **Penny**

1716	3	7	16	1725	3	6	15
1718	3	7	16	1726	5	10	20
1720	3	7	16	1727	5	10	20
1723	5	7	16				

3658 **Maundy Set.** As last four. Uniform dates

1723	40	95	220	1727	40	95	220

COPPER

3661   3662

3659   **Halfpenny.** "Dump" issue

	F	VF	EF		F	VF	EF
	£	£	£		£	£	£
1717	8	35	150	1718	8	35	150

3660   Second issue

	F	VF	EF		F	VF	EF
1719	5	35	175	1722	5	35	175
1720	5	35	175	1723	5	35	175
1721	5	35	175	1724	5	35	175

3661   **Farthing.** "Dump" issue, 1717 50   125   350

3662   Second issue

	F	VF	EF		F	VF	EF
1719	5	30	150	1722	6	35	165
1720	5	30	150	1723	6	35	165
1721	5	30	150	1724	6	35	165

GEORGE II, 1727–60

Silver was coined only spasmodically by the Mint during this reign and no copper was struck after 1754. Gold coins made from bullion supplied by the East India Company bear the company's initials; some of the treasure seized by Admiral Anson during his circumnavigation of the globe, 1740–4, and by other privateers, was made into coin which had the word LIMA below the king's bust to celebrate the expedition's successful harassment of the Spanish colonies in the New World. Hammered gold was finally demonetized in 1733.

GOLD

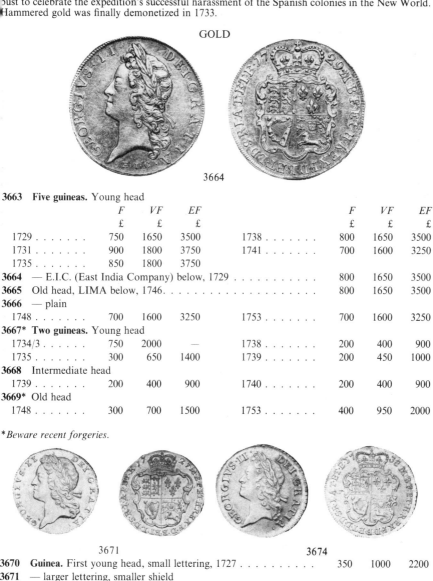

3664

3663 Five guineas. Young head

	F	VF	EF			F	VF	EF
	£	£	£			£	£	£
1729	750	1650	3500		1738	800	1650	3500
1731	900	1800	3750		1741	700	1600	3250
1735	850	1800	3750					

				F	VF	EF
3664 — E.I.C. (East India Company) below, 1729				800	1650	3500
3665 Old head, LIMA below, 1746.				800	1650	3500
3666 — plain						
1748	700	1600	3250	1753	700	1600	3250
3667* **Two guineas.** Young head						
1734/3	750	2000	—	1738	200	400	900
1735	300	650	1400	1739	200	450	1000
3668 Intermediate head						
1739	200	400	900	1740	200	400	900
3669* Old head						
1748	300	700	1500	1753	400	950	2000

Beware recent forgeries.

				F	VF	EF
3671		3674				
3670 **Guinea.** First young head, small lettering, 1727				350	1000	2200
3671 — larger lettering, smaller shield						
1727	250	650	1500	1728	300	700	1650

Overstruck dates are listed only if commoner than normal date or if no normal date is known.

3672 Guinea. Second (narrower) young head

	F £	VF £	EF £		F £	VF £	E* *
1729 *proof only FDC* £3600				1731	160	400	125*
1730	200	500	1500	1732	200	500	150*

3673 — E.I.C. below

1729	350	900	2500	1732	250	600	165*
1731	250	600	1650				

3674 — larger lettering on *obv.*

1732		*Extremely rare*		1736	180	450	125*
1733	150	375	950	1737	200	500	145*
1734	150	375	950	1738	180	450	125*
1735	160	350	1100				

3675 — — E.I.C. below, 1732 . . . . 300 700 175*

3676 Intermediate head

1739	150	375	900	1741/39		*Extremely rare*	
1740	160	450	1250	1743		*Extremely rare*	

3677 — E.I.C. below, 1739 . . . . 300 700 175C

3678 — larger lettering on *obv.*

1745	225	500	1450	1746	200	450	110C

3679 — LIMA below, 1745 . . . . 275 500 130C

3680 Old head

1747	150	350	800	1753	125	300	70C
1748	125	300	700	1755	175	375	850
1749	125	300	700	1756	125	275	65C
1750	150	350	700	1758	115	250	60C
1751	125	300	650	1759	115	250	600
1752	125	300	650	1760	120	275	650

3681   3679   3685

3681 Half-guinea. Young head

	F	VF	EF		F	VF	EF
1728	150	375	900	1734	120	350	800
1729	120	400	1000	1735			*? exists*
1730		*Extremely rare*		1736	120	400	1000
1731	200	600	1500	1737		*Extremely rare*	
1732	150	425	1100	1738	110	325	800
1733			*? exists*	1739	110	325	800

3682 — E.I.C. below

1729	250	500	1500	1732		*Extremely rare*	
1730	300	1000	—	1739		*Extremely rare*	
1731		*Extremely rare*					

3683 Intermediate head

1740	200	600	1500	1745	200	600	1500
1743			*? Unique*	1746	120	350	800

	F £	VF £	EF £		F £	VF £	EF £
3684 — LIMA below, 1745					350	900	1850
3685 Old head							
1747	160	500	1200	1753	100	250	500
1748	130	300	625	1755	100	250	500
1749		*Extremely rare*		1756	90	225	450
1750	110	275	550	1758	90	225	450
1751	120	325	700	1759	80	175	400
1752	120	325	700	1760	80	175	400

SILVER

	F £	VF £	EF £		F £	VF £	EF £
3686 Crown. Young bust. Ŗ. Roses and plumes in angles							
1732	80	200	500	1735	80	200	500
1734	110	275	600	1736	80	200	500
3687 Ŗ. Roses in angles							
1739	80	200	500	1741	80	200	500
3688 Old head. Ŗ. Roses in angles, 1743					80	200	500
3689 — LIMA below, 1746					80	200	500
3690 Plain (i.e. no marks either side)							
1746 *proof only FDC* £1750							
1750	100	275	600	1751	135	325	700

3692

	F £	VF £	EF £		F £	VF £	EF £
3691 Halfcrown. Young bust; plain (proof only), 1731 *FDC* £1650							
3692 Ŗ. Roses and plumes							
1731	25	80	275	1735	30	90	325
1732	25	80	275	1736	35	125	400
1734	30	90	325				
3693 — Ŗ. Roses							
1739	22	70	225	1741	22	75	300
3694 Old bust. Ŗ. Roses							
1743	20	65	200	1745	20	65	200
3695 — LIMA below							
1745	18	45	135	1746	18	45	135
3696 — plain							
1746 *proof only FDC* £700							
1750	35	130	350	1751	50	175	400
3697 Shilling. Young bust. Ŗ. Plumes							
1727	35	100	300	1731	50	175	450

3701

3698 Shilling. — R. Roses and plumes

	F	VF	EF		F	VF	EF
	£	£	£		£	£	£
1727	20	45	135	1731	20	45	135
1728	30	75	175	1732	30	75	175
1729	30	75	175				

3699 Young bust, larger lettering. R. Roses and plumes

1734	12	35	110	1736	12	35	110
1735	12	35	110	1737	12	35	110

3700 — plain, 1728 . . . . 40 125 350

3701 — R. Roses

1739	10	35	85	1741	12	35	95

3702 Old bust. R. Roses

1743	10	30	75	1747	12	35	100
1745	20	55	150				

3703 — LIMA below

1745	10	30	75	1746	30	90	250

3704 — plain

1746 *proof only* FDC £450				1751	30	90	200
1750	20	55	125	1758	4	12	35

3708   3710

3705 Sixpence. Young bust, plain, 1728 . . . . 30 90 250

3706 — R. Plumes, 1728 . . . . 25 70 175

3707 — R. Roses and plumes

1728	12	32	90	1734	25	50	135
1731	12	32	90	1735	25	50	135
1732	12	32	90	1736	20	45	125

3708 — R. Roses

1739	12	32	90	1741	12	32	90

3709 — Old bust. R. Roses

1743	12	32	90	1745	15	35	100

3710 — LIMA below

1745	10	30	75	1746	7	20	50

3711 — plain

	F	VF	EF		F	VF	EF
	£	£	£		£	£	£
1746 *proof only* FDC £325							
1750	20	50	145	1757	3	8	22
1751	25	75	200	1758	3	8	22

3712 Fourpence. Young head. R. Crowned 4

1729	4	10	17	1739	4	10	17
1731	4	10	17	1740	4	10	17
1732	4	10	17	1743	4	10	17
1735	4	10	17	1746	4	10	17
1737	4	10	17	1760	4	10	17

3713 Threepence. Young head. R. Crowned 3

1729	5	11	18	1739	5	11	18
1731	5	11	18	1740	5	11	18
1732	5	11	18	1743	5	11	18
1735	5	11	18	1746	5	11	18
1737	5	11	18	1760	5	11	18

3714 Twopence. Young head. R. Crowned 2

1729	3	7	14	1740	4	9	16
1731	3	7	14	1743	3	7	14
1732	3	7	14	1746	3	7	14
1735	3	7	14	1756	3	7	14
1737	3	7	14	1759	3	7	14
1739	4	8	15	1760	3	7	14

3715 Penny. Young head. R. Crowned 1

1729	3	5	10	1752	3	5	10
1731	3	5	10	1753	3	5	10
1732	3	5	10	1754	3	5	10
1735	3	5	10	1755	3	5	10
1737	3	5	10	1756	3	5	10
1739	3	5	10	1757	3	5	10
1740	3	5	10	1758	3	5	10
1743	3	5	10	1759	3	5	10
1746	3	5	10	1760	3	5	10
1750	3	5	10				

3716

3716 Maundy Set. As last four. Uniform dates

1729	30	60	120	1739	28	55	100
1731	30	60	120	1740	28	55	110
1732	28	55	110	1743	28	55	110
1735	28	55	110	1746	28	55	110
1737	28	55	110	1760	30	60	120

COPPER

3717 Halfpenny. Young bust

	F	VF	EF		F	VF	EF
	£	£	£		£	£	£
1729	5	22	90	1735	5	22	90
1730	5	22	90	1736	5	22	90
1731	5	22	90	1737	5	22	90
1732	5	22	90	1738	4	20	80
1733	5	22	90	1739	5	22	90
1734	5	22	90				

3718 Old bust, GEORGIUS

1740	4	20	80	1744	4	18	70
1742	4	20	80	1745	4	18	70
1743	4	18	70				

3719 — GEORGIVS

1746	4	20	80	1751	4	18	70
1747	4	20	80	1752	4	18	70
1748	4	18	70	1753	4	18	70
1749	4	18	70	1754	4	18	70
1750	4	18	70				

3720   3722

3720 Farthing. Young bust

1730	5	25	85	1735	4	20	75
1731	5	25	85	1736	5	25	85
1732	6	30	90	1737	4	20	75
1733	5	25	85	1739	4	20	75
1734	6	30	90				

3721 Old bust. GEORGIUS

1741	5	30	100	1744	5	30	100

3722 — GEORGIVS

1746	4	18	65	1750	5	25	85
1749	5	22	70	1754	1	10	35

GEORGE III, 1760–1820

During the second half of the 18th century very little silver or copper was minted. In 1797 Matthew Boulton's "cartwheels", the first copper pennies and twopences, demonstrated the improvement from the application of steam power to the coining press.

During the Napoleonic Wars bank notes came into general use when the issue of guineas was stopped between 1797 and 1813, but gold 7s. pieces were minted to relieve the shortage of smaller money. As an emergency measure Spanish "dollars" were put into circulation for a short period after being countermarked, and in 1804 Spanish dollars were overstruck and issued as Bank of England dollars.

The transition to a "token" silver coinage began in 1811 when the Bank of England had 3s. and 1s. 6d. tokens made for general circulation. Private issues of token money in the years 1788–95 and 1811–15 helped to alleviate the shortage of regal coinage. A change over to a gold standard and a regular "token" silver coinage came in 1816 when the Mint, which was moved from its old quarters in the Tower of London to a new site on Tower Hill, began a complete re-coinage. The guinea was replaced by a 20s. sovereign, and silver coins were made which had an intrinsic value lower than their face value. The St. George design used on the sovereign and crown was the work of Benedetto Pistrucci.

Early coinages

GOLD

3724

3723	**Five guineas.** Pattern only		
	1770 *FDC* £42,000		1777 *FDC* £42,000
	1773 *FDC* £42,000		
3724	**Two guineas.** Pattern only		
	1768 *FDC* £13,500		1777 *FDC* £13,500
	1773 *FDC* £13,500		

There are different bust varieties for 3723 and 3724, for further details see Douglas-Morris, November 1974, lots 127–132.

	F £	VF £	EF £
3725 **Guinea.** First head, 1761 (also with three leaves at top of wreath).	350	800	2250

3725   3726   3727

3726 Guinea. Second head

	F	VF	EF		F	VF	EF
	£	£	£		£	£	£
1763	250	650	1250	1764	200	550	1000

3727 Third head

1765	100	225	500	1770	110	250	525
1766	90	175	375	1771	100	200	475
1767	110	275	575	1772	90	175	375
1768	100	200	450	1773	90	175	375
1769	100	200	450				

3728 Fourth head

1774	80	150	325	1781	90	175	375
1775	80	150	325	1782	90	175	375
1776	80	150	325	1783	90	175	375
1777	80	150	325	1784	90	175	375
1778	100	190	400	1785	80	150	325
1779	90	175	375	1786	80	150	325

3728   3729

3729 Fifth head. R. "Spade"-shaped shield

1787	80	130	250	1794	80	130	250
1788	80	130	250	1795	105	175	400
1789	80	135	275	1796	105	175	400
1790	80	130	250	1797	90	140	275
1791	80	130	250	1798 . . . . ,	80	130	250
1792	80	135	250	1799	100	150	350
1793	80	130	250				

3730 Sixth head. R. Shield in Garter, known as the Military guinea, 1813 . . .   300   600

3731 Half-guinea. First head

1762	150	400	1200	1763	200	600	1350

3732 Second head

1764	90	225	475	1772		*Extremely rare*	
1765/4	250	600	—	1773	110	275	575
1766	100	250	500	1774	175	400	1200
1768	110	275	575	1775	175	400	1200
1769	100	250	500				

3733 Third head (less fine style)

1774		*Extremely rare*		1775	175	450	1250

3734 Fourth head

1775	70	135	275	1781	80	140	300
1776	70	135	275	1783	300	800	—
1777	65	120	250	1784	70	135	275
1778	80	140	300	1785	65	120	250
1779	95	200	500	1786	65	120	250

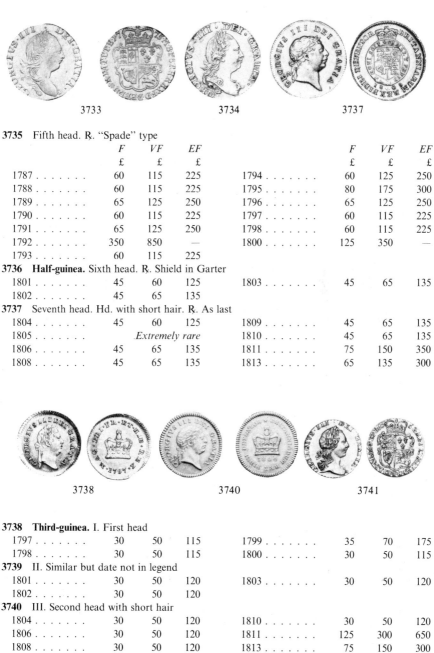

3733   3734   3737

3735 Fifth head. R. "Spade" type

	F	VF	EF		F	VF	EF
	£	£	£		£	£	£
1787	60	115	225	1794	60	125	250
1788	60	115	225	1795	80	175	300
1789	65	125	250	1796	65	125	250
1790	60	115	225	1797	60	115	225
1791	65	125	250	1798	60	115	225
1792	350	850	—	1800	125	350	—
1793	60	115	225				

3736 Half-guinea. Sixth head. R. Shield in Garter

1801	45	60	125	1803	45	65	135
1802	45	65	135				

3737 Seventh head. Hd. with short hair. R. As last

1804	45	60	125	1809	45	65	135
1805		*Extremely rare*		1810	45	65	135
1806	45	65	135	1811	75	150	350
1808	45	65	135	1813	65	135	300

3738   3740   3741

3738 Third-guinea. I. First head

1797	30	50	115	1799	35	70	175
1798	30	50	115	1800	30	50	115

3739 II. Similar but date not in legend

1801	30	50	120	1803	30	50	120
1802	30	50	120				

3740 III. Second head with short hair

1804	30	50	120	1810	30	50	120
1806	30	50	120	1811	125	300	650
1808	30	50	120	1813	75	150	300
1809	30	50	120				

3741 Quarter-guinea, 1762 . . . . 35 75 150

For gold of the "new coinage", 1817–20, see page 261.

SILVER

3742

		F	VF	EF
		£	£	£
3742	**Shilling.** Young bust, known as the "Northumberland" shilling, 1763.	100	175	350
3743	Older bust, no semée of hearts in the Hanoverian shield, 1787.	2	4	25
3744	— — no stop over head, 1787	3	6	40
3745	— — no stops at date, 1787	3	8	45
3745A	— — no stops on *obv.*, 1787	30	100	250

3746   no hearts   with hearts

		F	VF	EF
3746	— with semée of hearts, 1787.	2	4	25
3747	— no stop over head, 1798: known as the "Dorrien and Magens" shilling		*UNC*	£2750
3748	**Sixpence.** Without hearts, 1787.	1	3	18
3749	— with hearts, 1787.	1	3	20
3750	**Fourpence.** Young bust			

	F	VF	EF		F	VF	EF
	£	£	£		£	£	£
1763	3	8	16	1776	4	8	16
1765	100	250	600	1780	4	8	16
1766	5	9	17	1784	5	9	17
1770	5	9	17	1786	5	9	17
1772	5	9	17				

		F	VF	EF
3751	— Older bust. ℞. Thin 4 ("Wire Money"), 1792	7	15	30
3752	— — ℞. Normal 4			

	F	VF	EF		F	VF	EF
1795	3	7	15	1800	3	7.	15

3750   3751   3755

3753   Threepence. Young bust

	F	VF	EF		F	VF	EF
	£	£	£		£	£	£
1762	2	5	9	1772	3	6	14
1763	2	5	9	1780	3	6	14
1765	100	250	600	1784	3	7	15
1766	3	6	14	1786	3	6	14
1770	3	6	14				

3754   — Older bust. ℞. Thin 3 ("Wire Money"), 1792   7   15   30
3755   — — ℞. Normal 3

1795	3	7	14	1800	3	7	14

3756   Twopence. Young bust

1763	2	5	11	1776	2	5	11
1765	75	175	450	1780	2	5	11
1766	2	5	11	1784	2	5	11
1772	2	5	11	1786	2	5	11

3757   — Older bust. ℞. Thin 2 ("Wire Money"), 1792   5   12   25
3758   — — ℞. Normal 2

1795	2	4	7	1800	2	4	7

3759   Penny. Young bust

1763	2	5	11	1779	2	5	10
1765			*? Exists*	1780	2	5	11
1766	2	5	10	1781	2	5	10
1770	2	5	10	1784	2	5	10
1772	2	5	10	1786	2	5	10
1776	2	5	11				

3760   — Older bust. ℞. Thin 1 ("Wire Money"), 1792   2   5   8
3761   — — ℞. Normal 1

1795	1	2	6	1800	1	2	6

3762   Maundy Set. Uniform dates

1763	26	45	115	1780	26	45	115
1766	26	45	115	1784	26	45	115
1772	26	45	115	1786	26	45	115

3763   — Older bust. ℞. Thin numerals ("Wire Money"), 1792   50   80   175
3764   — ℞. Normal numerals. Uniform dates

1795	20	35	80	1800	20	35	75

Emergency issue

3765

3767

3766

	F	VF	EF
	£	£	£
3765 **Dollar** (current for 4s. 9d.). Spanish American 8 *reales* counter-marked with head of George III in oval	50	125	250
3766 — — octagonal countermark	60	135	300
3767 **Half-dollar** with similar oval countermark	60	135	300

Bank of England issue

3768

3768 **Dollar** (current for 5s.). Laureate bust of king. ℞. Britannia seated
l., 1804   35   70   175

These dollars were re-struck from Spanish–American 8 reales until at least 1811. Dollars that show dates of original coin are worth rather more.

3769 **Three shillings.** Draped bust in armour. ℞. BANK / TOKEN / 3 SHILL / date (in oak wreath)

	F	VF	EF			F	VF	EF
	£	£	£			£	£	£
1811	8	15	40		1812	9	16	45

3770 — Laureate head r. ℞. As before but wreath of oak and laurel

1812	8	15	40		1815	8	15	40
1813	8	15	40		1816	90	175	450
1814	8	15	40					

3771   3772

3771 **Eighteen pence.** Draped bust in armour
1811   5   12   30   1812   5   12   30

3772 — Laureate head

	F	VF	EF		F	VF	EF
	£	£	£		£	£	£
1812	4	11	25	1815	4	11	25
1813	4	11	25	1816	4	11	25
1814	4	11	25				

3773 **Ninepence.** Similar, 1812 (pattern only) *FDC* £750

For the last or "new coinage", 1816-20, see page 261.

COPPER

First issue—London

3774

3774 **Halfpenny.** Cuirassed bust r. R. Britannia

	F	VF	EF		F	VF	EF
1770	3	12	55	1773	2	10	50
1771	2	10	50	1774	3	12	55
1772	2	10	50	1775	3	15	60

3775 **Farthing**

	F	VF	EF
1771	15	35	90
1773	2	8	45
1774	3	12	60
1775	4	15	65

Second issue—Soho mint. "Cartwheel" coinage

3776

3776 **Twopence.** Legends incuse on raised rim, 1797 . . . . 6 18 80
3777 **Penny,** 1797. Similar. 5 15 50

Halfpence and farthings of this issue are patterns.

	VF	EF
	£	£
Third issue—Soho mint		
3778 Halfpenny. Draped bust r., 1799	3	25
3779 Farthing, 1799	3	25

3778   3782

Fourth issue—Soho mint

3780 Penny. Different bust

	F	VF	EF		F	VF	EF
	£	£	£		£	£	£
1806	1	4	45	1807	1	6	50
3781 Halfpenny							
1806		2	30	1807		3	40
3782 Farthing							
1806		2	30	1807		3	40

EIGHTEENTH-CENTURY TOKENS

In 1787 the regal copper coinage was very scanty, and so pennies and halfpennies were struck by the Anglesey Copper Mining Company and a fresh token epoch began. They present an immense variety of types, persons, buildings, coats of arms, local legends, political events, etc., all drawn upon for subjects of design. They were struck by many firms in most cities and towns in the country and are to be found in good condition. Circulated specimens are so common that they have little value.

For further details of 18th-century tokens see *The Provincial Token-Coinage of the Eighteenth Century*, by Dalton and Hamer, and Seaby's *British Tokens and Their Values*.

	VF	EF
	£	£
Price of commoner pennies	5	14
— — — halfpennies	4	11
— — — farthings.	3	9

Bury St. Edmunds penny

Coventry halfpenny

Isaac Newton farthing

NINETEENTH-CENTURY TOKENS

With the issue of the copper coinage of 1797 tokens were made illegal, but the dearth of silver currency was still felt. During the Napoleonic wars, a small wave of prosperity in the industrial districts brought the inevitable need for small change, so in 1811 tokens again made their appearance. On this occasion silver ones were made as well as copper. These, with two exceptions, were suppressed before the last coinage of George III.

For further details of 19th-century silver tokens see *The Nineteenth Century Token Coinage* by W. J. Davis and *Silver Token-Coinage 1811–1812*, by R. Dalton, also Seaby's *British Tokens and Their Values.*

	VF	EF
	£	£
Price of the commoner shillings	10	20
——— sixpences	10	20

Newcastle Shilling   Charing Cross Sixpence

	VF	EF
	£	£
Price of the commoner pennies	3	13
——— halfpennies	2	8
——— farthings	2	9

Withymoor Scythe Works Penny, 1813

London Halfpenny

GEORGE III

Last or new coinage, 1816–20

The year 1816 is a landmark in the history of our coinage. For some years at the beginning of the 19th century, Mint production was virtually confined to small gold denominations, regular full production being resumed only after the Mint had been moved from the Tower of London to a new site on Tower Hill. Steam-powered minting machinery made by Boulton and Watt replaced the old hand-operated presses and these produced coins which were technically much superior to the older milled coins.

In 1816 for the first time British silver coins were produced with an intrinsic value substantially below their face value, the first official token coinage.

Our present "silver" coins are made to the same weight standard and are still legal tender back to 1816 with the exception of the halfcrown. The old guinea was replaced by a sovereign of twenty shillings in 1817, the standard of 22 carat (.916) fineness still being retained.

Engraver's and/or designer's initials:

B.P. (Benedetto Pistrucci)

GOLD

3783

3783*	**Five pounds,** 1820 (Pattern only)	*FDC*.....	£20,000
3784	**Two pounds,** 1820 (Pattern only)	*FDC*.....	£8000
3785	**Sovereign.** ℞. St. George		

	F	VF	EF		F	VF	EF
	£	£	£		£	£	£
1817	75	125	375	1819	*Extremely rare*		
1818	85	150	450	1820	75	125	375

3785   3786

3785   3786

3786	**Half-sovereign.** ℞. Crowned shield						
1817	50	85	200	1820	55	90	225
1818	55	90	225				

* Beware counterfeits.

SILVER

3787

3787   Crown. Laureate head r. R. Pistrucci's St. George and dragon within Garter

		F	VF	EF
		£	£	£
1818, edge LVIII		8	25	115
— —	LIX	9	30	120
1819 —	LIX	8	25	115
— —	LX.	9	30	120
1820 —	LX.	8	25	115

3788

3788   Halfcrown. Large or "bull" head

	F	VF	EF				
	£	£	£				
1816	5	18	80	1817	5	18	80

3789

3789   — Small head

1817	5	18	80	1819	6	20	90
1818	6	20	90	1820	7	28	130

3790   3791

3790 Shilling. ℞. Shield in Garter

	F	VF	EF		F	VF	EF
	£	£	£		£	£	£
1816	2	5	25	1819	2	6	30
1817	2	6	30	1820	2	6	30
1818	5	18	85				

3791 Sixpence. ℞. Shield in Garter

	F	VF	EF		F	VF	EF
1816	1	4	20	1819	1	6	30
1817	1	5	25	1820	1	6	30
1818	1	6	30				

3792

3792 Maundy Set (4d., 3d., 2d. and 1d.)

	EF	FDC		EF	FDC
	£	£		£	£
1817	80	150	1820	80	150
1818	80	150			

		EF	FDC
3793 — **fourpence,** 1817, 1818, 1820 . . . . *from*		14	30
3794 — **threepence,** 1817, 1818, 1820 . . . . *from*		14	30
3795 — **twopence,** 1817, 1818, 1820 . . . . *from*		8	13
3796 — **penny,** 1817, 1818, 1820 . . . . *from*		7	11

GEORGE IV, 1820–30

The Mint resumed the coinage of copper farthings in 1821, and pennies and halfpennies in 1825. A gold two pound piece was first issued for general circulation in 1823.

Engraver's and/or designer's initials:
B. P. (Benedetto Pistrucci)
J. B. M. (Jean Baptiste Merlen)

GOLD

3797

		VF	EF
		£	£
3797 **Five pounds,** 1826 (proof only). ℞. Shield	*FDC* £7000		

3798

	VF	EF
	£	£
3798 **Two pounds,** 1823. Large bare head. ℞. St. George	275	550
3799 — 1826. Type as 3797 (proof only) . . . . *FDC* £3250		

3800

3800 **Sovereign.** Laureate head. ℞. St. George

	F	VF	EF		F	VF	EF
	£	£	£		£	£	£
1821	75	130	375	1824	75	135	400
1822*	75	130	375	1825	100	275	1000
1823	110	300	1100				

* Beware counterfeits.

3801

3801 Sovereign. Bare head. R. Crowned shield

	F £	VF £	EF £		F £	VF £	EF £
1825	75	125	375	1828*	500	1250	2500
1826	75	125	375	1829	85	135	400
— Proof *FDC* £1500				1830	85	135	400
1827*	85	135	400				

| 3802 | 3803 | 3804 |

3802 Half-sovereign. Laureate head. R. Ornately garnished shield.

1821	175	450	950

3803 — As last. R. Plain shield

1823	65	125	375	1825	60	110	325
1824	60	120	350				

3804 — Bare head. R. Garnished shield

1826	60	110	300	1827	60	110	300
— Proof *FDC* £875				1828	55	100	250

*Beware counterfeits

SILVER

3805

3805 Crown. Laureate head. R. St. George

1821, edge SECUNDO.	12	40	225
1822 — SECUNDO.	15	50	300
— — TERTIO	14	45	250

3806

3806   Crown. Bare head. R. Shield with crest (proof only), 1826   *FDC*   £2250

3807   3808

3807   Halfcrown. Laureate head. R. Garnished shield

	F	VF	EF		F	VF	EF
	£	£	£		£	£	£
1820	7	25	95	1823	225	650	1950
1821	7	25	95				

3808   — Similar. R. Shield in Garter and collar

	F	VF	EF		F	VF	EF
1823	7	30	110	1824	9	40	150

3809

3809   — Bare head. R. Shield with crest

1824		*Extremely rare*		1826 Proof *FDC* £400			
1825	7	25	85	1828	12	40	175
1826	6	22	80	1829	10	35	150

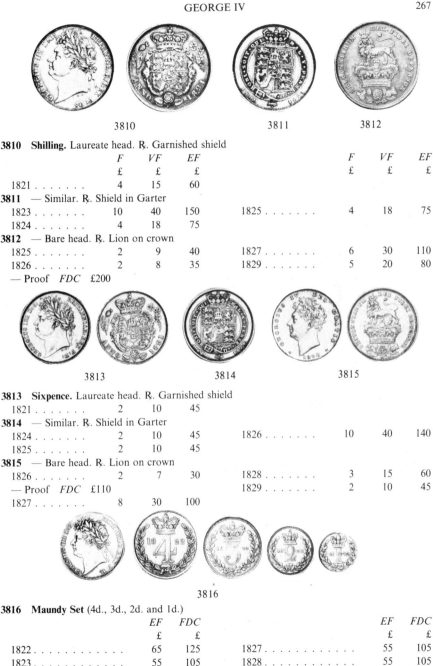

3810   3811   3812

3810   **Shilling.** Laureate head. R. Garnished shield

	F	VF	EF		F	VF	EF
	£	£	£		£	£	£
1821	4	15	60				

3811   — Similar. R. Shield in Garter

1823	10	40	150	1825	4	18	75
1824	4	18	75				

3812   — Bare head. R. Lion on crown

1825	2	9	40	1827	6	30	110
1826	2	8	35	1829	5	20	80
— Proof *FDC* £200							

3813   3814   3815

3813   **Sixpence.** Laureate head. R. Garnished shield

1821	2	10	45

3814   — Similar. R. Shield in Garter

1824	2	10	45	1826	10	40	140
1825	2	10	45				

3815   — Bare head. R. Lion on crown

1826	2	7	30	1828	3	15	60
— Proof *FDC* £110				1829	2	10	45
1827	8	30	100				

3816

3816   **Maundy Set** (4d., 3d., 2d. and 1d.)

	EF	FDC		EF	FDC
	£	£		£	£
1822	65	125	1827	55	105
1823	55	105	1828	55	105
1824	60	115	1829	55	105
1825	55	105	1830	55	105
1826	55	105			

			EF	FDC
			£	£
3817	**Maundy fourpence**, 1822–30.	*from*	11	18
3818	— **threepence**, small head, 1822.		20	35
3819	— — normal head, 1823–30	*from*	10	17
3820	— **twopence**, 1822–30	*from*	8	10
3821	— **penny**, 1822–30	*from*	5	8

COPPER

First issue, 1821–6

3822

3822 Farthing. Laureate bust, draped

	F	VF	EF		F	VF	EF
	£	£	£		£	£	£
1821		3	20	1825		3	18
1822		3	18	1826	1	5	30
1823		3	22				

3823

3827

Second issue, 1825–30

3823 Penny. Laureate head. R. Britannia

1825	2	12	50	1826 Proof *FDC* £200			
1826	2	10	40	1827	25	80	900

3824 Halfpenny. Similar

1825	9	25	90	1826 Proof *FDC* £90			
1826		3	24	1827	1	4	40

3825 Farthing. Similar

1826		3	15	1828		3	20
— Proof *FDC* £100				1829		5	35
1827		4	25	1830		4	20

3826 Half-farthing (for use in Ceylon). Similar

1828	2	12	45	1830	2	12	45

3827 Third-farthing (for use in Malta). Similar

1827		2	15

WILLIAM IV, 1830–7

In order to prevent confusion between the sixpence and half-sovereign the size of the latter was reduced in 1834, but the smaller gold piece was not acceptable to the public and in the following year it was made to the normal size. In 1836 the silver groat was again issued for general circulation: it is the only British silver coin which has a seated Britannia as the type. Crowns were not struck during this reign for general circulation; but proofs or patterns of this denomination were made and are greatly sought after. Silver threepences and three-halfpence were minted for use in the Colonies.

Engraver's and/or designer's initials:
W. W. (William Wyon)

GOLD

3828

3828	**Two pounds,** 1831 (proof only)					*FDC*	£5000
3829	**Sovereign.** ℞. Crowned shield						

	F	VF	EF		F	VF	EF
	£	£	£		£	£	£
1831	90	165	600	1835	85	150	450
— Proof *FDC* £2000				1836	85	150	425
1832*	85	150	425	1837	85	150	425
1833	85	150	425				

* *Beware counterfeits.*

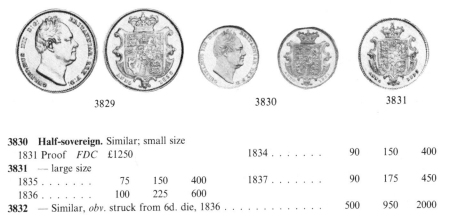

3829   3830   3831

3830	**Half-sovereign.** Similar; small size						
	1831 Proof *FDC* £1250			1834		90	150	400
3831	— large size						
	1835	75	150	400	1837	90	175	450
	1836	100	225	600				
3832	— Similar, *obv.* struck from 6d. die, 1836				500	950	2000

SILVER

3833

3833 Crown. ℞. Shield on mantle, 1831 (proof only) . . . . *FDC* £3500

3834

3834 Halfcrown. ℞. Shield on mantle

	F	VF	EF			F	VF	EF
	£	£	£			£	£	£
1831 Proof *FDC* £400					1836	9	30	125
1834	8	25	95		1837	12	50	200
1835	12	50	175					

3835

3836

3835 Shilling. ℞. Value in wreath

1831 Proof *FDC* £225					1836	4	18	80
1834	4	18	80		1837	5	30	125
1835	5	22	95					

3836 Sixpence. ℞. Value in wreath

1831	2	9	40		1835	2	9	40
— Proof *FDC* £150					1836	6	20	90
1834	2	10	40		1837	4	18	80

3837

3837 Groat. R̥. Britannia seated

	F	VF	EF			F	VF	EF
	£	£	£			£	£	£
1836		2	16		1837		2	16

3838 Threepence (for use in the West Indies). As Maundy threepence but with a dull surface

1834	1	6	30		1836	1	5	28
1835	1	5	28		1837	2	7	36

3839

3839 Three-halfpence (for Colonial use). R̥. Value

1834		2	16		1836		3	20
1835		2	18		1837	4	20	75

3840

3840 Maundy Set (4d., 3d., 2d. and 1d.).

	EF	FDC			EF	FDC
	£	£			£	£
1831	80	150		1834	75	140
— Proof *FDC* £250				1835	75	140
1832	75	140		1836	75	140
1833	75	140		1837	75	140
3841 — **fourpence,** 1831–7 . . . . *from*	11	20
3842 — **threepence,** 1831–7 . . . . *from*	20	30
3843 — **twopence,** 1831–7 . . . . *from*	7	13
3844 — **penny,** 1831–7 . . . . *from*	7	12

COPPER

3845

3845 Penny. No initials on truncation

	F	VF	EF		F	VF	EF
	£	£	£		£	£	£
1831	5	25	90	1834	5	30	100
— Proof *FDC* £225				1837	8	40	150
3846 — WW on truncation, 1831					7	35	125
3847 Halfpenny. As penny							
1831	1	6	30	1834	1	6	35
— Proof *FDC* £90				1837		5	25
3848 Farthing. Similar							
1831		2	16	1835		2	16
— Proof *FDC* £120				1836		3	20
1834		2	16	1837		2	16

3848   3849

3849 Half-farthing (for use in Ceylon). Similar

1837   12   40   175

3850 Third-farthing (for use in Malta). Similar

1835   2   15

VICTORIA, 1837–1901

In 1849, as a first step towards decimalization, a silver florin ($\frac{1}{10}$th pound) was introduced, but the coins of 1849 omitted the usual *Dei Gratia* and these so-called "Godless" florins were replaced in 1851 by the "Gothic" issue. The halfcrown was temporarily discontinued but was minted again from 1874 onwards. Between 1863 and 1880 reverse dies of the gold and silver coins were numbered in the course of Mint experiments into the wear of dies. The exception was the florin where the die number is on the obverse below the bust.

The gold and silver coins were redesigned for the Queen's Golden Jubilee in 1887. The double-florin which was then issued was abandoned after only four years; the Jubilee sixpence of 1887, known as the "withdrawn" type, was changed to avoid confusion with the half-sovereign. Gold and silver were again redesigned in 1893 with an older portrait of the Queen, but the "old head" was not used on the bronze coinage until 1895. The heavy copper penny had been replaced by the lighter bronze "bun" penny in 1860. In 1874–6 and 1881–2 some of the bronze was made by Heaton in Birmingham, and these have a letter H below the date. From 1897 farthings were issued with a dark surface.

Early sovereigns had a shield-type reverse, but Pistrucci's St. George design was used again from 1871. In order to increase the output of gold coinage, branches of the Royal Mint were set up in Australia at Sydney and Melbourne and, later, at Perth for coining gold of imperial type.

Engraver's and/or designer's initials:
W. W. (William Wyon)
L. C. W. (Leonard Charles Wyon)

J. E. B. (Joseph Boehm)
T. B. (Thomas Brock)

GOLD

Note. Over the past few years there has been substantial variation in the bullion price of gold and, as it has fluctuated, it has affected the value of British gold coins, particularly from Victorian issues onwards. The values given here were calculated at a time when the gold price was approximately $450 per fine oz. Most modern gold below EF condition sells at only a small premium above the quoted daily price for sovereigns (except scarce and rarer dates or mints).

Young head coinage, 1838–87

3851

3851

3851   **Five pounds,** 1839. R. "Una and the lion" (proof only) . . . . .   *FDC* £16,500

3852   3853

3852 Sovereign, type I. R. Shield. London mint

	F	VF	EF			VF	EF
	£	£	£			£	£
1838	75	100	275		1852		130
1839	100	250	800		1853		130
— Proof *FDC* £2500					— Proof *FDC* £4000		
1841	400	800	2500		1854		140
1842			140		1855		130
1843			140		1856		140
1844			150		1857		140
1845			150		1858		175
1846			150		1859		140
1847			140		1860		150
1848			150		1861		130
1849			150		1862		130
1850			175		1863		130
1851			140		1872		130

3853 — — die number below wreath

			EF			VF	EF
1863			130		1870		130
1864			120		1871		120
1865			140		1872		120
1866			120		1873		130
1868			130		1874		1100 —
1869			120				

 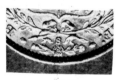

3854   3855

3854 — — M below wreath for Melbourne mint

		VF	EF			VF	EF
1872 M		70	175		1883 M	200	600
1874 M		70	175		1884 M	70	175
1875 M		*? None issued*			1885 M	70	175
1880 M		1000	3000		1886 M	1750	4250
1881 M		80	250		1887 M	1000	2750
1882 M		70	175				

3855 — — S below wreath for Sydney mint

	VF	EF			VF	EF
	£	£			£	£
1871 S.	90	175		1881 S.		150
1872 S.	90	175		1882 S.		150
1873 S.	90	175		1883 S.		150
1875 S.		150		1884 S.		150
1877 S.		150		1885 S.		180
1878 S.		150		1886 S.		180
1879 S.		150		1887 S.		200
1880 S.		150				

3856

3856 — Sovereign, type II. R̟. St. George. London mint

1871.	90		1878.		100
1872.	90		1879.	150	500
1873.	100		1880.		90
1874.	110		1884.		100
1876.	90		1885.		110

3857   3858

3857 — — M below head for Melbourne mint

1872 M	100	300		1880 M		95
1873 M		175		1881 M		95
1874 M		175		1882 M		95
1875 M		115		1883 M		95
1876 M		115		1884 M		95
1877 M		95		1885 M		95
1878 M		95		1886 M		95
1879 M		115		1887 M		95

3858   — **Sovereign.** S below head for Sydney mint

	EF £		EF £
1871 S.	200	1881 S.	95
1872 S.	175	1882 S.	95
1873 S.	150	1883 S.	95
1874 S.	100	1884 S.	95
1875 S.	100	1885 S.	95
1876 S.	100 ·	1886 S.	95
1879 S.	175	1887 S.	95
1880 S.	95		

Gold bullion at the time of printing $363 per oz at $1.57 to the £1 sterling.

3859   3860

3859   **Half-sovereign.** R. Shield. London mint

	VF £	EF £		VF £	EF £
1838	75	200	1852	80	175
1839 Proof only *FDC* £1000			1853	60	135
1841	90	250	— Proof *FDC* £2250		
1842	60	135	1854	*Extremely rare*	
1843	90	250	1855	65	140
1844	70	200	1856	65	140
1845	250	800	1857	80	175
1846	75	200	1858	60	140
1847	75	200	1859	60	140
1848	75	200	1860	60	135
1849	65	175	1861	60	150
1850	150	450	1862	750	—
1851	65	150	1863	65	135
3860 — — die number below shield					
1863	80	200	1873	55	150
1864	60	135	1874	65	150
1865	60	135	1875	55	135
1866	60	135	1876	55	130
1867	60	135	1877	55	130
1869	60	135	1878	55	130
1870	70	135	1879	75	250
1871	60	135	1880	55	130
1872	60	135			

3861 — — As 3859 (no die number) but head in slightly lower relief

	VF £	EF £		VF £	EF £
1880	60	135	1884	55	115
1883	55	115	1885	55	115

3862

3863

3862 — — S below shield for Sydney mint

	VF	EF		VF	EF
1871 S	110	475	1881 S	175	650
1872 S	120	500	1882 S	250	1250
1875 S	115	400	1883 S	120	350
1879 S	120	450	1886 S	120	450
1880 S	120	475	1887 S	120	450

3863 — — M below shield for Melbourne mint

	VF	EF		VF	EF
1873 M	125	450	1884 M	200	1000
1877 M	150	500	1885 M	300	1500
1881 M	200	700	1886 M	150	550
1882 M	150	500	1887 M	250	1250

Jubilee coinage, 1887–93

3864

3864 Five pounds. ℞. St. George
| 1887 | 425 | 650 |
— Proof *FDC* £1650

3865 Two pounds. Similar
| 1887 | 160 | 300 |
— Proof *FDC* £750

3866 Sovereign. ℞. St. George. London mint

1887	80	1890		80
— Proof *FDC* £500		1891		80
1888	80	1892		80
1889	80			

3866   3867   3869

3867 — **Sovereign.** M on ground for Melbourne mint

	VF £	EF £		VF £	EF £
1887 M		80	1891 M		80
1888 M		80	1892 M		80
1889 M		80	1893 M		80
1890 M		80			

3868 — — S on ground for Sydney mint

	VF £	EF £		VF £	EF £
1887 S	125	325	1891 S		80
1888 S		110	1892 S		90
1889 S		80	1893 S		90
1890 S		80			

3869 **Half-sovereign.** R. Shield. London mint

		EF £			EF £
1887		70	1891		80
— Proof *FDC* £350			1892		75
1890		70	1893		80

3870 — — M below shield for Melbourne mint

	VF	EF		VF	EF
1887 M	95	275	1893 M	110	350

3871 — — S below shield for Sydney mint

	VF	EF		VF	EF
1887 S	90	250	1891 S	90	250
1889 S	110	350			

Old head coinage, 1891–1901

3972 **Five pounds.** R. St. George

	VF	EF
1893	500	850
— Proof *FDC* £1800		

3873

3873 **Two pounds.** Similar

	VF	EF
1893	250	450
— Proof *FDC* £950		

3874 Sovereign. ℞. St. George, London mint

	VF	EF		VF		EF
	£	£			£	£
1893		70	1898			70
— Proof *FDC* £600			1899			70
1894		70	1900			70
1895		70	1901			70
1896		70				

3876

3877

3875 Sovereign. ℞. St. George. M on ground for Melbourne mint

1893 M	70	1898 M	70
1894 M	70	1899 M	70
1895 M	70	1900 M	70
1896 M	70	1901 M	70
1897 M	70		

3876 — — P on ground for Perth mint

1899 P	105	1901 P	70
1900 P	70		

3877 — — S on ground for Sydney mint

1893 S	70	1898 S	75
1894 S	70	1899 S	70
1895 S	70	1900 S	70
1896 S	75	1901 S	70
1897 S	75		

3878

3878 Half-sovereign. ℞. St. George. London mint

1893	60	1897	60
— Proof *FDC* £400		1898	60
1894	60	1899	60
1895	60	1900	60
1896	60	1901	60

3879 — — M on ground for Melbourne mint

1893 M		*Extremely rare*	1899 M	75	200
1896 M	75	200	1900 M	75	200

3880 — **Half-sovereign.** P on ground for Perth mint

	F	VF	EF		F	VF	EF
	£	£	£		£	£	£
1899 P		Proof *unique*		1900 P		90	300

3881 — — S on ground for Sydney mint

	F	VF			F	VF
1893 S	70	200		1900 S	60	150
1897 S	70	200				

SILVER

Young head coinage

3882

3882 Crown. Young head. ℞. Crowned shield

		F	VF	EF			F	VF	EF
1839 Proof only	*FDC* £2500				1845		16	45	375
1844		16	55	400	1847		18	60	500

3883

	VF	EF	FDC
	£	£	£
3883* Crown. "Gothic" type, as illustration; inscribed edge, mdcccxlvii = 1847	275	450	850
— Proof, Plain edge *FDC* £950			

* *Beware of recent forgeries.*

3884 — mdcccliii = 1853. Proof *FDC* £3000

3888

	F £	VF £	EF £		F £	VF £	EF £
3885 **Halfcrown,** type A[1]. Young head with one ornate and one plain fillet binding hair. WW in relief on truncation, 1839	250	600	2000				
3886 — Proof *FDC* £650							
3887 — type A[3]. Two plain fillets. WW incuse							
1839	250	600	2000	1840	12	40	175
3888 — type A[4]. Similar but no initials on truncation							
1841	30	100	400	1846	9	35	120
1842	10	35	150	1848/6	30	100	500
1843	18	60	275	1849	15	60	225
1844	9	35	120	1850	12	45	200
1845	9	35	120	1853 Proof *FDC* £1000			
3889 **Halfcrown,** type A[5]. As last but inferior workmanship							
1874	5	18	75	1881	5	18	75
1875	5	22	80	1882	5	22	80
1876	5	22	85	1883	5	18	75
1877	5	22	80	1884	5	18	75
1878	5	22	80	1885	5	18	75
1879	6	30	110	1886	5	18	75
1880	5	22	80	1887	5	18	80

3890   3892

		F	VF	EF
3890	**Florin,** "Godless" type (i.e. without D.G.), 1849	4	20	65

3891 Florin. "Gothic" type B[1], reads brit:, WW below bust, date at end of obverse legend in gothic numerals (1851 to 1863)

	F	VF	EF		F	VF	EF
	£	£	£		£	£	£
mdcccli		? *Proof only*		mdccclvii	5	25	100
mdccclii	4	20	85	mdccclviii	5	25	100
mdcccliii.	4	22	95	mdccclix	5	25	100
— Proof *FDC* £1100				mdccclx	6	30	135
mdcccliv.	200	500	1750	mdccclxii	20	100	300
mdccclv	5	25	100	mdccclxiii	50	175	650
mdccclvi.	5	27	120				

3892 — — type B[2]; as last but die number below bust (1864 to 1867)

mdccclxiv	5	25	100	mdccclxvi	6	30	130
mdccclxv	5	27	110	mdccclxvii. . . .	14	60	175

3893 — — type B[3], reads britt:, die number (1868 to 1879)

mdccclxviii . . .	5	27	120	mdccclxxiv . . .	5	25	100
mdccclxix	5	25	100	mdccclxxv	5	25	100
mdccclxx	5	25	100	mdccclxxvi . . .	5	25	110
mdccclxxi	5	25	100	mdccclxxvii . . .	5	25	110
mdccclxxii. . . .	4	20	80	mdcccclxxix . . .		*Extremely rare*	
mdccclxxiii . . .	4	20	80				

3894 — — type B[4]. As last but with border of 48 arcs and no WW

1877 mdccclxxvii	*Extremely rare*

3895 — — type B[5]. Similar but 42 arcs (1867, 1877 and 1878)

mdccclxvii. . . .		*Extremely rare*		mdccclxxviii. . .	5	25	100
mdccclxxvii . . .	5	25	110				

3896 — — type B[5/6]. As last but no die number (1877, 1879)

mdccclxxvii . . .	*Extremely rare*	mdccclxxix . . .	*Extremely rare*

3897 — — type B[6], reads britt:, WW; 48 arcs (1879)

mdccclxxix . . .	5	25	100

3898 — — type B[7]. As last but no WW, 38 arcs (1879)

mdccclxxix . . .	5	25	100

3899 Florin, "Gothic" type B[3/8]. As next but younger portrait (1880)

mdccclxxx	*Extremely rare*

3900 — — type B[8]. Similar but 34 arcs (1880 to 1887)

mdccclxxx	5	25	100	mdccclxxxv . . .	4	20	90
mdccclxxxi . . .	4	20	90	mdccclxxxvi . . .	4	22	95
mdccclxxxiii. . .	4	20	90	mdccclxxxvii . .		? *exists*	
mdccclxxxiv . . .	4	20	90				

3901 — — type B[9]. Similar but 46 arcs

1887 mdcclxxxvii	7	30	140

3902 Shilling, type A¹. First head, WW on truncation

	F £	VF £	EF £		F £	VF £	EF £
1838	3	15	60	1839	4	15	65

3903 — type A². Second head, WW (proof only), 1839 *FDC* £225

3904 — type A³. Second head, no initials on truncation

	F	VF	EF		F	VF	EF
1839	3	13	50	1853	3	14	50
1840	7	30	130	— Proof *FDC* £400			
1841	7	30	130	1854	30	110	400
1842	6	15	55	1855	3	13	50
1843	3	20	85	1856	3	13	50
1844	5	14	55	1857	3	13	50
1845	3	15	65	1858	3	13	50
1846	3	15	55	1859	3	13	50
1848 over 6	24	70	350	1860	5	22	80
1849	3	20	70	1861	5	22	80
1850	· 90	300	800	1862	9	35	110
1851	20	60	200	1863	9	55	175
1852	3	14	55				

3905 —type A⁴. As before but die number above date

	F	VF	EF		F	VF	EF
1864	3	13	50	1866	3	13	50
1865	3	13	50	1867	3	14	55

3906 — type A⁶. Third head, die number above date

	F	VF	EF		F	VF	EF
1867	20	65	225	1874	2	9	35
1868	3	13	50	1875	2	9	35
1869	3	16	70	1876	2	13	55
1870	3	16	70	1877	2	9	35
1871	2	9	35	1878	2	9	35
1872	2	9	35	1879	6	30	150
1873	2	9	35				

3907 — type A⁷. Fourth head; no die number

	F	VF	EF		F	VF	EF
1879	3	14	50	1884	2	7	27
1880	2	7	27	1885	2	5	20
1881	2	7	27	1886	2	5	20
1882	6	28	80	1887	4	15	60
1883	2	7	27				

3908 Sixpence, type A¹. First head

	F	VF	EF		F	VF	EF
1838	1	9	35	1852	2	10	40
1839	1	9	35	1853	1	9	35
— Proof *FDC* £150				— Proof *FDC* £250			
1840	2	10	40	1854	30	100	350
1841	3	15	50	1855	1	9	35
1842	2	10	37	1856	2	10	37
1843	2	11	40	1857	2	10	40
1844	1	9	35	1858	2	10	37
1845	2	10	37	1859	1	9	35
1846	1	9	35	1860	2	10	40
1848	20	65	250	1862	15	60	250
1850	2	10	37	1863	8	30	120
1851	2	10	37	1866		*Extremely rare*	

3909   3912

3909   Sixpence, type A[2]. First head; die number above date

	F	VF	EF		F	VF	EF
	£	£	£		£	£	£
1864	2	8	40	1866	2	8	40
1865	3	12	50				

3910   — type A[3]. Second head; die number above date

1867	3	14	55	1874	1	7	35
1868	3	14	55	1875	1	7	35
1869	3	20	80	1876	3	14	60
1870	3	20	80	1877	1	7	35
1871	2	8	37	1878	1	7	35
1872	2	8	37	1879	3	16	60
1873	1	7	35				

3911   —type A[4]. Second head; no die number

1871	3	12	50	1879	2	8	37
1877	2	8	37	1880	3	12	50

3912   — type A[5]. Third head

1880	1	5	22	1884	1	5	20
1881	1	5	20	1885	1	5	20
1882	3	16	60	1886	1	5	20
1883	1	5	20	1887	1	4	18

3913   3914   3915

3913   Groat (4d.). ℞. Britannia

1838	2	20	1847/6 (or 8)	12	40	135
1839	3	25	1848		2	22
— Proof *FDC* £110			1849		2	22
1840	3	22	1851	15	50	150
1841	4	32	1852	22	75	225
1842	3	27	1853	30	90	275
1843	3	27	— Proof *FDC* £275			
1844	3	30	1854		2	22
1845	3	30	1855		2	22
1846	3	27				

3914 Threepence. R. Crowned 3; as Maundy threepence but with a less prooflike surface

	YF £	EF £		YF £	EF £
1838*	3	30	1864	3	30
1839*	5	40	1865	5	45
— Proof (see Maundy)			1866	3	30
1840*	5	45	1867	3	35
1841*	5	50	1868	3	25
1842*	5	50	1869*	5	55
1843*	3	30	1870	3	22
1844*	5	45	1871	3	30
1845	3	22	1872	3	25
1846	6	60	1873	2	18
1849	5	45	1874	2	18
1850	3	25	1875	2	18
1851	3	35	1876	2	18
1853	5	60	1877	2	18
1854	5	35	1878	2	18
1855	5	50	1879	2	18
1856	5	45	1880	3	20
1857	5	45	1881	3	20
1858	3	35	1882	3	35
1859	3	20	1883	2	15
1860	3	30	1884	2	15
1861	3	25	1885	2	12
1862	3	35	1886	2	12
1863	5	45	1887	2	15

* Issued for Colonial use only.

3915 Three-halfpence (for Colonial use). R. Value, etc.

1838	2	18	1842	2	25
1839	2	16	1843	1	14
1840	3	35	1860	3	40
1841	2	16	1862	3	35

3916

˙*Overstruck dates are listed only if commoner than the normal date or if no normal date is known.*

3916   Maundy Set (4d., 3d., 2d. and 1.)

	EF	FDC		EF	FDC
	£	£		£	£
1838	35	60	1862	35	55
1839	35	60	1863	35	55
— Proof *FDC* £200			1864	35	55
1840	35	60	1865	35	55
1841	40	60	1866	35	55
1842	35	60	1867	35	55
1843	35	60	1868	35	55
1844	35	60	1869	35	55
1845	35	60	1870	35	55
1846	35	60	1871	35	55
1847	35	60	1872	35	55
1848	35	60	1873	35	55
1849	40	70	1874	35	55
1850	35	60	1875	35	55
1851	35	60	1876	35	55
1852	35	60	1877	35	55
1853	35	60	1878	35	55
— Proof *FDC* £300			1879	35	55
1854	35	60	1880	35	55
1855	40	70	1881	35	55
1856	35	60	1882	35	55
1857	35	60	1883	35	55
1858	35	60	1884	35	55
1859	35	60	1885	35	55
1860	35	60	1886	35	55
1861	35	60	1887	35	55

		EF	FDC
3917	— **fourpence**, 1838–87 .... *from*	6	10
3918	— **threepence**, 1838–87 .... *from*	12	20
3919	— **twopence**, 1838–87 .... *from*	4	7
3920	— **penny**, 1838–87 .... *from*	3	6

Maundy Sets in the original dated cases are worth approximately £5 more than the prices quoted.

Jubilee Coinage

3921

3921 Crown. ℞. St. George

	F	VF	EF			F	VF	EF
	£	£	£			£	£	£
1887	5	15	30		1890	7	22	55
— Proof FDC £375					1891	7	24	65
1888	8	22	50		1892	9	25	80
1889	5	15	30					

3922

3922 Double-florin (4s.). ℞. Cruciform shields. Roman I in date

| 1887 | 4 | 8 | 25 |

3923 — Similar but Arabic 1 in date

	F	VF	EF			F	VF	EF
1887	4	8	25		1889	5	10	30
— Proof FDC £175					1890	5	12	35
1888	5	12	35					

3924   3925

3924 Halfcrown. ℞. Shield in collar

	F	VF	EF			F	VF	EF
1887	2	4	16		1890	2	12	45
— Proof FDC £115					1891	2	12	45
1888	2	7	30		1892	2	12	45
1889	2	7	30					

3925 Florin. ℞. Cruciform shields

	F	VF	EF			F	VF	EF
1887	2	3	14					
— Proof FDC £75					1890	4	20	60
1888	2	5	20		1891	7	35	125
1889	2	6	24		1892	7	30	110

3926   3927

3926 Shilling. Small head. R. Shield in Garter

	F	VF	EF		F	VF	EF
	£	£	£		£	£	£
1887		1	7	1888		3	15
— Proof *FDC* £55				1889	12	50	200

3927 — Large head. R. As before

1889	1	4	20	1891	1	4	30
1890	1	4	25	1892	1	4	30

3928   3929   3930

3928 Sixpence. R. Shield in Garter (withdrawn type)

1887	1	6

— Proof   *FDC*   £40

3929 — R. Value in wreath

1887	1	6	1891	3	18
1888	3	15	1892	3	18
1889	3	15	1893	80	300	850
1890	3	16			

3930 Groat (for use in British Guiana). R. Britannia

1888	3	10	25

3931 Threepence. As Maundy but less prooflike surface

1887	1	4	1890	1	7
— Proof *FDC* £27			1891	1	7
1888	2	9	1892	2	10
1889	1	7	1893	4	22	90

3932 Maundy Set (4d., 3d., 2d. and 1d.)

	EF	FDC		EF	FDC
	£	£		£	£
1888	35	55	1891	35	55
1889	35	55	1892	35	55
1890	35	55			

Maundy Sets in the original dated cases are worth approximately £5 more than the prices quoted.

3932

	F	VF	EF
	£	£	£
3933 — fourpence, 1888–92 . . . . *from*	9	13
3934 — threepence, 1888–92 . . . . *from*	11	21
3935 — twopence, 1888–92 . . . . *from*	5	10
3936 — penny, 1888–92 . . . . *from*	5	10

Old head coinage

3937

3937 Crown. R. St. George. Regnal date on edge

	F	VF	EF
1893 — LVI	5	20	95
— — Proof *FDC* £375			
— — LVII	12	35	150
1894 — LVII	5	25	110
— — LVIII	5	25	110
1895 — LVIII	5	22	100
— — LIX	5	22	100
1896 — LIX	9	30	135
— — LX	5	22	100
1897 — LX	5	22	100
— — LXI	5	20	95
1898 — LXI	12	35	150
— — LXII	5	25	110
1899 — LXII	5	25	110
— — LXIII	5	25	110
1900 — LXIII	5	20	95
— — LXIV	5	20	95

3938

3938   Halfcrown. R. Shield in collar

	F £	VF £	EF £		F £	VF £	EF £
1893	2	7	25	1897	2	7	25
— Proof *FDC* £110				1898	2	7	30
1894	2	9	40	1899	2	7	30
1895	2	7	30	1900	2	7	25
1896	2	7	30	1901	2	7	25

3939   Florin. R. Three shields within Garter

1893	2	6	25	1897	2	6	25
— Proof *FDC* £80				1898	2	6	30
1894	2	9	40	1899	2	6	25
1895	2	7	35	1900	2	6	25
1896	2	6	30	1901	2	6	25

3939   3940

3940   Shilling. R. Three shields within Garter

1893	2	12	1897	2	12
— Proof *FDC* £60			1898	2	12
1894	3	18	1899	2	14
1895	2	14	1900	2	12
1896	2	12	1901	2	12

3941   Sixpence. R. Value in wreath

1893	2	10	1897	2	12
— Proof *FDC* £40			1898	2	12
1894	3	16	1899	2	12
1895	2	12	1900	2	10
1896	2	12	1901	2	10

3942 Threepence. ℞. Crowned 3. As Maundy but less prooflike surface

	EF £			EF
1893	3	1897		4
— Proof *FDC* £30		1898		4
1894	6	1899		3
1895	6	1900		3
1896	4	1901		3

3943

3943 Maundy Set (4d., 3d., 2d. and 1d.)

	EF £	FDC £		EF £	FDC £
1893	30	45	1898	30	45
1894	30	45	1899	30	45
1895	30	45	1900	30	45
1896	30	45	1901	30	45
1897	30	45			

		EF	FDC
3944 — **fourpence**, 1893–1901	*from*	5	8
3945 — **threepence**, 1893–1901	*from*	10	17
3946 — **twopence**, 1893–1901	*from*	5	6
3947 — **penny**, 1893–1901	*from*	5	6

Maundy Sets in the original dated cases are worth approximately £5 more than the prices quoted.

COPPER AND BRONZE

3948

Young head copper coinage, 1838–60

3948   Penny. ℞. Británnia

	F	VF	EF			F	VF	EF
	£	£	£			£	£	£
1839 Bronzed proof	FDC	£200			1853		3	16
1841			4	25	— Proof *FDC* £225			
1843	20	75	300		1854		3	16
1844	2	5	35		1855		3	16
1845	3	12	60		1856	5	18	80
1846	2	8	45		1857		3	20
1847	2	6	35		1858		3	18
1848/7	2	6	30		1859		4	22
1849	20	75	300		1860*		225	400
1851	2	8	45					

3949

3949   Halfpenny. ℞. Britannia

	F	VF	EF			F	VF	EF
1838		2	16		1852		3	24
1839 Bronzed proof	FDC	£90			1853		2	9
1841		2	14		— Proof *FDC* £125			
1843	1	8	40		1854		2	9
1844		3	20		1855		2	9
1845	15	45	150		1856		3	22
1846		4	25		1857		3	14
1847		4	25		1858		2	16
1848		5	30		1859		3	18
1851		3	22		1860*			2750

Overstruck dates are listed only if commoner than normal date, or if no normal date is known.

Copper

3950

3950   Farthing. ℞. Britannia

	F	VF	EF		F	VF	EF
	£	£	£		£	£	£
1838		3	18	1850		3	20
1839		2	16	1851	3	10	45
— Bronzed proof *FDC* £110				1852	3	11	45
1840		2	16	1853		2	20
1841		2	16	— Proof *FDC* £250			
1842		6	40	1854		3	20
1843		2	16	1855		4	25
1844	15	40	150	1856	2	6	40
1845		3	20	1857		2	20
1846		6	35	1858		2	20
1847		3	20	1859	5	15	45
1848		3	20	1860*	—	—	2900
1849	7	25	90				

* These 1860 large copper pieces not to be confused with the smaller and commoner bronze issue with date on reverse (nos. 3954, 3956 and 3958).

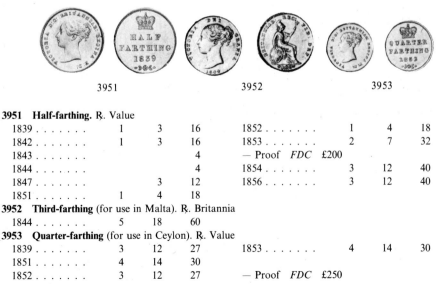

3951   3952   3953

3951   Half-farthing. ℞. Value

1839	1	3	16	1852	1	4	18
1842	1	3	16	1853	2	7	32
1843			4	— Proof *FDC* £200			
1844			4	1854	3	12	40
1847		3	12	1856	3	12	40
1851	1	4	18				

3952   Third-farthing (for use in Malta). **℞. Britannia**

1844	5	18	60

3953   Quarter-farthing (for use in Ceylon). **℞. Value**

1839	3	12	27	1853	4	14	30
1851	4	14	30				
1852	3	12	27	— Proof *FDC* £250			

Bronze coinage, "bun head" issue, 1860–95

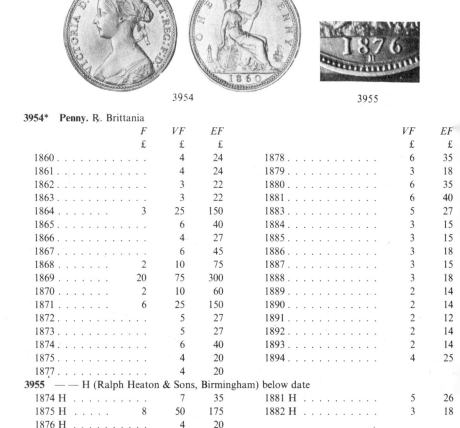

3954   3955

3954*   Penny. R. Brittania

	F	VF	EF			VF	EF
	£	£	£			£	£
1860		4	24	1878		6	35
1861		4	24	1879		3	18
1862		3	22	1880		6	35
1863		3	22	1881		6	40
1864	3	25	150	1883		5	27
1865		6	40	1884		3	15
1866		4	27	1885		3	15
1867		6	45	1886		3	18
1868	2	10	75	1887		3	15
1869	20	75	300	1888		3	18
1870	2	10	60	1889		2	14
1871	6	25	150	1890		2	14
1872		5	27	1891		2	12
1873		5	27	1892		2	14
1874		6	40	1893		2	14
1875		4	20	1894		4	25
1877		4	20				

3955   — — H (Ralph Heaton & Sons, Birmingham) below date

	F	VF	EF			VF	EF
1874 H		7	35	1881 H		5	26
1875 H	8	50	175	1882 H		3	18
1876 H		4	20				

**1882 without 'H' was sold in auction condition extremely fine for £1700, March 1988.*

3956

3956 Halfpenny. R. Britannia

	F	VF	EF		F	VF	EF
	£	£	£		£	£	£
1860		2	15	1878	2	6	40
1861		2	15	1879		2	15
1862		2	13	1880		4	25
1863		4	25	1881		4	25
1864		5	30	1883		3	22
1865	2	6	40	1884		2	12
1866		5	30	1885		2	12
1867	2	6	40	1886		2	12
1868		5	32	1887		1	10
1869	3	25	90	1888		2	12
1870		4	26	1889		2	12
1871	6	30	100	1890		1	10
1872		4	24	1891		1	10
1873		5	30	1892		2	20
1874	2	8	60	1893		2	12
1875		2	20	1894		3	22
1877		2	20				

3957 — — H below date

	F	VF	EF		F	VF	EF
1874 H		3	22	1881 H		2	20
1875 H		5	28	1882 H		2	20
1876 H		2	20				

3958

3960

3958 Farthing. R. Britannia

	F	VF	EF		F	VF	EF
1860		1	10	1880		2	14
1861		1	12	1881		1	8
1862		2	12	1883		4	20
1863	10	30	90	1884			5
1864		2	18	1885			5
1865		1	12	1886			5
1866		1	10	1887			8
1867		2	16	1888			7
1868		2	16	1890			7
1869		5	22	1891			5
1872		2	12	1892	1	6	20
1873		1	9	1893			5
1875	4	10	35	1894			7
1878			7	1895	3	8	30
1879			7				

3959 —**Farthing**. H below date

	F	VF	EF			VF	E
	£	£	£			£	
1874 H			14	1881 H			1
1875 H			6	1882 H			1
1876 H	4	10	30				

3960 **Third-farthing** (for use in Malta). R. Value

1866		8	1881		1
1868		9	1884		
1876		10	1885		
1878		9			

Old head issue, 1895–1901

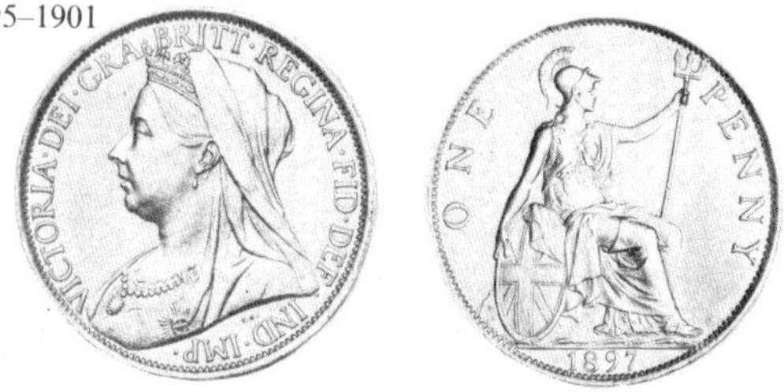

3961

3961 **Penny**. R. Britannia

1895		6	1899		5
1896		5	1900		3
1897		5	1901		2
1898		10			

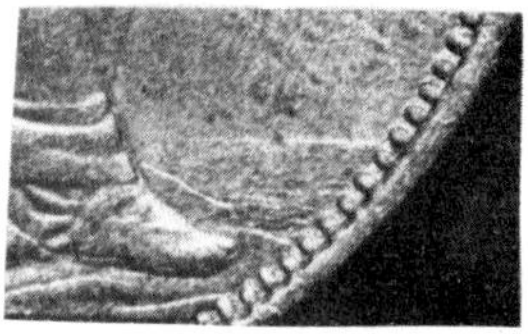

3961   "High tide" 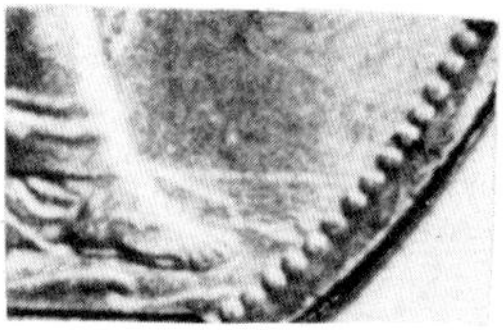   3961A   "Low tide"

3961A As last but "Low tide", 1895   18   75

3962 **Halfpenny**. Type as Penny. R. Britannia

1895	.6	1899	4
1896	.5	1900	3
1897	.5	1901	2
1898	.5		

3963 **Farthing**. R. Britannia. Bright finish

1895	.4	1897	5
1896	.4		

3964

	EF £		EF £
3964 — — Dark finish			
1897	4	1900	3
1898	4	1901	2
1899	4		

EDWARD VII, 1901–10

Five pound pieces, two pound pieces and crowns were only issued in 1902. A branch of the Royal Mint was opened at Ottawa and coined sovereigns of imperial type from 1908.

Unlike the coins in most other proof sets, the proofs issued for the Coronation in 1902 have a matt surface in place of the more usual brilliant finish.

Designer's initials:
De S. (G. W. de Saulles)

GOLD

3965

		VF	EF	UNC.
		£	£	£
3965	**Five pounds.** 1902. R̃. St. George	450	650	800
3966	— Proof. 1902. *Matt surface* FDC £750			
3967	**Two pounds.** 1902. Similar	200	300	500
3968	— Proof. 1902. *Matt surface* FDC £425			

3967

3969

3969 Sovereign.* R̃. St. George. London mint

	EF	UNC.		EF	UNC.
	£	£		£	£
1902 Matt proof *FDC* £140			1906	70	75
1902	70	75	1907	70	75
1903	70	75	1908	70	75
1904	70	75	1909	70	75
1905	70	75	1910	70	75
3970 — — C on ground for Ottawa mint					
1908 C (Satin proof only) *FDC* £3250			1910 C	200	300
1909 C	200	300			

3971 Sovereign. R. St. George. M on ground for Melbourne mint

	VF	EF	UNC.		VF	EF	UNC.
	£	£	£		£	£	£
1902 M		70	75	1907 M		70	75
1903 M		70	75	1908 M		70	75
1904 M		70	75	1909 M		70	75
1905 M		70	75	1910 M		70	75
1906 M		70	75				

The price of common sovereigns in lower grades of condition is closely related to the current gold price.

3972 Sovereign. R. St. George. P on ground for Perth mint

		EF	UNC.			EF	UNC.
1902 P.		70	75	1907 P.		70	75
1903 P.		70	75	1908 P.		70	75
1904 P.		70	75	1909 P.		70	75
1905 P.		70	75	1910 P.		70	75
1906 P.		70	75				

3973 — — S on ground for Sydney mint

		EF	UNC.			EF	UNC.
1902 S.		70	75	1907 S.		70	75
1903 S.		70	75	1908 S.		70	75
1904 S.		70	75	1909 S.		70	75
1905 S.		70	75	1910 S.		70	75
1906 S.		70	75				

3974

3974 Half-sovereign. R. St. George. London mint

	VF	EF	UNC.			EF	UNC.
1902 Matt proof *FDC* £100				1906		45	50
1902		45	50	1907		45	50
1903		45	50	1908		45	50
1904		45	50	1909		45	50
1905		45	50	1910		45	50

3975 — — M on ground for Melbourne mint

	VF	EF	UNC.		VF	EF	UNC.
1906 M	55	80	175	1908 M	55	80	200
1907 M	55	80	175	1909 M	55	80	175

3976 — — P on ground for Perth mint

	VF	EF	UNC.		VF	EF	UNC.
1904 P.	175	550	—	1909 P	140	400	—
1908 P	175	600	—				

3977 — — S on ground for Sydney mint

	VF	EF	UNC.		VF	EF	UNC.
1902 S	60	125	250	1908 S	55	110	175
1903 S	55	110	175	1910 S	55	110	175
1906 S	55	110	175				

Gold bullion price at the time of printing $363 per oz at $1.57 to the £1 sterling.

SILVER

3978

	F	VF	EF	UNC
	£	£	£	£
3978 Crown. ℞. St. George				
1902	20	35	65	11

3979 — Similar, but *matt proof FDC* £100
3980 Halfcrown. ℞. Shield in Garter

3980

	F	VF	EF	UNC.		F	VF	EF	UNC.
	£	£	£	£		£	£	£	£
1902		6	30	55	1906		8	70	110
— Matt proof *FDC* £55					1907		9	75	120
1903		20	75	350	550 | 1908		12	100	150
1904		10	55	250	400 | 1909		10	80	130
1905*		70	250	750	950 | 1910		8	55	90

3981 Florin. ℞. Britannia standing

1902		5	30	50	1906		6	50	75
— Matt proof *FDC* £40					1907		2	8	60	90
1903		2	6	50	75 | 1908		2	10	80	120
1904		2	10	60	90 | 1909		2	9	75	110
1905*		10	30	175	300 | 1910		4	40	65

Beware of recent forgeries.

3981   3982   3983

	F	VF	EF	UNC.		F	VF	EF	UNC.
	£	£	£	£		£	£	£	£

3982 Shilling. R. Lion on crown

1902		2	15	25	1906		2	20	35
— Matt proof *FDC* £25					1907		4	25	40
1903	1	5	50	90	1908	1	6	60	90
1904	1	5	40	65	1909	1	5	50	85
1905*	25	75	300	475	1910		2	15	25

3983 Sixpence. R. Value in wreath

1902		1	15	25	1906		2	20	35
— Matt proof *FDC* £20					1907		2	25	40
1903		2	20	35	1908		3	30	50
1904	1	4	35	55	1909		2	25	40
1905		2	25	40	1910		1	15	25

* Beware of recent forgeries.

3984 Threepence. As Maundy but dull finish

1902		3	5	1907		8	14
1903		8	14	1908		8	14
1904	3	30	45	1909		8	14
1905	2	20	35	1910		6	10
1906	1	20	35				

3985

3985 Maundy Set (4d., 3d., 2d. and 1d.)

	EF	FDC		EF	FDC
	£	£		£	£
1902	25	40	1906	25	40
— Matt proof *FDC* £40			1907	25	40
1903	25	40	1908	25	40
1904	25	40	1909	30	50
1905	25	40	1910	35	55

			EF	FD
			£	
3986	— **fourpence**, 1902–10 .... *from*	5	
3987	— **threepence**, 1902–10 .... *from*	5	1
3988	— **twopence**, 1902–10 .... *from*	5	
3989	— **penny**, 1902–10 .... *from*	5	

Maundy sets in the original dated cases are worth approximately £5 more than the prices quoted.

BRONZE

3990

3990   "High tide"   3990A   "Low tide"

3990   Penny. ℞. Britannia

	EF	UNC.		VF	EF	UNC.
	£	£		£	£	£
1902...........	4	8				
1903...........	8	20	1907...........		8	20
1904...........	12	25	1908...........		8	20
1905...........	10	22	1909...........		8	20
1906...........	8	20	1910...........		7	14
3990A As last but "Low tide", 1902.				3	20	40

3991

3991 Halfpenny. R. Britannia

	EF	UNC.		VF	EF	UNC.
	£	£		£	£	£
1902	4	8	1907		5	12
1903	6	14	1908		5	12
1904	8	20	1909		8	20
1905	8	20	1910		7	15
1906	7	15				

3991A As last but "Low tide", 1902.   10   25   45

3992   3993

3992 Farthing. Britannia. Dark finish

1902	3	6	1907		5	10
1903	5	10	1908		5	10
1904	7	14	1909		5	10
1905	5	10	1910		7	14
1906	5	10				

3993 Third-farthing (for use in Malta)

1902   R. Value   3   6

No proofs of the bronze coins were issued in 1902.

GEORGE V, 1910–36

Paper money issued by the Treasury during the First World War replaced gold for internal use afte
1915 but the branch mints in Australia and South Africa (the main Commonwealth gold producin
countries) continued striking sovereigns until 1930–2. Owing to the steep rise in the price of silver i
1919/20 the issue of standard (.925) silver was discontinued and coins of .500 silver were minted

In 1912, 1918 and 1919 some pennies were made under contract by private mints in Birmingham
In 1918, as half-sovereigns were no longer being minted, farthings were again issued with th
ordinary bright bronze finish. Crown pieces had not been issued for general circulation but the
were struck in small numbers about Christmas time for people to give as presents in the years 1927
36, and in 1935 a special commemorative crown was issued in celebration of the Silver Jubilee.

As George V died in January, it is likely that all coins dated 1936 were struck during the reign o
Edward VIII.

Designer's initials:
B. M. (Bertram Mackennal)
P. M. (Percy Metcalfe)
K. G. (Kruger Gray)

GOLD

3994

		FDC
		£
3994	**Five pounds.*** R̟. St. George, 1911 (Proof only).	1200
3995	**Two pounds.*** R̟. St. George, 1911 (Proof only).	525

Forgeries exist.

3996

3996 Sovereign. R̟. St. George. London mint

	EF	UNC.		VF	EF	UNC.
	£	£		£	£	£
1911.	70	75	1915.		70	75
— Proof *FDC* £275			1916.		90	110
1912.	70	75	1917*.	3000	6000	—
1913.	70	75	1925.		70	75
1914.	70	75				

* *Counterfeits exist of these and of most other dates and mints.*

3997 Sovereign. R. St. George. C on ground for the Ottawa mint

	VF	EF	UNC.		VF	EF	UNC.
	£	£	£		£	£	£
1911 C		95	110	1917 C		95	110
1913 C	225	450	—	1918 C		95	110
1914 C	225	450	—	1919 C		95	110
1916 C	*Extremely rare*						

3997   3998   4004

3998 — I on ground for India (Bombay) mint, 1918 95   110

3999 — M on ground for Melbourne mint

	VF	EF	UNC.		VF	EF	UNC.
1911M		70	75	1920 M	450	950	1400
1912 M		70	75	1921 M	4000	5000	
1913 M		70	75	1922 M	1200	3500	4750
1914 M		70	75	1923 M		75	90
1915 M		70	75	1924 M		75	90
1916 M		70	75	1925 M		70	75
1917 M		70	75	1926 M		75	90
1918 M		70	75	1928 M	300	950	1400
1919 M		90	110				

4000 — — — small head

	VF	EF	UNC.		VF	EF	UNC.
1929 M	250	950	—	1931 M	90	250	—
1930 M	135	175					

4001   4002

4001 — — P on ground for Perth mint

	VF	EF		VF	EF
1911 P	70	75	1920 P	70	75
1912 P	70	75	1921 P	70	75
1913 P	70	75	1922 P	70	75
1914 P	70	75	1923 P	70	75
1915 P	70	75	1924 P	75	80
1916 P	70	75	1925 P	75	80
1917 P	70	75	1926 P	75	80
1918 P	70	75	1927 P	75	80
1919 P	70	75	1928 P	75	80

	VF	EF	UNC.		VF	EF	UNC
	£	£	£		£	£	
4002 **Sovereign.** — — — small head							
1929 P.	75	85		1931 P.		75	8
1930 P.	75	85					
4003 ℞. St. George. S on ground for Sydney mint							
1911 S.	70	75		1919 S.		70	7
1912 S.	70	75		1920 S.	*Extremely rare*		
1913 S.	70	75		1921 S.	350	700	120
1914 S.	70	75		1922 S.	775	2000	475
1915 S.	70	75		1923 S.	775	2000	475
1916 S.	70	75		1924 S.	300	600	100
1917 S.	70	75		1925 S.		75	8
1918 S.	70	75		1926 S.	800	2350	500
4004 — — SA on ground for Pretoria mint							
1923 SA	*Extremely rare*			1926 SA.		70	7
1923 SA Proof *FDC* £750				1927 SA.		70	7
1924 SA.	2250	—		1928 SA.		70	7
1925 SA.	70	75					
4005 — — — small head							
1929 SA.	80	90		1931 SA.		80	9
1930 SA.	80	90		1932 SA.		95	11

4006

4006 **Half-sovereign.** ℞. St. George. London mint							
1911.	45	50		1913.		45	5
— Proof *FDC* £200				1914.		45	5
1912.	45	50		1915.		45	5
4007 — — M on ground for Melbourne mint							
1915 M					55	80	12
4008 — — P on ground for Perth mint							
1911 P.	55	70	80	1918 P.	200	350	500
1915 P.	55	70	80	1919 P, 1920 P (*Not circulated*)			
4009 — — S on ground for Sydney mint							
1911 S.	50	70	90	1915 S.	45	50	6
1912 S.	50	70	90	1916 S.	45	50	6
1914 S.	50	60	75				
4010 — — SA on ground for Pretoria mint							
1923 SA Proof *FDC* £475				1926 SA.		45	5
1925 SA.	45	50					

Gold bullion price at the time of printing $363 per oz at $1.57 to the £1 sterling.

SILVER

First coinage. Sterling silver (.925 fine)
4011   Halfcrown. R. Crowned shield in Garter

4011

	EF	UNC			EF	UNC
	£	£			£	£
1911	25	45		1915	12	20
— Proof *FDC* £70				1916	12	20
1912	30	50		1917	18	30
1913	35	65		1918	12	20
1914	12	25		1919	18	30

4012

4012   Florin. R. Cruciform shields

	EF	UNC			EF	UNC
1911	20	35		1915	12	20
— Proof *FDC* £50				1916	12	20
1912	25	40		1917	18	30
1913	35	60		1918	12	20
1914	12	20		1919	18	30

4013   Shilling. R. Lion on crown, inner circles

	EF	UNC			EF	UNC
1911	8	15		1915	8	15
— Proof *FDC* £35				1916	8	15
1912	18	30		1917	10	17
1913	25	50		1918	8	15
1914	8	15		1919	12	20

4013   4014

4014   Sixpence. ℞. Similar

	EF £	UNC £		EF £	UNC £
1911	8	13			
— Proof *FDC* £30			1916	8	15
1912	12	20	1917	14	35
1913	16	25	1918	8	15
1914	8	15	1919	10	18
1915	8	15	1920	12	20

4015   Threepences. As Maundy but dull finish

1911	3	5	1916	3	5
1912	3	5	1917	3	5
1913	3	5	1918	3	5
1914	3	5	1919	3	5
1915	3	5	1920	4	6

4016

4016   Maundy Set (4d., 3d., 2d. and 1d.)

	EF £	FDC £		EF £	FDC £
1911	25	45	1916	25	40
— Proof *FDC* £60			1917	25	40
1912	25	40	1918	25	40
1913	25	40	1919	25	40
1914	25	40	1920	25	40
1915	25	40			

		EF	FDC
4017 — **fourpence,** 1911–20	*from*	5	8
4018 — **threepence,** 1911–20	*from*	8	12
4019 — **twopence,** 1911–20	*from*	5	8
4020 — **penny,** 1911–20	*from*	7	10

Second coinage. Debased silver (.500 fine). Types as before.

4021 Halfcrown

	EF	UNC		VF	EF	UNC
	£	£		£	£	£
1920	20	40	1924		30	50
1921	25	50	1925	15	100	175
1922	20	40	1926		30	55
1923	12	20				

4022 Florin

1920	20	35	1924		30	50
1921	20	35	1925	8	75	135
1922	16	30	1926		30	50
1923	14	25				

4023 Shilling

1920	16	30	1924	20	35
1921	20	50	1925	35	55
1922	16	30	1926	12	27
1923	14	25			

4024 Sixpence

1920	10	18	1923	16	30
1921	10	18	1924	10	18
1922	11	20	1925	12	20

4025   4026

4025 — new beading and broader rim

1925	10	18	1926	12	20

4026 Threepence

1920	3	5	1925	10	20
1921	3	5	1926	10	20
1922	4	6			

4027 Maundy Set (4d., 3d., 2d. and 1d.)

	EF	FDC		EF	FDC
	£	£		£	£
1921	25	40	1925	25	40
1922	25	40	1926	25	40
1923	25	40	1927	25	40
1924	25	40			

4028 — **fourpence**, 1921–7	from	6	9
4029 — **threepence**, 1921–7	from	8	12
4030 — **twopence**, 1921–7	from	6	10
4031 — **penny**, 1921–7	from	7	11

2nd coinage   3rd coinage

Third coinage. As before but **modified effigy**, with details of head more clearly defined. The BM on truncation is nearer to the back of the neck and without stops; beading is more pronounced.

	VF £	EF £	UNC. £		VF £	EF £	UNC. £
4032 Halfcrown							
1926	4	30	50	1927		18	30
4033 Shilling							
1926		12	20	1927		18	30
4034 Sixpence							
1926		9	16	1927		10	18
4035 Threepence							
1926						3	5

Fourth coinage. New types, 1927–35

4036

4036 Crown. ℞. Crown in wreath

1927 Proof only	FDC	£110		1932	75	165	250
1928	45	90	150	1933	50	110	175
1929	50	110	175	1934	350	600	900
1930	50	110	175	1936	75	165	250
1931	55	130	200				

4037   4038

4037 Halfcrown. R. Shield

	VF £	EF £	UNC £		VF £	EF £	UNC £
1927 Proof only *FDC* £30				1932		10	30
1928		8	14	1933		9	16
1829		8	14	1934		25	40
1930	8	75	130	1935		6	12
1931		9	16	1936		5	10

4038 Florin. R. Cruciform sceptres, shield in each angle

1927 Proof only *FDC* £35				1932	7	70	125
1928		7	12	1933		9	16
1929		7	12	1935		7	12
1930		11	18	1936		6	10
1931		8	18				

4039   4040

4039 Shilling. R. Lion on crown, no inner circles

1927	12	20			
— Proof *FDC* £20			1932	8	14
1928	7	12	1933	7	12
1929	7	12	1934	14	25
1930	18	30	1935	7	12
1931	8	14	1936	6	10

4040 Sixpence. R. Three oak sprigs with six acorns

1927 Proof only *FDC* £18			1929	3	6
1928	3	6	1930	4	6

4041 — — closer milling

1931	7	14	1934	8	16
1932	12	20	1935	5	10
1933	6	12	1936	3	6

4042

4042   Threepence. ℞. Three oak sprigs with three acorns

	EF	UNC.		EF	UNC
	£	£		£	
1927 Proof only *FDC* £35			1933	1	
1928	10	18	1934	1	
1930	8	14	1935	1	
1931	1	2	1936	1	
1932	1	2			

4043   Maundy Set. As earlier sets

	EF	FDC		EF	FDC
	£	£		£	
1928	30	45	1933	30	45
1929	30	45	1934	30	45
1930	30	45	1935	30	45
1931	30	45	1936	35	50
1932	30	45			

	EF	FDC
4044 — fourpence, 1928–36 . . . . *from*	6	10
4045 — threepence, 1928–36 . . . . *from*	7	12
4046 — twopence, 1928–36 . . . . *from*	6	9
4047 — penny, 1928–36 . . . . *from*	8	13

Silver Jubilee Commemorative issue

4048

	VF	EF	UNC.
	£	£	£
4048 Crown, 1935. ℞. St. George, incuse lettering on edge	3	8	15
4049 — Similar. Specimen striking issued in box. . . . . *UNC.* 30			
4050 — — raised lettering on edge. Proof (.925 Æ̷R) *FDC* £200			

4051

4051   Penny. ℞. Britannia

	F	VF	EF	UNC			F	VF	EF	UNC
	£	£	£	£			£	£	£	£
1911			4	9		1918			4	9
1912			4	9		1919			3	7
1913			4	9		1920			3	7
1914			5	12		1921			3	7
1915			5	12		1922			12	25
1916			4	9		1926			15	35
1917			3	7						

4052   — — H (The Mint, Birmingham, Ltd.) to l. of date

	F	VF	EF	UNC			F	VF	EF	UNC
1912 H		1	20	45		1919 H		7	65	125
1918 H		8	75	135						

4053   — — KN (King's Norton Metal Co.) to l. of date

	F	VF	EF	UNC			F	VF	EF	UNC
1918 KN	2	10	90	175		1919 KN	2	12	110	200

4054   — — modified effigy

	F	VF	EF	UNC			F	VF	EF	UNC
1926	3	25	250	450		1927			3	5

4055   — — small head

	F	VF	EF	UNC			F	VF	EF	UNC
1928			3	5		1933*			*Extremely rare*	
1929			3	5		1934			10	18
1930			4	6		1935			2	4
1931			5	9		1936			1	2
1932			12	20						

* *An extremely fine specimen sold at auction for £15,000 in November 1985.*

4056   4058

4056 Halfpenny. ℞. Britannia

	EF £	UNC. £		EF £	UNC
1911	4	9	1919	4	
1912	4	9	1920	4	
1913	4	9	1921	4	
1914	4	9	1922	7	1
1915	4	9	1923	5	1
1916	4	9	1924	4	
1917	4	9	1925	5	1
1918	4	9			

4057 —— modified effigy

	EF	UNC		EF	
1925	7	15	1927	4	
1926	6	14			

4058 —— small head

	EF	UNC		EF	
1928	2	5	1933	2	
1929	2	5	1934	4	
1930	2	5	1935	2	
1931	2	5	1936	1	
1932	2	5			

4059   4062

4059 Farthing. ℞. Britannia. Dark finish

	EF	UNC		EF	
1911	3	6	1915	4	
1912	2	4	1916	2	
1913	2	4	1917	1	
1914	2	4	1918	9	1

4060 —— Bright finish, 1918–25 1

4061 Farthing. ℞. Britannia. Modified effigy

	EF	UNC		EF	
1926	1	2	1932	.50	
1927	1	2	1933	1	
1928	1	2	1934	2	
1929	1	2	1935	2	
1930	1	2	1936	.75	
1931	1	2			

4062 Third-farthing (for use in Malta). ℞. Value

1913 3

EDWARD VIII, Jan.–Dec. 1936

Abdicated 10 December. Created Duke of Windsor (1936–72)

coins of Edward VIII were issued for currency within the United Kingdom bearing his name and trait. The mint had commenced work on a new coinage prior to the Abdication, and various terns were made. No proof sets were issued for sale and only a small number of sets were struck. 'oins bearing Edward's name, but not his portrait, were issued for the colonial territories of tish East Africa, British West Africa, Fiji and New Guinea. The projected U.K. coins were to ude a shilling of essentially 'Scottish' type and a nickel brass threepence with twelve sides which ght supplement and possibly supersede the inconveniently small silver threepence.

signer's initials:
I. P. (T. Humphrey Paget)
K. G. (Kruger Gray)

4063

63* Proof Set
Gold, £5, £2 and £1, 1937. . . . .   *not issued*

Silver Crown, Halfcrown, Florin, Scottish shilling, sixpence and three-
pence, 1937. . . . .   *not issued*

The following coins were sold at auction in December 1984 and October 1985.

Sovereign, brilliant, with some hair lines in field 40
Halfcrown, brilliant mint state 16
Shilling, brilliant mint state 12
Sixpence, brilliant mint state 9

Nickel brass. Threepence, 1937. . . . .   *not iss*
Bronze. Penny. Halfpenny and Farthing, 1937 . . . .   *not iss*

Pattern

4064 Nickel brass dodecagonal threepence, 1937. R. Thrift plant of more   *Extremely r*
naturalistic style than the modified proof coin. A small number of these
coins were produced for experimental purposes and a few did get into
circulation . . . .

Colonial issues

4068   4071

ne coins of East Africa and West Africa occur without mm. (London) and with H (Heaton)
ningham and KN (King's Norton) Birmingham. The prices quoted are for the commonest of
type, regardless of mm.

GEORGE VI, 1936–52

Though they were at first issued concurrently, the twelve-sided nickel-brass threepence superse
the small silver threepence in 1942. Those dated 1943–4 were not issued for circulation in the L
In addition to the usual English "lion" shilling, a shilling, of Scottish type was issued concurrer
This depicts the Scottish lion and crown flanked by the shield of St. Andrew and a thistle. In 194
silver was needed to repay the bullion lent by the U.S.A. during the war, silver coins were repl
by coins of the same type and weight made of cupro-nickel. In 1949, after India had attai
independence, the title *Indiae Imperator* was dropped from the coinage. Commemorative cr
pieces were issued for the Coronation and the 1951 Festival of Britain.

Designer's initials:
  K. G. (Kruger Gray)
  H. P. (T. Humphrey Paget)
  W. P. (Wilson Parker)

GOLD

4074

F

4074	**Five pounds.** R. St. George, 1937. Proof.	
4075	**Two pounds.** Similar, 1937. Proof	
4076	**Sovereign.** Similar, 1937. Proof.	
4077	**Half-sovereign.** Similar, 1937. Proof	

SILVER

First coinage. Silver, .500 fine, with title IND:IMP

4078

	VF	EF	UNC.
	£	£	£
4078 **Crown.** Coronation commemorative, 1937. ℞. Arms and supporters	4	10	18
4079 — — Proof *FDC* £40			

4080   4081

4080 Halfcrown. ℞. Shield

	EF	UNC.		UNC.
	£	£		£
1937		6	1942	5
— Proof *FDC* £10			1943	6
1938	3	16	1944	4
1939		6	1945	4
1940		6	1946	4
1941		6		

4081 Florin. ℞. Crowned rose, etc.

	EF	UNC.		UNC.
1937		6	1942	4
— Proof *FDC* £8			1943	4
1938	3	15	1944	4
1939		5	1945	4
1940		5	1946	4
1941		4		

4082   4083

4082 Shilling. "English". ℞. Lion on large crown

	EF	UNC.		UNC.
1937		5	1942	4
— Proof *FDC* £6			1943	4
1938	2	15	1944	4
1939		5	1945	3
1940		5	1946	3
1941		5		

	EF	UNC.			VF	EF	UNC
	£	£			£	£	

4083 Shilling. "Scottish". R. Lion seated facing on crown, etc.

1937		5		1942			
— Proof *FDC* £7				1943			
1938	2	15		1944			
1939		5		1945			
1940		6		1946			
1941		6					

4084   4085

4084 Sixpence. R. GRI crowned

1937		3		1942			2
— Proof *FDC* £4				1943			2
2 1938		1	6	1944			2
1939		4		1945			2
1940		4		1946			2
1941		4					

4085 Threepence. R. Shield on rose

1937		2		1941		1	3
— Proof *FDC* £4				1942*	1	5	12
1938		2		1943*	2	8	15
1939	3	8		1944*	3	12	25
1940		3					

* *For colonial use only.*

4086

4086 Maundy Set. Silver, .500 fine. Uniform dates

	FDC			FDC
	£			£
1937	45		1942	45
— Proof *FDC* £50			1943	45
1938	45		1944	45
1939	45		1945	45
1940	45		1946	45
1941	45			

		FDC £		FDC £

)87   — **fourpence,** 1937–46. . . . . *from*   9
)88   — **threepence,** 1937–46 . . . . *from*   9
)89   — **twopence,** 1937–46 . . . . *from*   9
090   — **penny,** 1937–46. . . . . *from* 12

Second coinage. Silver, .925 fine, with title IND.IMP (Maundy only)
091   Maundy Set (4d., 3d., 2d. and 1d.). Uniform dates

1947.	45	1948.	45

092   — **fourpence,** 1947–8   9
093   — **threepence,** 1947–8. 10
094   — **twopence,** 1947–8.   9
095   — **penny,** 1947–8 12

Third coinage. Silver, .925 fine, but omitting IND.IMP. (Maundy only)
096   Maundy Set (4d., 3d., 2d. and 1d.). Uniform dates

1949.	45	1951.	45
1950.	45	1952.	45

The 1952 Maundy was distributed by Queen Elizabeth II.

097   — **fourpence,** 1949–52. . . . . *from*   9
098   — **threepence,** 1949–52 . . . . *from*   9
099   — **twopence,** 1949–52 . . . . *from*   9
100   — **penny,** 1949–52. . . . . *from* 12

CUPRO-NICKEL

Second coinage. Types as first (silver) coinage, IND.IMP.
101   Halfcrown. R. Shield

		UNC. £		UNC. £
1947.		4	1948.	4

102   Florin. R. Crowned rose

1947.	4	1948.	3

103   Shilling. "English" type

1947.	5	1948.	3

104   "Scottish" type

1947.	4	1948.	3

105   Sixpence. GRI crowned

1947.	3	1948.	2

Third coinage. Types as before but title IND.IMP. omitted

4106   4110

4106 Halfcrown

	UNC £		UN
1949.	5	1951.	
1950.	6	— Proof *FDC* £9	
— Proof *FDC* £9		1952.	*Extremely rar*

4107 Florin

1949.	7	1951.	
1950.	7	— Proof *FDC* £8	
— Proof *FDC* £8			

4108 Shilling. "English" type

1949.	6	1951.	
1950.	6	— Proof *FDC* £6	
— Proof *FDC* £6			

4109 — "Scottish" type

1949.	8	1951.	
1950.	7	— Proof *FDC* £6	
— Proof *FDC* £6			

Cupro-nickel

4110 Sixpence. As illustration

	Unc. £		VF £	EF £	Unc
1949	4	1951			
1950	4	— Proof *FDC* £4			
— Proof *FDC* £4		1952	1	10	3

estival of Britain issue

4111

	EF	UNC.
	£	£

4111   Crown. ℞. St. George, 1951. *Proof-like* 2   5

NICKEL BRASS

4112   4113

First issue, with title IND.IMP.

4112   Threepence (dodecagonal). ℞. Thrift

	VF	EF	UNC.		VF	EF	UNC.
	£	£	£		£	£	£
1937			2	1942			2
— Proof *FDC* £4				1943			2
1938		2	6	1944			3
1939		3	15	1945			5
1940			5	1946		3	30	110
1941			3	1948			3	15

Second issue, omitting IND.IMP.

4113   Threepence

	VF	EF	UNC.		VF	EF	UNC.
1949	4	35	120	1951		8	30
1950		8	25	— Proof *FDC* £25			
— Proof *FDC* £25				1952			3

BRONZE

First issue, with title IND.IMP.
4114 Penny. ℞. Britannia

4114

	UNC. £		UNC
1937.	2	1944.	
— Proof *FDC* £6		1945.	
1938.	2	1946.	
1939.	5	1947.	
1940.	6	1948.	

4115 Halfpenny. ℞. Ship

4115   4116

1937.	2	1943.	2
— Proof *FDC* £4		1944.	2
1938.	3	1945.	3
1939.	4	1946.	6
1940.	6	1947.	3
1941.	5	1948.	2
1942.	2		

4116 Farthing. ℞. Wren

1937.	1	1943.	.65
— Proof *FDC* £4		1944.	.65
1938.	2	1945.	.65
1939.	.65	1946.	.65
1940.	1	1947.	.65
1941.	.75	1948.	.75
1942.	.75		

Bronze
Second issue, without IND.IMP. Types as before
4117 Penny

	VF £	EF £	Unc. £		VF £	EF £	Unc. £
1949			2	1951	6	12	18
1950	4	10	20	— Proof *FDC* £16			
— Proof *FDC* £16							

4118   4119

4118 Halfpenny

1949	5	1951	5
1950	4	— Proof *FDC* £4	
— Proof *FDC* £4		1952	3

4119 Farthing

1949	1	1951	.70
1950	.70	— Proof *FDC* £3	
— Proof *FDC* £4		1952	.80

The coins dated 1952 were issued during the reign of Elizabeth II.

ELIZABETH II, acc. 1952

The earliest coins of this reign have the title BRITT·OMN, but in 1954 this was omitted from the Queen's titles owing to the changing status of so many Commonwealth territories. The minting of "English" and "Scottish" shillings was continued. A Coronation commemorative crown was issued in 1953, another crown was struck on the occasion of the 1960 British Exhibition in New York and a third was issued in honour of Sir Winston Churchill in 1965. A very small number of proof gold coins were struck in 1953 for the national museum collections, but between 1957 and 1968 gold sovereigns were minted again in quantity for sale in the international bullion market and to counteract the activities of counterfeiters.

Owing to inflation the farthing had now become practically valueless; production of these coins ceased after 1956 and the coins were demonetized at the end of 1960. In 1965 it was decided to change to a decimal system of coinage in the year 1971. As part of the transition to decimal coinage the halfpenny was demonetized in August 1969 and the halfcrown in January 1970. (See also introduction to Decimal Coinage on p. 332.)

Designer's initials:

G. L. (Gilbert Ledward)
W. P. (Wilson Parker)
M. G. (Mary Gillick)
W. G. (William Gardner)
E. F. (Edgar Fuller)
C. T. (Cecil Thomas)
P. N. (Philip Nathan)
R. D. M. (Raphael David Maklouf)
N. S. (Norman Sillman)

Other designers whose initials
do not appear on the coins:
Christopher Ironside
Arnold Machin
David Wynne
Professor Richard Guyatt
Eric Sewell
Leslie Durbin
Derek Gorringe

PRE-DECIMAL ISSUES

GOLD

First coinage, with title BRITT·OMN, 1953. *Proof only*

4120 **Five pounds.** ℞. St. George . . . . *None issued for collectors*
4121 **Two pounds.** Similar . . . . *None issued for collectors*
4122* **Sovereign.** Similar. . . . . *None issued for collectors*

* *A brilliant mint state specimen sold at auction for £24,000 in June 1985.*

4123 **Half-sovereign.** Similar . . . . *None issued for collectors*

Second issue, BRITT·OMN omitted

4125

	UNC. £
4124 **Sovereign.** ℞. St. George	
1957	70

1957   75

4125 — Similar, but coarser graining on edge

	UNC.		UNC.
	£		£
1958	75	1965	75
1959	75	1966	75
1962	75	1967	75
1963	75	1968	75
1964	75		

Note: *Gold bullion price at the time of printing $363 per oz at $1.57 to the £1 sterling.*

SILVER

The Queen's Maundy are now the only coins struck regularly in silver.
The location of the Maundy ceremony is given for each year.

First issue, with title BRITT·OMN.

		FDC
		£
4126	**Maundy Set** (4d., 3d., 2d. and 1d.), 1953. *St Paul's*	225
4127	— **fourpence**, 1953	40
4128	— **threepence**, 1953	40
4129	— **twopence**, 1953	40
4130	— **penny**, 1953	50

Second issue, with BRITT·OMN omitted

4131

4131 **Maundy Set** (4d., 3d., 2d. and 1d.). Uniform dates

	FDC		FDC
	£		£
1954 *Westminster*	50	1963 *Chelmsford*	50
1955 *Southwark*	50	1964 *Westminster*	50
1956 *Westminster*	50	1965 *Canterbury*	50
1957 *St. Albans*	50	1966 *Westminster*	50
1958 *Westminster*	50	1967 *Durham*	50
1959 *Windsor*	50	1968 *Westminster*	50
1960 *Westminster*	50	1969 *Selby*	50
1961 *Rochester*	50	1970 *Westminster*	50
1962 *Westminster*	50	*See also p. 333.*	

4132	— **fourpence**, 1954–70	*from*	10
4133	— **threepence**, 1954–70	*from*	10
4134	— **twopence**, 1954–70	*from*	10
4135	— **penny**, 1954–70	*from*	11

CUPRO-NICKEL

First issue, 1953, with title BRITT·OMN.

4136

		EF	UNC.	Proof FDC
		£	£	£
4136	**Crown.** Queen on horseback. ℞. Crown in centre of cross, shield in each angle, 1953	1	3	25

4137   4138

| 4137 | **Halfcrown,** with title BRITT·OMN. ℞. Arms, 1953 . . . . | 3 | 8 |
| 4138 | **Florin.** ℞. Double rose, 1953 . . . . | 3 | 6 |

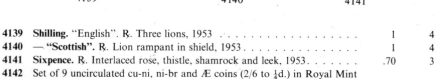

4139   4140   4141

4139	**Shilling.** "English". ℞. Three lions, 1953	1	4
4140	— **"Scottish".** ℞. Lion rampant in shield, 1953	1	4
4141	**Sixpence.** ℞. Interlaced rose, thistle, shamrock and leek, 1953	.70	3
4142	Set of 9 uncirculated cu-ni, ni-br and Æ coins (2/6 to ¼d.) in Royal Mint plastic envelope	8	

upro-nickel
cond issue, similar types but omitting BRITT·OMN.

4143   4144

		EF	UNC.
		£	£
143	**Crown,** 1960. Bust r. R. As 4136	2	5
—	— Similar, from polished dies (New York Exhibition issue)	4	18
144	— Churchill commemorative, 1965. As illustration. R. Bust of Winston		
	Churchill r.		.75
—	— Similar, satin-finish. *Specimen*		250

145 Halfcrown. R. As 4137

	EF	UNC.		
	£	£		
1954	2	15	1961	1
1955		4	1962	1
1956		5	1963	1
1957		2	1964	3
1958	2	12	1965	1
1959	2	15	1966	.60
1960		3	1967	.60

4146

146 Florin. R. As 4138

1954	3	30	1961	2
1955		3	1962	1
1956		3	1963	.75
1957	2	20	1964	.60
1958	1	10	1965	.50
1959	2	25	1966	.45
1960		2	1967	.40

4147 Shilling. "English" type. R. As 4139

	EF £	Unc. £		EF £	Unc.
1954		2	1961		
1955		2	1962		
1956		7	1963		
1957		1	1964		
1958	2	15	1965		
1959		1	1966		
1960		1			

4148 Shilling. "Scottish" type. R. As 4140

	EF	Unc.		EF	Unc.
1954		2	1961		
1955		3	1962		
1956		7	1963		
1957	2	15	1964		
1958		1	1965		
1959	2	15	1966		
1960		1			

4149 Sixpence. R. As 4141

	Unc.		Unc.
1954	3	1961	
1955	1	1962	
1956	1	1963	
1957	.65	1964	
1958	4	1965	
1959	.35	1966	
1960	4	1967	

NICKEL BRASS

4152   4153

First issue, with title BRITT.OMN.

4152 Threepence (dodecagonal). R. Crowned portcullis, 1953 . . . .

— Proof *FDC* £4

Second issue (omitting BRIT.OMN)

4153 Threepence. Similar type

	Unc.		Unc.
1954	4	1961	.3
1955	5	1962	.3
1956	5	1963	.2
1957	3	1964	.2
1958	6	1965	.2
1959	3	1966	.1
1960	3	1967	.1

BRONZE

First issue, with title BRITT.OMN.

4154   4158

	VF £	EF £	Unc. £	Proof FDC £
4154 **Penny.** R. Britannia (only issued with Royal Mint set in plastic envelope), 1953	.60	2	5	6
4155 **Halfpenny.** R. Ship, 1953			2	4
4156 **Farthing.** R. Wren, 1953			.75	3

Second issue, omitting BRITT.OMN.

4157 **Penny.** R. Britannia (1954–60 *not issued*)

	Unc. £		Unc. £
1954	*Extremely rare*	1964	.10
1961	.50	1965	.10
1962	.15	1966	.10
1963	.15	1967	.10

4158 **Halfpenny.** R. Ship (1961 *not issued*)

1954	4	1962	.10
1955	4	1963	.10
1956	4	1964	.10
1957	.40	1965	.10
1958	.35	1966	.10
1959	.20	1967	.10
1960	.20		

4156   4159

4159 **Farthing.** R. Wren

			EF £	Unc. £
1954	.80	1956	.55	2
1955	.75			

DECIMAL COINAGE

In December 1967 a decision to build a new mint at Llantrisant in South Wales was announced. Th first phase was completed by December 1968 when H.M. The Queen struck the first coins at th official opening. The second phase was completed during late 1975 at which time all coin productio at Tower Hill ceased.

Though the official change-over to a decimal currency did not take place until 15th Februar 1971, three decimal denominations were circulated prior to this date. The 10 and 5 *new pence* equivalent to the former florin and shilling, were introduced in 1968 and the seven-sided 50 *new pence* (equal to 10 shillings) was issued during October 1969. The old halfpenny was demonetized o 1st August 1969, and the halfcrown was withdrawn on 1st January 1970.

In 1968 bronze 2, 1 and ½ *new pence* dated 1971 were issued, together with the 1968 10 and 5 *new pence*, as specimens of the new coinage, but these bronze coins were not legalized for current use until 1971.

Britain's accession to the E.E.C. was commemorated by a special 50 pence piece in 1973. A crown-sized 25 pence has been issued to celebrate the Silver Wedding of H.M. The Queen and Prince Philip in 1972, the Queen's Silver Jubilee in 1977, the 80th birthday of Queen Elizabeth, the Queen Mother and for the Royal Wedding in 1981.

In 1979 the first proof sovereign since 1937 was issued and 1980 saw a proof five pound, two pound and half-sovereign.

Britain's first 20 pence piece appeared in 1982 and 1983 saw the first circulating non-precious metal £1 coin. In 1986 the Royal Mint has introduced a nickel-brass £2 piece specially struck in honour of the XIII Commonwealth Games to be held in Scotland (see illus. 4279). The word "NEW" was omitted from the 1982 cupro-nickel coins which now bear the denomination in words and figures. The ½ pence was demonetized in December 1984.

GOLD

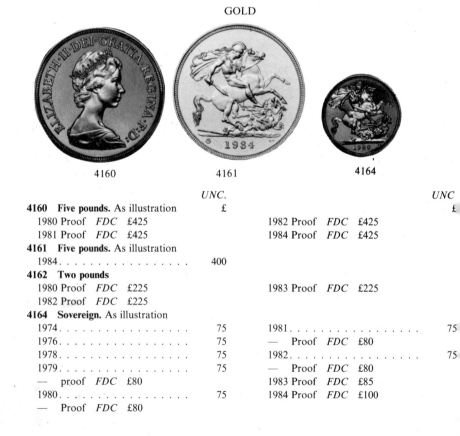

4160   4161   4164

	UNC. £			UNC £
4160 Five pounds. As illustration				
1980 Proof *FDC* £425		1982 Proof *FDC* £425		
1981 Proof *FDC* £425		1984 Proof *FDC* £425		
4161 Five pounds. As illustration				
1984	400			
4162 Two pounds				
1980 Proof *FDC* £225		1983 Proof *FDC* £225		
1982 Proof *FDC* £225				
4164 Sovereign. As illustration				
1974	75	1981		75
1976	75	— Proof *FDC* £80		
1978	75	1982		75
1979	75	— Proof *FDC* £80		
— proof *FDC* £80		1983 Proof *FDC* £85		
1980	75	1984 Proof *FDC* £100		
— Proof *FDC* £80				

4166 Half-sovereign

UNC.
£

1980 Proof *FDC* £50		1983 Proof *FDC* £50		
1982.	45	1984 Proof *FDC* £55		
— Proof *FDC* £50				

(For proof sets which include some or all of the above coins, see the list on pages 343–4.)

SILVER

4170 Maundy Set (4p, 3p, 2p and 1p). Uniform dates. Types as 4131

	FDC £		FDC £
1971 *Tewkesbury Abbey*	55	1988 *Lichfield Cathedral*	75
1972 *York Minster*	55	1989 *Birmingham Cathedral*	75
1973 *Westminster Abbey*	55		
1974 *Salisbury Cathedral*	55		
1975 *Peterborough Cathedral* . . .	55		
1976 *Hereford Cathedral*	55		
1977 *Westminster Abbey*	65		
1978 *Carlisle Cathedral*	55		
1979 *Winchester Cathedral*	55		
1980 *Worcester Cathedral*	55		
1981 *Westminster Abbey*	55		
1982 *St. David's Cathedral*	55		
1983 *Exeter Cathedral*	55		
1984 *Southwell Minster*	55		
1985 *Ripon Cathedral*	55		
1986 *Chichester Cathedral*	75		
1987 *Ely Cathedral*	75		

4180 — **fourpence**, 1971–89	*from*	13
4181 — **threepence**, 1971–89	*from*	13
4182 — **twopence**, 1971–89	*from*	13
4183 — **penny**, 1971–89	*from*	15

The Queen's Maundy are now the only coins struck regularly in .925 silver. The place of distribution is shown after each date.

NICKEL-BRASS

4185   4186

UNC.
£

4185 One pound (U.K. type). Edge DECUS ET TUTAMEN

1983	2
— Specimen in presentation folder	3
— Proof in *Æ*R	30
— Proof piedfort in *Æ*R	160

UNC

4186 One pound (Scottish type). Edge NEMO ME IMPUNE LACESSIT
         1984 . . . .
         — Specimen in presentation folder . . . .
         — Proof in *Æ*   *FDC* £21
         — Proof piedfort in *Æ*   *FDC* £70

CUPRO-NICKEL

4190   4191

4190 Fifty new pence (seven-sided). ℞. Britannia r.

| | *UNC.* | | *UNC.* |
	£		£
1969.	2	1978.	.75
1970.	4	1979.	.75
1976.	1	1980.	.75
1977.	1	1981.	.75

4191 Fifty (50) pence. "New" omitted. As illustration
         1982. . . . .   1984* (*See note on p. 337*). . . . .
         1983. . . . .

4195 Accession to European Economic Community. ℞. Clasped hands, 1973 . . . . . .   1.25
         — — (Proof in case)   *FDC*   £2

4195

Unc.
£

4200

4200 **Twenty-five new pence** (crown). Silver Wedding Commemorative, 1972. 75

— — (Cu.-ni. proof.) Issued in 1972/Mint set. See PS22. 4

— — (Æ proof in case)   *FDC*   £18

4201

4201 Silver Jubilee Commemorative, 1977 60

— — (Æ proof in case)   *FDC*   £12

— — (Cu.-ni. proof.) Only issued in 1977/Mint set. See PS27 on p. 343 4

— — (Cu.-ni. Specimen striking.) Issued in Royal Mint folder). 2

4202

4202 Queen Mother 80th Birthday Commemorative, 1980. 45

— — (Æ proof in case)   *FDC*   £35

— — (Cu.-ni. Specimen striking.) Issued in Royal Mint folder 1

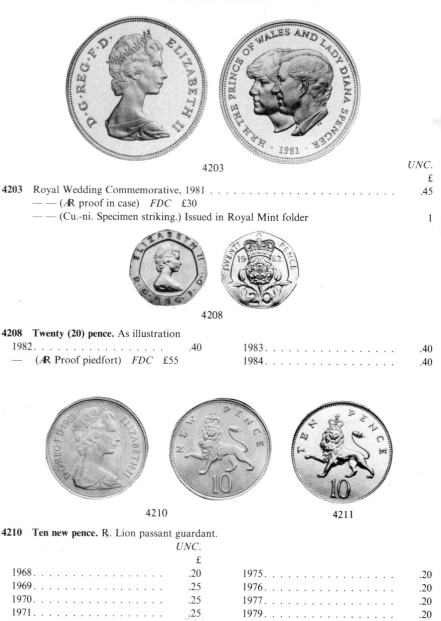

4203

4203 Royal Wedding Commemorative, 1981 45
    —— (*Æ* proof in case)   *FDC*   £30
    —— (Cu.-ni. Specimen striking.) Issued in Royal Mint folder   1

4208

4208 Twenty (20) pence. As illustration
1982. 40   1983. 40
    —   (*Æ* Proof piedfort)   *FDC*   £55   1984. 40

4210   4211

4210 Ten new pence. ℞. Lion passant guardant.
                                          UNC.
                                            £
1968. 20   1975. 20
1969. 25   1976. 20
1970. 25   1977. 20
1971. 25   1979. 20
1973. 20   1980. 20
1974. 20   1981. 20
4211 Ten (10) pence. As illustration
1982* . . . .   1984* (*See note on p. 337*)
1983* . . . .

| 4220 | 4221 |

4220   Five new pence. ℞. Crowned thistle

	Unc.		Unc.
	£		£
1968	.10	1977	.10
1969	.12	1978	.10
1970	.12	1979	.10
1971	.10	1980	.10
1975	.10	1981 Proof only	

4221   Five (5) pence. As illustration

1982*		1984*	
1983*			

BRONZE

| 4230 | 4231 |

4230   Two new pence. ℞. Plumes

1971	.05	1978	.08
1975	.08	1979	.08
1976	.08	1980	.08
1977	.08	1981	.08

4231   Two (2) pence. As illustration

1982*		1984*	
1983*			

* Coins which occur in the Royal Mint specimen or proof sets, there being none made for general circulation at the time of going to press.

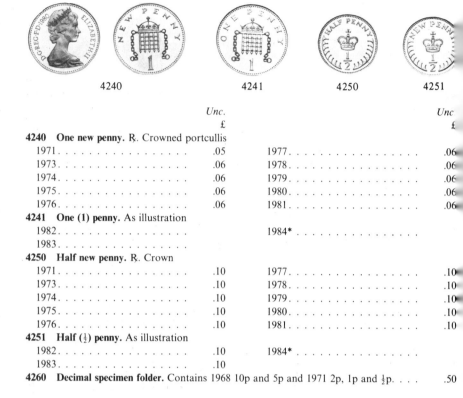

| 4240 | 4241 | 4250 | 4251 |

	Unc.		*Unc*
	£		£

4240 One new penny. ℞. Crowned portcullis

1971	.05	1977	.06
1973	.06	1978	.06
1974	.06	1979	.06
1975	.06	1980	.06
1976	.06	1981	.06

4241 One (1) penny. As illustration

| 1982 | | 1984* | |
| 1983 | | | |

4250 Half new penny. ℞. Crown

1971	.10	1977	.10
1973	.10	1978	.10
1974	.10	1979	.10
1975	.10	1980	.10
1976	.10	1981	.10

4251 Half (½) penny. As illustration

| 1982 | .10 | 1984* | |
| 1983 | .10 | | |

4260 Decimal specimen folder. Contains 1968 10p and 5p and 1971 2p, 1p and ½p. 50

NEW PORTRAIT

The new effigy is designed by Raphael David Maklouf, FRSA. It is only the third portrait of the Queen to be used on U.K. coinage, the previous change of portrait being in 1968 with the introduction of decimal coins. The designer's initials R.D.M. appear on the truncation. There is no portrait change on the Maundy coins.

GOLD

| 4261 | 4263 | 4276 |

UNC.
£

4261* **Five pounds.** Ŗ. St. George
1985 Proof *FDC* £450

4262 **Five pounds.** Ŗ. St. George, "U" in a circle to left of date
1985 400
1986 400

4263 **Five pounds.** Uncouped portrait of Queen Elizabeth II. As illustration. Ŗ. St. George, 'U' in a circle to left of date.
1987 450
1988 450

4264 **Five pounds.** 500th Anniversary of sovereign
1989 495
1989 Proof *FDC* £470

4266 **Two pounds.** Ŗ. St. George
*1985 Proof *FDC* £225   1988 Proof *FDC* £300
1987 Proof *FDC* £225

4267 **Two pounds.** Ŗ. St. Andrew's cross surmounted by a thistle of Scotland. Edge XIII
COMMONWEALTH GAMES SCOTLAND 1986 (*See illus. 4279*)
1986 Proof *FDC* £300

4268 **Two pounds.** 500th Anniversary
1989 Proof *FDC* £300

4271 **Sovereign.** Ŗ. St. George
1985 Proof *FDC* £90   1987 Proof *FDC* £100
1986 Proof *FDC* £100   1988 Proof *FDC* £150

4272 **Sovereign.** 500th Anniversary
1989 Proof *FDC* £150

4276 **Half-sovereign.** Ŗ. St. George
1985 Proof *FDC* £55   1987 Proof *FDC* £60
1986 Proof *FDC* £60   1988 Proof *FDC* £80

4276A

4276A **Half-sovereign.** 500th Anniversary
1989 Proof *FDC* £80

4277

4277 Britannia. One hundred pounds. (1oz of fine gold).
R. Britannia standing.

	UNC. £
1987	
— Proof *FDC* £555	275
1988	
1988 Proof *FDC* £500	275
1989	275

4278

4278 Britannia. Fifty pounds. ($\frac{1}{2}$oz of fine gold).
R. Britannia standing.

1987	
— Proof *FDC* £295	140
1988	
— Proof *FDC* £255	140
1989	140

4278A

4278A Britannia. Twenty five pounds. ($\frac{1}{4}$oz of fine gold).
R. Britannia standing.

1987	
— Proof *FDC* £155	75
1988	
— Proof *FDC* £130	75
1989	75

4278B

4278B Britannia. Ten pounds. ($\frac{1}{10}$oz of fine gold).

R̥. Britannia standing.

1987	35
— Proof *FDC* £65	
1988	35
— Proof *FDC* £65	
1989	35

NICKEL-BRASS

4279

4279 Two pounds. R̥. St. Andrew's cross surmounted by a thistle of Scotland. Edge XIII COMMONWEALTH GAMES SCOTLAND 1986

1986	3
— Struck in ·500 silver................................	12
— Proof in Æ *FDC* £20	
— Specimen in presentation folder	5

4280   4280A

4280 Two pounds. 300th Anniversary of Bill of Rights. Cypher of William and Mary, House of Commons mace and St. Edward's crown.

1989	3
— Specimen in presentation folder	5
— Proof Æ *FDC* £23	
— Proof piedfort in Æ *FDC* £40	

4280A   Two pounds. 300th Anniversary of Claim of Right (Scotland). R̥. As   £
4280, but with crown of Scotland.
  —1989   3
  — Specimen in presentation folder   5
  — Proof in Æ   *FDC* £23
  — Proof piedfort in Æ   *FDC*   £40

4281

4281   One pound (Welsh type). Edge PLEIDIOL WYF I'M GWLAD
  1985   2
  — Specimen in presentation folder   3
  — Proof in Æ   *FDC* £21
  — Proof piedfort in Æ   *FDC*   £55

4282   4283   4284

4282   One pound (Northern Ireland). Edge DECUS ET TUTAMEN
  1986   2
  — Specimen in presentation folder   3
  — Proof in Æ   *FDC*   £21
  — Proof piedfort in Æ   *FDC*   £45
4283   One pound (English type). Edge DECUS ET TUTAMEN
  1987   2
  — Specimen in presentation folder   3
  — Proof in Æ   *FDC*   £21
  — Proof piedfort in Æ   *FDC*   £45
4284   One pound (Royal arms). Edge DECUS ET TUTAMEN
  1988   2
  — Specimen in presentation folder   3
  — Proof in Æ   *FDC*   £21
  — Proof piedfort Æ   *FDC*   £45
4285   One pound (Scottish type). Edge NEMO ME IMPUNE LACESSIT (Illus. as 4186)
  1989   2
  — Proof in Æ   *FDC*   £21
  — Proof piedfort in Æ   *FDC*   £45

4286

4286 Fifty pence. ℞. Britannia r.

1985 2
1986* . . . .
1987* . . . .
1988* . . . .
1989 . . . .

4291

4291 Twenty pence. ℞. Crowned double rose

1985 . . . .
1986* . . . .
1987 . . . .
1988 . . . .
1989 . . . .

4301

4301 Ten pence. ℞. Lion passant guardant

1985* . . . .
1986* . . . .
1987* . . . .
1988* . . . .
1989 . . . .

BRONZE

4306

4306 Five pence. R. Crowned thistle

1985* . . . .
1986* . . . .
1987 . . . .
1988 . . . .
1989 . . . .

4311

4311 Two pence. R. Plumes

1985 . . . .
1986 . . . .
1987 . . . .
1988 . . . .
1989 . . . .

* These coins occur in the Royal Mint specimen or proof sets. There were none made for general circulation at the time of going to press.

4316

4316 One penny. R. Portcullis with chains

1985 . . . .
1986 . . . .
1987 . . . .
1988 . . . .

PROOF or SPECIMEN SETS

sued by the Royal Mint in official case from 1887 onwards, but earlier sets were issued privately by
~~e~~ engraver.
All pieces have a finish superior to that of the current coins.

		No. of coins	FDC £
S1	**George IV.** New issue, **1826.** Five pounds to farthing	11	17,000
S2	**William IV.** Coronation, **1831.** Two pounds to farthing	14	16,000
S3	**Victoria,** young head, **1839.** "Una and the Lion" five pounds, and sovereign to farthing	15	21,000
S4	— **1853.** Sovereign to quarter-farthing, including Gothic type crown . . .	16	18,000
S5	Jubilee head. Golden Jubilee, **1887.** Five pounds to threepence	11	3,750
S6	— — Crown to threepence	7	850
S7	Old head, **1893.** Five pounds to threepence	10	4,250
S8	— — Crown to threepence . . :	6	900
S9	**Edward VII.** Coronation, **1902.** Five pounds to Maundy penny. Matt surface	13	1,450
S10	— — Sovereign to Maundy penny. Matt surface	11	375
S11	**George V.** Coronation, **1911.** Five pounds to Maundy penny	12	2,450
S12	— — Sovereign to Maundy penny	10	650
S13	— — Halfcrown to Maundy penny	8	300
S14	New types, **1927.** Crown to threepence	6	200
S15	**George VI.** Coronation, **1937.** Gold. Five pounds to half-sovereign	4	1,450
S16	— — — Silver, etc. Crown to farthing, including Maundy	15	110
S17	Mid-Century, **1950.** Halfcrown to farthing	10	35
S18	Festival of Britain, **1951.** Crown to farthing.	10	50
S19	**Elizabeth II.** Coronation, **1953.** Crown to farthing	10	35
S20	"Last Sterling" set, **1970.** Halfcrown to halfpenny plus medallion	8	10
S21	Decimal coinage set, **1971.** 50 new pence ("Britannia") to $\frac{1}{2}$ penny, plus medallion.	6	6
S22	— **1972.** As last, but includes the cu.-ni. Silver Wedding crown	7	8
S23	— **1973.** As PS21 but "EEC" 50p	6	5
S24	— **1974.** As PS21 . . . . :	6	5
S25	— **1975.** As last	6	5
S26	— **1976.** As last	6	5
S27	— **1977.** As PS21 but including the proof Silver Jubilee crown struck in cupro-nickel	7	8
S28	— **1978.** As PS21	6	8
S29	— **1979.** As last . . . . . ~~.~~	6	10
S30	— **1980.** As last	6	6
S31	— — Five pounds to half-sovereign	4	750
S32	— **1981.** U.K. Proof coin Commemorative collection. (Consists of £5, £1, Royal Wedding crown (25p) in ÆR, plus base metal proofs as PS21.) .	9	500
S33	— — As PS21	6	6
S34	**Elizabeth II, 1982.** U.K. Uncirculated (specimen) set in Royal Mint folder. New reverse types, including 20 pence	7	3
S35	— — As last but proofs in Royal Mint sealed plastic case, plus medallion.	7	10
S36	— Æ Five pounds to half-sovereign	4	850
S37	— **1983.** As PS34, includes "U.K." £1	8	8
S38	— — As PS35, includes "U.K." £1	8	12

PS39	— — N £2, £1, £½ in case.	3	3.
PS40	— **1984**. As PS37 but with "Scottish" £1	8	
PS41	— — As PS38 but with "Scottish" £1	8	
PS42	— — N £5, £1, £½ in case.	3	6(
PS43	— **1985**. As PS37 but with new portrait, also includes "Welsh" £1. The set does not contain the now discontinued halfpenny	7	
PS44	— — As last but proofs in Royal Mint sealed plastic case, plus medallion	7	
PS45	— — As last but within a deluxe red leather case.	7	
PS46	— — N £5, £2, £1, £½ in case.	4	8.
PS47	— **1986**. As PS43 but with a new two pounds and the Northern Ireland .	8	
PS48	— — As PS44 but with two pounds and Northern Ireland £1.	8	
PS49	— — As last but within a deluxe red leather case.	8	
PS50	— — N £2 (as 4267), £1, £½ in a deluxe red leather case.	3	35
PS51	— **1987**. As PS43 but with "English" £1	7	
PS52	— — As last but proofs in Royal Mint sealed plastic case, plus medallion	7	
PS53	— — As last but within a deluxe red leather case.	7	2
PS54	— — N £2 (as 4266), £1, £½ in a deluxe red leather case.	3	40
PS55	— — **Britannia** N proofs. £100, £50, £25, £10 in a deluxe case	4	90
PS56	— — As last but only containing the £25, £10 in a deluxe case	2	21
PS57	— **1988**. As PS43 but with "Royal Arms" £1.	7	
PS58	— — As last but proofs in Royal Mint sealed plastic case, plus medallion	7	1
PS59	— — As last but within a deluxe leather case.	7	2
PS60	— — N £2 (as 4266), £1, £½ in a deluxe case	3	50
PS61	— — **Britannia** proofs. As PS55	4	90
PS62	— — As PS56	2	21
PS63	— **1989**. As PS43 but with Scotland £1	7	
PS64	— — As last but proofs and with 2 × £2.	9	2
PS65	— — As last but within red leather case.	9	3
PS66	— — Sovereign Anniversary N £5, £2, £1, £½	4	115
PS67	— — As last but only containing £2, £1, £½.	3	50
PS68	— — 2 × £2 in Royal Mint folder	2	
PS69	— — As last but silver piedfort proofs	2	8
PS70	— — As last but silver proofs	2	4

The prices given are for absolutely perfect sets with uncleaned, brilliant or matt surfaces. Sets are ofte seen with one or more coins showing imperfections such as scratches, bumps on the edge, etc. Any flaw will substantially affect the value of a set.

APPENDIX I

A SELECT NUMISMATIC BIBLIOGRAPHY

Listed below is a selection of general books on British numismatics and other works that the specialist collector will need to consult.

General Books:

NORTH, J. J. *English Hammered Coins*, Vol. I, *c. 650–1272*; Vol. II, *1272–1662*.
BROOKE, G. C. *English Coins*. (3rd Ed., 1951).
SUTHERLAND, C. H. V. *English Coinage, 600–1900*.
KENYON, R. LL. *Gold Coins of England*.
GRUEBER, H. A. *Handbook of the Coins of Great Britain and Ireland*.

Specialist Works:

MACK, R. P. *The Coinage of Ancient Britain*.
ALLEN, D. *The Origins of Coinage in Britain: A Reappraisal*.
DOLLEY, R. H. M. (ED.). *Anglo-Saxon Coins; studies presented to Sir Frank Stenton*.
KEARY, C. and GREUBER, H. *English Coins in the British Museum: Anglo-Saxon Series*.
BROOKE, G. C. *English Coins in the British Museum: The Norman Kings*.
ALLEN, D. F. *English Coins in the British Museum: The Cross-and-Crosslets ("Tealby") type of Henry II*.
LAWRENCE, L. A. *The Coinage of Edward III from 1351*.
WHITTON, C. A. *The Heavy Coinage of Henry VI*.
BLUNT, C. E. and WHITTON, C. A. *The Coinages of Edward IV and of Henry VI (Restored)*.
MORRIESON, LT.-COL. H. W. *The Coinages of Thomas Bushell, 1636–1648*.
SEABY, H. A. *The English Silver Coinage from 1649*.
SPINK & SON, LTD. *The Milled Coinage of England, 1662–1946*.
PECK, C. W. *English Copper, Tin and Bronze Coins in the British Museum, 1558–1958*.
LINECAR, H. W. A. *British Coin Designs and Designers*.
COPE, G. M. and RAYNER, P. A. *English Milled Coinage 1662–1972*.

and other authoritative papers published in the *Numismatic Chronicle* and *British Numismatic Journal*.

APPENDIX II

LATIN LEGENDS ON ENGLISH COINS

A DOMINO FACTUM EST ISTUD ET EST MIRABILE IN OCULIS NOSTRIS. (This is the Lord's doing and it is marvellous in our eyes: *Psalm* 118, 23.) First used on "fine" sovereign of Mary.

AMOR POPULI PRAESIDIUM REGIS. (The love of the people is the King's protection.) Reverse legend on angels of Charles I.

ANNO REGNI PRIMO, etc. (In the first year of the reign, etc.) Used around the edge of many of the larger milled denominations.

CHRISTO AUSPICE REGNO. (I reign under the auspice of Christ.) Used extensively in the reign of Charles I.

CIVIUM INDUSTRIA FLORET CIVITAS. (By the industry of its people the State flourishes.) On the 1951 Festival crown of George VI.

CULTORES SUI DEUS PROTEGIT. (God protects His worshippers.) On gold double crowns and crowns of Charles I.

DECUS ET TUTAMEN. (An ornament and a safeguard.) This inscription on the edge of all early large milled silver was suggested by Evelyn, he having seen it on the vignette in Card. Richelieu's Greek Testament, and of course refers to the device as a means to prevent clipping. (Virgil, *Aen* v.262.) This legend also appears on the edge of U.K. and Northern Ireland one pound coins.

DIRIGE DEUS GRESSUS MEOS. (May the Lord direct my steps.) On the "Una" 5 pounds of Queen Victoria.

DOMINE NE IN FURORE TUO ARGUAS ME. (O Lord, rebuke me not in Thine anger: *Psalm* 6, 1.). First used on the half-florin of Edward III and then on all half-nobles.

DOMINUS DEUS OMNIPOTENS REX. (Lord God, Almighty King.) (Viking coins.)

DUM SPIRO SPERO. (Whilst I live, I hope.) On the coins struck at Pontefract Castle during the Civil War after Charles I had been imprisoned.

EXALTABITUR IN GLORIA. (He shall be exalted in glory.) On all quarter-nobles.

EXURGAT DEUS ET DISSIPENTUR INIMICI EIUS. (Let God arise and let His enemies be scattered: *Psalm* 68, 1.) On the Scottish ducat and early English coins of James I (VI) and was chosen by the King himself.

FACIAM EOS IN GENTEM UNAM. (I will make them one nation: *Ezek.* 37, 22.) On unites and laurels of James I.

FLORENT CONCORDIA REGNA. (Through concord kingdoms flourish.) On gold unite of Charles I and broad of Charles II.

HANC DEUS DEDIT. (God has given this, *i.e.* crown.) On siege-pieces of Pontefract struck in the name of Charles II.

HAS NISI PERITURUS MIHI ADIMAT NEMO. (Let no one remove these [letters] from me under penalty of death.) On the edge of crowns and half-crowns of Cromwell.

HENRICUS ROSAS REGNA JACOBUS. (Henry *united* the roses, James the kingdoms.) On English and Scottish gold coins of James I (VI).

INIMICOS EJUS INDUAM CONFUSIONE. (As for his enemies I shall clothe them with shame: *Psalm* 132, 18.) On shillings of Edward VI struck at Durham House, Strand.

JESUS AUTEM TRANSIENS PER MEDIUM ILLORUM IBAT. (But Jesus, passing through the midst of them, went His way: *Luke* iv. 30.) The usual reverse legend on English nobles, ryals and hammered sovereigns before James I; also on the very rare Scottish noble of David II of Scotland and the unique Anglo-Gallic noble of Edward the Black Prince.

JUSTITIA THRONUM FIRMAT. (Justice strengthens the throne.) On Charles I half-groats and pennies and Scottish twenty-penny pieces.

LUCERNA PEDIBUS MEIS VERBUM EST. (Thy word is a lamp unto my feet: *Psalm* 119, 105.) Obverse legend on a rare half-sovereign of Edward VI struck at Durham House, Strand.

MIRABILIA FECIT. (He made marvellously.) On the Viking coins of (?) York.

NEMO ME IMPUNE LACESSIT. (No one provokes me with impunity.) On the 1984 Scottish one pound.

NUMMORUM FAMULUS. (The servant of the coinage.) The legend on the edge of the English tin coinage at the end of the seventeenth century.

O CRUX AVE SPES UNICA. (Hail! O Cross, our only hope.) On the reverse of all half-angels.

PAX MISSA PER ORBEM. (Peace sent throughout the world.) The reverse legend of a pattern farthing of Anne.

PAX QUÆRITUR BELLO. (Peace is sought by war.) The reverse legend of the Cromwell broad.

PER CRUCEM TUAM SALVA NOS CHRISTE REDEMPTOR. (By Thy cross, save us, O Christ, our Redeemer.) The normal reverse of English angels.

PLEIDIOL WYF I'M GWLAD. (True am I to my country.) Taken from the Welsh National Anthem. Used on the 1985 Welsh one pound.

POST MORTEM PATRIS PRO FILIO. (For the son after the death of the father.) On siege-pieces struck at Pontefract in 1648 (old style) after the execution of Charles I.

POSUI DEUM ADJUTOREM MEUM. (I have made God my Helper: *comp. Psalm* 54, 4.) Used on many English and Irish silver coins from Edward III until 1603. Altered to POSUIMUS and NOSTRUM on the coins of Philip and Mary.

PROTECTOR LITERIS LITERÆ NUMMIS CORONA ET SALUS. (A protection to the letters [on the face of the coin], the letters [on the edge] are a garland and a safeguard to the coinage.) On the edge of the rare fifty-shilling piece of Cromwell.

QUÆ DEUS CONJUNXIT NEMO SEPARET. (What God hath joined together let no man put asunder: *Matt.* 19, 6.) On the larger silver English and Scottish coins of James I after he succeeded to the English throne.

REDDE CUIQUE QUOD SUUM EST. (Render to each that which is his own.) On a Henry VIII type groat of Edward VI struck by Sir Martin Bowes at Durham House, Strand.

RELIGIO PROTESTANTIVM LEGES ANGLIÆ LIBERTAS PARLIAMENTI. (The religion of the Protestants, the laws of England, the liberty of the Parliament.) This is known as the "Declaration" and refers to Charles I's declaration to the Privy Council at Wellington, 19th Sept., 1642; it is found on many of his coins struck at the provincial mints during the Civil War. Usually abbreviated to REL : PROT : LEG : ANG : LIB : PAR :

ROSA SINE SPINA. (A rose without a thorn.) Found on some gold and small coins of Henry VIII and later reigns.

RUTILANS ROSA SINE SPINA. (A dazzling rose without a thorn.) As last but on small gold only.

SCUTUM FIDEI PROTEGET EUM *or* EAM. (The shield of faith shall protect him *or* her.) On much of the gold of Edward VI and Elizabeth.

TALI DICATA SIGNO MENS FLUCTUARI NEQUIT. (Consecrated by such a sign the mind cannot waver: from a hymn by Prudentius written in the fourth century, entitled "Hymnus ante Somnum".) Only on the gold "George noble" of Henry VIII.

TIMOR DOMINI FONS VITÆ. (The fear of the Lord is a fountain of life: *Prov.* 14, 27.) On many shillings of Edward VI.

TUEATUR UNITA DEUS. (May God guard these united, i.e. kingdoms.) On many English Scottish and Irish coins of James I.

VERITAS TEMPORIS FILIA. (Truth, the daughter of Time.) On English and Irish coins of Mary Tudor.

ICH DIEN. (I serve.) Aberystwyth Furnace 2d, and Decimal 2p.

Some Royal Titles:

REX ANGL*orum*—King of the English.

Rex saxonum occidentalium—King of the West Saxons.

DEI GRA*tia* ANGL*iae* ET FRANC*iae* DOMIN*us* HYB*erniae* ET AQVIT*aniae*—By the Grace of God, King of England and France, Lord of Ireland and Aquitaine.

D*ei* G*ratia* M*agnae* B*ritanniae*, FR*anciae* ET H*iberniae* REX F*idei* D*efensor* BR*unsviciensis* ET L*uneburgensis* D*ux*, S*acri* R*omani* *i*mperii A*rchi*-TH*esaurarius* ET EL*ector*=By the Grace of God, King of Great Britain, France and Ireland, Defender of the Faith, Duke of Brunswick and Luneburg, High Treasurer and Elector of the Holy Roman Empire.

BRITANNIARUM REX—King of the Britains (i.e. Britain and British territories overseas).

BRITT:OMN :REX :FID :DEF :IND :IMP—King of all the Britains, Defender of the Faith, Emperor of India.

Although not *Latin* legends, the following Norman-French mottoes might usefully be added here

DIEU ET MON DROIT. (God and my right.) On halfcrowns of George IV and later monarchs.

HONI SOIT QUI MAL Y PENSE. (Evil to him who evil thinks.) The Motto of the Order of the Garter, first used on the Hereford (?) halfcrowns of Charles I. It also occurs on the Garter Star in the centre of the reverse of the silver coins of Charles II, but being so small it is usually illegible; it is more prominent on the coinage of George III.

Seaby's Coin and Medal Bulletin
This is a magazine published for all interested in numismatics. It contains articles and notes on coins and medals; details of numismatic society meetings; answers to questions; letters to the Editor cuttings from the press, etc., etc.; also many pages of coins and medals of all kinds offered for sale These are well catalogued and act as a good guide to help collectors to catalogue and classify their own coins. Please send for a specimen copy and current subscription rates to B.A. Seaby Ltd, Cavendish Square, London W1M 0AJ. Bound Bulletins for some previous years are available (prices upon request).

Numismatic Clubs and Societies
There are well over one hundred numismatic societies and clubs in the British Isles, a number of which form part of the social and cultural activities of scholastic institutions or commercial industrial concerns.

The two principal learned societies are the Royal Numismatic Society and the British Numismatic Society, both of which publish an annual journal.

Many local clubs and societies are affiliated to the British Association of Numismatic Societies (the B.A.N.S., which holds an annual conference). Details of your nearest local club may be obtained from: The Hon. Sec., B.A.N.S., K. F. Sugden, Dept. of Numismatics, Manchester Museum, the University, Oxford Road, Manchester.

APPENDIX III

MINTMARKS AND OTHER SYMBOLS ON ENGLISH COINS

A MINTMARK (*mm.*), a term borrowed from Roman and Greek numismatics where it showed the place of mintage, was generally used on English coins to show where the legend began (a religious age preferred a cross for the purpose). Later, this mark, since the dating of coins was not usual, had a periodic significance, changing from time to time. Hence it was of a secret or "privy" nature; other privy marks on a coin might be the code-mark of a particular workshop or workman. Thus a privy mark (including the *mm.*) might show when a coin was made, or who made it. In the use of precious metals this knowledge was necessary to guard against fraud and counterfeiting.

Mintmarks are sometimes termed "initial marks" as they are normally placed at the commencement of the inscription. Some of the symbols chosen were personal badges of the ruling monarch such as the rose and sun of York, the boar's head of Richard III, the dragon of Henry Tudor or the thistle of James I; others are heraldic symbols or may allude to the mint master responsible for the coinage, e.g. the *mm.* bow used on the Durham House coins struck under John Bowes and the ws mark of William Sharrington of Bristol.

A table of mintmarks is given on the next page. Where mintmarks appear in the catalogue they are sometimes referred to only by the reference number, in order to save space, i.e. *mm.* 28 (= mintmark Sun), *mm.* 28/74 (= *mm.* Sun on obverse, *mm.* Coronet on reverse), *mm.* 28/- (= *mm.* Sun on obverse only).

MINTMARKS AND OTHER SYMBOLS

Edward III, Cross 1 (Class B + C).
Edward III, broken Cross 1 (Class D).
Edward III, Cross 2 (Class E).
Edward III, Cross 3 (Class G).
Cross Potent (Edw. III Treaty).
Cross Pattée (Edw. III Post Treaty)
Rich. III).
(a) Plain of Greek Cross.
(b) Cross Moline.
Cross Patonce.
Cross Fleurée.
Cross Calvary (Cross on steps).
Long Cross Fitchée.
Short Cross Fitchée.
Restoration Cross (Hen. VI).
Latin Cross.
Voided Cross (Henry VI).
Saltire Cross.
Cross and 4 pellets.
Pierced Cross.
Pierced Cross & pellet.
Pierced Cross & central pellet.
Cross Crosslet.
Curved Star (rayant).
Star.
Spur Rowel.
Mullet.
Pierced Mullet.
Eglantine.
Sun (Edw. IV).
Mullet (Henry V).
Pansy.
Heraldic Cinquefoil (Edw. IV).
Heraldic Cinquefoil (James I).
Rose (Edw. IV).
Rosette (Edw. IV).
Rose (Chas. I).
Catherine Wheel.
Cross in circle.
Halved Sun (6 rays) & Rose.
Halved Sun (4 rays) & Rose.
Lis-upon-Half-Rose.
Lis-upon-Sun & Rose.
Lis-Rose dimidiated.
Lis-issuant-from-Rose.
Trefoil.
Slipped Trefoil, James I (1).
Slipped Trefoil, James I (2).
Quatrefoil.
Saltire.
Pinecone.
Leaf (-mascle, Hen. VI).
Leaf (-trefoil, Hen. VI).
Arrow.
Pheon.
A.
Annulet.
Annulet-with-pellet.
Anchor.
Anchor & B.
Flower & B.
Bell.
Book.
Boar's Head (early Richard III).
Boar's Head (later Richard III).
Boar's Head, Charles I.
Acorn (a) Hen. VIII (b) Elizabeth.
Bow.
Br. (Bristol, Chas. I).

68 Cardinal's Hat.
69 Castle (Henry VIII).
70 Castle with H.
71 Castle (Chas. I).
72 Crescent (a) Henry VIII (b) Elizabeth.
73 Pomegranate. (Mary; Henry VIII's is broader).
74 Coronet.
75 Crown.
76 Crozier (a) Edw. III (b) Hen. VIII.
77 Ermine.
78 Escallop (Hen. VII).
79 Escallop (James I).
80 Eye (in legend Edw. IV).
81 Eye (Parliament).
82 Radiate Eye (Hen. VII).
83 Gerb.
84 Grapes.
85 Greyhound's Head.
86 Hand.
87 Harp.
88 Heart.
89 Helmet.
90 Key.
91 Leopard's Head.
91A Crowned Leopard's Head with
     collar (Edw. VII).
92 Lion.
93 Lion rampant.
94 Martlet.
95 Mascle.
96 Negro's Head.
97 Ostrich's Head.
98 P in brackets.
99 Pall.
100 Pear.
101 Plume.
102 Plume. Aberystwyth and Bristol.
103 Plume. Oxford.
104 Plume. Shrewsbury.
105 Lis.
106 Lis.
107 Portcullis.
108 Portcullis. Crowned.
109 Sceptre.
110 Sunburst.
111 Swan.
112 R in brackets.
113 Sword.
114 T (Henry VIII).
115 TC monogram.
116 WS monogram.
117 y or Y.
118 Dragon (Henry VII).
119 (a) Triangle (b) Triangle in Circle.
120 Sun (Parliament).
121 Uncertain mark.
122 Grapple.
123 Tun.
124 Woolpack.
125 Thistle.
126 Figure 6 (Edw. VI).
127 Floriated cross.
128 Lozenge.
129 Billet.
130 Plume. Lundy Is.
131 Two lions.
132 Clasped book.
133 Cross pomee.
134 Bugle.

The reign after a mintmark indicates that from which the drawing is taken. A similar mm. may have been used in another reign and will be found in the chronological list at the beginning of each reign.

1	2	3	4	5	6	7a	7b	8	
10	11	12	13	14	15	16	17	18	
20	21	22	23	24	25	26	27	28	
30	31	32	33	34	35	36	37	38	
40	41	42	43	44	45	46	47	48	
50	51	52	53	54	55	56	57	58	
60	61	62	63	64	65a	65b	66	67	
69	70	71	72a	72b	73	74	75	76	
78	79	80	81	82	83	84	85	86	
88	89	90a	90b	90c	91	92	93	94	
96	97	98	99	100	101	102	103	104	
106	107	108	109	110	111	112	113	114	
116	117a	117b	118	119a	119b	120	121	122	
124	125	126	127	128	129	130	131	132	
134									